AN ELIZABETHAN PROBLEM

AN ELIZABETHAN PROBLEM

Some Aspects of the Careers of
Two Exile-Adventurers

by

L. HICKS, S.J.

FORDHAM UNIVERSITY PRESS
NEW YORK

CONTENTS

TABLE OF ABBREVIATIONS

Spanish Cal.	*Calendar of Letters and State Papers relating to English Affairs preserved in, or originally belonging to the Archives of Simancas.*
Stonyhurst, Coll. M. or P.	Manuscripts preserved at Stonyhurst College, in the series of Grene's Collectanea, M. or P.
Tierney-Dodd	M. A. Tierney, *Dodd's Church History of England*, 5 vols., London, 1839–43.
Vat. Arch.	Various manuscript collections in the Vatican Archives.
Venetian Cal.	*Calendar of State Papers, Venetian.*
West. Arch.	Manuscripts in Westminster Cathedral Archives, Main Series.

FOREWORD

The two exiles, Thomas Morgan and Charles Paget, may claim the attention of historians of the reign of Queen Elizabeth I on more than one ground. In the first place they were closely associated with Mary, Queen of Scots. Morgan, on the recommendation of Sir William Cecil, the Secretary, joined the staff of the Earl of Shrewsbury, her gaoler, soon after she was imprisoned at Sheffield in 1569, and from that time to her execution in 1587, he was involved, in one way or another, in her affairs. When, as an exile, he was, in 1581, appointed by her as cipher clerk to her ambassador in France, Archbishop Beaton, he obtained a fateful control of her secret correspondence. Charles Paget, who went into voluntary exile in 1581, owed his connection with her, it would seem, to the intimate friendship which he formed with Morgan in Paris.

Then these two, according to official accounts and other documents, were involved in various ways in three plots: the Throckmorton plot in 1583, the Parry plot in 1585, and the Babington plot in 1586. Thirdly, in the sphere of the religious troubles of the time, Morgan and Paget were, from 1582, the spear-heads of the opposition to Dr. William Allen, the founder of the English seminary at Douay, later Cardinal, and to the Jesuit, Fr. Robert Persons, who in the reign of Queen Elizabeth were the leaders of the Catholic exiles. It was in this last context, particularly, that the author's attention was first drawn to them some years ago.

In the following pages an outline is given of the rise, growth and composition of that opposition, and the close association of Morgan and Paget with the Scottish Queen is traced. The Throckmorton and Parry plots are submitted to a critical examination, and the connection of these two exiles with the Babington plot is indicated, without entering, however, into an exhaustive discussion of the plot itself, for this would require a whole book. From all these aspects, the actions of these two men will obviously receive different interpretations according as they are either seen to be, as they themselves alleged, faithful servants of the Queen of Scots, or can, on the contrary, be shown to be agents of the Elizabethan Government. It is this particular question of interpretation which is the object of this work, and which is pursued throughout the book. From a study of the evidence up to roughly 1590, the author has come to the conclusion that they were agents of the Councillors of Queen Elizabeth. The evidence, however, partly direct, and partly circumstantial, has been so presented, it is hoped, as to enable the reader to form his own judgment. The work is divided into two parts. Part one gives something of the historical events directly affecting their careers during the later years of the Queen of Scots' imprisonment in England, and outlines their connection with them. More particularly it is concerned with Morgan's intimate friend, Charles Paget, portraying some of the evidence, completed in part two, leading to the conclusion that the latter was an agent of the Government in Mary's last years. Part two deals in more detail with Thomas Morgan, starting from the convenient focal point of his arrest and examination in 1590 by the Spanish authorities in Flanders, and thence retracing his earlier career in the light of that examination. The conclusion reached is that he played the same rôle as his associate, though for a longer period.

This arrangement of the book necessarily involves some repetition, for which the author begs the indulgence of the reader; but the nature of the evidence surviving of matters obviously intended to be kept secret, precluded an easily flowing narrative, and seemed to demand the type of episodic treatment which has, in fact, been adopted. Throughout the book it has been thought advisable to modernise the spelling in quotations from contemporary English documents, to make them more readily understandable. The notes, as will be seen, are very numerous. They contain, however, matter intimately bound up with the general theme of the book, but which could not be inserted in the text without causing excessive fragmentation.

It only remains for the author to express his gratitude to those who have assisted him. His colleague, Fr. B. FitzGibbon, s.j., gave considerable help from his extensive knowledge of the period, calling attention to several documents connected with the subject, aiding, too, with continual advice and encouragement over many years in discussion of these topics at every stage of the research. The author also owes a great debt of thanks to Miss P. Renold, M.A., F.R.HIST.S. Not only has she checked references, when preparing the manuscript for publication, but she transcribed several important papers, which might otherwise have been overlooked. Her knowledge, moreover, of the various hands met with in the documents has been the author's guide in assigning anonymous items to particular persons. Finally, thanks are due to the officials of the various archives, whence the documents have been drawn, for their unfailing and courteous help.

PART I

CHAPTER I

Thomas Morgan, an enigma: some remarks on his career—Scottish affairs: the rise of Lennox and the invasion plan, 1582—Career of Charles Paget—The Welsh faction—1582 invasion plan abandoned: new plan 1583—Paget's visit to England to wreck the plan

1. *Thomas Morgan, an enigma: some remarks on his career*

Few acquainted with the career of Thomas Morgan would deny that he is somewhat a man of mystery. A private individual holding no high position as her representative, he yet directed from Paris the interchange of letters between the imprisoned Queen of Scots and her followers, and was trusted by her even to the neglect of her own ambassador to the French court, James Beaton, Archbishop of Glasgow,[1] though she was warned against placing confidence in him by some of her undoubted adherents. Supposedly a loyal servant of the captive Queen, he yet recommended her, as will be seen, to put her trust in such men as Christopher Blunt, William Greene, Robert Poly and the like, known to him as followers of the Earl of Leicester, her mortal enemy. He treated familiarly, not only with William Parry and Solomon Aldred, who were looked upon as spies and servants of the Elizabethan Government by the English Catholic exiles in Paris, and who were such in point of fact, but also with servants of the English ambassador there, as well as with Thomas Phelippes, the decipherer employed by Walsingham and one of his trusted agents in the Babington plot of 1586. He was distrusted by the leaders of the Queen of Scots' party in France, the Duke of Guise, and the Archbishop of Glasgow. To the acknowledged leaders of the English Catholics, Dr. Allen and his collaborator, Fr. Robert Persons, s.j., both of whom worked in close conjunction with the Duke of Guise, Morgan and his intimate friend, Charles Paget, showed from 1582 continuous

[1] James Beaton fled from Scotland to France in 1546 after the assassination of his uncle, Cardinal Beaton, Archbishop of St. Andrews. In 1552 he was consecrated in Rome Archbishop of Glasgow and returned to Paris, where he lived till his death in 1603. He was appointed by the Queen of Scots her ambassador to the French court, and continued to hold that office until her execution in February 1587. He was a prelate of unblemished reputation.

opposition. Morgan even encouraged and aided Gilbert Gifford and the priest, Edward Gratley, to write against them and to offer one of the books to Walsingham for printing.[2] As early as 1585 in the circle of English Catholic exiles in Paris, despite his pretension of being a faithful servant of the Scottish Queen, Morgan, together with Charles Paget, was held to be a spy and agent of the English Government. No less than four times was he imprisoned, first in England in the Tower in 1572, then in the Bastille in 1585, again in Flanders in 1590, and yet again in the Bastille in 1604, in connection with an intrigue with a discarded mistress of Henry IV. When arrested in 1590 many ciphers were found in his possession by means of which, though but a private individual of no position, he corresponded with many highly placed persons in the various courts of Europe, treating of grave matters of state, and even intriguing to displace the Duke of Parma in his government of Flanders, by the Duke of Savoy.

Yet despite these puzzling and mysterious elements in his career, historians in general have held the view that he was a loyal follower of the Queen of Scots; but this opinion they have rather taken for granted, than based it upon an extensive study of the documents concerned with his activities and career. To some, indeed, it never seems to have occurred that possibly Morgan was not what he pretended to be. The fact is, little or no research has been made on the subject. It is, then, one of the purposes of this study to present the case for a less favourable judgment of his character and career by giving some account of the evidence that suggests, to put it no stronger, that far from being a true servant of Mary, Queen of Scots, he was in fact, an agent of the English Government; for certainly such was the conviction of the majority of the English Catholic exiles of his time. Before, however, examining that evidence, in order that the reader may be able to weigh it, it will be necessary to give, in the first three chapters, not only a résumé of his early life, but an outline of the chief events connected with the period of his life under review.

From an examination of the pedigree of the Morgans, W. Llewelyn Williams concluded with some hesitation that Thomas Morgan was the son of John Morgan of Bassaleg, a "scion of the Tredegar house", and as the facts and dates of his career all fit in with this conclusion, there appears no reason for questioning it.[3] At his trial in Flanders, in

[2] Cf. *infra* Chapter III, section 3 and Note 388.
[3] W. Llewelyn Williams, *Welsh Catholics on the Continent*, in *Transactions of the Honourable Society of Cymmrodorion*, Session 1901–1902, London 1903, pp. 124–127. There are, however, one or two errors in his short account of Thomas Morgan's career.

February 1590, Morgan stated that he was forty-seven years old, which would place his birth in 1542 or early in 1543. He had two brothers, Rowland, a Douay priest, who later apostatised, and was twice married,[4] and Henry, who was employed by the English Government as "Customer" of Cardiff.[5]

It will be recalled that Mary, Queen of Scots, after her defeat at Langside by her rebellious subjects in May 1568 fled to England to appeal to Queen Elizabeth, and there, after the inconclusive conferences of York and Westminster between her accusers and her representatives, began her unjust and illegal imprisonment by the English Government, which ended only with her execution in February 1587. Her first gaoler was the Earl of Shrewsbury, and Morgan began his connection with the captive Queen when he entered the Earl's service on the recommendation of Sir William Cecil, and acted as Shrewsbury's secretary.[6] Whilst thus employed, according to his own statement, which will be examined later, he gave information to Mary of the intrigues against her at the English court, and directed her correspondence. On the latter becoming known to the Government he was dismissed from the Earl's service and, a short while later, imprisoned for ten months in the Tower. Set free on condition of not meddling further in the affairs of the imprisoned Queen and of not leaving the kingdom for a year, he remained in England till 1575, when a further investigation being made into Mary's correspondence and who were her responsible agents in the matter, he betook himself secretly to France rather than incur the danger of another spell of imprisonment. There he made Paris his headquarters, and became an intimate friend

---

[4] *Ibid.* Cf. also Cardinal Sega's Report of his visitation of the English College, Rome, 14 March 1596, in Foley, *Records VI*, p. 15. The Douay Diaries record his ordination on the vigil of Pentecost 1583, Knox, *Douay Diaries*, p. 195. Thomas Morgan's trial in 1590 is dealt with in detail in Part II.

[5] Cf. Thomas Morgan [*alias* Charles Thomas] to his brother, Henry Morgan, s.d., Information against Henry Morgan, s.d. and Henry Morgan's Examination, 7 May 1585 (Dom. Eliz. 178, nn. 64–66). Henry appears to have been one of those whose names were, in 1598, submitted to Sir Robert Cecil for the office of Sheriff of Monmouthshire (cf. W. Cooke to R. Cecil, 25 November 1598, *Cal. Salisbury MSS. VIII*, p. 454).

[6] Cf. W. Cecil to Shrewsbury, 15 May 1569, recommending the bearer, Morgan, to the Earl (Lodge, *Illustrations of British History*, London, 1838 Ed. I, p. 473). From his own statement too, at his trial in 1590, that he was in the Earl's service for three years and some months, and that he was dismissed by the Earl in 1572 (cf. *infra* Chapter V, section 2), it is clear that he joined the Earl's staff very soon after the Earl's appointment as gaoler of the Queen of Scots. Shrewsbury's instructions are dated 26 January 1569 (*Scot. Cal. II*, p. 609). Mary arrived at Sheffield, the place of her captivity, 4 February of that year (cf. Shrewsbury and Knollys to Cecil, 5 February 1569, *Ibid.*, p. 616). Morgan is referred to as having been secretary to the Earl in the "Interrogation ministered to Alexander Hamilton", point 7, 26 June 1574, and in the Memorial drawn up by Burghley, for the examination of Henry Cockyn, 16 January 1575 (*Scot. Cal. V*, pp. 11 and 83).

of Charles Paget when the latter left England. About 1580 he was appointed cipher clerk to the Scottish Queen's ambassador, the Archbishop of Glasgow; and by thus controlling her correspondence acquired a position of trust in her service.

2. *Scottish affairs: the rise of Lennox and the invasion plan, 1582*

About this time, too, affairs in Scotland took a turn more favourable to the Catholics and to the Queen's party. At James VI's invitation his cousin, Esmé Stuart, Lord d'Aubigny, came to Scotland in 1579 and quickly rose to high favour with the youthful King, who created him Earl of Lennox. With the aid of Captain James Stewart, later Earl of Arran, he brought about the fall of the all-powerful Earl of Morton, who had ruled Scotland as Regent since the death of the Earl of Mar in October 1572. On the last day of December 1580, Captain Stewart accused Morton before the Privy Council of Scotland of having been implicated, at least by foreknowledge, in the assassination in 1567 of James's father, Darnley. He was, in consequence, arrested, and despite the efforts of the English Government to prevent it, was tried and executed 2 June 1581. Lennox and Stewart, now Earl of Arran, thus secured supreme power, and the English party in Scotland was for the time being overthrown. In France Lennox had been brought up as a Catholic and remained such at heart, but to retain his position he signed the new confession of the Protestant faith together with the King and his courtiers. His position, however, was by no means secure; for Arran, a Protestant, was not one tamely to take second place. When, therefore, W. Crichton, s.j. early in 1582 came to Scotland to view the possibility of sending fellow Jesuits there as missionaries, a step which had long been considered, he was presented by Lennox with a plan for the landing of foreign troops to restore the old faith and set free the Queen of Scots. In this Lennox was, without doubt, encouraged by the intrigues which, since the autumn of 1581, Mendoza, the Spanish ambassador in England, had been conducting by his secret agents for the overthrow of the English party in Scotland and the restoration of the Catholic faith.

This plan of invasion which Crichton brought back to France about the middle of April 1582 was considered by the leading supporters of the Queen of Scots there, the Duke of Guise, her cousin, the Nuncio, Monsignor Castelli, Juan Baptista de Tassis, the Spanish agent in France, Mary's ambassador, the Archbishop of Glasgow, Dr. Allen and the two Jesuits, William Crichton and Robert Persons. Some modifications were introduced, and it was decided to send the Scottish Jesuit to Rome to obtain the support of the Pope for the plan, and the English Jesuit to Lisbon, where since the conquest of Portugal in 1580, Philip II was residing, to secure the desired forces from the Spanish King.[7]

To these conferences at Paris to consider the plan of Lennox, Morgan and his friend, Charles Paget, had not been called, and they took umbrage on account of it, and became henceforth the leaders of the opposition to Dr. Allen and Robert Persons.

"There were living in Paris", wrote the Jesuit, "two English gentlemen, servants (as they kept asserting) of the Queen of Scots, one named Charles Paget, brother of Lord Paget, the other Thomas Morgan, a Welshman, who had been servant to the said Queen in Lord Shrewsbury's house. They took it very ill that they had not been called to the conference which had been convened by the Apostolic Nuncio and other lords above mentioned, or at least that the affair had not been communicated to them, while its execution had been entrusted to two Fathers of the Society. The truth is that the Duke of Guise and the Archbishop of Glasgow did not consider these two men as trustworthy, fearing lest they might hold secret correspondence with some of the Council in England,[8] though the said Queen of Scots trusted greatly in them contrary to the wish and opinion of the said Duke and Archbishop, her ambassadors".[9]

Nor did the two men approve of Persons's journey to Lisbon. Recalling these events years later, Persons wrote to Charles Paget:

"Witnesses also are not lacking for your desertion of me and Dr. Allen, afterwards Cardinal, caused by my undertaking the journey to Spain".[10]

3. *Career of Charles Paget*

This Charles Paget was the fourth son of William, first Baron Paget, who had had a chequered career under the Tudor sovereigns, and who

---

[7] A succinct account of these invasion schemes of 1582 to 1584 is given with the pertinent authorities in *Letters and Memorials of Fr. Robert Persons, S.J., C.R.S. XXXIX*, pp. xli–lxiii. Many of the documents are printed in *Kretzschmar*.

[8] Charles was corresponding with Walsingham in that very year 1582, cf. *infra* section 3 of this chapter.

[9] Persons, *Notes Concerning the English Mission, C.R.S. IV*, p. 63; also Persons, *Autobiography, C.R.S. II*, p. 31, and Persons to Paget, Rome, 20 December 1597 (Stonyhurst Coll. P. 452), and Same to Same, Rome, 14 February 1598 (Arch. S.J. Rom. Anglia 31. II. f. 711).

[10] Persons to Paget, Rome, 14 February 1598, *ut supra;* cf. also Same to Same, 20 December 1597, *ut supra*. It is probably to this journey to Spain that the captive priest, Younger alias Dingley, referred when he wrote: "He [Morgan] was grieved when Persons was to go to Spain to solicit the Spaniard" . . . (Dingley to Puckering, 14 September 1592, *Dom. Cal. Eliz. 1591–1594*, p. 269).

appears to have accommodated his religion to the varying circumstances of the time; though he seems to have preserved the adherence to the old faith which he had professed under the Catholic Queen, Mary Tudor, after the accession of Queen Elizabeth. In 1581 Charles Paget retired to France, possibly because of his dissatisfaction with the religious changes, but possibly also because of certain quarrels in which he seems to have been involved.[11] He settled in Paris, where he became a close friend of Thomas Morgan.

The distrust felt of him in 1582 by the Duke of Guise and the Archbishop of Glasgow was not without foundation. When Walsingham came to Paris on a special embassy in July 1581, Paget had an interview with him and was given to understand that the English Secretary of State would be his friend and patron in regaining the favour of Queen Elizabeth, which he had lost by leaving England without licence.[12] After the Secretary's return to England in the September of that year, they continued to interchange letters.[13] What Paget desired was either to live in England with liberty of conscience, or to dwell abroad and be allowed to enjoy the revenue of his small estate.[14] Apart, however, from his religion, he promised to follow the advice of Walsingham in all his actions.[15] It is true, there was a rift

[11] Cf. A letter from a Catholic at Brussels to his friend, a monk at Liège, Brussels, 14 July 1599 (Dom. Eliz. 271, n. 74), and Persons, *Domesticall Difficulties* (*C.R.S. II*, p. 183). The year of his leaving England is given in the D.N.B. as 1572, which is the year assigned also by Gillow in his *Biographical Dictionary of English Catholics* (*V*, p. 231). Persons, however, who was in a position to know, states definitely that he left England in 1581 (*Domesticall Difficulties, ut supra*, and Responsiones ad praecipuas calumnias Caroli Pageti, 22 August 1598, Vat. Arch. Nunz. Diverse, 264, f. 229). This later year agrees better with the date at which the English ambassador in Paris began to take notice of him as a Catholic exile, and it is confirmed by the Earl of Arundel in his examination, 24 December 1583, in which he stated "that he never received letters from Charles Paget, or message since his [*Paget's*] first departure over without licence, which he thinketh to be iii years past" (Dom. Eliz. 164, f. 115 printed in *C.R.S. XXI*, p. 48 note). He was certainly in England about 1578 (cf. George More to Walsingham, 20 December 1583, Dom. Eliz. 164, n. 44).

[12] "I do assure myself", Paget wrote to him later, "that as God was the chief and only mean that ministered the occasion, whereby most happily I became known to you in this town, and put me in mind to offer unto you mine unfeigned affection and service, and likewise in respect thereof caused you to render unto me promise of your honourable favour and friendship for the relief of my lamentable estate: so he will give me grace by mine actions to maintain myself in your good favour" (Paget to Walsingham, Paris, 8 January 1582, Dom. Eliz. Add. 27A, n. 56). Cf. also Same to Same, Paris, 4 March and 30 May 1582, and Doyley to Walsingham, 16 March 1582, wrongly calendared under 1583 (*Dom. Cal. Add. 1580–1625*, pp. 52, 60 and 86).

[13] That Walsingham wrote to Paget is clear from Paget's letter to Walsingham, Paris, 8 January 1582, and from Doyley to Walsingham, Paris 16 March 1582, *ut supra*.

[14] Cf. Paget to Walsingham, Paris, 28 September 1582, and to Q. Elizabeth, Paris, same date (*Dom. Cal. Add. 1580–1625*, pp. 74 and 77).

[15] Paget to Walsingham, Paris, 8 January, *ut supra*, and 6 April 1582, *Dom. Cal. Add. 1580–1625*, p. 55.

between the two in the same year, 1582, owing to the report of the ambassador, Sir Henry Cobham. In it he expressed his fear that Paget was endeavouring to convert to the Catholic faith the young Lord Percy, then in Paris, whom his father, the Earl of Northumberland, had asked Paget to keep watch over as regards his "conversation and study".[16] Paget, however, repudiated the charge as unfounded and ascribed it to the enmity towards him of the ambassador as well on account of his religion as of the favour shown to him by Walsingham.[17] Lord Percy, too, protested against the sinister suspicion, and wrote both to his father and to Walsingham, exculpating both himself and Paget, and blaming the ambassador for his passionate speeches.[18] So far, indeed, was Paget from persuading Lord Percy to change his religion, that he was at this very time counteracting successfully a plan of Allen and Persons to get the young lord to stay abroad and go to Italy in the hope of his conversion there to the Catholic faith, Captain Pullen being sent over to England to obtain the Earl's consent.[19] Paget, however, gave contrary advice and prevailed, and this occurred just before Persons set out for Spain and Portugal in May 1582.[20]

The rift, indeed, between Paget and Walsingham appears to have been settled, though the Catholic exile still refused to return to England, if liberty of conscience was not allowed him there.[21] Cobham,

---

[16] Cf. Cobham to Walsingham, Paris, 3 and 13 March 1582 (*For. Cal. January 1581–April 1582*, pp. 512 and 552); Walsingham to Paget, the Court, 4 May 1582; Paget to Walsingham, Paris, 30 May 1582 (*Dom. Cal. Add. 1580–1625*, pp. 58 and 60); Doyley to Walsingham, Paris, 16 March 1582 (*Ibid.*, p. 86), and the Examination of the Earl of Northumberland, 11 May 1585 (printed in *C.R.S. XXI*, p. 120). The Calendarist suggested that the young lord might be Lord Hamilton: the documents make it quite clear that he was Lord Percy.

[17] Paget to Walsingham, Paris, 4 March 1582 (*Dom. Cal. Add. 1580–1625*, p. 52), and Cobham to Walsingham, Paris, 4 October 1582 (*Ibid.*, p. 76).

[18] Lord Percy to Walsingham, Paris, 5 April, and to the Earl of Northumberland, Paris, 5 April 1582 (*Ibid.*, p. 55).

[19] Later, relying on the testimony of Captain Pullen, the intermediary in the matter, who eventually became a priest, Persons himself charged Paget with wrecking the scheme (cf. Persons to Paget, Rome, 14 February 1598, Arch. S.J. Rom. Anglia 31. II. f. 711; also Persons, *Notes Concerning the English Mission, C.R.S. IV*, pp. 97–99).

[20] Persons states that at the time of the consultation with Captain Pullen, there was question of himself going to Spain. This would place the incident between mid-April and 28 May 1582; for Persons's journey to Spain was only resolved upon at the conferences held in Paris after Crichton's return from Scotland in the middle of April 1582, and Persons actually left for Spain on 28 May of that year (cf. *C.R.S. XXXIX*, pp. lii–liv).

[21] Cf. Cobham to Walsingham, Paris, 26 September 1582 (*For. Cal. May–December 1582*, p. 351); Paget to Walsingham, Paris, 28 September 1582, and Same to Q. Elizabeth, Paris, 28 September 1582 (*Dom. Cal. Add. 1580–1625*, pp. 74 and 77). In his examination, 11 May 1585, the Earl of Northumberland stated: "his l. thinketh that the L. Treasurer, or Mr. Secretary, told him of her Majesty's misliking that the L. Percy, being in France should frequent the company of Charles Paget: he never heard notwithstanding that

in a letter to Walsingham, denied that he himself had acted out of malice, but had only discharged his duty, and he prayed the Secretary to let his loyal and honest manner be defended and not injured, adding a postscript, that he would be glad if Paget were informed that he had had no sinister dealing in the matter, but rather wished the exile restored to the Queen's favour.[22] At the same time he sounded the praises of the young lord whom but a few months before he had traduced.[23] Paget, on his part, notified Cobham of his intended departure from Paris to dwell at Rouen, adding:

> "I tell you hereof that if you have any occasion to use me in her Majesty's service, you may know where to have me. Pray report favourably of this and all my other actions".[24]

He also informed Walsingham of his intended change of abode.

> "And although I know", he wrote, "there is no air nor anything in this world will heal me of my diseases but the favour of her Majesty, which prostrate at her feet I crave: yet as one that is in pain and torment doth try all manner of means to give himself relief: so do I intend (God Willing) to obey the physician's advice, and forthwith to go to Rouen, and there to lie for a trial of my better health. And the rather because I trust the place will be more agreable unto her Majesty than this. And for that by enjoying of my living I perceive her Majesty doth hold me still in the number of her subjects, I think it my bounden duty to advertise your honour where I bestow myself, to the end that if it please her Majesty to command me any service, it may be known how her pleasure may be addressed to me, which I will ever perform with the loss of my life, matter of conscience in religion only excepted. And in like sort if it shall please your honour to employ me in any thing that may be accountable to you, your honour shall find I will endeavour to do that which shall be to your satisfaction. Humbly beseeching your honour to think, that I will not leave to carry a most affectionate devotion towards you so long

[22] Cobham to Walsingham, Paris, 4 October 1582 (*Dom. Cal. Add. 1580–1625*, p. 76).
[23] Cobham to Walsingham, Paris, 4 October 1582 (*For. Cal. May–December 1582*, p. 367).
[24] Paget to Cobham, Paris, 23 October 1582 (*Dom. Cal. Add. 1580–1625*, p. 78).

Charles Paget at this time was charged with any disloyalty. And after the admonition given to his L. he heard that Paget hath cleared himself of such suspicions as were conceived of him . . . His l. thought that Paget had cleared himself of all suspicion by reason that his l. heard Charles Paget did use often to resort to her Majesty's Ambassador in France and to Mr. Secretary whilst he was in France: and did always think that the greatest matters that were objected against Paget were for religion" (printed in *C.R.S. XXI*, p. 120).

as I be kept from desperate terms, which I suppose next unto her Majesty chiefly proceedeth from your self".[25]

Finally, there is a curious letter of Walsingham to Phelippes amid all the excitement following the discovery of the Babington plot.

"I pray you," he wrote, "send me word what course you have taken for young Paget's despatch. It touches my poor credit—how hardly soever I am dealt withal—to see our friend beyond the seas comforted".[26]

This son of Lord Paget became a ward of Sir G. Carey in the February following the date of this letter,[27] and in the May of that year 1587, Charles Paget, under the alias of T. Nauris, asked Berden to learn what had become of Lord Paget's son, and if her Majesty had allowed anything for his maintenance.[28] All this suggests, at least, that neither Lord Paget nor Charles were regarded as the traitors to the Elizabethan Government which they were represented to be in the published pamphlets of only a few years earlier.

It would be going beyond the evidence to ascribe to the Duke of Guise and the Archbishop of Glasgow a knowledge of the correspondence between Paget and Walsingham in 1582, but it may be that some rumour of it had reached them to arouse their suspicion, which would only be increased by Paget's wrecking the plan of Allen and Persons as regards the young Lord Percy. At all events the correspondence shows clearly that Paget was quite an unsuitable person to be taken into their confidence, a fact which proved only too true, as will be shown shortly, when the next year they did impart their plans to him and Thomas Morgan.

4. *The Welsh faction*

Around these two, whilst Persons was away in Portugal and Spain, the factions opposed to Allen and himself coalesced. The most important group that joined the Morgan-Paget party was what became known as the Welsh faction. To some extent this is an incorrect name for it; for though it undoubtedly arose out of the rivalry and hostility between the English and Welsh students in the English College, Rome, in 1578, it embraced not only Welsh but also English Catholic exiles, nor were

[25] Paget to Walsingham, Paris, 23 October 1582 (Dom. Eliz. 155, n. 79).
[26] Walsingham to Phelippes, 3 September 1586 (*Scot. Cal. VIII*, p. 666).
[27] *Dasent, XIV*, p. 352. He was sent to Oxford the same year 1587, matriculating 22 November (*Complete Peerage*, 1895, *VI*, p. 184).
[28] T. Nauris to [Berden], 10 May 1587 (*Dom. Cal. Eliz. 1581–1590*, p. 410).

all Welshmen in sympathy with it.[29] Rather might it be called the faction of Dr. Owen Lewis: for he was undoubtedly considered, and was, in fact, its leader.

This Owen Lewis, of Welsh extraction, was a fellow of New College, Oxford, when the religious changes, introduced by Queen Elizabeth and her councillors, forced him about 1562 to retire to Flanders.[30] There his undoubted ability gained rapid recognition and he was nominated Regius Professor of Canon Law in the recently founded University of Douay. Further promotion followed in his appointment to the Archdeanery of Hainault and to a Canonry in the Metropolitan See of Cambray. Being sent by the Archbishop of that see to Rome in connection with a lawsuit,[31] he there won the favour of Gregory XIII, who appointed him "Referendarius Utriusque Signaturae". He took a prominent part and became a leading adviser in all matters that concerned England and was closely connected with the Inquisition or Congregation of the Holy Office which managed these affairs: and, as formerly he had helped Allen in the foundation of the seminary at Douay and its later removal to Rheims, so was he instrumental in the establishment of the English College at Rome. Through his influence, his friend and fellow Welshman, Dr. Maurice Clenog, one of the chaplains of the English Hospice in Rome, who had taken a leading part in its affairs, was chosen to direct the new seminary. Unfortunately he was not fitted for such a charge,[32] and troubles soon arose between the English and the Welsh students, whom he was accused of favouring at the expense of the English.[33] The upshot of the quarrel was that Gregory XIII acceded to the request of the English students, more numerous than the Welsh, and much against the wishes of Owen Lewis, who strove by all means to keep his friend in office, dismissed

[29] In a letter some years later to Thomas Throckmorton, a follower of Morgan, Allen wrote: "As though this matter of Morgan were a matter of countries, whereas some beguiled Englishmen may follow his seditious humour, so many good Welshmen do detest these false and dishonourable suggestions" (Allen to T. Throckmorton, Rome, 4 January and 20 February 1591, Knox, *Allen*, pp. 320 and 326).

[30] In a letter of 8 February 1590 Hugh Griffin, the nephew of Owen Lewis, stated that his uncle had lived twenty-eight years out of England. This would place his withdrawal to Flanders about 1562, and not, as usually stated, in 1559 (H. Griffin to T. Morgan, 8 February 1590, R.O. S.P. 85, I, ff. 69–71.

[31] According to Persons, he came to Rome "poco avanti l'anno santo", which would place his arrival there in 1574 (cf. Persons, *Autobiography*, C.R.S. II, p. 23).

[32] Cf. Allen to O. Lewis, Paris, 12 May 1579, Knox, *Allen*, p. 78, and Persons, *Domesticall Difficulties*, C.R.S. II, p. 97.

[33] A good number of the documents concerning this episode are printed in Persons, *Domesticall Difficulties*, C.R.S. II, pp. 85 ff. Others are to be found in *Tierney-Dodd II*, Appendix. Cf. also J. H. Pollen, s.j., *The English Catholics in the Reign of Queen Elizabeth*, London, 1920, pp. 271 ff.

Maurice Clenog and ordered the administration of the College to be committed to the Jesuits, who were already in charge of several of the seminaries in Rome.[34]

Already a short while before this, Owen Lewis had lost prestige by his advocacy of Stukeley, whose Irish expedition, financed by the Pope, had ended in a fiasco by his diverting it to Africa. This resulted in his own death and that of King Sebastian of Portugal and the general slaughter of his army by the Moorish King at the battle of Alcazar, 4 August 1578.[35] These further troubles at the new seminary and his choice and defence of his friend and compatriot did but add to his temporary loss of position. Twice, thus, within a short time, he had supported with all the weight of his influence men who had failed miserably in the task assigned to them, the one, Stukely, a buccaneering adventurer whose deceit had led to a fruitless loss of papal funds and some discredit to papal policy; the other, Maurice Clenog, who by sheer incompetence had nearly brought the new seminary to ruin and caused a considerable stir throughout the city of Rome. For the sake of peace, then, and to remove Owen Lewis from Rome, it was arranged that Charles Borromeo, Cardinal Archbishop of Milan, should employ him as one of his Vicars-General.[36]

To be relegated to Milan away from the centre of affairs in Rome, however much it was softened by his appointment as Vicar-General, could not but be a severe blow to Lewis, seeing that he had previously taken a leading part in matters concerning England: and especially was it so to one of his character; for though he had estimable qualities, he was ambitious beyond measure and ready to employ intrigue to gain his desired ends.[37] But despite his withdrawal to Milan, he still

[34] This step was quite in accord with Allen's wishes (cf. Allen to O. Lewis, 12 May 1579, *ut supra*, and Allen to Alfonso Agazzari, the first Jesuit Rector of the College, Douay, 28 June 1579, *C.R.S. IX*, p. 15).

[35] Cf. M. V. Ronan, *The Reformation in Ireland under Elizabeth*, London, 1930, pp. 576–586.

[36] Cf. Borromeo to Como, 24 July 1580, Vat. Arch. Lettere di Cardinali 93, f. 89; Persons, *Notes Concerning the English Mission*, *C.R.S. IV*, p. 67, and Sega's Report on his visitation of the English College, 14 March 1596, Foley, *Records VI*, p. 8. Owen Lewis reached Milan 16 June 1580 (cf. O. Lewis to Agazzari, Milan, 8 July 1580, *C.R.S. IX*, p. 41).

[37] Of his ambition and intrigue there can be no doubt. Allen himself was well aware of it, as is clear from a despatch of Olivares, the Spanish ambassador in Rome. "Allen" he wrote, "says that the Bishop of Cassano [*Owen Lewis*] causes him no end of trouble, because although he is a man of good life, his ambition and want of judgement are terrible" (Olivares to Philip II, Rome, 22 February 1588, Simancas Est. Leg. 950). Further, in a Memorial concerning future appointments to English sees in view of the coming Armada, it is stated: "Owen Lewis, Bishop of Cassano, and some of his friends, when they have entertained hopes of the undertaking succeeding, have endeavoured to take steps that he be appointed to the Archbishopric of York". This Allen deemed

endeavoured to exercise some influence in English affairs by means of his nephew, Hugh Griffin; for as Persons states,

"he commended him to Cardinal Savello[38] and others of the Inquisition in all matters touching England and that Tribunal, to

[38] Jacopo Savelli, created Cardinal by Pope Paul III, was head of the Inquisition or Holy Office, that had charge of English affairs. He died in Rome in 1587, aged 75, having been a cardinal for 47 years (cf. Cardella, *Memorie Storiche de' Cardinali, IV*, p. 232).

undesirable, nor was he willing to let him stay behind in Italy, lest he intrigue behind his back. "The Cardinal [*Allen*]" the same document continues, "considering the Bishop of Cassano's turn of mind, his endeavours to stir up opposition to him, and the favour he enjoys with many cardinals, thinks it advisable not to leave him in Italy, for fear he should come to Rome to engage in new and underhand intrigues, as he has begun to do" (Memorandum drawn up by Olivares and Allen regarding future appointments in England, 1588, Knox, *Allen*, p. 303). Lewis's own letters, moreover, reveal his ambition and the use he made of friends and patrons to achieve it. Thus on 14 December 1587, when not yet appointed to the see of Cassano, he wrote to Arnold, the prior of the English Carthusians: "If you write to S^r. Juan Idiaquez [*the Spanish Secretary of State*] excuse me that I write never to his honour for modesty's sake, lest I should seem importunate for myself, but when he doth me a good turn he shall have letters from me and others enough to thank him, and shall have honour and joy in me. And truly I remember him daily at Mass; if he knew the means that are wrought to persecute me and blind the world, he would love me above all my nation, to the which truly I have done more service than all others of them, be it spoken to the glory of God". Again on 2 January 1588, he wrote to Arnold: "What you write to Spain to the good Secretary [*Idiaquez*], and my L. Duchess [*of Feria*] of me, I know it shall be loving and modest, and if there were therein a few lines pithy and short and effectual separately written as your own attestation to be shewed to the King [*Philip II*], it were well that the Secretary, if he listed, might read it to the King". Both letters are quoted by Persons, *A Briefe Apologie*, 1601, ff. 34v–35. With these letters should be read his commendation from Cardinal Melino to Philip II, Rome, 30 June 1587, and that of Giulio Battaglino to the Same, Madrid, 3 August 1587, apparently presented to the King at the request of Cardinal Medici (cf. *C.R.S. XXXIX*, pp. 358–360). There is a further undated eulogistic report of Lewis's career, given to the Duke of Savoy by Lewis's Carthusian friend, William Chisholm, Bishop of Dumblane and Vaison (cf. *infra* Note 243), and presented to Idiaquez by the Duke's agent, in which favour and support were requested that Lewis be raised to the purple (Simancas, K. 1448, n. 156, formerly at Paris). This document was certainly drawn up after the execution of the Queen of Scots, for in it she is referred to as "piae memoriae". It may have been connected with the above papers of 1587, but more probably should be referred to Prior Arnold's visit to Spain in 1589 for the same purpose (cf. Arnold to Philip II [after 26 May 1589], *Spanish Cal. 1587–1603*, p. 542, and Morgan to the Bishop of Dumblane, *Scot. Cal. X*, p. 229. The second letter is quoted in Persons's *Briefe Apologie*, ff. 31ff, where it is dated 20 August 1589; cf. also *infra* Note 221).

His efforts and those of his friends and patrons were to some extent rewarded; for he was nominated by Philip II to the see of Cassano in the kingdom of Naples, and the Pope agreeing, was consecrated 3 February 1588. Olivares, however, concluded that Philip II had so nominated him only to remove him from Rome, and insisted with the Pope, according to the mind of the King, that the new bishop should, in accord with the decrees of Trent, reside in his diocese (Olivares to Philip II, Rome, 22 February 1588, Simancas, Est. Leg. 950). The new bishop had to comply, and left Rome on 26 March 1588, only returning 22 December 1591 (Stonyhurst Coll. N. III, p. 73, referring to the contemporary Diary of Roger Baines). For his later ambitioning the purple, cf. Owen Lewis to Humphrey Ely, 16 March 1595, in Ely's *Certaine Briefe Notes*, pp. 95–97. It would certainly appear that in strong contrast to Allen, who was disinterested, Owen Lewis was a clerical careerist and used his friends and patrons to secure his own promotion. Cf. also Sega's Report of his visitation of the English College, Rome, 14 March 1596, Foley, *Records VI*, p. 8.

be believed as himself—and moreover he added (as Fr. Alphonsus Agazarius, Rector of the College affirmed to have seen and read written by the Doctor's own hand) that it should not be good to give overmuch credit to any of the said English College, about matters appertaining to the Inquisition, for that they might be partial, but that they should use his said nephew and one Friar Batson, a Franciscan, who newly was come from Flanders to Rome, and was no great friend to Jesuits, though he had a brother a scholar among them".[39]

The same nephew, however, was expelled from the English College for his unruly conduct[40] and Cardinal San Sisto, who succeeded Cardinal Morone as Protector, endeavoured further to persuade Owen Lewis to recall him from Rome, on account of the trouble he was causing to the new seminary, a step which Allen also counselled, but apparently without success.[41]

The removal of his friend, Dr. Maurice Clenog, from the direction of the English College, coupled with its assignment to the Society of Jesus, and the expulsion of his nephew, alienated Lewis from the

[39] Persons, *Domesticall Difficulties*, *C.R.S. II*, p. 184.

[40] In 1579 Allen begged Owen Lewis to restrain his nephew. "You must" he wrote, "temper your cousin (*sic*) Hugh's tongue and behaviour, who is of a bitter, odd and incompatible nature; for so not the students there any of them, but I assure you others have signified, that his disordered humours have been a great cause of your hatred and of all those garboils. And some have told me that I did an ill dieed to send him up, who for choler and other singularities was insupportable amongst his fellows here [*the seminary at Rheims*]. For God's love, therefore, correct his nature as much as you can" (Allen to O. Lewis, Paris, 12 May 1579, from the original at Milton House. Dodd's version of this letter, printed in Knox, *Allen*, p. 78, changes the sense of the passage by inserting a "not"). If Persons is correct in stating that Hugh Griffin was dismissed when Cardinal Moroni was Protector (*C.R.S. II*, p. 86), his dismissal from the college must have taken place before 1 December 1580, the date of Moroni's death.

[41] "Scripsit dominus Cardinal S. Sixtus ad me suadens ut illum ex Urbe revocarem; quod libenter facerem, si non esset ad quaedam mea et Archiepiscopi Cameracensis negotia illic persequenda necessarius." Allen wrote to Agazzari from Rheims, 7 February 1582, citing the above from Owen Lewis's letter to himself. Allen added: "Ego hac occasione literarum suadebo ipsi quantum possum, pertinere ad honorem suum ut nepotem suum revocet, ac id quoque esse ad salutem juvenis et collegii pacem omniumque animorum reconciliationem" (Knox, *Allen*, p. 110). Persons, too, refers to the disturbing influence of Hugh Griffin. "Yet little good" he wrote, "resulted [*i.e. from Lewis's withdrawal to Milan*], because the said nephew, remaining in Rome, kept writing to him things which tended to nourish his displeasure and augment his distrust of those who were governing the college, as is proved by many letters of Father Agazario, in which he says: 'As long as your Reverend Lordship will give credit to your nephew and other like passionate persons, without inquiring into the truth, it will not be possible to hope for union of hearts'" (*Notes Concerning the English Mission, C.R.S. IV*, p. 67). It seems odd, it may be added, that the business of the Archbishop of Cambray in Rome should be committed to a youth, who had only just finished his course of philosophy. Yet this was alleged by Owen Lewis as the reason for not calling his nephew from Rome, as both Cardinal San Sisto, the new Protector, and Allen desired.

Jesuits, and as Allen was closely united to these, to some degree from Allen also.[42]

"These two points", wrote Persons, "did put such a pike in the Archdeacon [*Owen Lewis*] and his nephew (afterwards made provost of Cambrai by the resignation of his uncle),[43] as they were never taken to be well united more unto the College, but that what scholar soever (especially if he were of their country) had any dislike or complaint against his Superior (as in a multitude where discipline is exacted it cannot pass without) he knew ever where to have recourse and where to be moved, and out of this fountain have ensued many great inconveniences since that time, as after shall appear, for now was it known that an opposite party was begun in Rome, and with it joined some other presently of the English nation abroad (as commonly it falleth) upon divers occasions, namely one Nicholas Fitzherbert, a gentleman that lived in Rome, and one Solomon Aldred that had been a tailor in Lyons but now was come to Rome with his wife, and procured a pension of his Holiness to live there, and had no other means to pass but to depend of the archdeacon as chief man in credit in that place,[44] and soon after in Paris two other gentlemen named Charles Paget and Thomas Morgan, for the causes that afterwards shall be touched, joined themselves in the same league, and by little and little drew in others both within and without the College, so as hereof began the very first root, as it were, of the great differences, that have fallen out since that time among Catholics of our nation".[45]

---

[42] "Sed vestri amici non sunt identidem mihi amici" (O. Lewis to Allen, cited by Allen in his letter to Agazzari, Rheims, 7 February 1582, *ut supra*). "El de Cassano [*Lewis*] fue sempre oposto del Cardenal Alano y de sus aficionados y assi podria ser inclinado a camino diverso que ellos" (Sessa, the Spanish ambassador in Rome, to Philip II, Rome, 26 October 1595, Simancas, Est. Leg. 967). At the time of this letter Owen Lewis had just died in Rome, 14 October 1595.

[43] Hugh Griffin was appointed Provost of Cambray, 21 June 1588 (L. Van Der Essen, *Correspondance d'Ottavio Mirto Frangipani. I*, p. 53, n. 1).

[44] Cf. L. Hicks, S.J., *An Elizabethan Propagandist: The Career of Solomon Aldred, The Month*, May–June 1945, p. 181, n. 3; also Sledd's Diary, Yelverton MSS. now B.M. Addit. 48029, ff. 122ff. This spy records that Aldred's pension, of 10 gold crowns a month, was granted on 16 August 1579.

[45] Persons, *Domesticall Difficulties, C.R.S. II*, p. 88. Cf. also *Notes Concerning the English Mission*, where he writes: "Nor did they [*Allen and Persons*] succeed better with Mgr. Owen, Referendary, who was in Milan, Vicar-General of Cardinal Borromeo, and was thought to be the head of the Welsh faction. He kept up a close correspondence with Paget and Morgan and others of that party, but had little intimacy with Allen and the fathers of the Society, and had his correspondents in Rome, chiefly Dr. Hugh Griffiths [*Griffin*], his nephew, as elsewhere was said, by which the government of the College was made very difficult as well for Allen as for the fathers and every day there arose great troubles on account of the disunion" (*C.R.S. IV*, p. 97). Some details of Griffin's later activities as a trouble-maker may be seen in Fisher's Confessions, printed in *C.R.S. LI*, n. XXXV.

To keep the seminary at Rheims free from such division, Allen took great pains,[46] but despite all his efforts it is clear from the letters of Dr. Barrett, who became Allen's assistant, that the Welsh faction soon penetrated into that seminary. In view of his later activities and his connection with the two Giffords, it may be that Solomon Aldred[47] had a part in this; for he was certainly closely associated with Owen Lewis and was a partisan of his faction. In a letter of 16 November 1582 Dr. Barrett related his meeting with Aldred and his journey with him to Lyons:

"I have written", runs the letter, "to Mr. George [*Gilbert*] about a certain conversation I had with Aldred during my journey. I came across him at Milan in the house of the Archdeacon [*Owen Lewis*] and setting out together for Lyons we talked in a familiar and friendly manner. That was the reason, I think, why he did not conceal from me, what he would never have mentioned, had he either been cautious about his own affairs or had consulted the Archdeacon beforehand. Your prudence will gather from that conversation of ours much more than it was necessary for me to write; for a trifling clue often reveals much. And the attitude of mind he revealed towards some of ours as well as towards some of yours I fear, he has derived from another source, namely from that poison that has infected the College from its foundation, and has spread far and wide to other parts. But I shall write at length about the matter on another occasion when I have gathered more information".[48]

This later letter which he promised may be that of 14 April 1583 which shows that the Welsh faction had gained considerable ground both within and without the seminary at Rheims. Allen, it is true, he reported, kept its partisans in some sort of obedience by not enquiring too closely into and overlooking excesses in their conduct and in their letters, so that those who were most opposed to him, offered and gave their services. Even "Morgan and his like" did so, and were employed by Allen in some financial business of the seminary, and for the time being there was outward peace. Nevertheless, Barrett continued, the Welsh were most industrious and displayed artful dexterity in their endeavours to win over recruits to their party. They kept watch to see if anyone had a complaint against or was alienated

---

[46] Cf. Allen to O. Lewis, Paris, 12 May 1579, *ut supra*, and Barrett to Agazzari, Rheims, 14 April 1583, Knox, *Douay Diaries*, p. 324.
[47] Cf. *infra* Chapter III, section 3.
[48] Barrett to Agazzari, Rheims, 16 November 1582, Knox, *Douay Diaries*, p. 320 (Latin).

from superiors, which was of frequent occurrence. To such a one they paid every attention and showed every kindness, supplying him with money, if needed, and inviting him to dine or sup with them. To gain him they never relinquished their efforts; and in this way they often perverted many of the English.[49]

That there was some bad feeling between the two parties at Rheims is shown by a comparatively trivial incident reported in a letter of Allen to Agazzari, which also reveals Allen's care to placate the Archdeacon. One of the students in a fit of temper smashed a portrait of Owen Lewis left in an out of the way room by one of the Welsh students, which gave cause for some stir between the friends of the Archdeacon and those of the president, Allen himself. To explain the incident and pacify Owen Lewis, Allen wrote a letter and begged Agazzari to forward it as quickly as possible, presumably so that the Archdeacon might hear of the incident and the explanation of it before he got to know of it from the partisans of the Welsh faction.[50] A year later there was open strife in the seminary between the two parties, and Stafford, the English ambassador in Paris, thought it of sufficient importance to report to Walsingham the great dissensions between the "Southern men and the Welshmen".[51] His reporting of it, however, is not really surprising, for the English Government strove by every means to promote such division.[52] It was part of their planned policy.

In fostering this Welsh faction in the seminary of Rheims, Persons singles out two English students from the English College, Rome, the two Giffords, William, from July 1582 a professor of the seminary at Rheims, and his cousin, Gilbert. Having stated that all those who had anything against their superiors in the English College, or any reason for dissatisfaction, at once placed themselves under the protection of Mgr. Owen [*Lewis*],[53] he continued:

"As among others did two young men of good family and rare talents named William and Gilbert Gifford, who coming to the

[49] Cf. Barrett to Agazzari, Rheims, 14 April 1583, *ut supra*. The whole letter very is revealing both as to the pressure of the Welsh faction in Rheims seminary, and to Allen's method in dealing with it. Cf. also Persons, *Notes Concerning the English Mission*, *C.R.S. IV*, p. 95.

[50] Allen to Agazzari, Rheims, 18 November 1583, Knox, *Allen*, p. 326.

[51] Stafford to Walsingham, Paris, 17 December 1584, *For. Cal. August 1585–August 1585*, p. 190.

[52] Cf. Barrett to Agazzari, Rheims, 14 April 1583, *ut supra*, and Persons, *Notes Concerning the English Mission*, *C.R.S. IV*, p. 69. On the opposition to Allen and Persons, cf. *infra* Chapter VI, section. 4.

[53] A later instance of this was recorded by Cardinal Sega in connection with the priest, Edward Gratley (cf. His report of his visitation of the English College, 14 March 1596, Foley, *Records VI*, p. 17).

seminary of Rheims helped much to form a faction amongst the the scholars. Among other things they united closely with two lay gentlemen, Paget and Morgan, one English, the other Welsh, heads of the lay faction".[54]

Certain it is that William was considered one of the Welsh party. Writing but a few months after the young man's arrival at Rheims from the English College, to become professor there, Barrett reported:

"They [*the Welsh*] think Father Gifford quite their own and I think he is so. No one, not even Doctor Allen, dares to admonish the man on this matter. In truth he behaves very well but he is infected with that disease, and is of an inconstant character [*mutabili ingenio*]. He behaves towards Allen with great deference and respect; and I hope he will later little by little lay aside his over-great familiarity with them [*the Welsh*]. My hopes of this would be stronger, if I did not mark that they showed him so many signs of favour, honour and esteem. I fear for human frailty which is wont to be overpleased by such things".[55]

Barrett's fears rather than his hopes were realised, as will appear in this narrative.[56] Such, then, was the so-called Welsh party.

When, therefore, Persons, who had been delayed by illness, arrived back in Paris in May 1583 from his mission to Philip II, he found that the Welsh party had joined with the Morgan-Paget faction. Recalling this in his Memoirs, composed years later, the Jesuit wrote:

"As soon as Dr. Allen heard that Father Persons had arrived in Paris, he went to meet him, and they remained together for some days to talk over together all that had happened in his absence.[57] And as on the one hand there were many things in England which were consoling . . . so on the other hand there were not wanting sorrows enough, both on account of the imprisonment and torture of Fr. William Holt, as was reported, and the revolution in Scotland,[58] and

[54] Persons, *Notes Concerning the English Mission*, C.R.S. IV, p. 69.

[55] Barrett to Agazzari, Rheims, 14 April 1583, *ut supra*.

[56] Cf. the intrigues of the English Government with the two Giffords after Allen had left for Rome in September 1585, *infra* Chapter III, section 3.

[57] "I had gone to Paris" wrote Allen on his return to Rheims, "to see Father Robert, and the heat and fatigue of the journey had affected my health, but in the mutual joy of our meeting all else was of no account" (Allen to Agazzari, Rheims, 26 June 1583, Knox, *Allen*, p. 197).

[58] William Holt, the Jesuit, was captured in Scotland 1 March 1583. The report of his torture proved incorrect, though the English Government had urged it. In fact, James promised the French envoy, De Mainville, that he would liberate him, as soon as he had shaken off the control of those who had seized his royal person at the Raid of Ruthven on 22 August 1582, the 'revolution' to which Persons referred to above (cf. *Letters and Memorials of Father Robert Persons*, C.R.S. XXXIX, pp. 202–203).

still more because it was understood that the faction begun the previous year by Paget and Morgan against Allen and the Fathers of the Society was much increased and had coalesced with that of the English and Welsh in Rome, which had already extended nearly everywhere, especially to the two seminaries of Rome and Rheims, where many of the scholars were drawn into it. For all those who became discontented with their superiors or for any other cause, or who did not want to observe the college discipline or to pursue their studies as they ought, took sides with that faction in order to strengthen themselves against the Fathers, and then immediately received favour from without. So the said Colleges, especially that of Rome, were continually disturbed and troubled".[59]

Persons and Allen, however, endeavoured to patch up the differences and at least in outward show succeeded.[60]

5. *1582 invasion plan abandoned: new plan 1583*

Meanwhile the first plan of invasion had come to naught. Philip II held back from giving military aid, and in August 1582 the English party among the Scottish nobles, led by the Earl of Gowrie, seized the young king and overthrew the government of Lennox, who was forced later to leave Scotland and return to France, where he died the following May.[61] The idea of invasion, however, was not abandoned. Several conferences were held in Paris between June and August 1583 and new plans devised. The main force, which it was hoped Philip II would supply, was to lead the attack from Scotland, whilst French troops were to make a diversionary movement somewhere on the Sussex coast after the principal body of soldiers had landed in the Northern parts. In this new plan the leaders were heartened by the news that James had regained his liberty and was showing distinct hostility to the English faction in Scotland.[62] Of this new plan of invasion Morgan and Paget were made cognisant, having been admitted, thanks to the peace-making efforts of Allen and Persons, to the confidence of the leaders of the Queen of Scots' party in France. At the conferences held in Paris it was decided to send Persons to Rome to lay the matter before Pope Gregory XIII, whilst Charles Paget, who volun-

[59] Persons, *Notes Concerning the English Mission*, C.R.S. *IV*, p. 95.

[60] Cf. Persons, *Autobiography*, C.R.S. *II*, p. 32, and Persons to Paget, Rome, 20 December 1597, *ut supra*.

[61] Lennox died in France 26 May 1583.

[62] James escaped from Falkland on 27 June 1583, and hurried to St. Andrews where his followers had gathered. The ground for his escape had been previously prepared by De Mainville who, as French envoy, was in Scotland from January till about April of that year.

teered for the task, was to undertake a journey to England in September
to obtain for the invasion the support of such persons as the Earl of
Northumberland and William Shelley of Michelgrove, and to see what
aid the Catholics could contribute to the venture. He was also to make
it clear that the aim of the expedition was not the conquest of the
country, but the liberation of the Queen of Scots, her elevation to the
English throne, to which by natural descent she was entitled, and
the restoration by these means of the old Faith.[63]

Paget certainly came to England in September 1583,[64] and stayed
at Petworth with the Earl of Northumberland, where at the invitation
of the Earl, Thomas, Lord Paget, came to meet his brother Charles.
Paget also met William Shelley there and a few days later lodged in a
house near Shelley's residence. But so far from carrying out the
instructions of the Duke of Guise and engaging in traitorous practices,
as the Government maintained—and this is a crucial point—he
crossed to England determined to overthrow the plan of invasion, as
the evidence which follows indicates.

6. *Paget's visit to England to wreck the plan*

In a letter to Charles Paget some years later, recalling to his mind the
activities of his faction, Persons wrote:

> "You cannot but remember . . . how after this we made a new com-
> position and atonement again with you in the same city of Paris,
> where it was concluded, that you should go to England and I to
> Rome, and that this league was broken again by you and not by us
> upon *the defeat of all the designments by that your journey*, and especi-

---

[63] Cf. *Letters and Memorials of Fr. Robert Persons, C.R.S. XXXIX*, pp. lvii–lx, where
the pertinent authorities are given. The Duke of Guise's Instructions for Charles Paget
are dated 28 August 1583, and are calendared in the *Spanish Cal. 1580–1586*, p. 505.

[64] From the examination of Haller, 20 December 1583, (Dom. Eliz. 164, n. 45), the
ship-master who conveyed Paget to England, can be ascertained sufficiently the date
of his arrival in England. Haller stated that he was at Dieppe "at Bartholemewtide
last" [24 August], waited there a fortnight before he had a favourable wind for a crossing,
and then made the journey in fourteen hours. One Watts, an Englishman (really a priest
and a friend of Persons, cf. *infra* section 6), dwelling at Rouen, covenanted with him to
bring over a gentleman to England, promising him £7 for this passage. He received
another £7 for the return journey later. Thus Haller would have sailed from Dieppe
about 7 September. On landing at Arundel Haven he accompanied the gentleman on
foot to William Davies's house at Patching, arriving there "about 2 of the clock after
midnight". Paget, thus, arrived about 8 September. Patching was but three miles from
Arundel Haven. According to Haller's examination, on the return journey the gentleman
went on board on "the Wednesday before Michaelmas", which in 1583 was 25 September,
Michaelmas Day, 29 September, falling that year on a Sunday. His stay in England,
therefore, was a very short one of less than three weeks. Though Haller himself said "he
knoweth not the gentleman's name", Thomas Wilkes, one of the examiners, noted in
the margin against this remark: "Ch. P".

ally upon the relation and oath of Mr. Watts,[65] the priest, who both affirmed to the Duke of Guise, to Fr. Claude Matheus, his confessor, Dr. Allen and to myself that you told him in secret at the sea's side, when you were to embark, that you meant in England to overthrow all our endeavours, and so the effect showed".[66]

Two months later he wrote again to him:

"Witnesses also are not lacking for your desertion of me and Dr. Allen, afterwards Cardinal, caused by my undertaking the journey to Spain [*1582*] and for our well known reconciliation in Paris, and eventually your defection again; just as also I recall what Mr. Watts, the priest, related to the Duke of Guise, Fr. Claude Matthieu, Dr. Allen and myself, of the words you used on the beach when you were setting out for England; and this, indeed, he told to many others as well".[67]

A little earlier, giving a summary account of the opposition throughout the years of Charles Paget and Morgan, he wrote to Juan de Idiaquez, the Spanish Secretary of State:

"Besides this, it is known that these two men at various times tried to persuade the Duke of Guise to take upon himself the liberation of the Queen of Scots, and place her on the thrones of England and Scotland, using the powers of France and her French friends and excluding the Spaniards, and as the Duke declined to agree to this, but determined once more in the year 1583, to ask again for help from his Majesty of Spain, Charles Paget, *not being able to prevent this decision, volunteered to go to England, and procure the Earl of Northumberland's collaboration with the Duke, but on his arrival he did the opposite and prevented him from becoming an ally.* This was told to many people afterwards by the Duke of Guise himself. Paget, too, when he was on the point of embarking for England, had himself told William Watts, an English priest, in confidence, that this was his intention. Moreover, it is known now on the testimony of the above-mentioned Samerie[68] and others that Paget and Morgan

[65] Italics mine. The priest, Watts, is the Englishman from Rouen mentioned in Haller's examination (cf. *supra* Note 64).

[66] Persons to C. Paget, Rome, 20 December 1597, Stonyhurst, Coll. P. 452.

[67] Persons to C. Paget, Rome, 14 February 1598, Arch. S.J. Rom. Anglia 31. II, f. 711 (Latin).

[68] H. Samerie or Samier, the Jesuit, was a loyal supporter of the Queen of Scots. He visited her three times during her captivity. He was with her for some months in 1582, and again in the summer of 1583 and a third time in 1584, using various disguises, once appearing as her physician and again as her valet. In his letters he used the aliases of La Rue and Hieronymo Martelli. His correspondence with her and her secretary, Nau, is in the *Scot. Cal. VII* and *VIII* under these names (cf. J. H. Pollen, s.j., *Mary Stuart's Jesuit Chaplain, The Month*, January and February 1911; also H. Fouqueray, s.j. *Histoire de la Compagnie de Jésus en France, II*, pp. 112–119).

had by means of letters alienated the Queen of Scots herself, and caused her to write to the Earl of Northumberland, to be sure not to associate himself with the Duke of Guise or the Spaniards in this project. And this was done by Paget and Morgan in Paris after they had been reconciled to the Duke of Guise and Dr. Allen and Fr. Persons, who out of their desire for peace and unity and to prevent these two men from obstructing their policy further, has admitted them to a share in all their secrets. But these two men were never loyal to them afterwards, as subsequent events will show".[69]

The Jesuit, Samerie, mentioned above by Persons, was certainly in a position to know the truth on this point for he had been sent by the Duke of Guise to give Mary an account of the resolution he had taken as regards the enterprise. Mendoza, the Spanish ambassador in England, reported to Philip II that he had seen Samerie, presumably on his return from his mission.[70] That the Scottish Queen, moreover, did oppose the Duke of Guise's project at this time is confirmed by the later testimony of Pasquier, master of the wardrobe in her prison household. In his examination, 2 September 1586, after the Babington plot, he swore that he had never been acquainted with any practice prejudicial to the Queen of England, and continued:

"True it is when M. Nau was in London two years ago,[71] Mr. Wilkes told me there was a Jesuit named Cruiton or Criton who had been taken with many papers of very great importance,[72] upon which the said Jesuit having been questioned, had confessed that there was an

[69] Persons's Account of the opposition of Paget and Morgan, 30 June 1597, enclosed in his letter to Juan de Idiaquez, English College, Rome, 3 July 1597, West. Arch. VI, nn. 41 and 42 (Spanish). Italics mine.

[70] Mendoza to Philip II, London, 19 August 1583, *Spanish Cal. 1580–1586,* p. 499. Mendoza does not name the priest, but he can be identified as Samerie by his reference to his visit to the Queen of Scots in the previous year (cf. *supra* Note 68).

[71] Nau, her French Secretary, was in London about the middle of November to the end of December 1584, negotiating on behalf of the Queen of Scots with Queen Elizabeth and her councillors. For these negotiations, cf. *Scot. Cal. VII.*

[72] Wilkes was certainly wrong in one point: for these papers referred to the plan of 1582 and not to that of 1583, and it is more than doubtful that they were found on the Jesuit (see Appendix II). At the end of August or the beginning of September 1584 the ship conveying two Jesuits, James Gordon and William Crichton, as well as the secular priest, Patrick Addy, chaplain to the Bishop of Ross, was intercepted "in St. John's Road" by the Admiral of Zealand, William van Bloys, alias de Treslong (Davison to Burghley, Edinburgh, 6 September 1584, *Scot. Cal. VII,* p. 318). The merchant, a Scottish Calvinist, who had chartered the ship, recognising Crichton and Gordon, betrayed Crichton to the Admiral, but fearing the vengeance of Gordon's nephew, the Earl of Huntley, he allowed Gordon to go free, substituting Patrick Addy in his place (Crichton's Memoirs, printed by J. H. Pollen, s.j. in *Mary, Queen of Scots and the Babington Plot,* Edinburgh, 1922, pp. 151ff). According to a report, however, that reached Davison, Gordon "redeemed his liberty with 100 crowns" (Davison to Burghley, 6 September, *ut supra*). It rather looks as if the interception was not just a chance event, for the English Government shortly before had been informed by Sir Edward Stafford

C

enterprise to be made against this realm; and the said Wilkes added to me that there had been a gentleman, Throckmorton a little before, a great friend from what he told me of the queen my mistress, who had been beheaded for this same cause. Being returned, I made report thereof to the queen, who told me that verily there had been a design to carry her off and re-establish the religion in England, but that forasmuch as in doing this it had been desired to constrain her to renounce her rights to the crown of England to the prejudice of her son to which she would never consent so long as she should live, offering to deliver to herself in recompense the government of such countries[73] beyond the seas with a revenue of a hundred thousand crowns and restitution of her dower in case the king of France wished to take it from her; that she had quite flatly refused it: moreover that such things being full of difficulties it could not be achieved without hazarding the life of many of her friends in England. But that if they would undertake such a thing in Scotland she would endeavour to dispose her son to it so much as should be in her, and a good part of the Scotch nobility".

Such was Pasquier's statement, and it is confirmed by the assertion of Nau, her French secretary, and by the Queen of Scots herself.[74]

That Paget, despite his crossing to England in September 1583, did not carry out the instructions of the Duke of Guise, is further confirmed by a report of Berden, alias Rogers, who had been sent to France in 1585 to act as a spy whilst pretending to be a Catholic.[75] On 13 August of that year he reported to Walsingham:

[73] In the sense, presumably, of counties, as the word is sometimes used in other documents of the time.

[74] Articles of Pasquier and his answers, 2 September 1586, *Scots. Cal. VIII*, p. 659; cf. also Berden to Walsingham, Rouen, 13 August 1585, Dom. Eliz. Add. 29, n. 39, printed in *C.R.S. XXI*, p. 78. For Nau's statement, 10 September 1586, cf. *Scot. Cal. IX*, pp. 1ff, and for the Queen's, *State Trials*, Ed. 1809, co. 1188; cf. also *infra* Chapter VIII, section 2. The leaders in France, it may be added, had no intention of depriving the Queen of Scots of her title to the English throne, as the documents clearly show (cf. *Kretzschmar*, pp. 166–171). The object of suggesting that the Duke of Guise should alone undertake the enterprise, was presumably to render it nugatory; for the Duke had himself neither the forces nor the money for such an undertaking.

[75] On Berden, alias Rogers, cf. *C.R.S. XXI*, pp. 66–93, where many extracts of his letters to Walsingham are printed.

of the intended departure of the Jesuits from Dieppe (cf. Stafford to Walsingham, Paris, 24 August 1584, *For. Cal. August 1584–August 1585*, p. 30, also Same to Same, Paris, 16 October 1584, *Ibid.*, p. 106). The two priests, Crichton and Addy, were taken off the ship and conveyed to Ostend. There, Crichton was on the point of being hanged by the Dutch Calvinists, but at the request of Queen Elizabeth, he was instead handed over to her, a ship being especially sent to bring him to England (*Crichton's Memoirs, ut supra;* cf. also Edmund Yorke to Walsingham, Middleburgh, 22 September 1584 and de Treslong to Ortell, Ostend, 4 October 1584, *For Cal. ut supra*, pp. 62 and 91).

"Charles Paget is now here in Rouen and writing a book in answer to that book that was set out against Throgmorton and also against the book of the Earl of Northumberland's death,[76] but he expecteth what shall be printed against William Shelley, and so to print his his book in English and Latin, Cledro the priest here doth stay to pen it[77] . . . It appeareth to be most true that Charles Paget did come into England to the late Earl of Northumberland and others to move a rebellion and to give them notice of an invasion which was then intended by the King of Spain, the Pope and the Duke of Guise, though he were specially sent unto by letters from the Queen of Scots not to proceed as then, for that the time did not fit for the purpose, and also he was sent unto by the Earl of Northumberland in like sort to stay his journey as then and Robotham his man was the messenger.[78] The said conspiracy was laboured with the Princes by Doctor Allen and Persons. *But Mr. Paget hath been blamed [by] those of this new conspiracy that he dealt not in the matter as he was directed, but rather that he did discover the same to the lords of the Council in England, and by that means he hath overthrown two great persons, so that they account him directly a spy, the rather for that he hath often protested that he never did deal with the Earl or Mr. Shelley on any matter of invasion, notwithstanding that he went into England for that purpose.* This brought him deeper in suspicion than before, and the

[76] The pamphlets referred to are *A discoverie of the treasons practised and attempted against the Queenes Majestie and the Realme by Francis Throckmorton*, London, 1584, and *A true and summarie Report of the Declaration of some of the Earl of Northumberland's treasons, delivered publiclie in the court of Star Chamber by the Lord Chancellor and others of her majesties most honorable privie councell, and councell learned by her majesties special commandment, together with the examinations and depositions of sundrie persons, touching the manner of his most wicked and violent murther committed upon him selfe with his own hand, in the Tower of London the 20* (sic) *daie of June 1585*, London, 1585. What appears to be a draft of this pamphlet, but wanting the pages on the Earl's death, is preserved at Hatfield, Vol. 138, ff. 108ff, and is well calendared in *Cal. Salisbury MSS. XIII*, pp. 270–281. The first pamphlet, of which there is also a draft (Dom. Eliz. 171, n. 86), was reprinted in Holinshed's *Chronicles*, Ed. 1807–8, *IV*, pp. 536ff. The second pamphlet was reprinted in *Somers's Tracts*, Ed. 1809, *I*, pp. 212ff.

[77] There is no evidence that such a book of Paget's, penned by Clitheroe, the priest, was ever printed, or that the Government produced a book concerning William Shelley (of whom cf. *infra* Chapter II). The purpose of Paget, possibly, of starting rumours that he was writing such a book was to screen his real position from his fellow Catholic exiles, who regarded him as an agent of the English Government.

[78] The Earl of Northumberland never denied that Charles Paget had come to see him at Petworth but only that there had been any talk of invasion. The Government's draft account in the manuscripts at Hatfield (*Cal. Salisbury MSS. XIII*, p. 276) states that according to the confessions of Wicliffe, the Earl's secretary, 20 December 1583 and 11 January 1584, Paget wrote to him enclosing another letter to be delivered to the Earl. This Wicliffe did, but when the Earl announced that the letter came from Charles Paget, Wicliffe wished his lordship to have no dealing with him. Whereupon the Earl replied: 'Well! he is come, and I cannot help it now". Robotham at the time was absent in France, but after he had returned the care of Paget was committed to him in place of Wicliffe. The remark of the Earl and Robotham's absence and return shortly agrees well with the above statement of Berden.

great suit which he maketh for the release of Thomas Morgan [*then in the Bastille*] (who of all the Papists here is generally accounted a spy). So that by all means possible they exclude him from their practices, and they daily labour to discredit him with the Duke of Guise, the Pope and King of Spain".[79]

Still further confirmation, and quite in agreement with his protestation, as reported by Berden, comes from Charles Paget himself. In a letter to the Queen of Scots, 18 July 1585, he wrote:

"The death of the Earl of Northumberland did not so much grieve me, for I knew he was mortal and must die; but the bruit given out that he killed himself because Mr. Shelley had confessed that I should say to him at my being in England that the Earl was content to take arms for the relief of your Majesty, and therefore I doubted not but he and all his 'parents' would do the like. As I shall answer at the day of judgement, I never spake word tending to any such end or sense to the said Shelley, but talked of such ordinary matter that the Council might have been privy thereof without offence. And I assure myself that Shelley, if he might be suffered to speak openly upon his conscience, would acquit me thereof. But he will, I fear, drink of the same cup the Earl of Northumberland has done, and so shall I with many more,[80] such are the devilish practices of the Earl of Leicester and his confederates.

The Earl of Northumberland was once poisoned before, but cured by Doctor Astlowe, and that not taking place, 'he is paid home with a dag [*pistol*]'. And they cannot be content to spoil him of his life, but they would take away his Christianity in making the world believe he killed himself.[81] If the Earl of Arundel had not been com-

---

[79] Berden to Walsingham, Rouen, 13 August 1585, Dom. Eliz. Add. 29, n. 39, printed in *C.R.S. XXI*, p. 78. Italics mine. Paget's "protests", reported by Berden, would equivalently mean that he had carried out the Queen of Scots' orders "not to proceed" then with the invasion plans. These orders would, presumably, have provided his excuse to his fellow exiles, for his failure to carry out Guise's instructions in England.

[80] There never was the slightest danger of Paget's "drinking the same cup" as the Earl. He protested too much, and the reason will be seen in a later note.

[81] The title of the pamphlet (cf. Note 76) gives the date of the Earl's death as 20 June, but in the text it gives the correct date 21 June. At Shelley's trial in 1586 it was stated: "Monday 21 June last about one o'clock in the morning he [*the Earl*] destroyed himself" (cf. Lansd. MSS. 45, n. 75). The Government maintained that he had shot himself in the Tower, where he had been confined since the beginning of January 1584, suspected of being involved in the Throckmorton-Paget plot. According to their statement he had been driven to take his life by the confessions in June 1585 of William Shelley, a fellow-prisoner in the Tower, implicating him in the invasion scheme, when Charles Paget visited the Earl at Petworth in September 1583. Suspicion was at once aroused that the Earl had really been murdered, as is clear from the Government's own enquiry relating into his death and his alleged treasons, held by the Council in the Star Chamber 23 June 1585, the pamphlet being published to allay this suspicion (cf. *A True and summarie Report*, etc., as in Note 76; cf. also Lord Francis Russell to Walsingham,

mitted when he was, within short time both the Earl of Northumberland and Shelley had been in liberty.[82] They both being examined were 'strongly' a twelvemonth together, and nothing could be found to touch them. And is it likely that Shelley of himself would

[82] Before being sent to the Tower, the Earl of Northumberland had been placed under house arrest in charge of Sir Thomas Leighton (cf. Walsingham to the Earl of Rutland, London, 17 December 1583, *Hist. MSS. Comm. 12th Report, Appendix, Part IV*, p. 156). About the same time the Earl of Arundel was also ordered to remain a prisoner in his own house (cf. F. V. to Charles Paget, 20 December 1583, Dom. Eliz. 164, n. 47, and Roger Manners to the Earl of Rutland, 5 January 1584, *Hist. MSS. Comm. ut supra*, p. 157). Arundel's examination and answers, 24 December 1583, are printed in *C.R.S. XXI*, pp. 45–48; cf. also his Protest, Arundel House, 12 January 1584 and Walsingham's reply on behalf of the Government, *Ibid.*, pp. 48–52). The Earl of Arundel was released early in April 1584, no evidence having been found against him (*Ibid.*, p. 56; cf. also Arundel to Queen Elizabeth, 11–14 April 1585, *Ibid.*, p. 99). Having become a Catholic, he was arrested again in April 1585, on his attempt to cross to France. He was confined in the Tower until his death on 19 October 1595, having meanwhile been declared guilty of treason at his trial 7 April 1589, at which, amongst other charges, he was again and quite falsely accused of having been implicated in the Throckmorton-Paget plot of 1583 (*Ibid.*, pp. 220–223. Compare Popham's brief there with his speech on the enquiry into the Earl of Northumberland's death).

William Shelley of Michelgrove, Sussex, appears to have been arrested about the same time as the two Earls. There is a reference to his examination 10 December 1583; in "The Case of William Shelley" (B.M. Egerton MSS. 2074, f. 73; cf. also "the Manner of Proceeding against William Shelley", B. M. Lansd. MSS. 45, n. 75).

Tynemouth, 26 June 1585, quoted by Cuthbert Sharpe, *Memorials of the Rebellion of 1569*, p. 359, from Dom. Eliz. Add. 29, n. 21). The Government's pamphlet, it may be added, does not stand up to critical examination, there being untruths, inaccuracies and inconsistent statements contained in it (cf. *infra* Chapter II, section 5).

Raleigh evidently did not think the Earl had committed suicide, and took it for granted that Sir Robert Cecil had the same conviction. Writing to the latter when Essex was in his power, Raleigh advised him: "The less you make him, the less he shall be able to harm you and yours. And if her Majesty's favour fail him, he will again decline to a common person.

For after-revenges, fear them not; for your own father that was esteemed to be the contriver of Norfolk's ruin, yet his son followeth your father's son and loveth him. Humours of men succeed not [*i.e. are not inherited*]; but grow by occasions, and accidents of time and power. Somerset made no revenge on the Duke of Northumberland's heirs. Northumberland that now is, thinks not of Hatton's issue. Kelloway lives, that murdered the brother of Horsey, and Horsey let him go by all his lifetime" (printed in *Murdin*, p. 811 and in E. Edwards, *The Life of Sir Walter Raleigh*, London, 1868, *II*, p 222). "In this passage" wrote Lingard, "Raleigh places Hatton, with respect to the death of Northumberland, in the same category with three other persons who had deprived their victims of life, either on the scaffold, or by assassination, and yet had never met with retribution from the friends or kindred of the sufferers. It appears to me, that his reasoning with Cecil is based on the admission by them both, that the violent death of Northumberland was owing to the contrivance of Hatton, as the death of the Duke of Norfolk and of the other victims mentioned by him had been owing to the contrivance of Lord Burghley and their respective persecutors; and, moreover, that Hatton's conduct on that occasion had been of such a description as to call loudly for vengeance from the house of Percy, 'Northumberland that now is, thinks not of Hatton's issue' " (Lingard, *History of England*, 1883 Ed. *VI*, p. 392, n. 1). Nor must it be overlooked that on the day before the Earl's death, his keeper was replaced by Bailiff, one of Hatton's servants. Moreover, if Paget on his visit to England did not, as the evidence shows, engage in treasonable practices with Northumberland and Shelley, the motive for the Earl's alleged suicide, falls to the ground: and the conclusion can only be that the motive was 'faked' by the Government.

confess an untruth, seeing himself free from danger? Or, on the other side, is it likely, if it were true, as it is not, that I should have said that abovesaid to Shelley, that the Earl of Northumberland had so little understanding as to know that he was not touched thereby in law? And to want Christianity as to kill himself? Or if God take so much of his grace from him, that with less suspicion and more facility he might have killed himself than with a dag? God, I trust, will reveal the truth to the enemy's shame, and give such punishment as such a practice merits".[83]

In line with this statement is Paget's correspondence with Walsingham in 1582, as outlined above, and with his conduct on his return from his mission to England at the end of September 1583.[84] Once the new ambassador, Sir Edward Stafford, reached Paris,[85] Paget lost no time in visiting him and offering his services. In his despatch of 27 October the ambassador reported:

"Charles Paget has been with me and offered all the service that might be, assuring me that he never did or would do anything against the Queen or his country. I desired him to do somewhat for proof thereof, as especially in discovering some practice against the State, which he being of that religion, as he was haunting with them that were papists of state and not of religion he might easily do without prejudice to his conscience, for every man was bound to discover anything done against his prince and country. And that I would not hide his good service under a bushel, but set it out with all the help to him that I could. *He desired me to judge of him by the effects.* I will have good watch over him and the rest".[86]

[83] Charles Paget to Queen of Scots, Paris, 18 July 1585, *Scot. Cal. VIII*, pp. 26–31. The extract quoted above is on pp. 28–29. Readers may wonder why he should have written thus to the Queen. But it must be recalled that the English Government in the pamphlet on the Earl of Northumberland's treasons and death, had represented Paget as obtaining the collaboration of the Earl and of William Shelley for the Duke of Guise's invasion scheme of 1583, when he visited them on his coming to England in that year under the alias of Mope. According to the letters of Persons and Berden cited above, he would so have appeared to have acted directly against her express directions. If, then, as the evidence tends to show, Paget was working in collusion with the English Government, he had to keep up his position with the Scottish Queen. The above passage, then, was to reassure her that he had not, in fact, acted contrary to her orders.

[84] The date of Paget's return to Dieppe can be ascertained from Haller's examination, 20 December 1583 (Dom. Eliz. 164, n. 45). He embarked on 25 September (cf. Note 64) and landed two days later, that is, on the 27th. Haller adds a graphic touch, that the "gentleman" was so sea-sick that they had no conversation together, and that the invalid stayed a day at Dieppe, evidently recovering from the effects of the crossing.

[85] Stafford arrived at Paris 17 October 1583, n.s. (cf. Stafford to Walsingham, 17 October 1583, *For. Cal. July 1583–July 1584*, p. 128).

[86] Stafford to Walsingham, Paris, 27 October 1583, *Ibid.*, p. 172. Italics mine. It was but a few days later that Francis Throckmorton was arrested and soon accused of being implicated in the Duke of Guise's plan of invasion, cf. *infra*.

All this evidence from different sources, Persons, Pasquier, Berden and Paget himself, hangs well together and shows that Paget on his visit to England in September 1583 did not endeavour to secure the collaboration of the Earl of Northumberland and others in the invasion scheme of that year. It is, moreover, in agreement with statements made by the Earl at his examination, 11 May 1585:

"He doth not remember", he asserted, "that any admonition was given him to take heed how he dealt with Charles Paget when he came to Petworth. . . .

His conference and talk with Charles Paget was only about the causes of his coming which he declared to be upon matters between him and the L. Paget his brother; and talked further with him of the state of France and matters occurrents beyond the seas.

He forsaketh God and his salvation if he knew any other cause of his coming: or knoweth with whom he had otherwise conference here within the Realm. . . .

He protesteth upon his salvation that he knoweth not what conference was between the L. Paget and Charles at that time; but sure he is that he saw a will written in parchment which was sealed there at his being at Petworth".[87]

---

[87] "Therle of Northumberland examined before the Chancellor, Mr. Vicechamberlain, Sir Walter Mildmay," printed from Egerton MSS. 2074, in *C.R.S. XXI*, pp. 120–122; cf. also *supra* Note 21. Though the Government stated that the Earl had been often examined, the dates of three of these being mentioned, of which two are referred to in the official account, the above is the only examination of which the replies of the Earl are extant, and no reference to this one was made by the Government! There are interrogatories for his examination 17 December 1583, but his replies have not been preserved. As regards the disappearance of all the main documents touched the Throckmorton-Paget plot, etc., cf. *infra* Note 100.

CHAPTER II

Francis Throckmorton's arrest: Lord Paget's flight abroad adversely interpreted—Throckmorton's denial of the truth of his confessions—Throckmorton's Submission and Declaration, 4 June 1584—William Shelley's confession at his trial, 12 February 1586—General criticism of the Government's case

1. *Francis Throckmorton's arrest: Lord Paget's flight abroad adversely interpreted*

Contrary to the evidence outlined in the last chapter, Queen Elizabeth's Government maintained that Paget *had* broached the subject of the invasion with the Earl of Northumberland during his stay at Petworth. As this was the central point of the charges in three political trials or enquiries in the following two or more years, which are connected with the theme of this book, the Government's case must now be examined in some detail.

In the first publication on the subject, that concerning Francis Throckmorton's Treasons, the case was based solely on his confessions. This Francis Throckmorton, eldest son of Sir John Throckmorton,[88] was arrested in November 1583, on suspicion of having conveyed letters to and from the Queen of Scots. When his house at Lewisham was searched two papers, according to the official account,

[88] "Throckmorton apprehended 5⁰ November" (Egerton MSS. 2074, f. 72, rough notes, undated, probably in the hand of Thomas Wilkes, one of the clerks of the Privy Council). The Diary of the Tower under 13 November records his being committed to that prison and confined in "Little Ease". His brother, George, was sent to the Tower, 17 November (Diary of the Tower). Before his committal Francis was held captive in the house of a gentleman called Randolph (An accusation of Sr. Francis Throckmorton for treason, Dom. Eliz. 171, n. 86). Sir John Throckmorton died 23 May 1580. His removal from the post of Justic of Chester within a year before his death was attributed by contemporaries to the malice of the Earl of Leicester (*Leicester's Commonwealth*, 1641 ed. p. 79, and Camden, *Annals*, English Translation, 1635, p. 261). There is extant a curious letter of Archbishop Whitgift to Burghley, 8 May 1584, i.e. two months or so before the execution of Francis Throckmorton. After complaining of the insolence of Beale, the trusted servant of Walsingham, he continued: "Sir John Throckmorton I loved whilst I lived with him, neither had I other occasion. He served her Majesty painfully in that place, I would there were (in that respect) the like now. His son Francis to my remembrance was never in my company but once in his father's time, when I sent for him by process to answer in certain matters wherewith he was to be charged, sithence which time, he hath not to my knowledge much remained within my jurisdiction" (*Hist. MSS. Comm. Longleat MSS. II*, p. 23). The name is spelt variously in the contemporary documents. I have used the spelling 'Throckmorton', except in quotations where it is written otherwise.

were found, the one in secretary hand and the other in Roman hand, containing the names of certain Catholic noblemen and gentlemen, and a list of havens suitable, so the Government maintained, for the landing of foreign forces.[89] He was, therefore, handed over to the Queen's Council and others, to draw the truth out of him by torture.[90] Then

[89] The official account was put forth in the pamphlet: *A Discoverie of the treasons practised . . . by Francis Throckmorton* (see Note 76). It was published on the very day of his execution, 10 July 1584 (*The Diary of the Tower*, printed at the end of Persons's Edition of Sander's *De Schismate*, Rome, 1586). The pamphlet was reprinted in Holinshed's *Chronicles*, 1807–8 Ed. *IV*, pp. 536ff. This version, however, omitted the "Note to the Reader" of some ten lines or so, and the prefatory letter of a certain "Q. Z. of Lyons Inn", 15 June 1584, to an unnamed friend who had professed to doubt the sufficiency of the evidence against Throckmorton. There is a rough draft of the pamphlet: "An accusation of Sr. Francis Throgmorton for treason" (Dom. Eliz. 171, n. 86). This is in the hand of Burghley's clerk, with corrections, etc., by Thomas Wilkes.

From the fact that the autographs and even some holographs of her letters are in British Archives and are not mentioned in the list of those seized at Chartley in 1586, it would certainly appear that the Government, long before the arrest of Throckmorton, were intercepting quite a number of the Queen of Scots' letters (cf. *Labanoff V, passim*). Moreover, as early as 3 September 1583 Cherelles, the secretary of Mauvissière, the French ambassador in England, was copying for Walsingham her letters received at the French embassy (cf. *Ibid.*, p. 361, and Cherelles to Walsingham, *Ibid.*, pp. 429–430). Already in April 1583 Henry Fagot, an official in the embassy, and Walsingham's spy, reported to the Secretary of State or to Burghley: "My Lord, I inform you also that if your Excellency wishes I will draw the Secretary of my Lord, the Ambassador [*i.e. Cherelles*] to be so much my friend, that if he is given a consideration of some little money, he will do nothing without informing me, of everything that will be done touching the Queen of Scots and the secret cipher which is written in such letters [*lettre quatale*]; and you must know that after your Excellency has read any packet addressed to her, that he [*Cherelles*] will not omit to put it back in the said bundle and that this is in no way known, I know, except by him. The great agents of the Queen of Scots are Sir Throckmorton and my Lord Henry Havard [*Howard*] who never come to bring anything from her except at night, and the Ambassador acts in like manner" (Henry Fagot to [Walsingham], April 1583, R.O. M.Q.S. XII, n. 61. The French used by Fagot is extremely obscure and ungrammatical, but the above translation gives what seems to be the sense, and is certainly much more intelligible than the rendering in *Scot. Cal. VI*, p. 430, which is made more obscure by some incorrect readings, such as 'mort' for 'nuit').

At his trial Francis Throckmorton acknowledged the paper in the secretary hand, but refused to recognise as his that in the Roman hand (cf. Stowe MSS. 1083, ff. 17–20). The paper in secretary hand, containing the list of the havens was drawn up, according to his own statement, with the aid of his father, which would make it at the time of his trial 21 May 1584 some four years old, and so, not made, as his accusers maintained, in view of the invasion plan of 1583.

[90] The *Diary of the Tower* records three rackings of Throckmorton: twice on 23 November and again on 2 December 1583. By 12 January n.s. the report had reached Persons at Paris that he had been "three times tortured cruelly on the rack" (Persons to Aquaviva, Paris, 12 January 1584, *C.R.S. XXXIX*, p. 187). A document entitled "Accounts of Events in England, December 1583" states that "they have put him to the torture dreadfully" (*Spanish Cal. 1580–1586*, p. 512). And on 20 December 1583 a correspondent wrote to Charles Paget that Throckmorton had been often racked, but according to report had confessed nothing (F. V. and F. R. to Paget, "from my house in the Counter", 20 December 1583, Dom. Eliz. 164, n. 47). It was doubtless in connection with this racking that Anne Throckmorton was asked in her examination, 18 December 1583; "Whether did you not speak to the boy of any ointment to be carried to your husband for his hands and back" (Dom. Eliz. 164, n. 41). The official account, however, states that "he was laid upon the rack and somewhat pinched, although not much: for at the end of three days following he had recovered himself and was in as good a plight

as before the time of his racking: which if it had then or any other time been ministered unto him with that violence that he and his favourers have endeavoured slanderously to give out, the signs thereof would have appeared upon his limbs for many years ... the second time he was put to the rack, before he was strained up to any purpose, he yielded to confess everything he knew, in the matters objected against him: whereupon he was loosed" (*Holinshed IV*, p. 535). The draft of the pamphlet after "put to the rack", adds, "being the 19th of November and the last time he suffered any torture, for although he was at other times brought to the place of the rack and there examined yet neither corded or pinched as he falsely enforced by speech to the auditory at his arraignment" (Dom. Eliz. 171, n. 86). This passage was crossed out and changed as in the pamphlet. That he was brought to the rack on 19 November is borne out by an autograph letter of Walsingham to Wilkes, written the day before: "You shall do well to give Mr. Norton [*the rackmaster*] warning this night or tomorrow in the morning early, to meet you at the Tower at such hour as by you shall be thought meet. I have seen as resolute men as Throgmorton stoop, notwithstanding the great show that he hath made of a Roman resolution. I suppose the grief of the last torture will suffice without any extremity of racking to make him more conformable than he hath hitherto shewed himself. And so I commit you to God. At the Court the 18th of November 1583, Your assured friend Fra: Walsingham" (Dom. Eliz. 163, n. 65). Of course, this does not necessarily imply that he was tortured for the last time on 19 November; certainly it hardly squares with the statement in the pamphlet, quoted above, "that he was somewhat pinched, although not much". One would scarcely compare Throckmorton's attitude under torture to Roman resolution, or think that the pain of his former racking would suffice to break down that determination, had he been only somewhat pinched but not much.

And in connection with these rackings it must be remembered that Englishmen, particularly of the legal profession have always prided themselves on the fact that the Common law of England has ever been adverse to torture being employed to extract a confession from one suspected or accused of a crime. Whatever the failures in practice, such methods are quite alien to its spirit. Magna Carta, indeed, laid it down that no free man should be destroyed in any way unless by legal judgment or by the law of the land, which lawyers have interpreted as excluding the use of torture. Coke himself, as Fortescue before him, declared its use to be contrary to the common law, and as one would expect, it was during a period of tyranny—that of the Tudors—that its application became so common. Particularly was this so during the reigns of Queen Elizabeth, when, as Hallam noted, the rack was rarely idle; but even in her reign, its use roused strong protest. It was the outcry caused by the appalling torture inflicted on Campion and his companions in 1581 that forced Burghley to pen that pamphlet in which he endeavoured to defend the Government's use of torture, and quite falsely to declare that such torture as had been inflicted was but slight (cf. *A Declaration of the favourable dealing of her Majesty's Commissioners, appointed for the examination of certain Traitors and of the Tortures unjustly reported to be done upon them for matter of Religion*", Somers Tracts I, pp. 209ff). It was of this same pamphlet that Hallam remarked: "Those who revere the memory of Lord Burghley must blush for this pitiful apology" (*Constitutional History*, 1842 *I*, p. 147). Hallam, however, did not realise the amount of deliberate falsehood it contained, as did also Burghley's *Execution of Justice in England*, issued in the same year 1583. Dr. Allen exposed him in *A True, Sincere and Modest Defence of English Catholics*, 1584 (modern edition, ed. J. H. Pollen, s.J. 1914). Similar slighting remarks of the lightness of the torture inflicted and similar falsehoods to those found in these two pamphlets of Burghley, appear also in the official account of the Throckmorton-Paget plot, with the composition of which he must have been connected, as its draft is in the hand of one of his clerks. One of the most odious traits in him and in Walsingham, indeed, which modern historians tend to pass over in silence, was the easy way they spoke of torture and its victims, and especially was this so of the former, who throughout his career was always so careful to avoid for himself any ill consequences of his actions. But even Burghley and Walsingham dared not apply torture to a nobleman. That is revealed in the official account of Northumberland's treasons, according to which Shelley told the Earl that his case was very different from Shelley's own: "for that the Earl in respect of his nobility, was not in danger to be dealt withal in such sort as he the said Shelley was like to be, being but a private gentleman, and therefore to be used with all extremity to be made to confess the truth" (*Somers Tracts I*, pp. 219–220).

shortly after the arrest of Throckmorton, Lord Paget and Sir Charles Arundel (Arundell) left England without licence, and retired to Paris.[91]

The Government seized on this flight, and linking it with the arrest of Throckmorton, endeavoured to show that they had fled because of the treasonable talks which, so they asserted, Lord Paget and his brother, Charles, had recently had with the Earl of Northumberland and William Shelley—overlooking the fact that this did not apply to Sir Charles Arundel. Thus, in the enquiry in the Star Chamber on 23 June 1585 concerning the Earl's death in the Tower two days before, the Solicitor-General, Egerton, asserted that the Earl, knowing how far he himself was touched with the said treasons and in what degree of danger he stood, if they should be revealed, found his only hope of safety to consist in cunning concealment of them. Therefore he endeavoured to cover them by all possible means he could devise. First, he had Lord Paget conveyed overseas,

"a man not only privy to the practices and treasons handled by Francis Throckmorton, but also to the treasons of his brother Charles, wherein the Earl and Lord Paget were *doubtless* both confederates with Charles, made acquainted by him with the causes of his coming over, as principal men with whom he dealt in those matters at Petworth".

The occasion, Egerton maintained, that provoked the Earl to convey away Lord Paget was the arrest of Throckmorton,

"who being committed to the Tower and charged with high matters was in case to be dealt withal by way of extremity, to be made to

[91] Lord Paget left London at the end of term, 23 November 1583, apparently to go to his house at Drayton, but really to cross over to France, though his secretary, William Warde, did not know of his purpose at the time (Examination of William Warde, Solicitor and secretary to Lord Paget, 14 and 20 December 1583, Dom. Eliz. 164, nn. 26 and 46). He was in Paris 2 December 1583, whence he wrote to Burghley (cf. *infra* text). With Lord Paget went Sir Charles Arundel, a servant named John and another unnamed person. The man who undertook their passage from a place called Fering was Thomas Clynsall, who was hired for the purpose by William Shelley at a fee of £30 (Extracts of various examinations, amongst other those of Clynsall 9 and 18 December, and another undated, Dom. Eliz. 167, n. 59). Clynsall further stated that Shelley, not the Earl of Northumberland, as the Government said, sent often "to enquire of the readiness of the bark". The baggage appears to have been taken to a tavern in Arundel kept by Christopher Haines, and two carriers, John Ramsden and "Thwaites of Stroode", conveyed it there, helped by Simon Smyth, a servant of the Earl (Examinations of Simon Smyth and John Ramsden, 28 December 1583, Dom. Eliz. 164, nn. 66 and 67). Haines knew nothing, so he stated, of Lord Paget's departure till after the event (Examination of Christopher Haines, 17 December 1583, Dom. Eliz. 164, n. 33). Nothing pertinent is to be found in other examinations. It seems, therefore, that both William Shelley and the Earl were responsible for the arrangements of their crossing.

confess the treasons charged upon him,[92] in revealing whereof
Charles Paget's coming to Petworth and the cause of his repair
thither could not be concealed. *No man at this time within the realm
could accuse the Earl of these confederacies, but the Lord Paget only,*
who stood in danger to be discovered by Francis Throckmorton.
The safety, therefore, of the Earl rested altogether upon Lord Paget's

[92] Italics mine. This appears to be in contradiction with the Government's other
statement that they knew nothing of the plot until Throckmorton had confessed, which
point is emphasised several times in the pamphlet concerning his treasons. "At the time
of his apprehension, there was no knowledge or doubt [*i.e. suspicion*] had of these treasons
or of his [*Throckmorton's*] privity unto them; but only an information and suspicion
delivered and conceived of some practice between him and the Scottish Queen" (*Holinshed
IV*, p. 540). How then could Throckmorton be charged with treason before he had been
forced "by extremity" to confess it? Being a messenger to convey letters to and from the
Queen of Scots was not treason, however much the Government disliked it. In stating
that they knew nothing of the plot or enterprise before Throckmorton's confessions, the
Government were certainly lying. The contemporary documents show that they had
knowledge of the invasion plan some months even before the arrest of Throckmorton.
The report of the ambassador in France concerning ships and men being prepared by the
Duke of Guise, shows that they had at least suspicions three months before his appre-
hension (cf. Cobham to Walsingham, 27 July 1583, *For. Cal. July 1583–July 1584*, p. 36;
cf. also Report concerning shipping on the coast of France (after 4 August 1583), Roger
Williams to Walsingham, Alost, 2 October 1583, Stafford to Walsingham, 27 October
and 19 November 1583, and Edmund Stansfielde to Stafford, Rouen, 31 October 1583,
Ibid., pp. 57, 123, 172, 222 and 185). The matter is placed beyond all doubt by a letter of
Robert Beale to Cobham in August 1583. "Being appointed" he wrote, "to attend in Mr.
Secretary's absence, whom her Majesty has sent into Scotland, she commands me to tell
you that being advertised that the Duke of Guise at Newhaven, Dieppe and other places of
Normandy was preparing ships, munition and soldiers, under good captains, to be sent
into Scotland, she (being then at Greenwich) sent for the French ambassador, and having
informed him of it, required him to advertise his master, and to pray him in her name,
according to his former promises of good will and protestations of friendship, to take
order that these preparations might be stayed, and not suffer anything to be attempted
in Scotland. For otherwise, seeing the parties were his subjects, and he himself now
forewarned of their designs, if anything were done, he could not well excuse it. The
ambassador has lately showed her a letter received from the King, wherein he assures
her of the continuance of his good will, and that he has heretofore hindered such enterprises and will continue the like course, whereupon she desired him to render his master
her hearty thanks and wishes you to do the like, signifying to the king how well she
accepted his friendly and courteous answer, and assuring him that she will requite him
with like good will" (R. Beale to Cobham, 27 August 1583, *Ibid.*, p. 82. Cf. also King of
France to Q. Elizabeth, 12 August 1583, *Cal. Salisbury MSS. XIII*, p. 204, wrongly
assigned, it seems, to 1582). Readers will remember that according to Guise's plan of
invasion, the main attack was to be made by way of Scotland if the state of that country
was favourable. Some days after Beale's letter, when Sir Edward Stafford was to be sent
to replace Cobham as ambassador in Paris, he was ordered in his instructions to render
hearty thanks to the King of France and the Queen Mother, for staying such preparations
as were being made by Guise for Scotland (Stafford's Instructions, September 1583,
Ibid., p. 115. "Then I" wrote Stafford, "according to your instructions, thanked him
[*Henry III*] for breaking the enterprise of Scotland" ... (Cobham and Stafford to Q.
Elizabeth, 21 October 1583, *Ibid.*, p. 154). Walsingham's letter of an even earlier date is
revealing, too. Writing on 20 August 1583, he informed Bowes of his opinion that "if
the Queen of England 'revoked' him [*Walsingham*] and suffered him [*James VI*] to run
this course that he takes, and to taste of the effects that are likely to ensue thereby to his
own harm, it would be the best way to daunt this new courage that he is of late grown to,
and make him to know himself better. For, as for any help that he may look for at the
French King's hands, upon the hope whereof it is to be thought that he bears himself

departing out of the realm, which was procured by the Earl with so great expedition, as that Throckmorton being committed to the Tower about the 7th day of November 1583, the Earl made means the twelfth day to have Lord Paget provided of shipping in all haste by William Shelley, wherein the Earl used such importunate entreaty, and sent so often to hasten the preparation of the ship, that the same was provided, and the Lord Paget embarked by the twenty-third day of the same month following or thereabouts".[93]

There is good reason to doubt, however, that such was the purpose

[93] Cf. *A True and summarie Report*, etc. (as in Note 76), reprinted in *Somers Tracts*, London, 1809, I, pp. 212ff. Italics mine. The above passage is on p. 218. What appears to be the draft of the pamphlet is at Hatfield (cf. Note 76). Egerton's argument was putting the cart before the horse. What had first to be proved was that the conferences between Lord Paget, Charles Paget and the Earl of Northumberland had been concerned with traitorous practices, and the evidence against this, already given, is very strong (cf. *supra* Chapter I). Nor does Egerton's argument hold for another reason. Even according to another part of the official account, Lord Paget was not the *only one* who could have accused the Earl, and the Earl, so they stated, knew it. There was William Shelley himself. Why otherwise, according to the same account, should he have begged Shelley to keep silent? That account, in fact, avers that not only could Shelley have revealed the Earl's alleged traitorous conduct, but actually did so; for the same pamphlet alleges that it was Shelley's confessions in June 1585, and his revealing to the Earl what he had confessed, that drove the Earl to despair and to commit suicide (*Somers Tracts I*, pp. 219–220, and *Cal. Salisbury MSS. XIII*, pp. 280–281). In Westminster Hall, 12 February 1586, Myles Sandes, Clerk of the Court, read the indictment against Shelley, part of which, in an English account of the trial runs: "The said William Shelley, knowing the said Charles Paget the said 7th day of September traitorously to have come from the parties beyond the seas unto Petworth aforesaid, traitorously to confer with the said Earl of Northumberland, etc." ("The Manner of Proceeding against Wm. Shelley", B. M. Lansd. 45, n. 75. The formal Latin indictment is still preserved in the Baga de Secretis, Pouch XLVII). The Government's statement, therefore, that the Earl knew that only Lord Paget could accuse him, was false, and the Queen's law-officers must have been aware of it. Had they, however, not asserted this, they would have had to explain why the Earl, on their own testimony, had made no attempt to get Shelley out of the country as he could have done, when Lord Paget and Sir Charles Arundel crossed to France. Later, indeed, at Shelley's own trial, they contradicted their statement above, by saying that the Earl had had others conveyed out of the country for fear that they might have revealed his alleged traitorous practices (cf. *infra* this chapter, section 4). This is only one instance of the trickery and falsehood practised by the Government that is revealed from a close study of the documents, and of their failure to achieve consistency in a fabricated story. Cf. also *infra* Note 100.

thus stoutly, the Queen of England has been certainly assured that there will be no such matter put in execution. For proof whereof he [*the King of France*] has given express commandment to the Duke of Guise to stay any preparations that way. For, indeed, he knows right well that her Majesty wants not the best means to keep him occupied at home, if he should attempt anything to her harm and prejudice" ... (Walsingham to R. Bowes, 20 August 1583, *Scot. Cal. VI*, p. 589). The last part of the letter no doubt refers to the power of preventing Henry III from favouring Guise's preparations by stirring up trouble for him with the Huguenots. Cf. also Walsingham to Q. Elizabeth, St. Johnstone, 12 September 1583, and Same to Same, 18 September 1583, *Ibid.*, pp. 611 and 612). Throckmorton was not arrested till early November and from the Government's own account had not confessed anything by 19 November (cf. Walsingham to Wilkes, 18 November 1583, quoted in Note 90).

of Lord Paget's leaving the country. The Earl of Northumberland, in
his examination of 11 May 1585, stated that

> "he knew of the Lord Paget's going half a year before he went over
> and that he had a purpose to go for matters of his conscience"; and
> that "Charles Paget declared to his L. that one cause of his coming
> was to have the L. his brother come over beyond the seas"; also that
> "he had in his L. hand 3 quarters of a year £30,000 of money of
> the L. Paget's which he had [prepared?] as his bank for his main-
> tenance beyond the seas, and so long he stayed the going away of
> L. Paget who would have departed so long before, if he had not
> stayed the L. Paget".[94]

This is confirmed by two letters of Lord Paget himself after his arrival
in Paris. Writing to his mother, he said that he had not done this upon
any sudden notion, but after a long time and deliberation, and felt
that what he had begun was by God's appointment and for His service,
and therefore it could not but be for the best. If they were to take all
from him, it would be very hard dealing, but that he would have to
leave to God and His cause. On the same day he wrote to Burghley,
that he had gone abroad without licence, but hoped Burghley would
weigh the reasons favourably. He travelled because of his gout and
because of his conscience, troubled these three years. He could not
persuade himself to remain contented with those terms that had been
granted to him. He was much in want of the sacraments, and could
not receive them at home,[95] especially as Catholics were so hardly
conceived of as at that time, "by the traitorous and villainous intent
of a mad beastly bedlem". His enemies had procured him great
misliking in the Queen, and he had gone abroad for his own security.
He, therefore, desired Burghley's intercession for the Queen's favour.
He had ever been a faithful servant and would not enter into any
practice or conference with any prince against the Queen.[96] Nor is his

---

[94] Printed in *C.R.S. XXI*, pp. 121–122.

[95] The Government had earlier harried him on the question of religion: and in November 1580 he had been in the custody of the Dean of Windsor for fourteen weeks, when
he yielded to have the Protestant service in his own house, and to attend it (Lord Paget
to the Lords of the Council, Windsor, 17 November 1580, Dom. Eliz. 144, n. 29; cf
also *Dasent XII*, pp. 134, 157). He boggled, however, at attending a sermon at St. Pauls,
and asked for delay (Lord Paget to Walsingham, London, 10 January 1581, Dom.
Eliz. n. 5).

[96] Cf. Lord Paget to Lady Paget, his mother, Paris, 2/12 December 1583, and Same
to Burghley, same date (Dom. Eliz. 164, nn. 5, 6). Treating of the Throckmorton plot,
the contemporary historian, Camden, wrote: "Thomas Lord Paget, and Charles Arundel,
a courtier, privily fled the land, and withdrew themselves unto France, who with others

letter to his brother, Charles, after the latter had returned to France, that of a conspirator who had conducted traitorous practices with him and the Earl of Northumberland in the preceding month.

"Brother Charles," he wrote, "as your abiding in Paris was not well liked, so is it now more misliked that you stay at Rouen, considering the company that is there, as the Bishop of Ross and such like.[97] It shall be therefore very good for you the better to avoid all suspicion to remove your self thence further into France as soon as you may and the rather because I do hear by some of my good friends that in some advertisments lately come you are touched as not to carry yourself so dutifully as you ought to do, which if they

---

[97] John Leslie was at one time professor of Canon Law in Aberdeen. He was one of the commissioners for Mary, Queen of Scots, at the conference in York in 1568, after her flight to England, and acted as her ambassador to Queen Elizabeth. He was imprisoned in the Tower in 1571 in connection with the Ridolfi plot, and was released in 1573 on condition of his leaving England. Bishop-designate of Ross in 1566, his appointment was only confirmed by the Pope in 1575, when he was consecrated. He became Vicar-General and suffragan of Rouen in 1579. A clerical careerist, a "politique" in outlook, and a friend of Thomas Morgan, he was distrusted by Mary's ambassador in France, the Archbishop of Glasgow, who suspected him of being in the pay of the Elizabethan Government (Glasgow to ——, Paris, 31 October 1580, *Labanoff VII*, p. 152. There is not the slightest ground for Labanoff's stating that this letter was addressed to the General of the Jesuits. It may well have been to Fentry, the Archbishop's nephew, who was at that time in Rome). The Archbishop's suspicion was not without foundation; for it was Ross who handed to Cobham, the English ambassador in Paris, the articles of the alleged Papal League of 1580 (cf. *infra* Chapter VI, section 3 and Appendix I). Ross was never called into the conferences in Paris, so it appears, of the leaders of the Scottish Queen's supporters during the years 1582 to 1584. He died in 1596 (Cf. *D.N.B. XXXIII*, and D. McN. Lockie, *The Political Career of the Bishop of Ross, 1566–1580, Historical Journal*, Birmingham University, *IV*, n. 2 (1954), pp. 98–143).

---

devoted to the Romish Religion, grievously bewailed and complained among themselves, that the Queen was without their desert alienated from them through the subtle practices of Leicester and Walsingham, that they were unworthily disgraced and ignominiously used, singular kinds of fraud were invented, privy snares laid, that they might whether they would or no, through improvidence be entangled in the snares of high treason, and that there was at home no hope of safety. And certainly to grope men's minds there were used some subtle devices indeed, counterfeit letters were privily sent under the name of the Queen of Scots, and the fugitives, and left in Papists' houses, spies were sent abroad everywhere to gather rumours, and lay hold of words, reporters of vain things were admitted, many called into suspicion, etc." (Camden, *Annals*, 3rd Edition, London, 1635, p. 261).

Lord Henry Howard appears to have been the recipient of such a forged letter at this time, which purported to have been written by the Queen of Scots (cf. His Examination, 11 December 1583, *Scot. Cal. VI*, p. 675). Howard, when accused of receiving such a letter, replied that having been "told by the messenger who delivered him the letter that he brought the same from the French ambassador, he repaired to the French ambassador to understand from him whether he had sent him any such letter; who denied the same, and avowed it on oath par le sang de Dieu, etc. as he has already set down to the Queen of England". Just before the Babington plot Mary herself received an "infinite number" of letters supposedly sent by Catholics (cf. *infra* Note 405). At the examination of the Earl of Arundel, 1 May 1585, a forged letter was produced (cf. *C.R.S. XXI*, pp. 14 and 15). Interesting light on the source of forged letters is to be seen in the "Confession of Thomas Harrison", *Scot. Cal. IX*, p. 530.

should be true I should be heartily sorry. I thought good therefore to give you warning thereof that you might be more wary and thus much assure your self that if you forget what duty and loyalty you owe here, I will forget to be your brother and shall be right sorry you are so near unto me. So praying God to send you His grace to do that which shall be for the best I leave you to His keeping. From London the 15 of October 1583".[98]

Further, it may be asked, what had Sir Charles Arundel, who crossed to France with Lord Paget, got to do with the whole business, and why did he leave the country without permission. The official account is strangely silent on this point. Norton, the Puritan lawyer and rack-master, evidently felt some explanation to be needed, and in his manuscript "Chain of Treasons", concerning this so-called Throckmorton plot, he wrote:

> "To be noted further that Charles Arundell, being a man of no power in the country to give assistance to the force, credit or counsel: and being also of no value or skill for conduct in war, and that way not able to do the confederates any service: and having nothing in him to avail any enterprise but only his nearness in court: his participation in those treasons doth give reasonable occasion to consider either of some intention to attempt against her person [*Queen Elizabeth*], which by him, if he tarried might have been disclosed".[99]

All this, it need hardly be said, is pure hypothesis, for which there is not a scrap of evidence. The Government in this instance, evidently thought it better to disregard the fervid imaginings of this hot Puritan and observe a discreet silence about Sir Charles Arundel.

2. *Throckmorton's denial of the truth of his confessions*

The central point of the Government's case, it must be again emphasised was that the conferences at Petworth between the Earl of Northumberland, Charles Paget and his brother, Lord Paget, were concerned with traitorous practices connected with the invasion plan of 1583. The case

[98] Lord Paget to his brother, Charles, 15 October 1583, Dom. Eliz. 163, n. 18, addressed in the same hand as that of the letter: "To my loving brother Mr. Charles Paget give these at Rouen". Endorsed 1583. The Government had apparently intercepted all these three letters of Ld. Paget.

[99] Yelverton MSS. XXXIII, now B.M. Addit. 48029, f. 68. Thomas Norton died 10 March 1584. Sir Charles Arundel was second cousin to Queen Elizabeth. Rather opposed to Norton's statement that Arundel was of no value or skill for conduct in war is the report of the spy Berden (alias Rogers) that Charles Arundel was commended to the Pope by the Duke of Guise for a man meet to have conduct of an army to invade England! (Berden to Walsingham, Paris, 30 September 1585, printed in *C.R.S. XXI*, p. 80; also Same to Same, Rouen, 13 August 1585, *Ibid.*, 78).

rested at first only on the alleged confessions of Throckmorton.[100] At his trial on 21 May 1584, however, he persistently denied the truth of these confessions, as they had been made under the influence of torture.

> "[He] denieth", a report of his trial notes, "all the material points of his examination to be true, holdeth himself not charged by law with the matters he hath confessed, because the rack forced him to say something for the ease of the torment, but with protestation that those things he should discover should not be of force to touch any man. He hath confessed nothing true, and therefore the law doth not bind him. . . . Denieth that Paget's coming doth touch him, professeth that his own confessions are false and may not touch him".[101]

[100] At Throckmorton's trial, however, a confession of W. Shelley was alleged in proof of the case (cf. *infra* Note 104). There is no means of checking, from the documents themselves, the Government's statements of what Throckmorton, the Earl of Northumberland and William Shelley confessed: for by a singular fate none of their confessions are now extant, save that of the Earl of Northumberland, 11 May 1585, which does not support the Government's case, and to which they did not refer. It is not as if confessions or examinations, connected in one way or another with the alleged Throckmorton-Paget plot, have all disappeared. There should be some seventy examinations, if those which have survived are added to those mentioned in the draft "Proceedings concerning the Earl of Northumberland" (*Cal. Salisbury MSS. XIII*, pp. 270–281. The dates of examinations as given in this document, are for the most part written in its margins, and not in the text, as in the calendarist's rendering). Yet of these seventy papers, well over twenty, and these the vital ones, have disappeared. There is reference to eleven different confessions of Francis Throckmorton himself, with their specific dates: only one confession is extant, and to that the Government did not refer, for it was practically useless for their purpose. Mention is made of no less than ten confessions of William Shelley on specified days: not one has survived. The Earl of Northumberland, the official account states, was often examined, two of his examinations being referred to by the Government, yet only one is extant, to which no reference was made, as it told against their case. The many examinations that do survive touch but the fringes of the story, such as the mere fact of Charles Paget's coming to England, his visit to the Earl at Petworth—which the Earl, indeed, acknowledged—the departure of Lord Paget and Sir Charles Arundel, and the like. But not one crucial point of the official account, such as the character of Charles Paget's activities in England, or the reason alleged for his brother's leaving the country, find support in any extant examination or confession. That surely is a remarkable fact. Can it be pure chance that so many non-vital confessions are today extant, yet not a single vital one, to which the Government appealed for proof of their statements? A similar disappearance of the main documents is true also of the Arden case in the same year (cf. Charlotte Stopes, *Shakespeare's Warwickshire Contemporaries*, Shakespeare Press, 1907, p. 107. Her verdict as to the cause of their disappearance was that they had been deliberately destroyed). But there is a further significant fact: all the dates of these confessions of Throckmorton, Shelley and the Earl of Northumberland and others, which are given in the Salisbury manuscript mentioned above, are omitted in the official printed account, so that no one, even in Government circles, could possibly have checked that printed version who did not have access to the alleged confessions themselves, and could thus have engaged himself in the laborious task of comparing official statements about undated confessions, as mentioned in the pamphlet, with the more than twenty given specific dates in the unprinted draft.

[101] The paper is endorsed "21 May [1584] Notes of Thr[ockmorton's arraigne]ment" (endorsement damaged) (B. M. Stowe MSS. 1083, ff. 17–20). These notes appear to be the only account of Throckmorton's trial extant. They are probably in the hand of Wilkes.

D

This denial caused considerable embarrassment to the Government, since they were seeking treasonable material with which to charge the Earl of Northumberland. Popham, the Attorney-General, in a paper in his own hand confessed as much:

> "The probability", he wrote, "of this matter for the coming over of Charles Paget into Sussex to such intent as is set down, being the principal point to touch the Earl of North[umberland] standeth *only* upon the confession of Fr. Trockmorton, which though it be strongly and resolutely to be *presumed* to be true, yet his testimony to touch any other than himself, is now so much enfeebled through his unstableness in persisting in his first accusation,[102] as it is not upon this point to be hastened to a Trial, especially of him that is to be tried by his peers. And of this opinion are both Mr. Solicitor[103] and myself. But if this point of Charles Paget's coming over to such end as aforesaid, had stood firmly proved, or may hereafter be made manifest, then we are of opinion that the matters following do fall out very plainly and strongly against the Earl".

He then proceeded to show this by instancing the fact of Paget's coming, his stay with the Earl, the visit of Paget's brother, Lord Paget, to Petworth at the Earl's invitation, William Shelley's coming there and his secret conference with Charles Paget some days later, Lord Paget's leaving the country soon after the arrest of Throckmorton, and so on.

> "All which with the rest", he concluded, "would have made way effectually against the Earl if the true cause of Charles Paget's being in Sussex the last summer might have been made probable and manifest without blemish or impeachment".[104]

[102] Italics mine. He was here referring to the carrying of letters to and from the Queen of Scots, which was the first accusation made against him by the Government. "Probability" is here used in the archaic sense of provableness.

[103] Solicitor-General, Egerton.

[104] "Probable" = proveable (see Note 102). "The Platt (*sic*) off the late Treason attempted by ffrancis Throckmorton and his confederates, deduced to the Earl of North" (Dom. Eliz. 171, n. 79). The document is in Popham's hand, and is signed by him. From internal evidence it was written after Throckmorton's denial of the truth of his confessions at his trial on 21 May 1584. It is surely condemnatory of the proceedings of the Government that because of his denial, and his persistence in his first accusation (cf. Note 102) they dared not risk bringing the Earl of Northumberland to trial, for he would have had to be tried by his fellow peers, and yet they could condemn Throckmorton himself to death. It is further to be noted that in the above document Popham declared that the treasonable purpose of Charles Paget's visit to Sussex "standeth only upon the confession of Fr. Throckmorton"; yet at that very trial on 21 May 1584, Popham himself, according to the only account of it that has come to light, referred for proof of its treasonable character to an alleged confession of William Shelley, 19 December 1583: "Popham proveth Paget's coming over to be for treasons by the examination of William Shelley 19 December" (Stowe MSS. 1083, *ut supra*). This same alleged confession is referred to in "The case of William Shelley", November 1585 (B. M. Egerton MSS. 2074, ff. 73–74), where it was stated: "Charles Paget came over into England about Bartholemewtide

3. *Throckmorton's Submission and Declaration, 4 June 1584*

The defect of proof, however, of the Earl's complicity, caused by Throckmorton's denial at his trial of the truth of his confessions, appears from the Government's own account to have been made good some three weeks later. At the end of the pamphlet on Throckmorton's treasons there was printed, as having been written by him *in his own hand* on 4 June 1584, a new Submission to the Queen, which was followed by his Declaration of the treasonable offences committed by him.[105] Now, in the domestic papers of Queen Elizabeth's reign

[105] *Holinshed IV*, p. 543. Italics mine. The Declaration comes immediately after the Submission. The Government stated that it was a *new* Submission, implying that there had been an earlier one. It was evidently to a previous one that reference was made at the trial. "Popham wondereth that he [*Throckmorton*] will deny the treasons: mentioneth

Anno 1583 to deal with the Earls of Arundel and Northumberland and others for the invading of the Realm"; and in the margin, among other confessions adduced as proof of this, is that of Shelley 10 and 19 December 1583. Nevertheless, they did not bring the Earl of Northumberland to trial. It is this sort of inconsistency, together with significant changes in the drafts, and the several manifest untruths that they contain, that make the official account, given in the two pamphlets, the one concerning Throckmorton, the other regarding the Earl's alleged treasons and death, quite unreliable (cf. *infra* this chapter section 5). Historians appear never to have submitted them to a critical examination, but blindly to have accepted them as true, though past and modern experience hardly guarantees the veracity of Governments.

Part of the explanation may be that the law-officers did not see the relevant papers of the cases, an impression that can be gathered from a study of the documents, but spoke from a brief prepared for them by Thomas Wilkes, and possibly by Thomas Norton. The latter's "Chain of Treasons" (Yelverton MSS. XXXIII, now B.M. Addit. 48029, ff. 68ff), may have been part of the briefing. Some confirmation of this view is given by a letter of Hatton to Wilkes, dated 20 June 1585, the day, that is, before the Earl's death. "Her Majesty" he wrote, "hath willed me to direct you to attend the judges with Mr. Attorney and Mr. Solicitor, and that you should earnestly call to your remembrance the first examination of the Earl of Northumberland, whereat those other gents were absent. Besides it pleaseth her to remember in Throckmorton's case you did travail both honestly and diligently, and may remember such parts thereof, which Mr. Attorney and Mr. Solicitor have not heard of, and therefore she would you should speed yourself presently to them, and to show these letters of her Majesty's pleasure herein to their satisfaction" (B.M. Egerton MSS. 2074, f. 64).

Whatever the explanation of the letter's date—and one need not necessarily jump to a sinister conclusion of Hatton's foreknowledge of the Earl's death before it took place, as the date may well have been a slip of the writer in the early hours of the 21st, soon after his decease—the letter itself appears to have had for its purpose the coaching of the judges and law-officers, in view of the meeting of the Queen's Councillors in the Star Chamber, 23 June, to declare the Earl's treasons and the manner of his death (For the comments of J. H. Pollen, s.j. on this and another letter of Hatton, cf. *C.R.S. XXI*, p. 126). But it is surprising, that the Government did not rely on a written record of Northumberland's first examination, but only on Wilkes's memory of it. Had such a document already disappeared, or was it ever in existence? But more surprising still is it, to find that Mr. Attorney (Popham) and Mr. Solicitor (Egerton), a year after Throckmorton's trial and condemnation were still not acquainted with all the details of the case, as is clear from the phrase: "In Throckmorton's case you did travail both honestly and diligently and may remember such parts thereof, which *Mr. Attorney and Mr. Solicitor have not heard of.*" Italics mine. At all events it confirms the impression that the law-officers were briefed by Wilkes and did not prepare their case from a study of the documents.

there is an undated manuscript, endorsed by Walsingham's clerk: "ffraunces Throgmortons submission to her Matie", which corresponds exactly with that printed in the pamphlet, but it is not, as the Government stated, in the prisoner's own hand, though signed by him. Its peculiarities will be discussed later: suffice it here to note that in it Throckmorton withdraws his denial of the truth of his confessions.

"The natural care in me of the defence of my life", the document states, "did lately move me to the undutiful gainsaying and denial of that which before had been by me in most humble sort confessed; nevertheless I most humbly beseech your Majesty that in imitation of the example of God whose image (both in respect of the happy place you hold and in regard of your singular wisdom and other rare princely virtues and perfections wherewith God and nature hath plentifully endowed your Majesty) you represent unto us here in the earth, it may like your highness to commiserate the lamentable estate of me your Majesty's poor distressed subject that do both humbly confess myself worthy of death, and in token of my repentance and sorrowful afflicted heart, do not only not crave the prolonging of my life if the grant thereof shall not stand with the good pleasure of your Majesty, but rather most humbly beseech the trebling of the torment by the law for mine heinous offence justly imposed upon me, if the same may be any satisfaction to your Majesty for the unnatural and undutiful crime whereof I rest by your laws justly condemned, or any mitigation of your Majesty's indignation rightfully conceived against me that desire not to live without your favour, and dying will wish from my heart that mine end may be the beginning of your Majesty's security, and an increase both to your highness and to this your Majesty's most flourishing commonwealth, of the happy blessings of Almighty God.

Your Majesty's most woeful subject in
that he hath offended you".[106]

About this document there are some peculiar circumstances. It would appear to have been enclosed in a letter of Sir Owen Hopton, Lieutenant of the Tower, to Walsingham of 1 June 1584.[107]

[106] Dom. Eliz. 171, n. 1(i), undated. The Submission is printed in full in the pamphlet about his treasons, where it received the date 4 June 1584.

[107] The Calendarist has no doubt about it, and definitely states that it was so enclosed (cf. *Dom. Cal. Eliz. 1581–1590*, p. 179).

---

a submission of Throckmorton's own hand to the Queen's Majesty. Town Clerk readeth the submission to the Queen. Popham repeateth the effect of Fra. Thro. submission and explaineth the same" (Account of the trial, Stowe MSS. 1083, ff. 17–20). Apart from the above references, there is no other evidence of such a first Submission. If it existed, it has not survived, as is the case with all the vital confessions of the persons concerned (cf. Note 100).

"Right honourable", he wrote, "for answer of your ii several letters touching Mr. Francis Throckmorton, first according to the effect of your first letter I delivered him both in speech and writing, as much as is mentioned in a note here-enclosed, and he promised to answer some part of those ii demands, and thereupon, I delivered him paper, pen and ink, nevertheless he left those ii principal points and did write a *supplication to the Queen's Majesty, which herein I have sent you.* Now touching your last letter, my Lady Throckmorton[108] came to him, and gave him good and motherly counsel to deal plainly and loyally with her Majesty, and to discover such practices as he knew, to be hurtful to her Majesty and State: [109] And for mine own part I declared as much to them as is mentioned in a bill[110] here-enclosed, and then, Throckmorton said he would declare the truth, and as much as he knew touching the state, and then I asked him if he had any special matter touching the state, more than he had uttered before, and unto that question he made no sufficient answer, but required to have pen and ink and some private conference with the lady, his mother, which I would not suffer till your further pleasure be known. Nevertheless I beseech your honour to license me to give him pen and ink, for else he will speak slanderously of me at the hour of his death, for he is very angry, that I have sent the supplication to your honour, written to her Majesty, and of your further pleasure herein I pray to be advertised for I could no sooner write unto you, my Lady coming to the Tower but at 4 of the clock. And thus I humbly take my leave. From the Tower the first of June 1584.

Your honours most bounden to command
Owen Hopton".[111]

The supplication mentioned in this letter and enclosed with it, would seem to be the Submission, which is really a supplication for

[108] Italics mine. He was referring to Lady Throckmorton, Francis's mother.

[109] This seems an odd phrase to use, considering that according to the official account he had already, in his many confessions, discovered such practices. It is true that he had denied the truth of these confessions at his trial, but in view of that, one would have expected a rather different phrasing.

[110] This "bill" seems to be the note above, which he had already said was enclosed. It runs: "First her Majesty's pleasure is, that the lady and your wife shall have access to you, to persuade you to discharge your duty towards her highness. And the speeches that shall pass between you and them, shall be in my hearing. And if I shall find by your speeches that you are inclined to discover your knowledge of such practices, as you have been made privy of tending to the disquieting of this state, then may I let you have some private conference with them both" (Dom. Eliz. 171, n. 2). Again let it be emphasised that his demand to disclose the practices, considering the many alleged confessions, seems strange.

[111] Dom. Eliz. 171, n. 1. The letter is in the hand of a clerk, but signed by Owen Hopton. It is addressed in the same clerk's hand, and is endorsed by Walsingham's clerk: "primo Junij 1584. From the Lieutenant of the Tower. Francis Throgmorton." "Supplication", is added in another hand.

mercy.[112] If this is so, then the Government's statement that he wrote it on 4 June can hardly be correct, seeing that Hopton's letter referring to it was written 1 June. Another false statement of the Government concerning this Submission is that he wrote it in his own hand, for the document is not in the same hand as the signature, but bears a remarkable resemblance to that of Francis Mills, Walsingham's secretary. The signature itself is the same as that of the only confession of Throckmorton extant;[113] but a curious feature of it is that it does not come immediately after the words "Your Majesty's most woeful subject in that he hath offended you", but at the end of the page after one-third of the sheet had been left blank.

Moreover, it is surely very odd that Hopton should state in the above letter that he had delivered to Throckmorton paper, pen and ink; yet further on in the same letter that his prisoner had asked for pen and ink, and that he should have begged Walsingham to allow him to give these things to him, else Throckmorton would speak slanderously of him at the hour of his death. From the same letter one gathers that only his mother came to visit him on this occasion at the Tower, nor is there any evidence that he was ever permitted to see his wife, in accordance with the "bill" mentioned by Hopton. Could it be that Throckmorton was tricked into signing a paper which had been substituted for that mentioned first by Hopton, which might well have been a supplication to the Queen to see his wife? For why should Throckmorton have been very angry with Hopton for having sent his supplication to Walsingham, and thus have given Hopton cause to fear what he might say against him on the scaffold, unless the Secretary allowed pen and ink to be given to him? Was it because Throckmorton had discovered that he had been tricked into signing the present "Submission", in which the signature is so oddly placed, and that Hopton feared that he might say at the time of his execution that he could not have written the paper, for he had not had in his possession for a sufficient length of time the means, pen and ink, to do so? Certainly, these two documents, the Submission and Hopton's letter, do suggest that some trickery was practised; nor must it be overlooked that the Submission was only published after Throckmorton's execution, when he could not expose any such trickery.

Furthermore, it is clear that the Government desired, if possible, to proceed against the Earl of Northumberland for his alleged treason-

---

[112] *Ibid.*, n. 1(i), quoted above in the text.
[113] That of 12 December 1583, Dom. Eliz. 164, n. 22. Cf. also Note 100.

able practices. The opinion of the Attorney-General, Popham, as shown already, had been that *proof* of the Earl's complicity, strong as its likelihood might appear, depended on Throckmorton's confessions, which had been so much enfeebled by his denial of their truth at his trial. Why then, since from their own account, this denial had been withdrawn by Throckmorton's new Submission and Declaration, did they not take measures to bring the Earl to trial? Yet they never did so, but rather published an account, containing definite untruths, of his alleged treasons only after his death, when, as with Throckmorton, they could be sure he could not expose them.[114]

It is also to be noted that there is no mention in Hopton's letter of Throckmorton's Declaration of his treasons, which is pages longer than his Submission, and which the Government stated the prisoner had penned the same day as the Submission, viz. 4 June 1585. Nor is there any evidence, apart from the Government's assertion in the pamphlet, that he ever wrote such a Declaration. In it he is alleged to have given an account concerning the correspondence of the Queen of Scots, and of his connection with the invasion scheme of 1583.

Finally, it may be remarked that neither the Submission nor the Declaration is in accord with Throckmorton's conduct on the scaffold a month or so later.

"... they have put to death", wrote Persons, "good Mr. Throckmorton, although they had promised to spare his life. God has willed it so, for he has made a very holy and edifying end. He would not ask pardon of the Queen ... at the hour of his death, but said that she ought to ask pardon of God and the state for her heresy and

---

[114] To give an instance of an insinuated untruth: in the pamphlet, which purports to give an account of the proceedings in the Council, hastily summoned to be held in the Star Chamber, 23 June 1585, Popham insinuated in his speech on that occasion that the Earl, when merely Sir Henry Percy, sided with the rebels in the Rebellion of the North in 1569, and that about that time had undertaken the conveying away of the Scottish Queen. But the documents themselves show that Sir Henry actively opposed his brother in that rising, joined the royal troops, and attacked the rebels. Queen Elizabeth, in fact, on that occasion wrote to him recognising his "constancy and forwardness in her service", and assuring him that in consideration of his fidelity she would have regard to the continuance of such a house in the person and blood of so faithful a servant (Queen Elizabeth to Sir Henry Percy, Yeven, 17 November 1569, Haynes, *State Papers*, London, 1740, p. 553). The Earl of Sussex, too, who had commanded the royal forces, wrote to Cecil, testifying to Sir Henry's "soundness" during the rebellion, his readiness to serve with all his force against the rebels, and "to venture his person with the first" (Sussex to Cecil, 7 January 1570, *Dom. Cal. Eliz. 1566–1579*, p. 182). Another example is the really absurd story about Allen having received the articles of the alleged Papal League of 1580, which was, in fact, completely bogus, and of his communicating them to John Hart, one of his priests, under the condition of the greatest secrecy (cf. Appendix I).

misgovernment in allowing innocent men be killed every day".[115]

Hunsdon, too, the Queen's cousin, in a letter to Davison, added a postscript that he did not doubt that his correspondent had heard of the execution of Francis Throckmorton, adding:

> "He died very stubbornly neither asking her Majesty's forgiveness nor would willingly have anybody to pray of them".[116]

4. *William Shelley's confession at his trial, 12 February 1586*

But, it may be asked, does not Shelley's acknowledgment at his arraignment on 12 February 1586, that during Paget's visit to England he *did* engage with him and the Earl in traitorous practices, support the Government's case? That the trial itself was a piece of Government propaganda is shown by an unusual proceeding during it. After the indictment had been read and Shelley had pleaded guilty,

> "her Majesty's counsel at Law moved the Commissioners that it would please them *for the better satisfaction of the hearers present and manifesting of the truth to the world abroad,* that the matter of this treason being so dangerous to her Majesty and the realm, and that in so high a degree as it was, might notwithstanding the confession of the indictment be laid open to the understanding of all men, whereunto Mr. Vicechamberlain [*Hatton*] after some conference had therein with the rest of the Commissioners assented".[117]

According to this decision the Queen's counsel proceeded to give a long account of the alleged treasons, and of the "suicide" of the Earl of Northumberland, owing to the confessions of Shelley in June 1585, implicating him in those treasons. Further, from these very examinations of Shelley, of the 3, 10, 12, 16 and 19 June, none of which is now extant,[118] the Government, according to their own statement, had enough material to condemn Shelley; nor are there any examinations subsequent to these which further disclose the treasonable nature of his practices. Yet they did not bring him to trial till nearly eight months after the Earl's death. More than this, from their own account, they

---

[115] Persons to Agazzari, Rector of the English College in Rome, Paris, 7 August 1584, n.s., printed in *Letters and Memorials of Fr. Robert Persons, C.R.S. XXXIX,* p. 226. Throckmorton was executed 10 July 1584, o.s.

[116] Hunsdon to Davison, Berwick, 23 July 1584, R.O. S.P. 52(Scottish)/35, n. 58. The Calendarist has erroneously printed "pray for them" (*Scot. Cal. VII,* p. 234).

[117] Italics mine. "The Manner of proceeding against Wm. Shelley", B.M. Lansd. 45, n. 75. This is an account in English of his trial; cf. also R.O. Baga de Secretis, Pouch XLVII.

[118] These dates appear in the draft of the Northumberland pamphlet (*Cal. Salisbury MSS. XIII, ut supra*), and in the document entitled "The Case of William Shelley how he standeth charged with treason" (B. M. Egerton MSS. 2074, ff. 73–74).

could prove even earlier the treasonable nature of Charles Paget's conferences in England in September 1583, not only from Throckmorton's confessions, his denial of their truth having been withdrawn, as they declared, by his Submission of 4 June 1584, but from a confession of Shelley himself of 19 December 1583.[119] At the trial, in fact, of Throckmorton, the Attorney-General, Popham, adduced this very confession as proof of the treasonable practices.[120]

As to Shelley's plea of guilty, consideration must be given to the Government's methods. In the Egerton manuscripts occur these undated Memoranda:

"The Earl [*of Northumberland*] to be drawn to confess the truth. His concealments of the truth to be considered ... The parties against him to be confronted. Before he be dealt with some meaner persons to be re-examined. And these to be drawn, by the presence of some of the commissioners and the show of the Rack. Those to be borne in hand that my L. has confessed, without shewing them what, in certainty. And the L. to be charged with what they confess, and to be borne in hand that they have confessed what is likely, probable".[121]

"Where such orders," comments J. H. Pollen, s.j., "both violent and dishonest, are officially issued, it is easy to see what terrible abuses of intimidation will follow, especially when subordinates are egged on with praises from the Queen, as is here done. Thus Hatton writes to Wylkes, of the 'great service' you may do 'if you can win any good guess from his [*Northumberland's*] hand' about a letter lately discovered. Two days later he adds, 'the arrest of Thomas Somerset ... will content the Queen much. Would God the others we want were in his case' ".[122]

Methods of dealing with prisoners could, however, be flexible. In Shelley's case, after an earlier proposal, made not long after his arrest,

[119] Cf. *supra* Note 104.

[120] *Ibid.*

[121] B.M. Egerton MSS. 2074, f. 79, quoted in *C.R.S. XXI*, p. 126. The date of the document is probably some time in May or June 1585, when the Earl of Northumberland was the particular object of the Government's inquisition. In a paper dated 27 May 1585, "What course is meet to be held in the causes of certain prisoners remaining in the Tower", the first entry runs: "The Earl of Northumberland to remain as he doth until William Shelley and Wicliffe be examined [to be examined W. Shelley, W. Wicklyffe]" (printed in *C.R.S. II*, p. 238). From the documents Shelley appears to have been examined, as shown above, on 3, 10, 12, 16 and 19 June 1585, but no reference has been found to any further examination of Wicliffe. It would seem, therefore, that the document quoted in the text should be placed about this period.

[122] *C.R.S. XXI*, p. 126, edited by J. H. Pollen, s.j. The charge against Somerset was of corresponding with Allen, and of having intelligence with the Queen of Scots (cf. The Several offences of D. Astlowe, Tho. Somerset and Pedro Cubiare, 12 February 1586, Dom. Eliz. 186, n. 61, printed *Ibid.*, p. 136).

that he should "be put to the rack and examined by the Lieutenant, the Attorney, the Solicitor and Norton", he appears already before November 1584 to have been played upon in a smoother way and been promised mitigations, at least, of his harsh fate. In a letter to Walsingham, he wrote:

> "Having through your honour's favour towards me obtained such special grace in this my great distress, besides the comfort I received of other good speeches it pleased your honour in communication with Sir Owen [*Hopton*] to use me of long times past, and withal understanding of your honour's now being at your house in the city: I held me not satisfied in any sort of duty, if I should omit any office to express the same: and not knowing for the present how to make better declaration thereof than in this sort, I thought it requisite in these few lines to make the same apparent: yielding myself to your honour's devotion and favourable consideration in these my distresses, as to your honour's wisdom shall seem meet: most humbly craving your honour's continuance of favour towards me in further relieving me out of these my miseries being not in any sort willing to make any recital of my negligence past: the remembrance whereof, so greatly irketh me as my former estate considered, how deeply I contemn myself therein none but God and myself can witness: and so ceasing to trouble your honour any further with discoursing of my troubled mind and unfortunate estate, I most humbly take my leave this 5th of November 1584".[123]

Shelley, clearly, was not the man to resist the Government's methods. As already stated, he was brought to trial, though not until over a year later, when he was condemned to death for high treason. The sentence was not carried out, however, but he was "respited at her Majesty's good pleasure". He was still in prison in July 1588, after which there is no further reference to him.[124]

---

[123] W. Shelley to Walsingham, 5 November 1584, Dom. Eliz. 175, n. 5, endorsed, possibly by Mills: "10 (*sic*) Novemb. 1584. Mr. Shelley *to be released of his imprisonment*". He was not in fact released. For the earlier proposal to put Shelley to the torture, cf. a document headed "To be propounded to ye LL in commission, etc. For the examining of such as are committed to ye Tower, etc." 12 February 1583/4, Dom. Eliz. 168, n. 14. In considering the letter given in the text it should be recalled that by Shelley's alleged confession of 19 December 1583, he had confessed the treasonable character of Paget's visit to England in September 1583 (cf. *supra* Note 104), and that according to the official account, by June 1584 Throckmorton had withdrawn the denial of the truth of his confessions, by his Submission of 4 June 1584.

[124] "William Shelley. He is attainted of high treason and respited at her Majesty's good pleasure" (The Lords' resolution upon the prisoners, 30 November 1586, Dom. Eliz. 95, n. 32, printed in *C.R.S. II*, p. 263; cf. also List of prisoners in the Tower, 2 July 1588, *Ibid.*, p. 281).

What value, then, can be attached to his plea of guilty made under such conditions? In another case during this period, William Parry also made a confession of guilt to a so-called assassination plot, and was, in fact, executed, though it is certain that he had been a spy and an agent-provocateur of the Government.[125] In any case, Shelley's solitary plea of guilty, stating that Charles Paget came over to win support from leading Catholics, including the Earl of Northumberland and Shelley himself, and had treasonable conferences during his visit to England in September 1583, cannot stand against the overwhelming evidence already given, that Paget did not carry out the instructions of the Duke of Guise, but deliberately intended to wreck the invasion plan.[126] At the same trial of Shelley, it may be added, the Government contradicted their own former statement that the Earl had got Lord Paget out of the country because he knew that he *alone* could convict him of these treasonable practices: for the Queen's counsel then declared that the Earl had contrived to send abroad, for the same reason, Davies, Robotham, and Clynsall, though in the case of the last named they knew that it was false; for though Clynsall conveyed Lord Paget to France in the last days of November 1583, he was certainly in their hands very soon after.[127]

5. *General criticism of the Government's case*

By February 1586, then, the complete ruin of three persons in England, Francis Throckmorton, the Earl of Northumberland and William Shelley, had been effected by or because of a case in which the *evidence*, as opposed to hypotheses or confessions obtained by torture or promises of leniency, contradicts its central point: namely, that Paget's visit to England in September 1583 had been for treasonable purposes. But in addition to the evidence already adduced, it may be well to conclude this chapter with some general appraisal of the Government's case, as it appears in the contemporary printed material and in the manuscript account of Shelley's trial: for the "plot" of which Throckmorton was the first victim became one integral part of the atmosphere in which the last years of the Queen of Scots' life were passed.

The fundamental error about the nature of Charles Paget's activities in England in 1583 is by no means the only error of fact to be found

---

[125] Cf. *infra* Chapter III, section 2.
[126] Cf. *supra* Chapter I, section 6.
[127] Cf. Extracts from various examinations (Dom. Eliz. 167, n. 59), where two of Clynsall's are dated 9 and 18 December.

in these writings. There are others which range over wide and not always obviously related fields. For instance, Philip II is represented as having been ready in 1579–80 to give all necessary aid for the reformation of religion in England, if the efforts were backed by such as were well-affected in this country.[128] By this statement the Government was evidently attempting to connect the Throckmorton-Paget plot with the alleged Papal League of 1580, which can be proved to have been bogus.[129]

Apart from any other considerations, the Spanish king was, in 1580, far too occupied with establishing by force of arms his claim to the Portuguese throne, to think of aiding an invasion plan of these isles. It was only after the return from Scotland of Crichton, the Jesuit, with the proposals of Lennox, that at the conferences in Paris of April and May 1582, a resolution was taken about the "enterprise", as the invasion plan was called.[130] Nor did Philip II, either in 1582 or in 1583, promise the aid of his forces: just the reverse, as is clearly evident from the contemporary documents. [131]

Then, it was further stated, Mendoza, the Spanish ambassador in England, told Francis Throckmorton that the King, his master, had promised to pay one-half of the expenses of the enterprise. This, so the official account declared, Throckmorton confessed on 4 December 1583. There is not the slightest support for this in the despatches of Mendoza, and it is certain that Philip II made no such promise. Among other reasons for his refusal to aid the enterprise with armed force was precisely the disagreement about the financial contribution to be made respectively by the Pope and himself.[132]

Again, it was asserted that the greatest ban to proceeding with the enterprise was that no way had been found to put the Scottish Queen

---

[128] Cf. *Somers Tracts I*, p. 216, and *Cal. Salisbury MSS. XIII*, p. 273.

[129] Cf. Appendix I, where the alleged league is shown to have been bogus.

[130] Cf. *supra* Chapter I, section 2.

[131] Although in 1582 he had been tentatively ready to help Lennox in Scotland with a gift of 10,000 crowns, he decidedly declined to supply military aid (cf. Philip II to Juan de Tassis, Spanish Chargé d'Affaires in France, Lisbon, 14/24 September, 1582, *Spanish Cal. 1580–1586*, p. 401). Referring to the plans of the "empresa" in 1582, the Papal Secretary of State wrote: "Ma sua Maestà non si risolve mai di farlo et cosi fu esclusa quella pratica" (Como to Taberna, Nuncio in Spain, Rome, 22 July/1 August 1583, printed in *Kretzschmar*, p. 172; further references will be found in *C.R.S. XXXIX*, p. lvi). In 1583 Philip again refused military aid (cf. Taberna to Como, Madrid, 2/12 September, 14/24 September 1583, and the report of Mgr. Sega, who had been sent on a special embassy by the Pope to Philip II in 1583, *Kretzschmar*, pp. 175, 177 and 212–215; cf. also Philip II to Olivares, Spanish ambassador in Rome, 10 February 1584, *Spanish Cal. 1580–1586*, p. 517).

[132] For the wrangling over their respective contributions, cf. the despatches of Como and Taberna, *Kretzschmar*, pp. 171–181, and Sega's report, *ut supra*.

in safety.[133] There is nothing in the contemporary records to support the statement: the documents show clearly that the irresolution of Philip II, his tardiness in replying to the Pope's petition, and his final refusal to support the enterprise with armed forces caused the stay of its execution.[134]

Finally, it was stated that the proposed landing in Sussex was later misliked. So far as the contemporary documents go, this is pure invention on the part of the Government. The landing in Sussex of French forces was to have been diversionary, whilst the main force, to be supplied by Spain, was to attack from Scotland, if the state of affairs there was favourable, or from the frontier between the two countries. It was laid down, moreover, that the main force was to be the first to arrive.[135] There is no evidence that any change on this point was discussed or contemplated. Other instances of errors of fact of this kind might be given, but let these suffice.

Besides errors of fact, the official accounts contain a large number of inconsistent and contradictory statements, which cumulatively cast a most curious light on their authors' intentions: some examples will here be given. It has already been pointed out that according to the account of the Earl's treasons, he got Lord Paget out of the country because he *alone* could reveal the Earl's traitorous practices connected with Charles Paget's visit to England, and that this was contradicted at the trial of Shelley, where several others were declared to have been conveyed away for the same purpose.[136] Neither statement is consistent with no attempt having apparently been made to remove Shelley himself who, according to the Government, was actually the one to implicate the Earl.

In the latter case they tried to weaken the apparent discrepancy, but here again inconsistency becomes evident. Thus, in the pamphlet concerning Francis Throckmorton, it is stated that Charles Paget endeavoured "in a sort" to find out the disposition of William Shelley and how he might stand affected to give assistance to the treasons, though Paget "discovered not directly his traitorous intents" to Shelley.[137]

---

[133] Cf. *Holinshed IV*, p. 547; *Somers Tracts I*, p. 216 and *Cal. Salisbury MSS. XIII*, p. 274.
[134] Cf. *supra* Note 131.
[135] Cf. "Disegno per l'impresa d'Inghilterra," in the despatch of the Nuncio in France, Castelli, 10/20 June 1583, *Kretzschmar*, p. 168.
[136] *Somers Tracts I*, p. 218; cf. *supra* last section.
[137] *Holinshed IV*, p. 542. The draft has "obliquely to sound William Shelley ... he discovered not directly his traitorous intents to Shelley with the forces appointed for invading the realm": but this was amended as in the text above.

Yet later, in the pamphlet concerning the Earl, it appears that at the meeting in a coppice near Davies's house, among other topics of conversation, Paget enquired of Shelley the strength and fortifications of Portsmouth, and what forces and strength the Queen had in other parts Westwards. Foreign princes, Paget declared, would seek revenge for the wrongs done to them by the Queen, as time and opportunity served their purpose; they disdained to see the Queen of Scots used as she was, and would employ all their forces for her delivery; the Duke of Guise would be a leader therein and had, indeed, forces in readiness for altering the state of religion here in England and her liberation; the Earl of Northumberland would lend his assistance, for he was well affected to the Scottish Queen and would do what he could for her advancement. The stir would be in the Northern parts, Paget said, because Sussex was not convenient, there being no safe landing-places on that coast, and it was near to London where the Queen would be ready to resist them. Thus, whensoever any stir should take place the Earl would leave Sussex and go into the North. By these and suchlike speeches, it was said, Shelley *gathered* that Paget had dealt with the Earl as a chief party. Paget, in fact, confessed to Shelley that he came over to break and deal in such matters.[138] One can scarcely be lost in admiration at Shelley's perspicacity in his inference from all this, but the whole passage is hardly consistent with the former statement, that Paget "discovered not directly his traitorous intents" to him!

In the draft of the pamphlet, indeed, the same inconsistency is even further remarkable. The anonymous princes of the pamphlet are there specified as the kings of France and Spain,[139] and there is added to the above that the Catholics would shortly find relief, and that Paget advised Shelley to follow the Earl. From all this Shelley *gathered* that Paget had dealt with the Earl as a chief party and a man forward in these actions. More than this, Paget revealed that the Duke of Guise would be a leader in the matter, the Earl as assistant, and that all Catholics would join. He told him further that he had come over to treat of this affair and relied on the Earl to be a man of the greatest force and able to stir most arms in the North, whither he would go as soon as the attempt was begun; for the stir would be in the North and

---

138 *Somers Tracts I*, pp. 217–218. Italics mine.
139 As regards France, the Government knew well that at Queen Elizabeth's request, Henry III had prevented any movement on the part of the Duke of Guise, and had been thanked for her by Sir Edward Stafford for the steps he had taken—even before the arrest of Throckmorton! (cf. *supra* Note 92).

foreign forces would be landed in Scotland, because Sussex was not suitable.[140] By the time of Shelley's trial, his *inference* from Paget's oblique talk of invasion, had become *foreknowledge* of his traitorous purpose. The indictment stated that Shelley,

> "*knowing* the said Charles Paget the said day 7th of September traitorously to have come from the parties beyond the seas unto Petworth aforesaid, traitorously to confer with the said Earl of Northumberland and other her Majesty's subjects, about his most wicked and traitorous purposes aforesaid, did etc."[141]

Inconsistency is also to be met with in the Government's statements about Francis Throckmorton and his treating with Mendoza. In one place it is stated that Thomas Throckmorton, *when last in England* imparted all the negotiation about the enterprise to his brother, Francis, who *thereupon* undertook to effectuate the plan here with the help of the Spanish ambassador, whom he instructed how and with whom to deal for the preparing of a party within the realm.[142] He also showed the ambassador the list of havens. Later in the same pamphlet it is declared that Francis, urged on by letters of Morgan, was already negotiating about the enterprise with Mendoza, who informed him that Persons had gone to Rome to understand the Pope's mind; and that *soon after* this Thomas Throckmorton came to England![143] In the pamphlet concerning the Earl of Northumberland it is asserted, that Francis was recommended from beyond the sea to Mendoza who told him what plot was laid for the enterprise, and with whom the Englishman was directed to confer in the matter, and that *therefore* Francis informed the ambassador of the havens and the noblemen and gentlemen that he had set down as fit to be dealt with in the cause.[144] Thus, in the one case it was Thomas, when in England, who revealed the negotiation to Francis, so that he resolved to aid the plan with the help of Mendoza; in the other it was because of letters from Morgan that Francis got in touch with the ambassador, who revealed the plot to him and treated with him: and all this, it is clearly stated, was *before* Thomas's arrival in England.

It may be added, that apart from the Government's statements, there is not the slightest evidence that Thomas Throckmorton came

---

[140] *Cal. Salisbury MSS. XIII*, pp. 277–278. All derived, according to them from Shelley's confessions of June 1585.
[141] B.M. Lansd. 45, n. 75. Italics mine.
[142] *Holinshed IV*, p. 539. Italics mine.
[143] In the Declaration, *Holinshed IV*, p. 545.
[144] *Somers Tracts I*, p. 216; *Cal. Salisbury MSS. XIII*, pp. 273–274.

to England for the purpose of the enterprise. So far as the contemporary documents dealing with it show—in which he is not even mentioned— he was not in the confidence of the leaders in France, and there are no instructions drawn up for him by the Duke of Guise, as there are for Charles Paget. Nor does it seem at all probable that these leaders should have sent Thomas to England after the middle of August 1583, seeing that they had decided in the same month to send Paget.[145] The official account states, indeed, that the latter was sent over because it was feared that the "enterprise by some casualty might fail in the only hands of one man", Thomas Throckmorton, and that Thomas was therefore covertly advertised of the decision to send Paget, so that he might not be offended at another man being joined with him in his labour.[146] In saying this the former statement was overlooked, that by this time the negotiation was no longer entrusted only to one, Thomas's brother, Francis, being deeply engaged therein with the Spanish ambassador !^[147] The truth seems rather to be, as Francis is said to have stated in one place, that his brother Thomas visited England to per- suade him to settle his affairs and leave the country, and that after making an end of his account with Francis, he returned to France, with the understanding agreed between them, that if the enterprise did not succeed between that time and the next spring, Francis would arrange his affairs and go abroad.[148]

Further inconsistency is apparent as regards the date when Charles Paget came to England. In the pamphlet about Francis Throckmorton he is stated to have arrived in August 1583,[149] and in that concerning the Earl of Northumberland, in September of that year,[150] though on the previous page of the same pamphlet Mendoza is said to have told

[145] Charles Paget's Instructions are dated 28 August 1583 (Teulet, *Relations Politiques de la France et de l'Espagne avec l'Ecosse au XVIe siècle, V*, p. 311). From the Govern- ment's account Thomas Throckmorton arrived in England after the middle of August; for in the Declaration it is stated that before his arrival Mendoza had told Francis, his brother, that Persons had gone to Rome to understand the Pope's mind, and that soon after that Thomas came to England. Persons's Instructions are dated 22 August, n.s. and he left on 26 August. "Infra quatuor dies exiturus est cum uno famulo viae comite" (Persons to Aquaviva, Paris, 22 August 1583, n.s. Arch. S.J. Rom. Fondo Gesuitico 651). Allowing time for the news of Persons's departure to reach Mendoza, and for the fact that the new style, used in France, was ten days ahead of the old style used in England, this would place Thomas Throckmorton's arrival in England after mid-August 1583. Charles Paget arrived about 8 September (cf. *supra* Note 64).

[146] *Holinshed IV*, p. 539. In the draft of the pamphlet (Dom. Eliz. 171, n. 86) there was added "And this letter was shown to his brother Francis", but the addition was crossed out and so omitted in the printed version.

[147] *Holinshed IV*, p. 539.

[148] *Holinshed IV*, p. 547.

[149] *Holinshed IV*, p. 539.

[150] *Somers Tracts I*, p. 217.

Francis about Bartholemewtide [*24 August*] of Paget's arrival,[151] at a time, that is, when Paget was still in France! In one unpublished Government document he is said to have come over about Bartholemewtide,[152] but in Shelley's indictment the date is given as 7 September; yet later in that same account of his trial, the Queen's counsel asserted that he had arrived on 5 September, and that Wicliffe took him to Connigar Lodge, near the Earl's house at Petworth, on "Friday night, being the 6th of September"![153] Such variations are all the more surprising, seeing that the correct date could have been ascertained from the examination of John Haller, 20 December 1583, the shipmaster who had actually brought Paget to England.[154] Variations like these, and there are many others, show the Government's utter disregard of consistency in their statements of their case, even to the extent that in the same document there are obvious inconsistencies about such an important fact as the date of Charles Paget's arrival in England.

The worst feature, however, of these accounts is the assertions of things known to be false. One instance of this has already been shown as regards the torture of Francis Throckmorton.[155] False, too, is their assertion that "at the time of his apprehension there was no knowledge or doubt [*suspicion*] had of the treasons or of his privity unto them",[156] as is also the statement that his Submission was written in his own hand.[157] Equally false is the insinuation that the Earl of Northumberland, when Sir Henry Percy, had sided with the rebels in the Rebellion of the North.[158] Other examples could be given, such as a statement that Edward Rishton, a priest, took a message to Allen informing him that preparations were ready on this side for the invasion, at a time when Rishton was a prisoner in their own hands![159] Then, too, there is the

---

[151] *Somers Tracts I*, p. 216.

[152] "The case of William Shelley how he standeth charged with treason," November 1585, B.M. Egerton MSS. 2074, ff. 73–74.

[153] "The Manner of proceeding against Wm. Shelley" B.M. Lansd. 45, n. 75.

[154] Paget arrived about 8 September (cf. *supra* Note 64).

[155] Cf. *supra* Note 90.

[156] *Holinshed IV*, p. 540; cf. also pp. 541 and 547. That they had knowledge of the invasion plan even before the arrest of Throckmorton has already been shown (cf. *supra* Note 92).

[157] Cf. *supra* section 3 of this chapter.

[158] Cf. *supra* Note 114.

[159] In the pamphlet it was asserted that a message was sent in November 1581 to Dr Allen from a subject of this realm by a seminary priest returning beyond the seas, viz. that he had received from Allen at All-Hallowtide before that men and all things were in readiness if the place of landing might be known, etc. (*Somers Tracts I*, p. 215). The draft (*Cal. Salisbury MSS. XIII*, pp. 272–273) gave more definite details, in striking contrast to the vague indefiniteness of the pamphlet. The priest is there named as Edward Rishton, who was alleged to have confessed on 22 November 1581 that Evan Haydock or Haddock at Shrovetide [i.e. 1581] willed him to tell Allen that, whereas he had received word from

E

whole story of the bogus Papal League and their assertions about the same.[160]

These features, the errors of fact, the inconsistencies, the false statements, and the frequent vagueness, especially as regards dates, of the printed versions of the Government's case, compared with the drafts of the same, give the impression that the authorities were simply making up a case, though a case, indeed, in which there was a shrewd admixture of truth and falsehood. That there was a plan of invasion is certain, but their own case about it falls down on the crucial point of Paget's visit to England. Undoubtedly he came over in September 1583, armed with instructions from the Duke of Guise, but far from carrying out these instructions he had crossed to England determined to wreck the plan of invasion. Then, though knowing of this plan well before the arrest of Francis Throckmorton, they concealed it under the false assertion that they had learnt of the plan from Throckmorton's confessions. As for Throckmorton himself, he had a list of havens—he did not deny it at his trial—but one made up, as he stated, with the help of his father, who had died in 1580, when there was no question of invasion. It seems, however, that he did have a general knowledge of an attempt to succour his fellow Catholics, acquired, it would appear, from Mendoza;[161] but there is no proof, nor is it prob-

[160] Cf. Appendix I.

[161] "This Throckmorton, as I understand from Claude [*Matthieu*] the Jesuit, has a general knowledge of the agreement which has been entered into to succour the Catholics" (Nuncio to Como, Paris, 12 December 1583, Knox, *Allen*, p. 419). "Throckmorton who

Allen at All-Hallowtide before [therefore 1580] that men and all things were in readiness, etc., as above. Further, it is stated, on 24 December Rishton confessed that Haydock said it was a message of great secrecy and that Allen had sent him word that it was the King of Spain that had the men in readiness. Apart from this statement of the Government there is no record of any of these examinations of Rishton! And it is sheer nonsense which he is supposed to have confessed about the Spanish forces being in readiness. It certainly seems odd, too, that Haydock who, as stated, had been informed by Allen at All-Hallowtide 1580, that all was prepared, should a few months later (Shrove-tide 1581) ask Allen if everything was in readiness. Readers, too, will have noticed the discrepancy between the accounts as regards the dates at which Haydock is supposed to have sent the message to Allen by Rishton, a seminary priest returning beyond the seas. In the pamphlet it is in November 1581, in the Salisbury MSS. it is at Shrove-tide 1581. Neither date, as a matter of fact, fits in with Rishton's career. By December 1580 he was in prison in England (Knox, *Douay Diaries*, p. 174) and was still there in June 1581 (Allen to Agazzari, Rheims, 23 June 1581, Knox, *Allen*, p. 95). With Campion and his companions he was arraigned at Westminster Hall 14 November 1581, and condemned to death, 20 November following. He was not, however, executed, but remained in prison till he was exiled with twenty others in January 1585 (the decree of banishment is dated 15 January 1585, Dom. Eliz. 175, n. 9, partly printed in Foley, *Records III*, p. 288; cf. also *C.R.S. V*, p. 102 and Knox, *Douay Diaries*, p. 204). Clearly he could not have been returning beyond the seas and giving a message to Allen either at Shrove-tide or in November 1581, being then a prisoner in the hands of the Government. The official statement is pure fiction, or rather falsehood.

able, considering that Paget himself was sent over, that Francis Throckmorton was employed as an active agent by the Duke of Guise. With their foreknowledge of the invasion plan, the Government ascribed that rôle to him, knowing that he had conveyed letters to and from the Queen of Scots, which gave a possible colour for the wider accusations. As for the Earl of Northumberland, the case against him fails absolutely because Paget did not fulfil his instructions. Their dealings against him have all the marks of a "frame-up". They dared not risk bringing him to trial by his fellow peers, even though, according to their own statements, they had evidence to convict him. With his case falling to the ground, so with it does the reason for his alleged suicide. Finally, it also follows that the ruin of Shelley was effected on the same false grounds as that of the Earl.

---

was informed by Don Bernardino [*Mendoza*] of our plans, made some admissions under torture, which have resulted in a twofold evil: for not only did this create danger for many people in England, but Don Bernardino himself seems to be somewhat alienated from the project" (Persons to ——, Tournai, 8 March 1584, *C.R.S. XXXIX*, p. 199).

CHAPTER III

Morgan's connection with the Throckmorton-Paget plot—Morgan and the Parry plot—Further intrigues 1585–1586

1. *Morgan's connection with the Throckmorton-Paget plot*

What, it may be asked, has all the above to do with Morgan, apart from the fact of his friend, Charles Paget, having been closely associated with these events? According to the Government's account Morgan, too, was intimately connected with the plot. It was he who had induced Francis Throckmorton to begin his connection with the Scottish Queen, "a little before Christmas was two years", after receiving a cipher from him for that purpose.[162]

> "He did voluntarily confess",[163] they stated, "that he had written divers letters to her, and had conveyed many to and fro, between her and Thomas Morgan in France, by whose means he was first made known to her, and that he had received as many letters from her. He also declared the effect of his letters to her and of hers to him; which letters between them were always written in cipher, and the cipher with the nullities and marks for names of princes and councillors he sent unto the Queen's Majesty, written with his own hand." And later on the same page: "He haunted continually two ambassadors in London, by whose means he sent and received letters to and from beyond the seas daily. To whom and from whom? Even to and from Thomas Morgan and Thomas Throgmorton at Paris, men known to her Majesty and her Council to be notorious

---

[162] *Holinshed IV*, p. 545, in the Declaration. As this document was said to have been sent to Queen Elizabeth at the same time as his "Submission", which was dated 4 June 1584, this would place the beginning of his intelligence with the Queen of Scots late in 1582. She, however, according to this account, wrote to him first, but before he had answered the letter, the Duke of Lennox died, 26 May 1583 (*Ibid.*, p. 545). Getting the captive queen to correspond with named persons and sending them a cipher for the purpose was typical of Morgan. There are several instances of his doing so recorded in his correspondence with her.

[163] The draft (Dom. Eliz. 171, n. 86) adds after "confess" "without toture or show of the rack". But this was wisely omitted in the pamphlet, as it was in flat contradiction with what had been stated earlier, viz. that he had confessed after first being tortured and on the second occasion shown the rack (*Holinshed IV*, p. 538; cf. *supra*, Note 90).

practisers, very inward with the Duke of Guise and contrivers of the treasons and devices for the invasion intended".[164]

It was Morgan again, according to the official account, who informed Francis Throckmorton

"that by the persuasion of the Pope and the King of Spain, the Duke of Guise had yielded to perform the journey in person;[165] and that it was thought that the next way to attain liberty for the the Scottish Queen and to reform Scotland was to begin here in England".

And therefore he desired to know whether, in Throckmorton's opinion, Catholics would back any such force as should be sent, considering tolerance in religion would follow from the well-performing of the enterprise; what their forces would amount to both of horse and foot, and where would be the fittest landing.[166] Throckmorton answered, according to the same account, that he saw no great probability of the good success of such an enterprise; for the Catholics were timorous, dispersed, the matter perilous to be communicated to many, without which he did not see how any estimate could be made of the forces, besides that it was an imminent danger to the Queen of Scots, for which he saw no remedy.[167] Morgan, therefore, desired him to confer with the Spanish ambassador, to whom he would be recommended: hence began his conferences with Mendoza, the ambassador sending for him and treating of the matter with him.[168]

It was Morgan, too, who had sent Throckmorton a letter revealing that Mope, who had come to England, was Charles Paget, and requesting him to assure the Spanish ambassador that this coming was not to

---

[164] *Ibid.* Yet in the same pamphlet Francis Throckmorton is made to declare that it was with Morgan "all my intelligence was (for with my brother [*Thomas*] I never had any, other than that the matters by me written to Morgan were by him imparted unto my brother most times) ..." (*Ibid.*, p. 545).

[165] *Holinshed IV*, p. 545. From the context they were referring to the year 1583. It is difficult to reconcile the Government's statements on the topic of invasion and of the Duke of Guise. In the pamphlet concerning the Earl of Northumberland the Duke is said to have solicited the Pope and other princes for two years to supply him with forces for the purpose (*Somers Tracts I*, p. 216; *Cal. Salisbury MSS. XIII*, p. 273). The mention in the context of the death of a "great personage", definitely named in the Salisbury MSS. as the Duke of Lennox, who died 26 May 1583, shows that they were referring to that year. The statement in the Northumberland pamphlet hardly agrees with that in the text above, and both seem somewhat strange, seeing that yet another statement of the Government avers that already in 1580 there had been formed a confederacy of the Pope, the King of Spain and other princes for the invasion of the realm (cf. *infra*, Appendix I).

[166] *Holinshed IV*, p. 545.

[167] *Ibid.*

[168] *Ibid.*

move any man, but only to view the country, for that the moving of any man was referred to Mendoza himself.[169]

From these passages it is clear that the Government represented not only Charles Paget, but also Thomas Morgan, as being deeply involved in the invasion scheme. How far the latter was so involved in reality must be judged from his relations with the English councillors, and his other activities depicted in the chapters that follow.

As for the scheme itself, with the definite refusal of Philip II in September 1583 to support it, the plan of that year came to an abortive end. The special mission to Spain of the Papal envoy, Sega, failed to shake the King's resolution. He simply reiterated his refusal, adding a further reason for it, to those that he had previously given to the Nuncio, Taberna, that the preparations and co-operation of Catholics in England, so the Duke of Guise had informed him, were not such as he had been led to expect.[170] Hope, however, was again revived the following year by the news of James VI's increasing favour to Catholics, his support of his mother's cause and his willingness to aid the enterprise. He wrote, in fact, two letters, one to the Duke of Guise, and the other to the Pope, requesting help against the intrigues of the English Government. In consequence, the Duke of Guise once again decided to lead an expedition against the English party in Scotland. Hopes were further raised by the overthrow of the Gowrie conspiracy, secretly favoured by Walsingham, with the consequent flight to England of the Earls of Mar and Angus, and the Master of Glamis, the leaders of the English faction, and the execution of the Earl of Gowrie. The Pope once again, through his Nuncio, urged Philip II to lend his aid to an invasion plan, but again in vain: and without that aid the

---

169 *Holinshed IV*, p. 547. Mendoza, it was stated, was aggrieved that such matters as the "moving of men" to support the invasion, had not been left to him (*Ibid.*, p. 546). According to a statement earlier in the pamphlet, the Spanish ambassador affirmed to Throckmorton that Charles Paget "was come over to view the havens and country for landing of such foreign forces about Arundel and specially to sound and confer with certain principal persons for assistance; and . . . that Charles Paget had accordingly done his message and had spoken with some principal persons here according to his commission" (*Ibid.*, p. 539). In the later pamphlet about the Earl of Northumberland, "Mendoza", it was stated, "told Francis Throckmorton about Bartholomewtide 1583, that one Mope, was come into England to sound the Earl of Northumberland, and other principal men in Sussex; and about the end of September following . . . that Mope was Charles Paget, and that he came not only to sound the men but to view the places, the havens, the provisions and means, etc." (*Somers Tracts I*, p. 216). The crucial point, in fact, of the Government's case was that Paget's purpose had been to obtain the support of the Earl of Northumberland and others, including William Shelley, for the intended invasion (cf. "The Manner of proceeding against Wm. Shelley", B.M. Lansd. 45, n. 75). Readers must judge how all this agrees with the other statement in the text above, that he was not to sound any man!
170 Cf. *Kretzschmar*, pp. 212–215.

Pope was unwilling to act. Then followed, in June 1584, the death of the Duke of Alençon, the heir to the French throne, leaving the Huguenot, Henry of Navarre, the next in succession, and making it imperative for the Duke of Guise, the leader of the Catholic League, not to leave the country. By the end of the year James, unwilling to wait any longer for help from the Catholic princes, abandoned his mother's cause and made the first tentative steps towards reconciliation with Queen Elizabeth, which in 1586 resulted in a league between their respective countries.

2. *Morgan and the Parry plot*

About this time, too, Morgan was implicated in another episode—the so-called assassination plot of Dr. William Parry.[171] For some years previous to the plot, this spendthrift and rather disreputable man, during his travels abroad, had acted as a spy or intelligencer for the Elizabethan Government, as is evidenced by his extant letters to Burghley and Walsingham. After his return to England in 1580 he was tried and condemned to death for entering the chambers of Hugh Hare, one of his creditors, with the intention of murdering and robbing him. The death penalty was, however, remitted by the Queen, but he remained in prison till the summer of 1582 and, when released, obtained licence to travel abroad for three years, and once again engaged in his former occupation of a spy.[172]

In Paris he was reconciled to the Catholic Church, but was regarded with suspicion by most of the Catholic exiles. Thence he went to Lyons, and later to Milan and Venice. At the latter city he endeavoured to get permission to visit Rome, with a written promise that he would be allowed to leave again and return to France. After some delay this was eventually granted, or should he prefer it, he was told that he could go to Milan and give there the important information which he avouched he wished to communicate; as he had returned to Lyons before the passport arrived, it was, at his request, forwarded to him there. But he went neither to Rome nor to Milan. Later, in a letter to the Cardinal of Como, the Papal Secretary of State, and also in his

---

[171] For a fuller treatment of the plot and the career of Parry, cf. L. Hicks, s.j., *The Strange Case of Dr. William Parry, the Career of an Agent-Provocateur, Studies*, Dublin 1948, pp. 343–362, where many of the documents are quoted.

[172] "M. Philips is at Bruges, and M. Parry, your old acquaintance, is presently to go over. He will, I take it, abide most at Paris. He hath found good friends in this place" (Nicholas Faunt [*Walsingham's secretary*] to Anthony Bacon, 1 August 1582, quoted by Birch, *op. cit. I*, p. 25).

confessions, he asserted that the passport had arrived too late. This was not, in fact, the case. The truth seems to be that he had never had any serious intention of going to Rome, but had wished to open up communication with the Holy See in view of his later schemes. And the reason stated by him for his proposed journey rather supports this. When at Venice, he had asserted that a design against the Church had been committed to him by the English Government, which he had decided to relinquish. Ignorance of this design would entail great and irreparable harm for Catholics: a knowledge of it, on the other hand, would enable the Pope not only to counter it, but to draw advantage from it.[173] His own conduct, however, makes his assertion improbable, for had it been true, instead of the vague language of the letter, he could have communicated the alleged design to the Nuncio there, or even have explained it in the letter itself. But he did neither. All this is evidenced by the strictly contemporary correspondence of the Nuncio, Campeggio, and Como, and should be compared with what he insinuated later in his confessions, viz. that he had discussed the assassination plot at Venice with the Jesuit, Benedetto Palmio, who had introduced him to the Nuncio and who had commended his devotion and encouraged him in his murderous plan.[174] Nor must it be overlooked that at this very time, as the extant letters show, he was acting as a spy for the English Government.[175]

In Lyons he pestered another Jesuit, William Crichton, on the subject of the assassination of the Queen, more as a speculative problem than as a concrete proposal of an attempt on her life; but in spite of all the arguments urged by Parry in support of assassination, the Jesuit categorically denied that it was morally justifiable.[176]

---

[173] Cf. his letter to Como, enclosed in the despatch of Campeggio, the Nuncio in Venice, to Como, Venice, 12 March 1583, R.O. Transcripts 31/9, bundle 80. A translation of Parry's letter is given in *Studies, ut supra*, pp. 347–348.

[174] Cf. his confession 13 February 1585, *Holinshed IV*, pp. 566–570; cf. also D. Jardine, *Criminal Trials*, London, 1846, *I*, p. 256. In his letter to Burghley and Leicester, the Tower, 18 February 1585, Parry wrote: "The matter [*i.e. of assassination of Q. Elizabeth*] first conceived at Venice, the service (in general words) presented to the Pope, continued and undertaken in Paris, and lastly, commended and warranted by his Holiness, digested and resolved in England, etc." (*Holinshed IV*, p. 571).

[175] Cf. Parry to Burghley, Venice, 28 January 1583, n.s., B.M. Lansd. 40, n. 24; Same to Same, Venice, 4 and 10 March 1583, *Ibid.*, 37, nn. 32 and 33; Same to Same, Lyons, 10 May 1583, *Ibid.*, 39, n. 21; Same to Same, Lyons, 18 June, 12 and 27 August 1583, *Ibid.*, 39, n. 24 and R.O. S.P/78/10, nn. 25 and 29; Same to Same, Lyons, 28 August, *Ibid.*, 78/10, n. 31, and Same to Walsingham, Lyons, 27 June 1583, *Ibid.*, 78/9, n. 132, and Same to Burghley and Walsingham, Lyons, 28 August 1583, *Ibid.*, 78/10, n. 30.

[176] Cf. Crichton to Walsingham, The Tower, 20 February 1585, printed in *Holinshed IV*, p. 572, and *Crichton's Memoirs 1582–1587*, printed by J. H. Pollen, s.j. in his *Mary Queen of Scots and the Babington Plot*, Edinburgh, 1922, p. 157.

From Lyons he went to Paris, arriving there some time in October,[177] and there renewed his intimacy with his own countryman, Thomas Morgan, and his associate, Charles Paget, leaders of the opposition to Allen and Persons. The Jesuit refused to have anything to do with him, considering him, as he undoubtedly was, a spy; and Allen, though he did not decline all conversation with him, treated him with circumspection.[178] At Paris, he once again raised the question of assassination, this time with Thomas Morgan who, so he declared, suggested that Parry himself should undertake it, and who thus became embroiled in a hypothetical plot—hypothetical, because Parry had first to be assured that it was morally justifiable, and because he never had any intention of putting it into execution. The Catholic divine, whom by Morgan's appointment he consulted, declared it to be utterly unlawful, and the priest whose counsel he sought in England gave the same answer.[179] It was Morgan, too, who took him to the Nuncio, Ragazzoni, but neither the circumstances of the introduction—Parry was muffled in a clerical cloak for disguise—nor the subsequent conversations gave the Nuncio any confidence in him: and though he forwarded

[177] Cf. Parry to Burghley, Paris, 24 October 1583, B.M. Lansd. 39, n. 43; also Stafford to Burghley, Paris, 21 October 1583, *For. Cal. July 1583–July 1584*, p. 158.
[178] Cf. Persons, *Autobiography, C.R.S. II*, p. 32, and *Notes Concerning the English Mission, C.R.S. IV*, pp. 122–125. In his confessions, speaking of consulting as to whether assassination was lawful, Parry wrote: "Dr. Allen I desired, Persons I refused" (*Holinshed IV*, p. 567), but it seems clear, in fact, that he never asked Allen's opinion on the subject. Later Charles Paget, in his charges against the Jesuits, charged Persons with having been an accomplice of Parry (cf. Persons to Cardinal Cajetan, enclosing Paget's charges and his own replies, 22 August 1598, Vat. Arch. Nunz. Diverse 264, ff. 229–240; also Persons to Juan de Idiaquez, Rome, 3 July 1597, with enclosure of 30 June, West. Arch VI, nn. 41 and 42; Persons to Paget, Rome, 20 December 1597 and 18 February 1598, Stonyhurst, Coll. P. 452 and Arch. S.J. Rom. Anglia 31. II. f. 711). "For touching the practice against her Majesty's person which he [*Paget*] fathereth upon Fa. Persons and other Jesuits, I know myself a great part of them to be false, and the rest are neither likely nor probable. At first where he chargeth Fa. Persons to have advanced the practice of Parry for killing her Majesty, besides that it is well known that the said father hath always abhorred such detestable actions, I know that if he had any such intention that of all men living he would never have employed Parry, for he knew him to be a spy for the Lord Treasurer Cecil, and so did both he and Dr. Allen ever esteem him. And therefore was there neither reason nor probability that he would commit such a matter unto him. But if any such matter were intended, no man more like than Mr. Paget and Morgan to be the debiters and setters on of Parry to execute it, for they had more intrinsical familiarity with him than all the rest of the nation beside" (A Catholic at Brussels to his friend, a monk at Liège, Brussels, 14 July 1599, Dom. Eliz. 271, n. 74; cf. also Note 352 *infra*).
[179] Cf. Parry to Morgan, London, 22 February 1584, Dom. Eliz. Add. 28, n. 61. At his trial he declared: " 'And yet [I] never intended to kill Queen Elizabeth: I appeal to her own knowledge and to my Lord Treasurer's and Master Secretary's' "; and later, "he cried out in a furious manner: 'I never meant to kill her: I will lay my blood upon Queen Elizabeth and you before God and the world' " (*Holinshed IV*, pp. 576 and 578). On the scaffold, too, he declared: "I die a true servant of Queen Elizabeth: for any evil thought that ever I had to harm her, it never came into my mind; she knoweth it and

a letter, written by Parry to the Cardinal of Como, he twice gave warning that Parry had a bad reputation.[180] Having received no reply to this letter, Parry on 1 January 1584 penned another to the Pope, which the Nuncio forwarded with a further warning that Parry was well known in Paris and of bad repute.[181] Neither the letter to Como nor that to the Pope contained any reference to assassination. The former explained, quite untruthfully, the reason for not availing himself of the passport, and begged the Papal Secretary of State not to give credence to malicious reports of his enemies, but to rely on those of the Archbishop of Glasgow, the Bishop of Ross, Charles Paget and Thomas Morgan.[182] In that to the Pope he declared vaguely that he had in mind to undertake an enterprise for the public good, the peace of the whole of Christendom, the restoration of England to its ancient obedience to the Apostolic See, and the liberation from her long and weary sufferings of the Queen of Scotland, the only true and undoubted heiress of the crown of England; and he begged the Pope, in view of this dangerous enterprise, to grant him a plenary indulgence.[183]

With the groundwork thus laid for his scheme, Parry crossed to England bearing two significant letters from Sir Edward Stafford, the English ambassador in Paris. One of these was a private note to Walsingham warmly recommending him, but stating that from the Secretary's last letter, thanking the ambassador for the way he had

---

[180] Ragazzoni to Como, Paris, 18 December 1583, enclosing Parry's letter of 10 December 1583, Vat. Arch. Nunz. di Francia XVII, f. 278; Same to Same, Paris, 25 December 1583, *Ibid.*, f. 280. For a translation of Parry's letter, cf. *Studies, ut supra* (Note 171).

[181] Ragazzoni to Como, Paris, 8 January 1584, enclosing Parry's letter to the Pope, 1 January 1584, Vat. Arch. Nunz. di Francia XVII, f. 287. A translation of Parry's letter is in *Studies, ut supra* (Note 171).

[182] The only testimony to Parry that is known is that of Crichton, the Jesuit. "Sta qui di continuo il Sig. Parry Inglese, il quale offerisce il suo servitio, se piacerà a N. Sre accettarlo in gratia et gia per mezzo del Pre. Benedetto Palmio col quale haveva conferito le cose sue, ho inteso ch'ha piaciuto a S. Stà. concederlo salvo condutto per andar liberamente per tutto il stato ecclesiastico; è realmente huomo di molto grande intelligentie per tutto et che ha bellissime qualità, ma il punto sta di cognoscere il suo interiore et fin tanto se puo fidarsi di lui, et in questo non posso io penetrare. Pur penso ch'il Sig. Archidiacono di Cambray [*Owen Lewis*] ch'è del suo paese et lo cognosce risponderà per lui" (Crichton to Como, Lyons, 17 July 1583, R. O. Transcripts 31/9, bundle 80).

[183] With the letter he had sent a testimony that he had been to confession and received communion (Vat. Arch. Nunz. di Francia XVII, f. 286).

---

her own conscience can tell her so . . . I die guiltless and free in mind from ever thinking hurt to her Majesty" (B.M. Lansd. 43, n. 53). The Government suppressed this speech in their official account (cf. *infra*). Parry was equivalently saying that he was an agent-provocateur of the Government, and was appealing to their knowledge that it was so. Later Morgan denied complicity, when he declared Parry's statements false (Morgan to Queen of Scots, Paris, 30 March 1585, *Scot. Cal. VII*, p. 602). So, too, did his friend Charles Paget (*Ibid.*, p. 628).

used Parry, it was superfluous to write in his favour. The other was to Queen Elizabeth, in which he declared that Parry's dutiful good-will to her Majesty and to most of her Council sufficiently recommend-ed him, yet was he bold enough to add his word of praise. Parry had both the ability and the means to do her good service. He added, more significantly still:

"Besides that I think he hath some matter of importance that he hath kept to deliver to yourself for the good will he hath to your service".[184]

From Rye, where he landed, Parry wrote to the court and advertised some that he had a special service to discover to the Queen's Majesty.[185] On arriving in London, accordingly, he obtained an audience with the Queen in her palace at Whitehall and related to her that he had been sent from France by the friends of the Queen of Scots, Thomas Morgan in particular, and by the Jesuits, with the approval of the Pope, to assassinate her, and that he himself had only entered into the conspiracy in order to discover these dangerous practices of her enemies.[186] This, then, was the matter of importance which Sir Edward Stafford had informed the Queen that Parry had kept to reveal to her.

In due course, to his two letters to Rome, Parry received a reply from the Cardinal of Como, stating that the Pope commended his good dispositions and his resolutions for the public service and benefit, exhorted him to effect what he had proposed, and granted him the indulgence for which he had petitioned.[187] This letter Parry was not slow in showing to some of the court and to the Queen herself as confirmation of his earlier statement of a plot to assassinate her: and so it was accepted. "He was welcomed with fine speeches", wrote Persons.[188] The Queen gave him several audiences, and granted him a liberal pension.[189] In the Parliament that met in November 1584 he was returned as member for Queenborough, Kent. His stock, indeed,

[184] Stafford to Queen Elizabeth, Paris, 29 December 1583; to Walsingham, of the same date, R.O. S.P. 78/10, nn. 115 and 117. Italics mine. Cf. also Parry to Walsingham, Paris, 17 December 1583, Dom. Eliz. Add. 28, n. 46.
[185] Parry's confessions, *Holinshed IV*, p. 568.
[186] *Ibid.*
[187] Como to Parry, 30 January 1584, B.M. Lansd. 96, n. 13. The minute of the letter is in Vat. Arch. (cf. R.O. Transcripts 31/9, bundle 81). This has a passage crossed out and another substituted, as in the original Italian letter; translation in *Holinshed IV*, p. 573. Cf. also *Studies, ut supra* (Note 171).
[188] Persons, *Notes Concerning the English Mission*, C.R.S. IV, p. 125.
[189] *Holinshed IV*, p. 562.

was so high, that Burghley's nephew, Sir E. Hoby, placed his affairs in his hands, empowering him to solicit his business at court, and begging his uncle to give to Parry the same credence as he would to himself.[190]

In December of that year, perhaps trading on his previous good fortune, he spoke in Parliament in vigorous terms against the further harsh measures against Catholics then under discussion,[191] and was placed, therefore, in custody of the Serjeant. Next day, however, the Queen declared by the Vice-Chamberlain, Sir Christopher Hatton, that she approved the conduct of the House in the matter, but that Parry by her appointment, and partly to her satisfaction, had revealed the reasons for his behaviour to some of the Lords in Council, and that a humble acknowledgment of his fault ought to be sufficient satisfaction.[192] With this Parry complied.

In the summer previous to this incident he had repeated the part he was said to have played with Morgan as regards assassination, this time with a certain Edmund Neville, who had recently returned from Rouen, where he had acted as a spy for the Government.[193] This Neville, who was in financial straits, had a grievance: he claimed to be the legal heir of the fourth and last Lord Latimer, whose daughter, married to Burghley's eldest son, Thomas, had possession of the estates. From the moment of his return the Government appears to have held him in suspicion and Parry himself, according to the contemporary Camden, had denounced him to the Queen as a disaffected person.[194] Some weeks after the incident in Parliament just recorded, Parry twice approached Neville again, on the subject of assassination, and two days or so later, on 9 February 1585, Neville laid an information against him.[195] The Queen then, according to the official account, instructed Walsingham, as a trusted friend of Parry, to call him to his house. There Parry was informed

[190] Sir E. Hoby to Burghley, 1 October 1584, *Cal. Salisbury MSS. III*, p. 67; cf. also Parry to Burghley, 3 September 1584, B.M. Lansd. 43, n. 16.

[191] The Bill was passed eventually in 1585, becoming the Statute by which most of the English Martyrs were thenceforth condemned.

[192] Cf. S. D'Ewes, *Journal of all the Parliaments during the Reign of Elizabeth*, London, 1682, pp. 340 and 342.

[193] Cf. Neville to Walsingham, Rouen, 15 September, 23 October and 8 November 1583 (*For. Cal. July 1583–July 1584*, pp. 109, 168, 199); also Lady Anne Lee to her brother, Charles Paget, Drayton, 29 January 1584, warning him against Parry and Neville, as they were both spies. (Dom. Eliz. 167, n. 51).

[194] Camden, *Annals*, 1635 Ed. p. 392.

[195] Cf. confessions of E. Neville, 9 February 1585, Dom. Eliz. 176, n. 47; his declaration, 10 February, *Holinshed IV*, p. 564, and his deposition, 11 February, Dom. Eliz. 176, n. 48.

"that her Majesty had been advertised, that there was somewhat intended presently against her own person, wherewith she thought he could not but be acquainted, considering the great trust that some of her worst affected subjects reposed in him: and that her pleasure therefore was that he should declare unto him his knowledge therein; and whether the said Parry himself had let fall any speech unto any person (*though with an intent only to have discovered his disposition*) that might draw him into suspicion, as though he himself had any such wicked intent".[196]

Parry denied that there had been any such speech, but later declared spontaneously that he recalled a talk with his kinsman, Neville, touching a point of doctrine, that it was lawful to take the life of a prince for the furtherance of the faith, contained in Allen's book.[197] A few days later, however, he made a full confession.[198]

At his trial on 25 February 1585, Parry was accused of having conspired to bring about the death of the Queen at Westminster, 1 February 1584, and "at divers other times and places in the same county".[199] Como's letter to him of 30 January 1584 was read as confirming this, and also a garbled version of Parry's letter from the Tower to Queen Elizabeth.[200] Of course, the revelation of the so-called plot by Parry himself on his arrival in England, the disclosing of the letter of Como on his receipt of it, together with the subsequent high favour shown to him on that account, proved awkward corners for the Government. But they turned them by lying boldly. They declared, somewhat paradoxically, that Parry's intent in discovering the plot in

[196] *Holinshed IV*, pp. 562–563. Italics mine. The words italicised surely betray that the Government was well aware of Parry's rôle as an agent-provocateur.

[197] *Ibid.* No such doctrine is contained in the book of Allen (*A True, Sincere, and Modest Defence of English Catholics*, 1584, modern ed. London, 1914) which was written in reply to Burghley's *Execution of Justice, etc.* 1583. The English Councillor never answered Allen, except in so far as the untruthful statements set out in the official account of the Parry "plot" may be considered to be an answer.

[198] At his trial Parry, according to the Government's account, which alone is extant, first acknowledged that he had made his confession "freely and without constraint", but after it had been read, he declared it had been made under threat of torture, which the Government denied.

[199] *Holinshed IV*, p. 574.

[200] Passages were omitted that told against the Government. This garbled version was printed in the official pamphlet, the only account, so far as is known, of his trial now extant. Parry's original holograph letter to the Queen, The Tower, 14 February 1585, is in B.M. Lansd. 43, n. 47. Strype was the first to discover how the letter had been doctored (cf. Strype, *Annals*, 1824 Ed. *III, I*, p. 380 and *III, II*, pp. 337–339; also D Jardine, *op. cit., I*, pp. 261–262). The pamphlet, *A True and plaine Declaration of the Horrible Treasons practised by W. Parry, etc.*, originally published in 1585, was reprinted in Holinshed's *Chronicles* (cf. Ed. 1807/8, *IV*, pp. 561–587). The doctored version of Parry's letter appears in this edition without any note about Strype's discovery of the original letter.

the first instance on his arrival in England, was only to make it easier
to execute later—and this, despite Parry's letter to Morgan, which
had apparently been intercepted, stating that the "plot" was abandoned.[201] The favours accorded him they ascribed to the wonderful
clemency of the Queen; and lest the ministers themselves might be
blamed for want of care for her safety, seeing that they emphasised
the extreme danger in which she had been all this time, they roundly
asserted that out of regard for Parry she had concealed the plot from
all, an assertion which, apart from its utter improbability, was contradicted by Parry's confessions![202]

The verdict at the trial was a foregone conclusion, and on 2 March
1585 the sentence was carried out in Palace Yard, Westminster. On
the scaffold, Parry once more avowed his innocence of all intent to
harm the Queen and denied the truth of his confessions.

" 'His offence' he confessed, 'was twofold. The one in being reconciled to the Church of Rome (whereof he was a member) both at
Milan and Paris, contrary to a positive law only.[203] The other in
entering into conference with his kinsman and friend (as he took
him) Mr. Neville, and in concealing what passed between them,
which he did *upon confidence of her Majesty, to whom he had before
bewrayed what he had been solicited to do*'.[204] Being charged with
Cardinal Como's letter by Mr. Topcliffe and that therein he had
promised to destroy her Majesty, and was by him as from the Pope
animated thereunto. 'O Master Topcliffe', said he, 'you clean mistake it. I deny any such matter to be in the letter; and I wish it
might be truly examined and considered of'. The sheriff requiring
him to cease to purge himself since the law had passed against him:
'O Mr. Sheriff', said he, 'give me leave to speak: for this is my last

[201] Parry to Morgan, London, 22 February 1584, Dom. Eliz. Add. 28, n. 61.

[202] Queen Elizabeth appears to have shown considerable partiality for Parry. She had
spared him when condemned to death over the Hare affair in 1580, and had intervened
in his favour when Parry spoke out against the measures against Catholics in December
1584. In his letter to the Queen from the Tower, 14 February 1585, he wrote: "Remember
your unfortunate servant, chiefly overthrown by your hard hand, etc." but the word
"servant" is blotted out, and "Parry" substituted (printed in Strype, *Annals*, 1824, *III*,
II, pp. 337–339). Needless to say the Government did not read this portion of the letter
at his trial, nor print it in the pamphlet (cf. Note 200). It may have been that the Earl of
Leicester resented the Queen's partiality; for he appears to have opposed Parry earlier,
endeavouring to get Burghley into trouble with the Queen, because of the favour
Burghley showed to him (T. Birch, *Memoirs of the Reign of Queen Elizabeth*, London,
1754, *I*, p. 12, using as his authority a letter of Anthony Bacon to Essex, 11 September
1596).

[203] Why he should have been reconciled twice does not appear. Was the second time
to impress the authorities at Milan with his good faith?

[204] Italics mine. Compare this with the question asked of him by order of the Queen
at his first interrogation by Walsingham.

farewell to you all, I die a true servant of Queen Elizabeth; for any evil thought that ever I had to harm her, it never came into my mind; she knoweth it and her own conscience can tell her so. God save Queen Elizabeth; for a more gracious princess and sovereign was never any. I avow it before you all, and seal it here with my blood. I die guiltless and free in mind from ever thinking hurt to her Majesty'."

After once more asserting his innocence and charging the Treasurer, who was present, to tell the Queen he died her faithful servant, he recited the Our Father in Latin. He was turned off the ladder, then cut down and disembowelled whilst still alive.[205] Clearly, it was not in the interest of the Government to publish the speech above; nor did they do so in the printed pamphlet, and it remained unknown until Strype included it in his Annals.[206]

Years later, long after Walsingham's death, Thomas Harrison, by his own account a friend and servant of the Secretary, and one who was expert, as was Thomas Phelippes, in imitating the handwriting of others, avowed that the plot was "wrought by them", i.e. Walsingham, Phelippes and himself.[207] Be that as it may, the Government certainly used it as good propaganda, issuing a pamphlet on the subject and having special prayers composed to be used at court, in Parliament and elsewhere, for the marvellous escape of the Queen! Such propaganda may not be unconnected with the Bond of Association, which the Queen of Scots regarded as her death warrant, and with the excessively severe laws against Catholics, passed in Parliament in 1585. Certainly, in this Parliament, on account of the plot there was a

[205] The speech is given in an account of his execution (B.M. Lansd. 43, n. 53), first printed by Strype, *Annals*, 1824, *III, I*, pp. 362ff. The document is endorsed by Burghley.

[206] That the Government was very concerned about what was printed about Parry is shown by two letters of Burghley. One of the printers was evidently committed to custody for an account that did not please them (cf. Burghley to Walsingham, 1 and 4 March 1584, Dom. Eliz. 177, nn. 1 and 4). This concern was also evidenced by a postscript to a despatch of Sir Edward Stafford to Walsingham, Paris, 12 March 1585. "Mr. Cooke", he wrote, "whom you sent me yesterday, has done some wrong to this service [*he was referring to the efforts to obtain the extradition of Thomas Morgan from the French King at Queen Elizabeth's request*] for he has given out 'that Parry denied at his death all that he had confessed, which the evil-affected here, I am afraid, will serve their turns of. I have sent for him and warned him, so that since I hear no speech of it,' and also warned those whom he told, that I know of, not to speak of it" (*For. Cal. August 1584–August 1585*, p. 349).

[207] Cf. "Confession of Thomas Harrison concerning the Conspiracy against Mary", signed Ch. Maire: Robert Mayre. Endorsed: "Harrisones Confession that served Secr. Walsingham". (*Scot. Cal. IX*, p. 530). The Calendarist has assigned the document to 1587, but the reference in it to "Ld. Buckhurst then Treasurer", shows that it was years later. Buckhurst became Treasurer in 1599, after the death of Burghley. Harrison, under the name of Roger Almond, alias Vavasour, was responsible for the capture of W. Holt, s.j. at Leith 1 March 1583 (cf. *Scot. Cal. VI*, pp. 318, 321, 345).

"motion made with general applause of the whole house to revive the former judicial proceedings" against the Queen of Scots, propounded thirteen years before. Queen Elizabeth, in fact, used the plot as an excuse for breaking off the negotiations with Mary which Nau, her French secretary, had begun in London in November 1584.[208]

It may be added that there seems to have been an attempt on the part of the Government to implicate de Courcelles, of the French Embassy, in the affairs of Francis Throckmorton and those of Parry.[209] Efforts, too, were made to have Thomas Morgan extradited as an accomplice of Parry, but the French King persistently refused to surrender him, though he was arrested and imprisoned in the Bastille.[210] As for Neville, he appears to have been pardoned in June 1585 and in the same month granted a pension of one hundred pounds a year—a big sum in the then value of money—to be reckoned as from the last Christmas [i.e. 1584];[211] but he was kept in the Tower till February 1598, when he was removed to the Fleet, and finally set free under bond on 31 December of that year.[212]

3. *Further intrigues 1585–1586*

Little remains to record of these years. In September 1585 Dr. Allen and Fr. Persons went to Rome, never to return to the scene of their former labours. One of the purposes of their visit was to expose the activities of a certain Solomon Aldred.[213] For some years this obscure man had been employed by Walsingham in spreading favourable reports on the Government's attitude towards Catholics, and to lead their co-religionists abroad, the highest authorities included, to believe that there was no real persecution in England—the thesis of Burghley's

---

[208] Cf. Q. Elizabeth to Queen of Scots, 22 March 1585, *Scots. Cal. VII*, p. 597; also Q. Elizabeth to Sir Amias Poulet, 13 September 1585, *Ibid., VIII*, p. 102. The special prayers composed on the occasion are printed in Strype, *Annals, III, I*, pp. 377ff and *III, II*, pp. 330ff. Ed. 1824.

[209] Cf. De Courcelles to Walsingham, London, 28 January 1585, *For. Cal. August 1584–August 1585*, p. 261. Attention may be called to the date of this letter, some days, that is, before E. Neville laid his information against Parry on 9 February. Cf. also Mauvissière, the French ambassador, to Walsingham, London, 24 February 1585, *Ibid.*, p. 301.

[210] For further treatment of these efforts to have Morgan extradited, and of his imprisonment, cf. *infra* Chapter IX.

[211] C. C. Stopes in *Shakespeare's Warwickshire Contemporaries*, 1907, p. 128, gives a verbatim quotation, in the old spelling, concerning Neville's pardon and pension, of several lines from a document, for which she gives a reference to *Coke MSS. Hist. MSS. Comm.* I have not, however, been able to trace the document, and feel she must have given an incorrect reference for it.

[212] Cf. *Dasent XXVIII*, p. 299 and *XXIX*, p. 422.

[213] Berden to Walsingham, Paris, 30 September 1585, *Dom. Cal. Add. 1580–1625*, p. 153; partly printed also in *C.R.S. XXI*, p. 80.

Execution of Justice—and that if only peaceful methods were employed, and Allen and Persons restrained from irritating the Government by their books and by their support of forceable methods, some accommodation could be effected as regards religious matters in England, even to the extent of granting toleration to Catholics.[214] A further purpose of this propaganda was to sow division among Catholics and to prevent, or at least delay, any combined movement for the relief of their afflicted brethren in England. For this purpose Aldred was also employed to bribe some of high standing in the Papal curia.[215]

For the same purposes, soon after the departure of Allen and Persons, the Government intrigued by means of Aldred, with two priests, Edward Gratley and Dr. William Gifford, a professor in the seminary of Rheims, and a passport was sent to the latter that he might cross to England; where, it appears, he was to act as a cover for the activities of his cousin, Gilbert Gifford, an agent-provocateur of the Babington plot.[216] Of all these "practices" of the two priests Thomas Morgan was cognisant, though he pretended to Mary, Queen of Scots, that their aim was to overtake Walsingham and not to serve him, which is not borne out by the documents.[217] With Morgan's help and encouragement Gratley and Gilbert Gifford composed a book justifying the proceedings of the English Government as regards

[214] It is hardly necessary to state that the Government had really no such intention, cf. L. Hicks, s.j., *An Elizabethan Propagandist, the Career of Solomon Aldred, The Month,* May–June 1945, pp. 188–191, where the authorities are given. What was given in that article rather as surmises can now be proved by further documents. Cf. in particular, Charles Arundel to Gregory XIII, Paris, 10 April 1585, R.O. Transcripts 31/9, bundle 82a; the Examination by the Nuncio in Paris, of Charles Arundel and Thomas Fitzherbert, 30 September 1585, Vat. Lib. Chigi M. II, 47, ff. 10–16, and Discorso del Sig. Thomaso Fitzherberto, etc. 1602, West. Arch. VII, n. 72; also Berden (alias Rogers) to Walsingham, Paris, 30 September 1585, printed in *C.R.S. XXI*, p. 80. Cf. also *infra* Note 615.
[215] Cf. *The Month, art. cit.;* also Persons, *Autobiography, C.R.S. II,* pp. 34 and 35; *Domesticall Difficulties, Ibid.,* pp. 184 and 185; *Notes Concerning the English Mission, C.R.S. IV,* pp. 126–129, and Sega's Report, 1596, Foley, *Records VI,* p. 13.
[216] These intrigues can be traced in the following documents: Berden to Walsingham, 28 December 1585, printed in *C.R.S. XXI,* pp. 83 and 84; Stafford to Walsingham, Paris, 2 January and 15 April 1586, *For. Cal. Sept. 1585–May 1586,* pp. 276 and 550; Aldred to Walsingham, Rouen, 27 March and 15 April 1586, *Dom. Cal. Add. 1580–1625,* pp. 170 and 174; John Foxley [*Gratley*] to Walsingham, 20 April, 18 and 21 June 1586, *Ibid.,* pp. 172 and 179; "the Reasons wherefore Mr. William Huntley [*William Gifford*] cannot presently repair to England," Dom. Eliz. 199, n. 95; Confession of Gilbert Gifford, Paris, 14 August 1588, *Cal. Salisbury MSS. III,* pp. 346–349 and Notata contra Gilbertum Giffordum, 20 March 1588, Simancas, Est. Leg. 950, f. 114. Cf. also *infra* Appendix V, and *Dr. Gifford in 1586,* by Dom. Butler, o.s.b. and J. H. Pollen, s.j., *The Month,* March and April 1904. Fr. Pollen's judgment of Dr. Gifford is, however, too favourable, in view of his subsequent career: his activities in the troubles of the English College, Rome, 1594–1597, and his later intrigues in 1603 and 1606. All this rather sinister part of his career was before he entered the Benedictine order.
[217] Cf. Morgan to Queen of Scots, 24 April 1586, *Murdin,* p. 510.

F

Catholics, which Gilbert Gifford brought to England for publication by Walsingham.[218] Both Morgan and Charles Paget, despite disclosure of the character and activities of Aldred, continued to work with him against the Catholic leaders, Allen and Persons. In his letter to Paget in 1597 recalling this, Persons wrote:

> "But we being in Rome, you cannot forget how you and your friends continued your treaties with Solomon Aldred, that came in and out of England to Paris from the Council and professed himself opposite to our proceedings. The sending also into England of Ballard and Savage without our privities or ever writing one syllable thereof unto us, though the one were a priest, thereby subject to Allen. Afterwards in like manner your dealings with Gilbert Gifford and Gratley, other two priests, were kept secret from us, as also their treaties in England with the enemy, their writing of two infamous books against Dr. Allen, Jesuits and Spaniards whereof ensued the general and particular hurts that all men know".[219]

It was certainly Morgan and Paget who were responsible for sending to England the priest Ballard, a leading figure in the Babington plot of 1586. Allen himself characterised this continued opposition of Thomas Morgan in a letter to the latter's friend, Thomas Throckmorton.

> "And to say more plainly," he wrote, "the things that have been done by that faction were never done against me for any particular

---

[218] Cf. Notata contra Edwardum Gratleum, 20 March 1588, Simancas, Est. Leg. 950, f. 113; the Confession of Gilbert Gifford, Paris, 14 August 1588, *ut supra*; Phelippes to Walsingham, 8 July 1586, printed in *The Letter-Books of Sir Amias Poulet*, Ed. J. Morris, S.J. London, 1874, p. 218; and Henry Caesar to Walsingham, 9 December 1588, *Ibid.*, p. 385, from Dom. Eliz. Add. 30, n. 120. The book apparently was never published. For further details about Gratley, cf. Sega's Report, 1596, Foley, *Records VI*, p. 17 and *infra* Note 388 and Chapter XII, section 3.

[219] Persons to Paget, Rome, 20 December 1597, Stonyhurst, Coll. P. 472. The second book referred to was one composed by Gilbert Gifford in reply to Allen's *Defence of the Surrender of the town of Deventer to the Spaniards by William Stanley* (cf. L. Hicks, S.J., *Allen and Deventer, The Month*, January 1934, pp. 514–517); cf. also H. Caesar to Walsingham, 9 December 1588, *ut supra*.
Already in 1584 Aldred was under suspicion and the Nuncio in Paris reported unfavourably of him, that he was regarded as a spy (cf. Nuncio to Como, Paris, 6 February, 19 March and 28 May 1584, Vat. Arch. Nunz. di Francia XVII, 53, 92 and 180; Como to Nuncio, 19 February 1584, *Ibid.*, XVI, 16; also Allen to Como, 20 July 1584, and Como to Allen, 27 August 1584, Knox, *Allen*, pp. 234 and 239; and Persons to Aquaviva, Paris, 23 July 1584, printed in *C.R.S. XXXIX*, p. 217). Rogers (alias Berden), the spy, in his letter to Walsingham of 30 September 1585, stated that Allen and Persons had concluded to sift Bateson, the Jesuit, in Rome who had been working with Aldred, and to discredit some of the Cardinals there, if they could, about the matters in which Aldred was dealing; and further on in the letter, that in Paris there was great looking into Aldred's affairs, and that they were very vigilant about him, etc. (T. Rogers [*Berden*] to Walsingham, Paris, 30 September 1585, *Dom. Cal. Add. 1580–1625*, p. 153; and *C.R.S. XXI*, p. 80; also *infra* Note 651).

or personal respect (myself neither before my promotion nor after never giving them any occasion in the world of offence) but to the offence and special hurt of the common cause".[220]

At the same time he wrote to Charles Paget:

"And to say more plainly (because you use plain dealing with me as you say, and I like well in everybody) I see no Jesuit nor other priest, clerk or religious of our nation that detesteth not Morgan's foul dealing towards me, and consequently against the common cause whereof you must needs give me leave to be the leader, because so it hath pleased God, his Holiness and his Majesty to count me, and not for my own private but for the advancement of that service have put me in this room, whereby it followeth that all those who seditiously conspire my disgrace ... the same do band themselves directly and traitorously against the good of their country, and against the service of the highest princes in Christendom by whom only we expect succours and relief for our afflicted and unfortunate country".[221]

It is against the background of the events narrated in these three chapters, and of the continued opposition to Allen and Persons, that those aspects of the careers of Charles Paget and Thomas Morgan particularly concerned with the Queen of Scots must be considered. The English Government represented them as being enemies of Queen Elizabeth. Evidence has already been adduced to show that Charles Paget was not such. In the following chapters further evidence will be given to add to it, as well as to indicate that Thomas Morgan, far from being an enemy of Queen Elizabeth and a loyal supporter of the Queen of Scots, was in reality an agent of the Elizabethan Government, though it will ever remain a problem as to how far Queen Elizabeth herself was made cognisant of the fact.

---

[220] Allen to T. Throckmorton, Rome, 4 January and 20 February 1591, Knox, *Allen*, pp. 320 and 325.

[221] Allen to C. Paget, Rome, 4 January 1592 (*vere* 1591), Stonyhurst, Coll. M. p. 129. Cf. also Persons, *A Briefe Apologie*, 1601, f. 36, where part of the letter is quoted. Allen was referring more particularly to the attempt of those opposing him in 1589 to traduce him to the King of Spain, and have Owen Lewis, Bishop of Cassano, raised to the purple in opposition to him (cf. Arnold, the Carthusian Prior, to Philip II [after 26 May 1589], and Morgan to the Bishop of Dumblane [20 August 1589], references as in Note 37 *supra*).

PART II

CHAPTER IV

Thomas Morgan's arrest and trial in Flanders in 1590—
His own statements—Statements of the witnesses
against him—Morgan considered an English Government agent

1. *Thomas Morgan's arrest and trial in Flanders in 1590*

Although by the beginning of 1590 the Queen of Scots had already
been dead for nearly three years, an event occurred then in the life of
Thomas Morgan which throws an unexpectedly clear light on his
alleged position with regard to her affairs. This was his arrest and
trial in Flanders at the beginning of that year; and it seems best to
begin the second part of this book with an account of these happenings:
for on that occasion many witnesses were called, both ecclesiastics and
laymen, some even being summoned from Paris, and their testimony,
given under oath, reveals clearly their opinion that Morgan was
nothing but an agent employed by Queen Elizabeth's councillors. The
reports of the trial, indeed, provide a convenient framework for the
consideration of the other evidence about his activities which will be
dealt with in later chapters.

There are three official documents, besides letters from the Duke of
Parma and others, that are concerned with the trial, but it must be
emphasised that only a summary of the process is given and that the
actual statements of the individual witnesses are not forthcoming,
though possibly they may yet be found in the Belgian or Spanish
Archives, or in what remains of the Farnese Correspondence.[222] The
first paper was forwarded by the Duke of Parma to Philip II, presumably immediately after the conclusion of the trial. It is dated 12 February
1590, and is signed by De Salinas, Auditor-General of the army in
Flanders. The second document was sent to the King at his own
command, by the Archduke Ernest in December 1594, and was
occasioned, no doubt, by the visit of Morgan to Spain in that year
which caused enquiries to be made about him. The result of these

---

[222] The great collection of Farnese papers in the Archivio di Stato, Naples, perished
by enemy action during the late war, but there are still some extant in Parma.

enquiries was that he was exiled from Spain in 1595, as he had been from Flanders by the Duke of Parma, three years earlier. This document in a few details supplements the first. The third paper is practically a repetition of the first, but appears to be incomplete, and adds nothing to the two already mentioned. It seems highly probable that it was sent to the King by the Archduke Ernest in 1594 along with the second document.[223] These three documents form the basis of the following account of Morgan's trial in 1590, which gives, in the first place, what he confessed or acknowledged, and then the assertions of the witnesses —to be followed by supporting evidence for these assertions from other sources: but first, a few details as to his arrest.

He was arrested by order of Parma and confined in the prison of the Provost-General of the army.[224] The date of this arrest appears to have been early in January 1590, for the news of it had reached Rome by 8 February of that year.[225] A quarrel had evidently broken out between a gentleman called Gage and Morgan, in which the latter was wounded, and which resulted in the apprehension of both combatants.[226] But in the case of Morgan this was but the occasion or apparent cause of his arrest, the real reason being the many signs reported to Parma of his being a spy for the Queen of England, and of his corresponding with Burghley, her Treasurer. His chief accusers were Colonel William Stanley and Hugh Owen, two well-known Catholic exiles in the service of the King of Spain.[227] It may very well have been that the failing health of Lord Paget, who died in Flanders early in 1590, made the arrest possible; for the exile, Charles Browne, bastard brother of Lord Montagu, reported to Philip II that though Morgan had long been suspected as a "pernicious instrument" in the Catholic state from the clear evidence of his evil practices, they had never until that time

[223] "Sumario de los cargos que resultan contra Thomas Morgan, assi de su propria y spontanea confession, como de lo que contra el deponen diversos testigos, assi ecclesiasticos como seglares, fecho en Bruxeles en doze de febrero 1590" (Simancas, Est. Leg. 839, f. 21); "Sobre el negocio de Morgan," amongst the papers and letters of the Archduke Ernest, December 1594 (*Ibid.*, Est. Leg. 607, f. 117). In connection with this second document, cf. Archduke Ernest to Philip II, Brussels, 20 December 1594 (*Ibid.*, f. 107). The third document is entitled "Sumario de los cargos, etc." as in the first (*Ibid.*, Est. Leg. 598, f. 72).

[224] Cf. Parma to Philip II, Brussels, 20 February 1590, Simancas, Est. Leg. 598, f. 23, and Charles Browne to Same, Brussels, 22 February 1590, *Ibid.*, Leg. 599, f. 87.

[225] Cf. Hugh Griffin to Morgan, Rome, 8 February 1590, R.O. S.P/85 (Italian States), I, f. 69.

[226] Cf. *Ibid.*, Lewkner, *The State of English Fugitives*, London, 1596, p. 52; and Sobre el negocio de Morgan, *ut supra*.

[227] Cf. Parma to Philip II, 20 February 1590, Charles Browne to Same, 22 February 1590, and "Sobre el negocio de Morgan", *ut supra*; also T. Barnes to [? Phelippes], Antwerp, 31 May 1590, *Dom. Cal. Add. 1580–1625*, p. 307.

been able to proceed against him, owing to the protection afforded him by this exiled lord and his brother, Charles, and their friends. In the same letter he suggested that it would be a great service to God, and for the royal interest, if Morgan were sent to Spain to answer before the Inquisition the charges made against him.[228]

Many ciphers were found in his lodging on his arrest, as well as letters from the Carthusian Bishop of Dumblane, William Chisholm, together with a reply of Morgan to the same. In this reply, among other points, he treated of placing ambassadors in the various courts of Europe, he himself selecting of preference to be stationed in Paris. The principal reason for this, at least for his wish to leave Flanders, appears to have been the report that Cardinal Allen was coming to the Low Countries, from whom he, as Morgan himself stated, could expect nothing but "hard favours". By means of the Carthusian Bishop, he hoped to lodge with the Carthusians near Paris or in their vicinity, and apparently at their expense. But the most important point of the letter was a strong recommendation to the Bishop, who enjoyed great credit with the Duke of Savoy and his wife, to persuade the Duke to procure from the King of Spain his own appointment as Governor of Flanders in place of the Duke of Parma, under whose rule, so Morgan reported, the state of affairs had deteriorated: and all this to the end that after Philip II's death, the Duke of Savoy, being in possession of the country, might seize it for himself as ruler of it, independent of Spain. It was for this and other seditious matters contained in these letters that Parma ordered his trial by the King's Attorney in presence of the Auditor-General.[229]

From the summary of the trial, however, it is clear that one of the main points selected for investigation was the real position of Morgan as regards the late Queen of Scots. This also appears from a letter of

[228] Charles Browne to Philip II, 20 February 1590, *ut supra*.
[229] A Spanish translation of Morgan's letter to the Bishop of Dumblane, together with the cipher, was sent by Parma to Philip II with the summary of the process, and is now in the Simancas archives (Est. Leg. 598, ff. 73ff). A copy of the letter in English, with a key to the names in cipher at the end of it, is to be found among the Scottish Papers in the Record Office (cf. *Scot. Cal.* X, pp. 229–237). This copy was evidently brought to the English Government by the priest, John Cecil, in 1591 (cf. List of Papers, *Dom. Cal. Eliz. 1591–1594*, p. 43). It is worthy of note that in June of the same year this priest-informer suggested to the English Government that Savoy might be used to spread their own propaganda. "I have thought" he wrote, "upon that point, how the King of Spain may be informed of the false foundations and vain hopes he is fed with of the state of things here; and that the information may take place, I find no more compendious and commodious way than by the Duke of Savoy, and *he to have it from Morgan*, and those he favoureth in Flanders, and they will easily be brought to perform any such office, and when not in their name, it may be done with greater facility, and I dare undertake to set it down in such order that it shall take effect" (Snowden [*John Cecil*] to R. Cecil, 3 July

Dr. Owen Lewis, Bishop of Cassano, which Morgan's friends, probably through the intervention of the Bishop's nephew, Hugh Griffin, caused Lewis to write in defence of the prisoner, and which is nothing but a quotation from a letter which the Queen of Scots had written to the Bishop in 1586 in commendation of Morgan, at that time a prisoner in the Bastille.[230] But while the Bishop was brought in for Morgan's defence, Cardinal Allen but a few weeks later wrote in a very different strain. In a letter to the Duke of Parma he said that it would be highly acceptable to him that Morgan should at least be exiled from the dominions of the King governed by his Highness, as he was a person who by his intrigues could cause serious trouble.[231] In the event, Allen's suggestion was acted upon, but not till two years later, when Morgan was at length released from prison and exiled by the Duke.[232]

2. *His own statements*

From his own statements at the trial, it transpires that though he called himself an Englishman, Morgan was in fact of Welsh origin, having been born of honourable and Catholic parents in the "province of Wales",[233] and was in 1590 some forty-seven years old. At the age of eighteen, the summary continues, he entered the service of the Protest-

---

[230] Cf. Testimonial from O. Lewis, Bishop of Cassano, to Mr. Thomas Morgan, Rome, 24 February 1590, Knox, *Allen*, p. 437; also H. Griffin to Morgan, Rome, 8 February 1590, *ut supra*. The letter quoted by Lewis is that written to him by the Queen of Scots, 30 April 1586 (R.O. Transcripts 31/9, bundle 82a, from Vat. Arch. Arm. I. 17, p. 11), and in point of fact was written by her at the instance of Morgan himself (cf. Morgan to Q. of Scots, 18/28 January 1586, *Murdin*, p. 470ff).

[231] 'Mi sarebbe gratissimo ... che almeno sia mandato fuori di quei dominii di S. Maestà, che sono sotto il governo dell'Altezza V. .... essendo egli persona che con suoi traffichi potrà dare disturbo" (Allen to Parma, Rome, 4 May 1590, Naples, Arch. di Stato, Carte Farnesiane, fascio 1706, cited by R. Léchat, *Les Refugiés Anglais*, Louvain, 1914, p. 163, n. 3). The letter is no longer extant owing to the destruction already referred to of the Farnese papers at Naples. Persons referred also to another letter written to Parma, 30 February 1592, on the same subject of the faction. The activities of this faction, the letter said, had resulted in the death of the Queen of Scots (*Briefe Apologie*, 37v).

[232] His being set free was reported by the spy Robinson [*Sterell*] in a letter to Monson [*Phelippes*], Liège, 13 June 1592, *Dom. Cal. Eliz. 1591–1594*, p. 234. C. Paget also referred to his release, as well as to his having been exiled, in a letter to [Barnes] (Brussels, 12 July 1592, *Ibid.*, p. 244).

[233] Cf. *supra* Chapter I, section 1.

1591, Dom. Eliz. 239, n. 78 (italics mine); cf. also *infra* Note 361). On the question of deposing Parma for the Duke of Savoy, cf. —— to Barnes, Antwerp, 31 May 1590, *Dom. Cal. Add. 1580–1625*, p. 307, and Dingley to Puckering, 7 September 1592, *Dom. Cal. Eliz. 1591–1594*, p. 267. For the comments of Cardinal Allen on the Carthusian bishop's part in these affairs, cf. Allen to Paget, Rome, 4 January 1592 (*vere* 1591), Stonyhurst, Coll. M. 129; cf. also Persons, *Certayne Aparent Judgments*, C.R.S. II, p. 205 and his *Briefe Apologie*, 1601, ff. 31ff, where he quoted part of Morgan's letter to the Bishop of Dumblane, giving the date of it as 20 August 1589; cf. also Note 243 *infra*.

ant Bishop of Exeter,[234] becoming a scrivener to the Archdeanery.
After three years he transferred his services to the Protestant Archbishop of York,[235] and was employed as a secretary till the Archbishop's
death in 1568, enjoying with him, so Morgan himself stated, such
credit as no other of the episcopal household. He acknowledged that
these two Protestant bishops were the "greatest heretics, most pertin-
acious followers of Calvin and the fiercest persecutors of the Catholic
Church that were in the Kingdom", and that all during this time he,
Morgan, conformed to the state religion, even so far as to receive the
Protestant communion, though, so he asserted, he was at heart a
Catholic. He had no patrimony, but prebends were given him for his
services to the value of four thousand crowns, as well as landed
property; but, as is duly noted in the summary, his statements as to the
value of these perquisites are not consistent, since he declared at
another time that it exceeded ten thousand pounds, lowering it again
on another to but eight hundred crowns.[236]

After the death of the Archbishop, so his confession runs, he joined
the staff of the Earl of Shrewsbury, who had been appointed gaoler of
the Queen of Scots, and was employed by him as his secretary. He
entered this service, so he gave it to be understood, with a view to
helping the Queen in her captivity. Before he had taken this step,
however, he had consulted about it with the Earl of Pembroke, the
Earl of Northumberland and William Shelley, all of whom he knew to
be friends of the captive Queen. All three approved of it, especially the
Earl of Pembroke. During these years in which he was in the employ

[234] William Alley (1510?–1570). He was consecrated 14 July 1560 and died 15 April
1570 (cf. *D.N.B.*). Morgan would have entered his service about 1561.
[235] Thomas Young (1507–1568). He was consecrated Bishop of St. David's 21 January
1560, and was transferred to the archiepiscopal see of York 27 January 1561. A friend
of the Earl of Leicester, he showed himself a very active President of the Council of the
North. He died 26 June 1568 (cf. *D.N.B.*).
[236] Ten thousand pounds appears to have been a favourite sum for Morgan. In addition
to the above reference to it, he stated that he was released from the Tower in 1572 or 1573
under a bond of ten thousand pounds, and in a letter to the Queen of Scots he asserted
that Queen Elizabeth had offered to pay that same sum for his extradition from France
(Morgan to Queen of Scots, 18/28 January 1586, *Murdin*, p. 470). All these statements
border on the fantastic. Ten thousand pounds in that age would have been a very large
sum indeed in modern values, running into six figures. It is quite beyond belief that the
parsimonious Elizabeth would have been willing to offer such a sum to the French King
for handing over a mere private individual of no position, seeing that it was only with
reluctance that she had paid the much lesser sum of two thousand pounds for the surrender
of the Earl of Northumberland by the Scots. Rather did Morgan use such a figure in his
deliberate and cunning megalomania to convey the impression of the great importance
attached to his own person by the English Government and those associated with it.
Other instances of this trait of megalomania will be given in due course (cf. *infra* Chapter
IX, section 4).

of Shrewsbury, he used to inform the Queen of Scots, so he asserted, of what measures were being considered and contrived against her at court; and when men were sent to search her rooms, he would give her previous notice,[237] and take into his own care papers of greater importance. He also directed the letters she wrote and those she received, both within and without the kingdom, making use for this purpose of the two French ambassadors, La Mothe Fénelon and Mauvissière.[238] But after three years and some months these services which he rendered to the Scottish Queen became known at court. He was, in consequence, apprehended and imprisoned in the Tower, the charge against him being that to the prejudice and harm of the state he had corresponded with leading Catholics inside and outside the realm.

According to his own statement, though imprisoned for a matter of state—it occurred in 1572—he was released after more or less ten months, under bond of ten thousand pounds not to leave the kingdom for a year and not to meddle in the affairs of the Queen of Scots. He agreed that it was the custom of the English Council not to release any prisoner accused of treasonable practice, unless the prisoner appeared apt for their purposes and promised under oath to do some signal service either at home or abroad, and that many persons in this way had been set free, as well clerics as laymen, who had afterwards been employed in the service of the Queen of England. He averred, however, that it was not in this way that he had been released from the Tower, but because he could give a good account of himself, and because of the favour shown to him by Burghley and Wilson, both of whom he had won over to the party of the Queen of Scots, though he did not state the means by which he had accomplished this. Moreover, they had set him free, he agreed, without ever having charged him by a formal written indictment, though he was imprisoned for a matter of grave importance to the state and to the life of Queen Elizabeth.

He further confessed that eighteen months after his release from the Tower, during which time he had spent some seven hundred crowns of his resources, he retired secretly to France: and that the Queen of Scots had sent letters of warm recommendation to her ambassador in Paris, the Archbishop of Glasgow, and to the Duke of

[237] He did not state how he himself obtained such previous knowledge. The implication seems to be that when Shrewsbury himself was forewarned of such a search he communicated the same to his secretary. Regarding his employment with Shrewsbury, cf. also Note 6.

[238] This seems to have been a bad slip on Morgan's part. Mauvissière did not replace La Mothe Fénélon as ambassador till the autumn of 1575, three years and more, that is, after the dismissal of Morgan from Shrewsbury's service (cf. *infra* Chapter V, section 2).

Guise, bidding them to employ him in her service as a person of trust who had well merited it. From her dowry in France, he asserted, she also assigned him a pension of thirty crowns a month. Thus, he remained in Paris, assisting the affairs of the Queen of Scots, and continuing to correspond with her as before. In this, he averred, he had given such satisfaction that she used no other ciphers than the ones he had sent her, even when she wrote to the Duke of Guise and her ambassador.

He acknowledged, too, that he had been arrested in Paris in 1585 by order of the King of France, at the instance of the Queen of England, because he had been denounced by some who had been executed, of conspiring her death.[239] In consequence, he had been imprisoned in the Bastille for two years, though without ever having been examined and interrogated as to the cause of his imprisonment. In fact, he had, so he stated, been very well treated in that prison, having been assigned two crowns a day by the King for his prison expenses, which had amounted to more than seven hundred crowns, and those who had so wished had come to visit him every day. At his arrest there had been found in his chambers seven or eight thousand crowns and many papers, of which he had not lost a page, but the money, so he asserted, had belonged to Lord Paget.

Morgan further acknowledged that he had been on terms of familiar friendship with Gilbert Gifford, a Catholic cleric who had since been arrested and was then in prison in Paris; that he had been concerned in several enterprises against the English state and against the person of its Queen, not one of which had taken effect.

By order, he said, of Bernard Mendoza, the Spanish ambassador in Paris, he had come to Flanders, having been told that the King of Spain's command was that he should go there with other English pensioners to serve his Majesty on any occasion that offered. He agreed, however, that notwithstanding this, from the time when he had arrived there in 1588, he had not spoken once to his Highness or to any minister of the court, nor given any information. Yet he confessed, and the facts prove it, that he had had a very considerable correspondence, and had been active in treating of public affairs of grave moment. But all this, he asserted, he had done with the knowledge of the King of Spain.

---

[239] It was at the instance of Queen Elizabeth that in 1585 he was arrested in Paris, being accused of having been implicated in the so-called Parry plot (cf. *infra* Chapter IX, section 1).

For the purpose of this correspondence he had thirteen different ciphers, which had been found in his possession, amongst which were two he did not know, so he said, or was unwilling to name the persons for whose correspondence he used them. There were also found two different seals for sealing his letters. Two of the ciphers he had used, so he confessed, in corresponding with his brother, a cleric in England, with a gentleman called Thomas Barnes residing in London,[240] and with one called Fernihurst, living in Scotland.[241] There were other ciphers found by which he corresponded with the Steward of the Princess of Béarne, the secretary of the Duchess of Feria,[242] the Governor of Montreuil in Picardy and the Bishop of Dumblane,[243] who had become a Carthusian in the monastery of his order in the Dauphiné, and who often passed to and from the Court of Savoy, and was a partisan of the Bishop of Cassano [*Dr. Owen Lewis*] in opposition to Cardinal Allen and the Jesuits.

But, though he had had such a large correspondence with all parts, very few letters had been found, save some from Cardinal Mondovi,[244] thanking him for the information he continually sent to him for his Holiness. There were also no drafts or copies of his replies. Morgan acknowledged, indeed, that he had torn up and burned the letters received from his correspondents together with his own notes and drafts; so it was inferred that they had referred to affairs of importance,

---

[240] Thomas Barnes, a spy of the English Government, was employed mostly in Flanders. His correspondence with Phelippes, the decipherer and servant of Walsingham, and with Charles Paget, is calendared in the *Domestic Calendars* and *Additional 1580–1625*. Other letters are to be found in the *Foreign Calendars*, Flanders Correspondence and Salisbury MSS. For his part in the Babington plot, cf. J. H. Pollen, s.j., *Mary Queen of Scots and the Babington Plot*, Edinburgh, 1922.

[241] This was Andrew Ker, Laird of Fernihurst, who had succeeded his father, Sir Thomas Ker, in 1586.

[242] The Duchess of Feria, *née* Jane Dormer, was widow of the 1st Duke of Feria, Spanish ambassador in England at the beginning of Elizabeth's reign. The secretary in question may have been Ralph Parsley or Parcely, an English Catholic exile (cf. Persons *Certayne Aparent Judgments*, *C.R.S. II*, p. 207). What Persons there related is supported by the Duke of Feria's Memorial to Philip II, Brussels, 3 September 1594, Simancas Est. Leg. K. 1594, f. 76; cf. also "Tratado de la Relacion que se dio a su Alt^a. sobre los entretenidos Ingleses", Brussels, 10 March 1596, *Ibid.*, Est. Leg. 612.

[243] William Chisholm, Bishop of Dumblane had been coadjutor to his uncle of the same name, the then Bishop of Dumblane, on whose death he had succeeded him in the see. Later he left Scotland and became Bishop of Vaison in France in 1574. He resigned that see on becoming a Carthusian monk in 1584. He died in 1593. He was of the Morgan-Paget faction. Cf. also Note 229 *supra*, and Prior Arnold to Philip II, n.d. *Spanish Cal. 1587–1603*, p. 542. The Bishop of Dumblane and Vaison is to be distinguished from his nephew, a third William Chisholm, who succeeded his uncle in the see of Vaison.

[244] Vincenzo Laureo, Bishop of Mondovi, was created Cardinal by Gregory XIII, and became Protector of Scotland in 1586 on the death of Cardinal Sermoneta. He died 26 December 1591 (cf. J. H. Pollen s.j., *Papal Negotiations with Mary Queen of Scots*, Edinburgh, 1901, p. cvii, and Cardella, *Storiche de Cardinali, V*, p. 204).

and that he was unwilling or afraid that anyone should know of them. Only the last two letters from the Bishop of Dumblane were discovered, together with a draft of one reply—now enclosed with the summary of the process—though Morgan agreed that their correspondence had continued for several years.

He further acknowledged that as soon as he had arrived in Flanders in 1588 he had gone to the house of the postmaster of Antwerp and informed himself by what way letters were directed to England, and where the couriers lived who made the crossing to that country; though to direct his own letters he could have gathered the information from his numerous countrymen, or been content with the answer given in the postmaster's house, that should he wish to write to England, his letters would be forwarded. Not content with this he had wormed himself into the confidence of particular couriers, "pumping" them as to whether they carried despatches from the Duke of Parma to England, and had tried to find out to whom these despatches were directed, by what way and at what time.

He confessed, too, that he proposed to a Scotch gentleman who had correspondents in Scotland and powerful friends there, to capture the King of Scots and take him to Rome, offering him funds for that purpose and urging him to communicate to the Bishop of Cassano in Rome his plans for effecting it ; though, it was evident, the summary continues, that this was but a device of the English Council, along with similar projects, which were intended to divert his Holiness from lending encouragement and support to the plans of his Catholic Majesty for the reduction of England. Indeed, he had openly avowed that he would be sorry to see his country subjugated by foreigners and especially by Spaniards.[245]

Many other circumstances, which to avoid prolixity were omitted, the summary concludes, increased the suspicion that his imprisonments had been ruses to increase his credit amongst Catholics and to lull into confidence the Queen of Scots. No further steps, however, had been taken to submit the prisoner to rigorous

---

[245] The scheme, if Prior Arnold, the Carthusian, is to be believed, involved the assassination of the Scottish Chancellor (cf. Arnold to Philip II, after 26 May 1589, *Spanish Cal. 1587–1603*, p. 542). In this letter to the King of Spain, in which the suggested capture of James VI was related, Arnold declared that the Bishop of Dumblane had sent him to his Catholic Majesty and had promised to see to the assassination of the said Chancellor! It is worthy of remark how these schemes of assassination are associated with Morgan and his faction, such as those of George Gifford, Parry, the agent-provocateur, Ballard, and Arnold and the Bishop of Dumblane. On Arnold, cf. also Persons, *Certayne Aparent Judgments, C.R.S. II*, p. 205, and *Briefe Apologie*, ff. 32v and 33.

examination,[246] as he had alleged that all that he had done and treated of had been with the knowledge and consent of his Catholic Majesty and for his service. His Majesty's orders in the matter were, therefore, awaited, after he had seen the relevant papers.[247]

3. *Statements of the witnesses against him*

Such is the summary given in these documents, of what Morgan confessed and acknowledged at his trial in Flanders. But the documents also contain some comments of those who examined him, as well as assertions of those who witnessed against him, which appear to have been made under oath.[248] Thus, as regards his taking service with the Earl of Shrewsbury in 1569, many witnesses were convinced that Morgan did so with the secret connivance of the Earl of Leicester, so that by winning the goodwill of the captive Queen of Scots, he might the better discover the designs of herself and her adherents both at home and abroad; and they declared that this conviction was confirmed by the execution of many gentlemen, among whom there had been some who had revealed themselves as partisans of the Scottish Queen only to Morgan. His religion, too, was very suspect, for though he had been brought up in heresy and had taken service with the Protestant Bishop of Exeter, it had never been discovered at what time he had been reconciled, if ever he was, to the Catholic Church: nor, during the many years he lived in Paris, was it ever known that he went to confession or received communion, though many had taken pains to find out whether he did so.[249]

Other factors, too, the witnesses stated, gave rise to suspicion: his being set free from the Tower, the disagreements that were found in

[246] By "rigorous examination" was meant examination under torture (cf. Parma to Philip II, 20 February 1590, *ut supra*.

[247] The last paragraph of the "sumario" is in the hand of De Salinas, Auditor-General of the army, who appended his signature. It runs: "These are the charges faithfully copied from the official examination of and the information laid against Thomas Morgan, a prisoner in the prison of the Provost-General". The reply of Philip II to Parma's letter, if extant, has not been found.

[248] "They sent Crichton, the Scotch Jesuit, to Paris to take [*Gilbert*] Gifford's examination, whose imprisonment they had procured: and withal, they caused all such as anyway relied upon them, to take their oath before the Auditor-General that in conscience they thought Morgan to be a traitor and a spy" (Lewkner, *The State of English Fugitives*, p. 53). Lewkner's statements are by no means always correct, but he was in Flanders at the time of Morgan's arrest, and might have known and reported the facts. He applied to Sir Robert Sidney for a passport to return to England in June 1590 (cf. Lewkner to Sidney, 4 June 1590, *Dom. Cal. Add. 1580–1625*, p. 307). Concerning Gifford, much more about this agent of Walsingham will be found elsewhere in this book.

[249] This is an addition from the second document, "Sobre el negocio de Morgan", *ut supra*.

his own statements, his leaving England in such safety, though nobody was allowed to do so without a licence—these circumstances, coupled with his ambitious eagerness to meddle in grave affairs of state, his possession of so many ciphers, which he had used to correspond with all sorts of people in all the courts of Christian princes, as well as persons of high standing and importance as those of little, and his frequent communication with England and Scotland—all these things compellingly induced a strong conviction that he was a spy. He was, so they asserted, freed from the Tower by the Treasurer, under a promise to act as such and he brought with him from England a cipher of Burghley's, by means of which the two might interchange letters, and which, indeed, they might still be using.[250] When, moreover, English Catholics summoned from Paris had attested that they had seen him treating and conversing with the servants of the English ambassador there, and of Walsingham, he cunningly passed it off without showing any concern about it.

As for his crossing to France in 1575 several witnesses were convinced that Morgan had done so the better to discover to the Queen of England the negotiations of the Pope, his Catholic Majesty and other Christian princes for the liberation of the Queen of Scots. Moreover, from his entrance into France he had begun to sow division and dissension between her and her adherents, the Duke of Guise, the Archbishop of Glasgow, Dr. Allen and the Jesuits, in order to open the way to his own advancement and to serve his ambition. Thus, in his letters he had persuaded her that these men were planning the conquest of England and Scotland in the interests of his Catholic Majesty, Philip II, under cover of her name and with the pretence or pretext of procuring her liberation. This the Queen of Scots had greatly resented, and giving credit to his malicious counsels, she had determined to take the management of her affairs out of their hands, forbidding them by letters to communicate with her or to negotiate any matter for her without the intervention of the said Morgan and his close collaborator, Charles Paget. For a long time, indeed, she had refrained from writing to the Duke and Glasgow, so that the Archbishop, aggrieved at this neglect, had begged her to discharge him from his post. In the same manner Morgan had continued to sow division among the English Catholic exiles, following the faction of those who proclaimed that the reduction of the kingdom and the liberation of the Queen of Scots could be procured and effected without

---

[250] This statement about the cipher is from the same document.

G

the employment of foreign forces. The leaders of this party were the Bishop of Cassano at the Court of Rome, and the Bishop of Dumblane: and these, with the prisoner, Morgan, strongly opposed and acted against Dr. Allen, the Jesuits and others who wished to reduce the kingdom by the forces of his Catholic Majesty, convinced, as they were, that any other way that was suggested was purely chimerical and a cunning ruse of the Council of England. Thus it was that Morgan and Paget had sent the priest Ballard to England to persuade Catholics to assassinate Queen Elizabeth, alleging for this the authority of Dr. Allen and Fr. Persons, though they knew nothing about it, and the discovery of this scheme led to the execution of fourteen gentlemen and of the Queen of Scots herself.[251] Morgan, indeed, had admitted that he had been concerned in several enterprises against the said kingdom and against the person of its Queen, and that not one had been brought to execution; and the majority of the Catholics who witnessed against him were convinced that it was he himself who had prevented their execution by secret information sent by him to England; for as he had confessed, he had a large correspondence with that country by way of the French ambassador.

Morgan had, in fact, according to these witnesses, always opposed the reduction of the realm by his Catholic Majesty; and all the time he was in her service in France, he had advised the Queen of Scots not to deal with the King of Spain and those of his nation, except to find out what money Philip II could contribute. Indeed, his confederate, Charles Paget, had so prevailed in this matter that for some time before she died, she had put no trust in the King of Spain or in the Duke of Guise, her most assured adherent, or in the Archbishop of Glasgow, her own ambassador in France.[252] Still less did she follow the advice of Dr. Allen, now Cardinal, or of Fr. Persons, or of those that depended on his Majesty; and Charles Paget, in fact, had expressly threatened her that he and his friends would leave her service, if she negotiated with the above-mentioned; and they had persuaded her to put complete trust in the party they had formed in England. So great faith did they persuade her to have in them, runs the summary, and so successfully did they contrive matters, that they obtained the management and disposal of her property and rents in France, and by this means

---

[251] "The sending also into England of Ballard and Savage without our privities or ever writing one syllable thereof unto us [*Allen and Persons*], though the one were a priest, thereby subject to Allen" (Persons to Paget 20 December 1597, reference, and further information about Ballard, *infra* Note 407).

[252] From "Sobre el negocio de Morgan".

had become very rich, if public report was to be believed, whilst she herself had become financially embarrassed and her creditors ill-satisfied.[253]

As for his incarceration in the Bastille in 1585, his good treatment there, the permission to visit him and the allowance of two crowns a day for his expenses, amounting to more than seven hundred crowns, all pointed, it was asserted, to the presumption that this imprisonment also had been a ruse—a ruse cunningly designed the better to discover secret plans, to make them known to the Queen of England, and so open the way for her to make herself secure and rid herself of her enemies one after the other, and even to do away with the Queen of Scots. Further suspicion was aroused by his admission that he had taken to France only three hundred crowns, and that his friends had sent him another five hundred; yet from divers of his answers it appeared that, apart from his personal expenses, he had spent on various occasions more than two thousand five hundred.

His admission, too, of familiar friendship with Gilbert Gifford added to that suspicion, for that cleric had been arrested and imprisoned in Paris for having written a book full of invective and lies against the authority of the Pope, and to prejudice the good reputation of his Catholic Majesty. In it he had attacked, too, those who relied on his Majesty for the reduction of England and had endeavoured to persuade the English that no favour was to be looked for at the hands of Philip II and from the designs of that nation, but only cruelty and tyranny. The said Gilbert Gifford asserted further in his confession that in the composition of that book he was assisted by another cleric called Gratley, then a prisoner of the Inquisition in Rome, and by the prisoner Thomas Morgan, who had given instructions for it. It was with his knowledge that Gifford had taken the book to England, and presented it to the Queen's Secretary of State, Morgan being quite aware that the said Gilbert Gifford was in the pay of Walsingham.[254]

4. *Morgan considered an English Government agent*
The official documents from which the above summary has been taken leave no doubt that the Catholic witnesses were convinced that Morgan was an agent of the English Government. The opinion of the Duke of Parma himself was scarcely less unfavourable. A few days

---

[253] *Ibid.*
[254] Gilbert Gifford's confession, to which the document refers, is at Hatfield (cf. *Cal. Salisbury MSS. III*, pp. 346–349). Cf. also *supra* Chapter III, section 3.

after the trial he wrote to Philip II that the number of ciphers found in Morgan's possession, his correspondence that had been discovered, and his schemes that had been revealed, caused grave suspicions in those who had conducted the case that he was a spy of the Queen of England and a 'bad Christian'. There was evidence enough to proceed to torture though, so far, they had not had recourse to it, but his papers, his replies when interrogated, and his whole manner of proceeding revealed him as a man of cunning and malice. He had endeavoured and, indeed, was still endeavouring to carry on intrigue, sow division, and counter the plans for bringing England back to the obedience of the Catholic Church, conceived by Dr. Allen, Fr. Persons and other good Catholics within and without the realm, who saw eye to eye with his Majesty. It would, therefore, be a great evil to allow him to continue in his courses. He awaited, however, his Majesty's orders in the matter. The reply of the King to this letter, if still extant, has not been found, but it could hardly have been favourable to Morgan, seeing that Parma kept him in prison for more than two years, and when releasing him in 1592 banished him from the Low Countries. He was lucky, really, to have escaped with his life[255] and, indeed, would have been executed as a seditious traitor, for he was supposedly in the service of the King of Spain and had a pension from him, had not Parma considered that such a punishment, though merited, might be interpreted as his own private vengeance for the wrongs done to his own person by Morgan.[256]

---

[255] "It is marvel that Morgan escaped only with banishment, which is an encouragement to Pooly [*Poley*] and other spies" (Verstegan to Persons and Englefield, Antwerp, 17 September 1593, Stonyhurst Coll. B. 127, printed in *C.R.S. LII*, p. 176). For Parma's letter above, cf. Note 224.

[256] "Y fuera ahorcado como sedicioso y traydor sino parecía al Duque de Parma que dandole el castigo que merecía todos entenderian que vengava los agravios particulares que le avia hecho" (cf. "Sobre el negocio de Morgan", *ut supra*).

CHAPTER V

Other evidence against Morgan: was he a Catholic?—
His alleged services to the Scottish Queen when
Shrewsbury's secretary—Imprisonment in the Tower,
1572—Flight to France, 1575

1. Other evidence against Morgan: was he a Catholic?

It is to be regretted that the individual statements of the witnesses at
the trial in Flanders are not forthcoming, but to make up for this
deficiency there are other documents extant which lend support to
their testimony, and which in most cases would not have been known
to them. In the first place, concerning his religion, Morgan may
possibly have been telling the truth when he said he had been brought
up as a Catholic, for he would have been but eleven years old when the
Catholic sovereign, Mary Tudor, began to reign. His brother, Rowland, certainly entered the seminary of Rheims, was duly ordained,
and returned to the mission-field of England in 1583.[257] Yet his
brother, Henry, spoke of this Rowland as "being perverted to popery",
which suggests that he, as least, was not brought up as a Catholic but
embraced that faith later.[258] He apostatised after some years, and,
despite his priestly vows, was twice married.[259] Henry himself, so far
as the records go, showed no sign of being a Catholic, and was
employed by the Government as Customer of Cardiff. The Morgan
household, therefore, hardly appears to have been strongly Catholic.

As for Thomas, it is true that the Nuncio in France in 1585, after
having given an earlier bad report of him, which will be quoted in due
course, later asserted that he was a good Catholic and a faithful servant
of the Queen of Scots;[260] but this was after Morgan had been in the
Bastille some months, and when it was the policy of himself and his
friends to seek the intervention of the Holy See to secure his release,
for which intervention there would have been no hope had they not

[257] His stay at Rheims can be traced in Knox, *Douay Diaries.*
[258] Examination of Henry Morgan, 22 May 1585, Dom. Eliz. 178, n. 66.
[259] Authorities as in Notes 3 and 4 *supra.*
[260] Nuncio to Secretary of State, Paris, 11 November 1585, R.O. Transcripts 31/9,
bundle 82a; cf. also *infra* Chapter IX, section 4.

represented the prisoner as a practising Catholic. The Nuncio's statement, in any case, can have little weight against the very positive assertion at the trial, of those who had made it their business over a considerable period to watch and find out, yet who had never seen him go to confession or receive communion as a Catholic during the years he had lived in Paris. Certainly, if he had been brought up in the Catholic faith, his religion could have weighed but little with him, for at the early age of eighteen he entered the service of a known episcopal persecutor of Catholics, and after three years, again found employment in the household of another Protestant bishop, also known as a persecutor.

Moreover, when William Wade in 1585 was sent over to France on a special embassy to demand Morgan's extradition, soon after he had been imprisoned in the Bastille, he expressed spontaneous surprise at finding that the prisoner was considered to be a Catholic. In the course of a despatch to Walsingham, relating the reluctance of the French King to hand over Morgan to the English Government, he wrote:

> "How this man [*Morgan*] is now made a Catholic and so thought worthy to be protected I understand not, unless those that favour him ... would have us to think as unreverently of the King as they in their open actions show little respect, sith they term this a war for religion".[261]

Wade, clearly, did not regard Morgan as really a Catholic, and considered Walsingham to have the same opinion of his religion as himself. This testimony is of considerable weight; for Wade was a high official, in the confidence of Burghley and Walsingham, had been employed in connection with Mary, Queen of Scots, and in several important missions abroad, and during the years that Morgan stayed in Paris, had himself been twice in France, first when Sir Amias Poulet or Paulet was ambassador, and later when Sir Henry Cobham filled that post. Of course, Morgan, if a spy, would have shown some signs of being a Catholic, as did other spies, such as Rogers or Berden, Poley, Moody, Barnes and Sterrell, for he would otherwise have defeated his own purpose and made it impossible to penetrate into the circle of the English Catholic exiles. This casual remark of Wade, however, certainly supports the witnesses at the trial who regarded Morgan as only a Catholic in appearance.

261 Wade to Walsingham, Paris, 1 April 1585, *For. Cal. August 1584–August 1585*, p. 391.

2. *His alleged services to the Scottish Queen when Shrewsbury's secretary*

Of his services to the Queen of Scots whilst he was employed by the Earl of Shrewsbury as his secretary, there is little evidence beyond his own statements. There are, indeed, a few documents dealing with his arrest and imprisonment in the Tower in 1572, and many others concerned with the enquiry into the correspondence of the captive Queen in 1574; but according to the witnesses at his trial in 1590 any services that he had rendered to the Queen of Scots had not been intended to help her, but to win her confidence, so that he might get to know her plans and secrets and the persons with whom she corresponded, and as agent of the English Councillors, and especially of Leicester, betray them to the Government. His arrest and imprisonment in the Tower was but a ruse, they maintained, to disguise the fact that he was such an agent. It is not unknown that the Government did so act with some of its agents: Robert Poley was imprisoned as a party to the Babington plot, though it is certain that in that connection he was but carrying out the orders of the Government itself; Colville, too, another agent, suggested that he should be imprisoned for a space, to disguise the rôle he was to play.[262]

Morgan's arrest in 1572 seems to have been connected with his dealings with the Bishop of Ross, and to have been an aftermath of the Ridolfi plot and the affair of the Duke of Norfolk: and there are certainly some curious circumstances about it. Already in April 1571 he was reported by a spy in the Marshalsea as "a dear and secret friend" of the Bishop:[263] and only a few months later, Ross himself was committed to the custody of the Bishop of Ely and, in October of that year, sent to the Tower. The several confessions he there made supplied the principal evidence that led to Norfolk's execution. Morgan was mentioned in the answers made to interrogatories, both by Ross and Norfolk, the latter declaring, on the testimony of Barker, that Morgan was a great intelligencer to the Bishop of Ross, though he

---

[262] "Under his honour's correction I think it very expedient—if he mind to use my service herein—that I should now presently after Christmas, be committed to the Marshalsea for a month or two upon colour of an escape to be purposed by me over sea" [R. Colville] to R. Bowes, 14 December 1586, *Scot. Cal. IX*, p. 191). For Poley, cf. Maliverey Catylin, another spy, to Walsingham, 19 September 1586, *Dom. Eliz.* 193, n. 52, and also R. Southwell, *A Humble Supplication, etc.* Ed. R. C. Bald, Cambridge, 1953, p. 18. For Catylin himself, cf. M. Catylin to Walsingham, Portsmouth, 25 June 1586, *Dom. Eliz.* 190, n. 51.

[263] "He [*Bartlett*] told me that one Morgan, who had been in Spain was a dear and secret friend of the bishop [*of Ross*], and so was Thomas Cobham" (W. Herle to Burghley, the Marshalsea, 16 April 1571, *Scot. Cal. III*, p. 544). Concerning Ross, cf. *supra* Note 97.

did not remember to have heard of Morgan's dealings in matters of state.[264] Yet despite this suspicious connection with the imprisoned Bishop, no concern at that time was shown by the Government about Morgan, nor was there any attempt to dismiss him then from his post as secretary to Shrewsbury.

It was, in fact, Queen Elizabeth herself, some months later, who took the initiative in proceeding against him, not, it may be conjectured, without some prompting from one of her councillors. Some remarks made by her in a conversation with Shrewsbury led the Earl on his return to Sheffield to make enquiries. Two boys came forward as accusers, one of them, a Scot, called John Steward, being the first to reveal that Morgan and two of the Earl's men, with others dwelling in a neighbouring town, conveyed letters to and from the Queen of Scots. At the same time, on 27 February 1572, there were most conveniently discovered on the bare ground, hidden under a stone, some letters of Mary which had been there at the mercy of damp and vermin since before Christmas! The unnamed messenger, so it was stated, fearing a search, had hidden and left them there.[265] In consequence of all this, Shrewsbury dismissed Morgan from his service, binding him in a recognisance to appear before any Privy Councillor at command. Burghley, however, did not consider this step sufficient, and Shrewsbury after a short time, once more getting hold of Morgan, sent him together with his chief accuser, the Scottish boy, John Steward,

---

[264] Interrogatories and Answers of the Duke of Norfolk, 31 October 1571, *Cal· Salisbury MSS. I*, p. 554; cf. also, Interrogatories of the Bishop of Ross, 31 October 1572, *Ibid.*, p. 555: "There was speech between this examinate and Morgan sundry times, but not of any matters of great importance. He gave into Morgan's custody certain household stuff, books of stories, and such other, but no other thing of secrecy. He obtained from the Queen of Scots for Morgan two letters to the Duchess of Feria, for procuring payment of Morgan's portions in Spain".

[265] One of the letters so conveniently found after being hidden for two months under a stone, was the alleged letter of the Queen of Scots to the Duke of Alva. Writing to the Earl of Shrewsbury Burghley stated: "I have disclosed the contents of some of the ciphered letters which your Lordship lately sent to me, being hidden under a stone. One was from that Q. to the D. of Alva, wherein she maketh plain mention of the practice of Ridolfi, imputing the discovery thereof to the negligence of others, and not of herself: Another of the letters was to Grange and Lyddyngton, to confirm them to stand fast, and to expect money from the Duke of Alva, with the L. Seton. The third letter is not yet deciphered. The L. Seton is indeed by stealth come through England, landed at Harwich, and so passed into Scotland by the Middle March, and is in the castle of Edinburgh, where he hindereth the accord" (Burghley to Shrewsbury, 4 March 1572, printed by E. Lodge, *Illustrations of British History*, 1838 Ed. *I*, p. 534; cf. also J. D. Leader, *Mary Queen of Scots*, London, 1880, p. 252). A similar story was told by Wade when the Queen of Scots' papers were seized in 1586: "The ambassador Châteauneuf writes that Wade asserts that he found a large quantity of ciphers buried in a garden, and amongst them the copy of a letter from me—a curious place to keep papers, forsooth!" (Mendoza to Philip II, Paris, 26 September 1586, *Spanish Cal. 1580–1586*, p. 624).

on March 15 to the Treasurer, who committed him to the Tower.[266]

The whole incident is probably not unconnected with the pressure the English councillors were bringing to bear upon Queen Elizabeth in 1572 to take extreme measures against the Queen of Scots. This resulted in the autumn of that year in Killigrew being sent to Scotland on a most secret commission—for apart from him it was known only to Elizabeth, Burghley and Leicester—to negotiate with the Earl of Morton and the Regent, the Earl of Mar, for the handing over to them of the Scottish Queen on condition that she should be put to death. The death of Mar stayed the matter for the time being, but the plan was revived again in 1574, just after enquiries had again been made about the correspondence of the Queen of Scots, in which Morgan was once more involved.[267]

3. *Imprisonment in the Tower, 1572*

There is no record, nor even a hint, in the extant documents, that Morgan, whilst in the Tower in 1572, was ever subjected to an inter-rogation, or that his chief accuser, John Steward, was examined at that time, though he was two years later in 1574. Still less was there any indictment, a point emphasised by the witnesses at Morgan's trial in Flanders in 1590. This in itself is a singular fact, especially when com-pared with the long series of examinations in 1574 and 1575—including that of John Steward—of those who were supposedly concerned with conveying letters to and from the Queen of Scots.[268] So far as it goes, this fact supports the contention that the Government knew that there was nothing for which to submit him to an examination or to try him, and

[266] Cf. Shrewsbury to Q. Elizabeth, 28 February 1572; to Burghley, 28 February, 4, 6 and 15 March 1572, *Scot. Cal. IV*, pp. 137, 138, 145, 146 and 164. Cf. also J. D. Leader, *op. cit.*, pp. 250–254. The exact date of Morgan's commitment to the Tower is not ascertainable. In a list of prisoners there, dated 14 June 1572, there is named a "Mr. Morgan ye Erle of Shrewsburys man: to have his brother to speak with him in presence of ye Erle" (*C.R.S. I*, p. 60). Presumably he was committed to the Tower soon after March 15.

[267] The "great matter" can be followed in the correspondence of Henry Killigrew, English ambassador to Scotland, with Burghley and Leicester during the months of September, October and November 1572, which is given in the *Scot. Cal. IV*, pp. 389–435. The death of Mar put an end to the business for a time, though it was not lost sight of altogether (cf. Killigrew to Burghley, 20 June 1573, *Ibid.*, p. 589). Negotiations were revived in 1574 with Morton, who had become Regent in place of Mar (cf. Killigrew to Walsingham, 21 June 1574, to Burghley, 23 June 1574, to Walsingham 23 June 1574 *Ibid.*, pp. 675, 677 and 678: cf. also *V*, pp. 25, 28, 32, 33 and 41). The demands of Morton, however, were considered exorbitant, and by the middle of August of that year the "great matter" was allowed to sleep (cf. Tytler, *History of Scotland*, London, 1866, *VII*, pp. 311–325 and 384–387, and *VIII*, pp. 7–13, and J. Hosack, *Mary, Queen of Scots*, Edinburgh, 1874, *II*, pp. 146–153, 166–167 and 181–185).

[268] These examinations are numerous and can be studied in *Scot. Cal. V*. One of the first to be interrogated was John Steward, whose examination was conducted by Killigrew in Edinburgh, 20 June 1574 (*Ibid.*, *IV*, p. 676).

that his imprisonment was a ruse to conceal the fact that he was their agent.

This contention, indeed, is strongly supported by a letter of Morgan himself to Burghley, written on 18 January 1577, some time, that is, after he had gone to France.

"About this time two years," he wrote, "upon the ripping up of certain matters, which seemed altogether tending to renew my unquietness: I did easily see, that either I must have yielded myself to imminent trouble (as once I did before) of long imprisonment, or else be of mind to forsake my country. A very hard choice good L., for the one affection and nature would scarce suffer me to brook of and the other my weakness of body, and the fresh remembrance of my former thraldom did cause me to fear. Notwithstanding, as a man that is desperately forced, I took it for my best advice, rather to want my friends and leave my native soil, than to leese [*lose*] my liberty, and the use of common air, whereof in such likelihood I saw myself deprived. For I protest before God and all his angels who judge me thereafter, if I speak not as the truth is, and as I mean. I stand so innocent in respect of attempting anything, either against the Queen Majesty's estate, or the wealth of my country, that if it were not, for that my former fear of hard usage and long imprisonment, I would in short time return, and present myself to yield an account of whatsoever demeanour, I can be charged withall. But because I dare not make the adventure, for the causes above remembered, I am thus constrained to lead my life with a heavy heart in a foreign land, which is done, I confess, without her Majesty's licence and therefore to be judged as a grievous offence. Howbeit, I do prostrate myself before her Highness, and acknowledge my fault therein, most humbly craving, it will please the same, so to pardon my absence, as this my special case doth in part require, and also further, until the contrary be apparent, to accept me, as one of her Highness' faithful and loyal subjects. Which as ever I have been, so I remain, and will while I live, whatsoever befall me. This profession of my bounden duty, for that opinion which I always conceived of courteous usage, and equity in your L. dealings, I have presumed thus overboldly to address in writing, most humbly beseeching your L. to dispense with me for the doing thereof, and to accept my simple meaning in good part. And as already, so hereafter shall I be bound to make my daily prayers for the long continuance of your honourable estate, as God knoweth to whose protection I commit your L. At Paris the 18 of January 1577".[269]

[269] Dom. Eliz. Add. 25, n. 1. The letter is addressed in the same hand: "To the Righte honorable the lorde Burleighe L. [Trea]surer of Englande". Seal mark; endorsed "Mr. Thomas Morgan to my L. from Paris".

This letter, it must be emphasised, was written to Burghley, who had been responsible for imprisoning Morgan in the Tower and was fully cognisant of his troubles in 1572. Yet in it Morgan mentions no charge made against him; still less does he acknowledge any offence committed by him, save that of leaving the kingdom without licence. On the contrary, he vigorously protests his innocence and gives as the reason for his leaving England the fear that he might have been imprisoned again as he had been in 1572. There is, too, an implicit plea for leave to return, which, as will be shown later, must, in fact, have been granted. It would have been complete folly on his part—and Morgan, whatever else he was, was no fool—so to address Burghley, had he in fact been guilty of any crime in 1572, even though imprisoned in the Tower: far from having any effect, it would have been treated by Burghley as a piece of gross impertinence. Rather is the letter that of one who was conscious of having been imprisoned for no crime committed by him, and who was well aware that Burghley himself knew it, and that there was nothing with which to charge him saving, as already stated, his leaving the realm at the beginning of 1575 without licence. The letter, in fact, supports the contention of the witnesses at his trial in 1590 that his imprisonment in the Tower in 1572 was for no offence, but was a ruse to conceal his employment by the Government.

His release, then, from the Tower, may well have been, as he declared in 1590, because he could give a good account of himself and by the favour of Burghley, though not precisely in the same sense as he would have given his judges to understand. But his further statement that he won over to the party that favoured the Queen of Scots both Burghley and Thomas Wilson is quite incredible.[270] Equally incredible

[270] Neither Burghley nor Wilson were won over to her party. It is just possible, but not at all probable, that Morgan was deceived in this matter by Burghley. "There are four principal advisers of Queen Elizabeth", wrote the French ambassador, Châteauneuf, "who conduct her affairs with great artifice, as well towards other Christian princes as towards Huguenots and Catholics. These are Christopher Hatton, the Chancellor, William Cecil, Lord Burghley, the Lord Treasurer of England, Robert Dudley, the Earl of Leicester, the Chamberlain and Francis Walsingham, the Secretary of State. These four have been raised by her from small beginnings to great honours for different reasons. The Chancellor and the Treasurer pretend to favour the affairs of the King of Spain and even the Catholics within the realm, whereas on the contrary, the Earl of Leicester and Walsingham, have always shown themselves great Protestants and well affected towards France. But, in point of fact, it is all dissimulation, known to their mistress, to deceive the ambassadors of the princes there, and to ruin the English Catholics and all those who favour the Queen of Scots" (Châteauneuf, Observations on the Babington Plot, *Labanoff*, *VI*, p. 280. Translation). Burghley can hardly be said to have been won over to the party of the Queen of Scots when in fact he was, in 1572, and in 1574, negotiating with the Scots to hand her over to them on condition she should be put to death! When, moreover, Wotton was sent on a special embassy to France after Mary's trial and condemnation in 1586, he gave out in private, according to the report of Stafford, the English ambassador,

is the condition on which, so Morgan stated, he had been released from the Tower, that he should not leave the kingdom for a year, seeing that leave was required to depart the realm in any case; and if he implied that such licence was given for his departure after a year, his statement contradicts what he wrote to Burghley in the letter already quoted, where he acknowledged that he had committed a grievous offence in leaving the country without licence in 1575, certainly more than a year after his release from the Tower. Still less credible was his assertion that as surety for the fulfilment of the alleged terms of his release, he had had to give a bond of ten thousand pounds, a huge sum in those days, and certainly one quite beyond his means.[271]

4. *Flight to France, 1575*

His escape from England, it will have been noticed, Morgan passed over very lightly in his confessions, merely stating that some eighteen months after he had been released from the Tower he had crossed over secretly to France. There is, however, a good deal more about it than that. In June 1574 enquiries were once more started concerning the conveyance of letters to and from the Queen of Scots, beginning with the examination of Alexander Hamilton, who was tutor to two of Shrewsbury's children in a house of the Earl's four miles or so from Sheffield.[272] At the time Hamilton was interrogated in London, there was examined in Edinburgh before Killigrew, the English ambassador there, John Steward, a youth of eighteen, who, when a stable-boy at Sheffield two years earlier, had been the first to accuse Morgan and

---

[271] Cf. *supra* Note 236.

[272] Shrewsbury to Walsingham, Sheffield, 6 June 1574, *Scot. Cal. IV*, p. 668. The examination of Alexander Hamilton took place on the 12 and 26 June 1574 (*Ibid., IV*, pp. 671–672, and *V*, pp. 6–12); cf. also Shrewsbury to Walsingham, Sheffield, 12 July 1574 (*Ibid., V*, p. 23).

---

that Burghley counselled her death more than anyone else. Wotton, further, told the Queen Mother that if Mary was executed, Burghley would make peace with her son, the King of Scots. Indeed, in this connection, Wotton spoke of almost nobody but Burghley. This, so Stafford reported to the Treasurer, was repeated to him by those to whom Wotton had said it, and who had asked Stafford about it (cf. Stafford to Burghley, Paris, 9 November 1586, *For. Cal. June 1586–June 1588*, p. 136). After the death of Robert Cecil, Burghley's son, in 1612, when it was safe to give expression to such thoughts, Henry Howard, Earl of Northampton, wrote *à propos* of the transference of Mary's remains to Westminster: "She is buried with honour, as dead rose leaves are preserved, when the liquor that makes the kingdom sweet has been distilled. Was reminded of the bedlam courses taken by the 'little one' [*Robert Cecil*] and his father, in inflaming the Queen's [*Elizabeth's*] ears, though they covered themselves by the passions of Walsingham. But when the Queen's decay threatened ruin to his house, he [*Cecil*] sang 'another song by the quille' and having aided the King's ascent to the throne, was supported by him" (H. Howard to [Rochester], [10 October] 1612, *Dom. Cal. James I, 1611–1618*, p. 152).

others.[273] On 1 August Walsingham, forwarding Killigrew's latest letter, wrote to Burghley, begging him to order the apprehension and examination of certain persons suspected to be dealers in the Queen of Scots' cause. He stated also that he had been secretly informed that Morgan was continuing to practise in her affairs and had access to the French ambassador.[274] Nothing seems to have come from these examinations for the time being. Nor is there evidence of any attempt to arrest Morgan; and as for Hamilton, Shrewsbury reported after his return, that the tutor considered himself bound to Walsingham.[275]

Some months later, however, the matter was again revived by the arrest of Henry Cockyn, a bookseller and stationer of London. After several examinations in which he admitted nothing,[276] he eventually, on 20 February 1575, made a long confession, extorted under threat of torture, promise of pardon for all past offences and reward for the future.[277] This confession Walsingham sent forthwith to the Queen.

It would be uncritical to place full confidence in a confession extorted by these methods, especially as those accused, Dr. Astlowe, Dr. Good and others persistently denied the statements that Cockyn had made against them.[278] There was moreover, a "hush-hush" about the whole

---

[273] Killigrew to Walsingham, Edinburgh, 21 June 1574, enclosing the examination of John Steward, 20 June 1574, *Ibid., IV*, p. 676; cf. also Killigrew to Walsingham, Edinburgh, 12 July 1574, *Ibid., V*, p. 23.

[274] Walsingham to Burghley, Woodstock, 1 August 1574, *Ibid., V*, p. 35. It was only on March 8 of that year that Morgan had been freed from further appearance before the Privy Council (*Dasent, VIII*, p. 203).

[275] Shrewsbury to Walsingham, Sheffield, 26 September 1574, *Scot. Cal. V*, p. 63.

[276] The papers concerning Cockyn are given in *Scot. Cal. V*, beginning with Burghley's memoranda for his examination, 16 January 1575.

[277] "Neither by examination nor threatening of torture could we get the party [*Cockyn*] (whose confession I send to your Majesty) to discover anything, so that I was almost void of all hope to do any good. In the end, having great cause to suspect that he received some secret pension at the Queen of Scots' hand (which he was loth to lose), I thought good, therefore, to run on that course with him, assuring him by my letters that if he would discover what he knew (accusing no man wrongfully) in the causes he was examined of, I would not only promise your pardon for his former offences, but also some such further consideration that both he and his should be the better for it, and besides that, the matter should be handled with such secrecy that he should not be discovered to be an accuser of others any further forth than he should assent to; which offer, if he should refuse, I assured him by torture he should be made to confess the bottom of the matter. This course being both faithfully and substantially executed by the Lieutenant of the Tower (who, therefore, deserves at your hands great thanks) the party was drawn to set down in writing the said confession" (Walsingham to Q. Elizabeth, London, 22 February 1575, *Ibid., V*, p. 94). Cf. also *Dasent VIII*, p. 336: "February 6 1575 Cockyn bookbinder in Paul's Churchyard to be examined and threatened with torture." It was only on 4 August 1574 that the Queen of Scots wrote to her ambassador in Paris to arrange for a pension to be paid to Cockyn (cf. Queen of Scots to Glasgow, Sheffield, 4 August 1574, *Labanoff, IV*, p. 190).

[278] The examinations of Astlowe, Good and others are given in *Scot. Cal. V*. There are over seventy documents dealing with the matter.

business even to the extent as to whether it should be communicated to members of the Council.[279] Yet, in consequence of Cockyn's confession several of Shrewsbury's men, including Alexander Hamilton, who just a few months before had expressed himself as bound to Walsingham, were ordered to be sent up under guard to be charged by their accusers.[280] Walsingham also advised the Queen to have Dr. Astlowe, Dr. Good and Morgan apprehended and sent to the Tower.[281] The former two were, in fact, arrested and though Elizabeth demurred, at first, at sending "such mean men" to the Tower, she eventually agreed to it.[282] Morgan escaped to France. The Queen herself did not share Walsingham's opinion of the whole business, and thought the matter confessed by Cockyn to be of small importance—merely the conveying of letters to the Queen of Scots—which was, in fact, the sum total of it.[283] She agreed, however, to all that Walsingham had promised the bookseller and gave leave for Cockyn's wife to visit him in the Tower, thinking that more might, thus, be got from him.[284] Yet, despite further confessions of Cockyn, the Queen herself was of opinion that the matters confessed were not "so sufficiently put down", that the parties detected by him to be practisers of the Queen of Scots might be convicted.[285] And so it proved. In April and May there followed examinations of Good, Astlowe and others, prisoners in the

---

[279] "Whereas you require my opinion whether the whole or part of the confession I sent your Majesty is to be communicated to such of your Council as you shall choose, as also who they be whom I think fit; if your Majesty makes choice of those that be loyal and secret, then you may without any difficulty impart the whole to them. For the second—whom I think fit—I must refer to your own choice whose long experience and trial had of them can best judge of them" ([Walsingham] to Q. Elizabeth, London, 26 February 1575, *Ibid.*, *V*, p. 95). Cf. also Edward Carey to [Walsingham], Hampton Court, 17 January 1575, which appears to refer to the beginning of the business and which emphasises the secrecy of it; also [Walsingham] to Q. Elizabeth, London, 22 February 1575, (*Ibid.*, *V*, pp. 84 and 94).

[280] The only known accuser was Cockyn. The use of the plural may possibly have suggested that Walsingham had some secret agent or agents who also accused them. If so, they never appeared or were revealed.

[281] Walsingham to Q. Elizabeth, London, 1 March 1575, *Ibid.*, *V*, p. 97.

[282] Walsingham to Burghley, London, 20 April 1575, *Ibid.*, *V*, p. 134.

[283] Edward Carey to Walsingham, Richmond, 11 March 1575, reporting the Queen's opinion (*Ibid.*, *V*, p. 102). There is a letter of Walsingham of the same date to the Earl of Sussex (Lord Chancellor), in which he bemoaned the fact that though he, the Chancellor, and the Solicitor (Randolph) had been appointed to examine a confession, the matter would come to nothing, "for that her Majesty is persuaded that the matters they are charged withal are of no great consequence, which I take to be a kind of watchword, that our travail therein will be to no great purpose" (Walsingham to Sussex, 11 March 1575, B.M. Harleian MSS. 6991, n. 64).

[284] E. Carey to Walsingham, 11 March 1575, *ut supra*.

[285] Walsingham to Leicester, 29 March 1575, *Scot. Cal. V*, p. 113; cf. also Sir Walter Mildmay to Walsingham, 10 March 1575, *Ibid.*, *V*, p. 101, and Q. of Scots to Glasgow, 20 February 1576, *Labanoff*, *IV*, p. 296, cited *infra* Note 289.

Tower, and Cockyn's replies to the same, but nothing came of it all save the keeping in prison without trial for some months of several men whom, as the Queen rightly foresaw, her councillors could not convict. They were, in fact, released a few months later from the Tower: Astlowe, Good and Berlie on bail September 11, and Nasmyth and Alexander Hamilton on December 10, Cockyn having already been released in the previous May.[286]

What lay behind all this commotion? It may have had some obscure connection, not apparent in the documents, with the marriage in November 1574 of Elizabeth Cavendish to Charles Darnley, brother-in-law of the Queen of Scots, which certainly aroused in Queen Elizabeth great resentment.[287] But the real cause is rather to be sought in the relations at that time between England, France and Scotland. On 30 May 1574 Charles IX died and was succeeded by his brother, Henry III, who was known to be more friendly to the house of Guise than the late King of France had been, and less favourable and accommodating as regards England. The ministers of Elizabeth, and especially Walsingham, appear to have been very apprehensive lest the new French King might actively intervene in Scotland in favour of the party there that looked to France, and in consequence, in favour, too, of the Queen of Scots.[288] Walsingham, in particular, had long desired Elizabeth to give open and efficient help to the French Huguenots, in alliance with the Protestant German princes, and at the same time to enter into a defensive alliance with the Earl of Morton, the Regent in Scotland. The plan of handing over the Queen of Scots, on condition that she should be put to death, actively revived in June 1574, had been abandoned by the end of August of that year, because Elizabeth would not agree to what she considered the exorbitant demands of the Regent. For the same parsimonious reason she was reluctant to enter into a closer alliance with the Regent, because it entailed an expenditure of money in pensions, both for him and for several of the Scottish nobility. Walsingham, in consequence, feared that the Regent, who had somewhat cooled in his friendly attitude to England, might transfer his offers and alliance to the French.

[286] Cf. *Dasent IX*, p. 23 and 60 and *VIII*, p. 392.
[287] Cf. Shrewsbury to Q. Elizabeth, Sheffield, 4 December 1574, exculpating himself (*Scot. Cal. V*, p. 68).
[288] Walsingham's letters at this time clearly reveal this apprehension (cf. Walsingham to Q. Elizabeth, 16 January 1575; to Leicester, 10 March 1575; to Q. Elizabeth, 20 March 7 and 14 April 1575; to Burghley, 16 April 1575, *Scot. Cal. V*, pp. 83, 102, 112, 115–118 and 119. Cf. also Tytler, *op. cit.*, *VIII*, pp. 6–16, and C. Read, *Mr. Secretary Walsingham*, *II*, pp. 126–138).

All this activity, then, of the discovery of conveyance of letters to the Queen of Scots, which, in point of fact, came to nothing, appears to have had for its purpose to rouse the fears of Queen Elizabeth, excite her resentment against her captive and so bring pressure upon her to follow the policy advocated so strongly by the Secretary of State.[289] Be this as it may, the driving force behind the whole commotion was clearly the fanatical enmity to the Queen of Scots shown by Walsingham, who considered that so long as she was alive "there would never grow accord in Scotland". This is evident from his letters of the period; and it led him at times to adopt a somewhat hectoring tone to Queen Elizabeth,[290] who though quite willing to have her captive done away with by the Scots, provided no public blame accrued to herself, was withal not in sympathy at this time with the rabid malevolence of her minister, nor convinced—and rightly so—of the effectiveness of his impetuous policy.

As for Morgan, though he was singled out by Queen Elizabeth herself as one directly touched and to be dealt with first, to avoid imprisonment he escaped to France—the only one of the eleven accused by Cockyn to do so. According to Dr. Good's account, which there seems no reason to doubt, it happened in this way. A fortnight or so after Good's examination before Burghley at the house of the Bishop of London, Good not yet being imprisoned, Morgan came to him and asked him upon what points he had been examined. Good told him and Morgan said he would find out as much as he could of Cockyn's confessions. Shortly after this he came to Good again and said that he and Good and divers others had been accused by the book-seller, Good as "a principal doer to the Scottish Queen", Morgan as the carrier of her letters. This, so he reported, he had learnt from Cockyn's wife, whom he wanted Good to invite to his house. This Good refused to do, but agreed to meet her in the White Friars. When, however, she met Morgan and Good there, she utterly denied that she knew anything about the matter. After her departure following upon this flat denial, Morgan said to Good that he could not endure torture, and

---

[289] Cf. Q. of Scots to Glasgow, 20 February 1576, (*Labanoff, IV*, p. 296). "Au surplus tous ceulx qui estoient en prison à Londres pour mon service sont maintenant en libertè, et n'a esté possible à Walsingham, ny aultres de mes plus mauvais ennemys, de découvrir aucune chose d'important par leur confession, ou aultres tesmoignages, sinon qu'ils avoient porté de mes lettres, sans pouvoir rien dire du contenu en icelles. Les auteurs de telles recherches ont esté bien faschez de ne pouvoir trouver subjet pour le faire valoir aupres de ceste Royne". . . .

[290] Cf. Walsingham to Q. Elizabeth, London 26 February and 7 April 1575, *Scot. Cal. V*, pp. 95 and 116; also Walsingham to Leicester, 9 and 10 March 1575, *Ibid., V*, pp. 100 and 102.

was not going to await the issue, another realm being as good for him as this.[291] At the same time he counselled Good to do what he thought best. From this account it certainly looks as if Morgan had already determined on flight and was giving Good a plausible motive for it by the knowledge which he pretended to have received from Cockyn's wife.[292]

In any case, this contradiction between her statement and the previous assertion of Morgan, together with the fact that though singled out by the Queen, he alone of the eleven accused by Cockyn escaped to France, as also his letter to Burghley two years later, acknowledging no other offence save that of leaving the country without licence, strongly suggest that he had derived his information from other sources than from Cockyn's wife; and that, knowing what was coming, found himself in the same position as did Gilbert Gifford later, at the time of the Babington plot.[293] It would seem, therefore, that having served as a tool in 1572 and been imprisoned despite it, he was determined not to suffer a bogus imprisonment a second time. If so, there was every reason why in his confessions in 1590 he should have passed lightly over his escape to France, just as he passed over in complete silence his return later to England.

[291] Contrast this with what Morgan wrote to Burghley, 18 January 1577, quoted in the previous section.

[292] Cf. Examination of Dr. Good in the Tower, 12 May 1575, *Scot. Cal. V*, p. 141.

[293] Gilbert Gifford, though working for the Government at the time of the Babington plot, but fearing he might be made a scapegoat and imprisoned in consequence, fled to France without the permission or knowledge of Walsingham (cf. G. Gifford to Walsingham, Paris, 3 September 1586, *Scot. Cal. VIII*, p. 672). Even so, a few days later, Walsingham wrote to Phelippes; "It shall now suffice to assure G. G. that both he and I have been greatly abused ... *He must be content that we both write and speak bitterly against him*". "In other words", commented J. H. Pollen, "Walsingham owns that Gilbert is not guilty (from Walsingham's point of view) but he says that he must submit to being indicted as if guilty" (J. H. Pollen, s.j. *Mary Queen of Scots and the Babington Plot*, Edinburgh, 1922, p. 119, where he quoted Walsingham's letter above. Pollen's italics).

H

CHAPTER VI

When was Morgan employed and pensioned in France by the Scottish Queen?—Morgan's reconciliation with the English Government: visits to England—His relations with the English ambassadors and Phelippes, the decipherer—His faction the cause of division between Mary and her adherents

1. *When was Morgan employed and pensioned in France by the Queen of Scots?*

In his confessions in 1590, it will be recalled, Morgan gave it to be understood that at his crossing to France in 1575 the Queen of Scots had sent letters to the Archbishop of Glasgow and the Duke of Guise, recommending that he be employed in her service as a person of trust, and also, that she had assigned him a pension of thirty crowns a month. There is, however, no evidence in the extant letters of the Scottish Queen to support the first part of his statement—rather the reverse, and the second part can be clearly shown to have been false. It is true that Mary did write to Glasgow recommending him as one who could give good information, but that was a year or more after his arrival in France: and far from suggesting that he be employed in *her* service, she suggested that if he were recognised and given employment *by the King of France*, he would render great services in the affairs of those parts.[294] It looks rather as if the Queen of Scots, anxious to help Morgan in his need, was trying to find a post for him with the King of France: but there seems to have been no question of employing him in her own service at that time. This is confirmed in the same letters in which she later expressed her gratification at the way the Archbishop of Glasgow had carried out her instructions in distributing alms to the English exiles, and made a further grant to Morgan of a hundred crowns, to complete a gift of six hundred livres which she had made

---

[294] "Je vous prie avoir le dict Morgan pour recommandé. Il est homme duquel vous pourriez tirer beaucoup de bons advis, et que feroit de grands services au Roi, s'il estoit recongnu et employé aux affaires de deça" (Q. of Scots to Glasgow, Sheffield, 21 May 1576, *Labanoff, IV*, p. 321).

to him that year.[295] Evidently the King of France did not give Morgan recognition or employment such as she wished, for a year later again she was still endeavouring to find a post for him, and urged Glasgow to try and place him with any one of her French relations.[296]

As for the annual pension, that was granted only in 1581, six years after he had left England, and amounted to only two hundred crowns a year. The purpose of it was the same that had inspired her to find him a post, namely, to free him from the needy circumstances in which, according to reports, he had found himself placed in these last years.[297] There was, too, a further reason for his pension, for it was at this time that she desired Glasgow to employ him in ciphering and deciphering letters regarding certain negotiations with Spain, fearing to use a Frenchman for this purpose.[298] She had, indeed, before this suggested that Morgan should be used as an intermediary between one of her adherents, Singleton, who went over to France in September 1580, and her ambassador, for the immediate payment to Singleton of five hundred crowns; but this was only in case Singleton, to whom she had also at once assigned a pension of twelve hundred livres, could not himself communicate with her ambassador.[299] And in passing, it may be remarked that the liberality shown by her to Singleton, as soon as he had crossed to France, by giving him an immediate grant of five hundred crowns, and a pension for the future, is in striking contrast to her treatment of Morgan after he had escaped to that country five years earlier. As Mary always felt obliged to reward those who had

[295] Cf. Q. of Scots to Glasgow, 18 March 1580, *Labanoff*, *V*, p. 138

[296] Q. of Scots to Glasgow, Sheffield, 12 July 1577, *Ibid.*, *IV*, p. 373.

[297] "Faictes délivrer à Morgan, sur la fin de ceste année, deux cens escuz, employez au rolle de pensions secrettes, sous le nom de Bérisson; et ainsi continuerez vous les années suivantes, l'ayant voulu asseurer de ceste pension certaine, affin qu'il ne tombe plus en la necessité ou j'ay entendu qu'il s'est trouvé ces années dernières" (Q. of Scots to Glasgow, Sheffield, 20 May 1581, *Ibid.*, *V*, p. 226).

[298] "Vous auriez les sieurs Singleton et Morgan pour vous y assister de ce qu'ils pourront, et jugerez estre besoing, les trouvant tous deux bien nécessaires pour ce qui sera à negotier en ce pays; et doresnavant je désire que vous employez le dict Morgan pour mettre en chiffre toutes les lettres que vous m'escrivez sur ce subject, et de mesmes pour deschiffrer les miennes escrites en ceste alphabet" (Q. of Scots to Glasgow, Sheffield, 21 May 1581, *Ibid.*, p. 234.

[299] "Partant, je vous prie affectueusement autant que vous avez ma personne propre en racommandation, qu'incontinent la présente, sans aucun délays vous délivrez cinq cens escuz à ce porteur, et, s'il n'a la commodité de communiquer avec vous, vous les luy faciez tenir par Morgan qui ira entre vous deux; et pour l'advenir, s'il est contrainct de séjourner plus longuement en France, mon intention est que vous luy faciez fournir la somme de douze cens lives par chacun an, sans que, pour quelque occasion que ce soit, il y aye faute ou retardement. Car je ne veulx, ny puis honnestement manquer, en telle necessité, à une personne à qui je suis tant obligée" (Q. of Scots to Glasgow, 27 September 1580, *Ibid.*, *V*, p. 180). She also desired Glasgow to obtain for Singleton a pension from the King of France.

helped her, this fact alone suggests that whatever services Morgan had rendered to her, they had not been of such great importance as he made them out to be at his trial in 1590. Indeed, his appointment as cipherer in 1581, already referred to, was deferred for a while by the Queen of Scots herself, to see how far the King of France would help in her renewed negotiations for associating her son with herself in the crown of Scotland.[300] But early the next year the Spanish negotiations were in full swing, and it was then, most probably, that Morgan took up his post.[301]

Thus, it was only gradually, and long after his arrival in France, that he succeeded in worming himself into her service—quite contrary to the impression he gave at his trial in Flanders. But from the date when he began his new employment, his position became one of increasing and commanding importance in her affairs, because of the use he made of his post as cipher clerk in these negotiations, which continued for three years. He became virtually the only channel for the Scottish Queen's secret correspondence.[302] His appointment, indeed, may be said to have been Mary's most fateful decision during these years, and one which undoubtedly led to her ruin.

2. *Morgan's reconciliation with the English Government: visits to England*

Before this fateful appointment took effect, it seems certain that Morgan had made his peace with the English Government for the only offence he acknowledged—leaving the country without permission—for he appears to have been in England in the early part of 1579. The evidence for this rests on a letter to Zayas, Secretary to the

---

300 "Ne vous hastez poinct de retirer Morgan chez vous jusques à ce que nous voyons quelle yssue prendra ceste négotiation mise en avant avec la France, laquelle succédant bien, je n'auray tel besoing dudict Morgan pour les aultres, où je vous avois mandé de l'employer" (Q. of Scots to Glasgow, Sheffield, 18 September 1581, *Ibid.*, *V*, p. 262).

301 He appears, however, to have taken up residence with Glasgow early in 1581 (cf. Cobham to [? Walsingham], Blois, 13 January 1581, *For. Cal. 1581–April 1582*, p. 18). "This is all I could learn of him [*Glasgow*] at that time, and in other conferences I have always found him in this manner of opinion; but I hear that Morgan, who lies at his [*Glasgow's*] house in Paris, *is privy to his more 'inward meanings'*." Italics mine. The last phrase suggests that Cobham was ready to use Morgan; cf. also section 3 of this chapter. A succinct account of the Spanish negotiations is given in *C.R.S. XXXIX*, pp. xlvff.

302 Cf. Q. of Scots to Englefield, 20 May 1586, *Murdin*, p. 514: "... nor by any means could I have advertised you of thus much if it had not been poor Morgan (the chief and almost the only finder out and director of all the intercourse of intelligence I have had *these many years past*) who hath, notwithstanding his troubles, appointed me this way for the present, ... ". Italics mine. Cf. Same to Liggons, 18 May, and to Foljambe, 29 May 1586, *Labanoff*, *VI*, pp. 303 and 330. This was especially true after the expulsion of the Spanish ambassador, Mendoza, from England at the end of 1583.

Spanish Council of State, from Mendoza, who had come to England as Spanish ambassador in 1578.

"An Englishman, named Morgan", he wrote on 26 July 1579, "left this country four months ago on the pretext that he was going to recover the wages owing to him as one of his Majesty's gentlemen, the Queen [*Elizabeth*] having given him licence to be absent four or five months. He returned a few days ago, saying that his Majesty had ordered him to be paid, and although I knew that he had permission to go, he did not tell me anything of his going, nor has he sent me word on his return. If the Queen of Scotland wrote recommending him, I still would like to say that these people are very fond of giving her permission to write, and by paying a little money to a servant of Walsingham, such letters are easily obtained, as the poor lady is pleased to give them rather than offend people. I suppose that Guarras'[303] long stay in Paris was in consequence of his carrying letters from her and as I gathered from him here, he did himself a great deal of injury in this way".[304]

Such was Mendoza's letter: and the Morgan mentioned in it can hardly be other than Thomas Morgan, the reputed servant of the Queen of Scots; for he certainly had had connections with Spain. In 1571 he was reported by a spy as a dear and secret friend of the Bishop of Ross[305] and as one who had been in Spain; and the Bishop, in his confession of 31 October of that year, stated that he had obtained from the Queen of Scots for Morgan two letters to the Duchess of Feria, for *procuring* payment of his portion in Spain.[306]

Finally, from Morgan's own testimony, it can be shown that he was contemplating going to Spain with a friend in the spring of 1578. On 25 December 1577 he wrote to the Countess of Northumberland, then in exile in Luxembourg:[307]

[303] After the expulsion of the Spanish ambassador, de Spes, in 1572, Antonio de Guarras, a Spanish merchant, though without formal commission, acted as representative of Philip II, sending despatches to the Duke of Alva in Flanders and to Zayas in Spain. He was imprisoned in October 1577 for alleged intrigues, and was not released by the English Government till May 1578, when he was expelled the country. The ambassadorial privilege which he claimed was not recognised by the English Government, on the ground that he had no formal commission to act as ambassador. This matter may be followed in *Spanish Cal. 1568–1579.*

[304] Mendoza to Zayas, London, 26 July 1579, *Ibid.*, p. 682.

[305] Cf. *supra* Note 263.

[306] *Cal. Salisbury MSS. I*, p. 555. Cf. *supra* Note 264.

[307] He appears to have visited the Countess in May of that year 1577. "Some part of the English", wrote the English ambassador, Sir Amias Poulet, "are departed already towards the Low Countries and many others go shortly. Morgan, once secretary to the Earl of Shrewsbury, is gone to Lille and thence to Luxemburg to the Countess of Northumberland" (Poulet to Walsingham, Paris, 9 May 1577, *For. Cal. 1575–1577*, p. 576).

"Before the receipt of your letters of the 9th of October and the 22nd of November last, specifying your carefulness of me, I was moved by an old friend of mine to go with him next spring into Spain, as I wrote to you already. I promised him that, having —— favour and commendation in my company, I would go with him and thereupon wrote —— for licence, not thinking that your ladyship had so great a respect to my poor estate, as evidently it appears you have. I expect —— pleasure for answer to my letters, before the receipt whereof I would be loth to trouble —— upon this occasion, at present, and especially in a matter that only concerns my own particular, and nothing else, and yet I will not forget to acknowledge to —— how greatly you mind to tender my well-doing for Ll sake. But whatsoever I receive from —— that tends to the allowance of the journey, I am like to give over the same upon the comfort that you give me, if I may easily satisfy my said friend, and that he urge me not with my promise to go with him. I do not perceive to whom you wish me to procure myself recommended in those parts. Wherefore, if it shall please your ladyship to let me understand your mind therein, I trust to find the personages in your letters 'remembered', ready to write for me. If I should deal with the Queen of Scots for her letters I may stay too long expecting the same, and, per-adventure, I shall require her letters to such as her Majesty will not write to".[308]

Apart, however, from the inference in Mendoza's letter, quoted above, there is no evidence that Morgan actually went to Spain at this period, but he certainly did go to Rome in the year 1579: for Sledd, the spy, in his long list of priests and laymen, included as living in Paris in the early part of 1580, "Thomas Morgan, gent. a Welshman", and added, "Mr. Morgan about a year since came from Rome", and that a Mr. Lovell had accompanied him, who was then "lodging in Bayon college".[309] In the light of these particulars it seems clear that the Morgan mentioned in the letter of Mendoza was Thomas Morgan, so-called adherent of the Scottish Queen. Not only had he returned to England, but he had been given licence in 1579 to leave the country

---

[308] Morgan to Countess of Northumberland, Paris, 25 December 1577, *Scot. Cal. V*, p. 250. The dashes represent undeciphered symbols.

[309] Sledd's Diary 1579–1580, Yelverton MSS. XXXIII, ff. 121ff, now B.M. Addit. 48029, recently printed in *C.R.S. LIII*, pp. 193–245. "Sledd that notorious varlet, and infamous Judas (I will not say wicked homicide) having intended to work some mischief, came from Rome in the company of divers Englishmen, whose names and marks he took diligently" (W. Allen, *A Briefe Historie of the Glorious Martyrdom of Twelve Reverend Priests*, 1582, Ed. J. H. Pollen, s.j., London, 1908, p. 83). According to his own diary Sledd arrived at Rome on 5 July 1579, and left in the company of Allen and his companions on 25 February 1580. Lovell, who according to Sledd "came from Rome with

for four or five months on the pretext, as Mendoza expressed it, of going, presumably to Spain, to "recover the wages owing to him", and during those months he had actually been to Rome.[310] Obviously he must have been pardoned for his offence of leaving the country in 1575 without permission and had come to terms with the Government, as he had implicitly desired in his letter to Burghley, already quoted.

He may have come to England again in 1580, for Sledd noted further on in his diary, that "Mr. Morgan ... departed from Paris towards England the 15 of April being Friday".[311] Furthermore, from a very cryptic letter of Walsingham, Morgan appears to have been engaged by him in this same year 1580, in some very secret business; for on 24 August the Secretary wrote to Burghley:

"Her Majesty upon earnest solicitation made by the party that followeth the secret cause that your L. and I are only made acquainted withal is pleased that £500 shall presently be delivered: it may please your L. to give order that the said sum may be left with Mr. *Alderman Martins* to be delivered to such person as by me shall be sent to receive the same bringing my letter with him to that purpose. Your Lordship's together with the letter enclosed from Mr. Pooley [*name crossed out in MS. and overwritten by the same writer* 'Jermyn']312 I have received and do mean to return such answer as may both stay Mr. Poole's preparations and yet not breed a thorough discouragement. I find her Majesty doubtful what to do in that cause. Of her own disposition (were she not stayed by secret dissuadements) I find her well enough inclined to go forward in the matters the rather for that there is daily just cause unto her Highness to yield timely remedy or else the disease will prove most dangerous if not uncurable. And to the end your L. may see how careful they are to advance

---

[310] It seems extraordinary that Mendoza made no remark on the oddness, for a subject of Queen Elizabeth, of this "pretext" which, it should be noted, would provide excellent cover for spying out in Spain, or in Rome, where Morgan actually went, what preparations were being made for the expedition to Ireland. Nor must it be forgotten that in 1578–1579 occurred in the new English College in Rome, the troubles between English and Welsh students which were, at least partially, only pacified for the time being by the College being handed over by the Pope to the care of the Jesuits on 19 March 1579.

[311] The 15th of April did fall on a Friday in 1580. Sledd himself arrived at Paris on 6 April, reached Rheims on the 17th and left again on the 20th, reaching Paris again on the 24th (cf. his Diary, *ut supra*).

[312] Jermyn was an alias of Thomas Morgan, cf. *infra* Note 325.

Mr. Morgan" in 1579, arrived at Rheims from Rome via Paris on 9 July 1579, and left again for Paris on 8 October the same year. Though the actual date of Morgan's arrival at Rheims does not appear in the College Diary, he is noted as having come from Rome in an entry of 28 July 1579, which records his departure thence for Paris (Knox, *Douay Diaries*, pp. 154 and 157). Lovell had previously been dismissed from the English College, Rome, as not willing to take the students' oath on 23 April 1579 (cf. *Liber Ruber, C.R.S. XXXVII*, p. 12).

their kingdom and increase their number I send you a letter written in Italian by an English Jesuit".[313]

Such was Walsingham's report, and whatever the secret matter was[314] it would certainly seem to have been some project of great importance and of the highest secrecy to counter the increase of Catholics. Jermyn or Germin, the name substituted for Poley or Pooley, was an alias of Thomas Morgan, well known to Phelippes, Walsingham's agent.[315] In view of Morgan's later connection with Poley, another agent, this letter suggests that it was Thomas Morgan who had written to Walsingham, and who was connected with the secret matter referred to in it.

Morgan appears once more to have been in England in the spring of 1582. In a letter of 14 March of that year the Bishop of Ross wrote from Rouen:

"This bearer has delivered me a letter from your good friend and mine, Mr. Morgan, in favour of two Englishmen who are in captivity in Rome, and therefore I have written to Mr. Chisholm [*the Carthusian, Bishop of Dumblane*] to do his diligence for their relief and give testimony on my behalf of their religion and honesty, and 'is referred' to the letter which I have received from Mr. Morgan, which you may send to Rome to Mr. Chisholm, if you think good; for it will have the more credit that it is written from London, and from a Catholic and I hope it will do good".[316]

From this it would seem that early in 1582 Morgan was in London, whence he wrote to his friend, the Bishop of Ross.

313 Walsingham to Burghley, the Court, 24 August 1580, Dom. Eliz. 141, n. 38. The italics are underlinings in the manuscript. He might at the end have been referring to the letter of Persons, written in Italian, to Agazzari, Rector of the English College in Rome, dated 5 August 1580 (cf. *C.R.S. XXXIX*, p. 41).

314 It may possibly have been connected with the later bribing of some of the Cardinals in Rome. Cobham, in a postscript to his despatch of 7 July 1580, wrote: "I have in my hands the names of the Cardinals, with their dispositions and manner of dealing in several countries, ready to send you when you command" (*For. Cal. 1579–1580*, p. 341). Cf. Notes 214, 615 and 651.

315 Cf. *infra* Note 325. The above reference to Poley appears to be the earliest yet discovered showing that Walsingham was in 1580 considering employing him. F. S. Boas, in his chapter on Poley, writes that "our first certain knowledge of him is in the earlier part of 1583" (cf. *Christopher Marlowe*, Oxford, 1940, p. 117). Cf. also Poley to Earl of Leicester, undated [1585], R.O. S.P. 78 (France), 17, n. 26bis. This interesting letter is quoted fully in Appendix IV *infra*. Regarding its dating, cf. Note 727.

316 *Scot. Cal. VI*, p. 109. The document is endorsed: "Secret advertisementes. France. Out of the B. of Rosses lettre. 13 March 1581". Its heading runs: "The coppie of the note taken out of the bishoppe of Rosse his lettre dated the xiiiith of March 1581, written from Roan to Thomas Morgan in Paris". It will be noted that the endorsement gives the date as the 13 March, the heading as the 14 March. This latter date is the correct one, for the

3. *His relations with the English ambassadors and Phelippes, the decipherer*

His having made his peace with the Government for the offence of leaving the country without licence, is also reflected in their treatment of him. In January 1578 Sir Amias Poulet, ambassador in Paris, wrote

heading appears to have been taken from the despatch of Cobham, the English ambassador in Paris. At the end of his despatch, 20 March 1581/2, he wrote: "I enclose a copy of Morgan of Islingtons lettre written in favour of some which are imprisoned in Roome, directed to the Bishop of Rosse withall a note owte of the Bishop of Rosses lettre, directed to Thomas Morgan in Paris" (R.O. French Correspondence).

At first sight, it would seem from this that Thomas Morgan was not in England but in Paris. But this would mean postulating another Morgan, the Morgan of Islington, otherwise unknown, who was an intimate friend of Ross, well known to Chisholm, the Bishop of Dumblane, and of sufficient influence in Rome for his letter to have had some effect: and that is highly improbable. The only Morgan known, who was intimately acquainted with Ross, well known to Chisholm, and who also, through Owen Lewis and Hugh Griffin, had some pull in Rome, was Thomas Morgan, the reputed servant of the Queen of Scots. As may be seen the paper itself is only a copy of a letter, on which no original address appears. It may be that the creation of this second unknown Morgan— Morgan of Islington—arose out of the letter to Ross having been signed "Morgan"; for it is strange that Cobham only designated this person by his surname and place, Islington, where he was staying, which was presumably on the address, without giving the Christian name, as he did when referring to the Morgan in Paris. The further statement that Ross's letter was directed to Thomas Morgan in Paris, may be possibly have been due to the ambiguity of the passage in Ross's letter: "This bearer has delivered me a letter from your good friend and mine, Mr. Morgan, in favour of," etc. If "Mr. Morgan" in that passage is taken as the person addressed, it would mean: "Mr. Morgan, this bearer has delivered me a letter from your good friend and mine in favour of, etc.", and Cobham, from the other phrase, "the letter which I received from Mr. Morgan" would have taken the addressee to have been Thomas Morgan, whom he knew lived in Paris. He would thus have created two Morgans, one the Morgan of Islington, who had written the enclosed letter to Ross and the other, Thomas Morgan in Paris. If, however, "Mr. Morgan" be taken as in apposition to "your good friend and mine", the passage would mean: "This bearer has delivered me a letter from Mr. Morgan, your good friend and mine", etc., and there would be no indication to whom Ross's letter was directed. On the first interpretation one must, as already said, postulate two Morgans, both friends of Ross, acquainted with Chisholm and of some influence in Rome, one of which, Morgan of Islington, is otherwise unknown. As this is highly unlikely, the second interpretation seems preferable. According to this, then, Ross sent the bearer to one in Paris with a letter to be forwarded to Chisholm in Rome, in favour of two Englishmen in captivity there. At the same time he enclosed a letter from their common friend, Mr. Morgan, in the same sense, and suggested that this also might be sent to Chisholm, as it would have more effect, coming from a Catholic in London. That Morgan was in Wales in 1582 is known from a letter of Allen, in which he wrote: "De Morgano aliquoties rescripsi P.V. illum jam diu in Wallia sua esse, nec Lutetiae multum moratum esse" (Allen to Agazzari, Rheims, 13 September 1582, Knox, *Allen*, p. 162).

In connection with the Englishmen imprisoned in Rome, it may be noted that in the previous July Cobham had written to Walsingham: "I am informed that the Englishmen imprisoned in Rome will not be released from captivity until there come 'relation' from England, giving notice what quality, condition, and profession each of them are of. I hear that Don Bernardino de Mendoza deals very badly with her Majesty and her subjects in this cause, hearkening after all evil relations" (Cobham to Walsingham, Paris, 21 July 1581, *For. Cal. 1581–April 1582*, p. 268). The two Englishmen referred to in Ross's letter may have been Nicholas Faunt, Walsingham's servant, and Fane or Vane, as Cobham in October reported that these two had been imprisoned in Rome (Same to Same, Paris, 22 October 1581, *Ibid.*, p. 344).

to Walsingham of a scheme to kidnap Morgan and send him to England, Massimo Dalbene, the proposer of it, having laid down the condition that Morgan's life should be spared.[317] This was a year before he came to England and obtained licence to go abroad again to "recover" his Spanish wages. But in October 1579, after his peace had been made and his visit to England earlier in the year, Morgan appears to have been giving information to the same ambassador.[318] It is clear, too, that he treated with Poulet's successor, Sir Henry Cobham, and that in this activity his friend, the Bishop of Ross, had also some part. In a despatch of 15 April 1580, Cobham reported:

"The Bishop of Ross and Thomas Morgan received the other day letters from Sir Francis Englefield, dated at Madrid the 12th ult., wherein he shows himself a passionate Castilian and very desirous to advance the King of Spain's practices, ..." After other details, he added: "By the same packet came letters from him [*Englefield*] to the Queen of Scots and one Throckmorton, and a great packet to Dacres, called Lord Dacres, now at Rheims, as I am informed". Then, further in the same letter: "*Morgan reports* that the servant of Lord Talbot who was here is put in prison [*in Paris*], doubting he shall be ill-handled; but Tempest is greatly in fear, because he kept him most company. The Scottish bishops and Morgan received letters from Scotland on the 11th inst. mostly written in cipher".[319]

It seems most probable that Cobham acquired the details of the letters received, from Morgan and Ross. Certainly, less than three months later, Ross handed to Cobham the articles of the bogus Papal League, and asserted that Bishop Goldwell and the priests coming at that time to England were to be instruments of that league.[320] It is not surprising, therefore, that the Archbishop of Glasgow should have written in the

---

317 Poulet to Walsingham, Paris, 8 January 1578, quoted by J. Morris, s.j. *The Letter-Books of Sir Amias Poulet*, London, 1874, p. xxv, from the Rawlinson MSS. There is no evidence that any attempt was made to carry out the suggestion. As regards the attitude to Morgan at this time, cf. Same to Same, Paris, 24 January 1578, *For. Cal. 1577–1578*, p. 470.

318 Cf. Poulet to Walsingham, Paris, 26 October 1579, *For. Cal. 1579–1580*, p. 77: "*Morgan tells me* that Mr. Wilson opened a packet of letters sent by her of Scotland, wherein were letters for the Emperor, the Empress, Archduke Ernest, the King of France, the Queen regnant, the Bishop of Ross, and that after being seen they were returned. *He tells me* that they dealt only with certain abbeys and benefices affecting the Scots and the Bishop of Ross; and that if they had been on business of consequence they would have gone by that hand . . . " Italics mine.

319 Cobham to [the Secretaries], Paris, 15 April 1580, *For. Cal. 1579–1580*, p. 232. Italics mine.

320 Cobham to [Walsingham], Vanves, 12 July 1580, *Ibid.*, p. 355. He stated that he had enclosed the articles in his last despatch which, according to the Calendar would, presumably, be that of 7 July, *Ibid.*, p. 341. On the bogus Papal Leauge of 1580, cf. *infra* Appendix I.

same year that he had communicated none of their affairs to Ross, for he did not doubt but that he was receiving money from England, evidently considering him to be an agent of the English Government.[321]

Then, it must also be remembered that during his trial in 1590, English Catholics summoned from Paris attested that they had seen Morgan treating and conversing with servants of the English ambassador and of Walsingham.[322] One of these servants of Walsingham here referred to, was undoubtedly the decipherer, Thomas Phelippes, who in the years 1578–1583 was employed in Paris, first by Sir Amias Poulet and on his recall by his successor, Sir Henry Cobham.[323] That Morgan was, in fact, on terms of close friendship with Phelippes during some part of the latter's stay in France is testified to by Gilbert Gifford in his confessions.

"Phelippes" he stated, "one of the servants and spies of Walsingham, frequently told me that Morgan was a great and intimate friend of his, and also spoke to me of the times they would dine and eat together in Paris: and all this seemed to me most certainly true; for Phelippes in conversation could take off Morgan to the life, and seemed to have an excellent understanding of his character. What they treated of and for what purpose I do not know, but Morgan once told me that Phelippes had given him a summary of some letters written in cipher".

From the same source the suspicion arises that Morgan acted as paymaster to Gilbert Gifford for Walsingham.

"I received no money from Walsingham", so runs the confession, "except shortly before my arrest [*in December 1587*]; Walsingham made this known to Morgan in a general way, and certainly knew that I had received money from Morgan. This is clear from my letters to Walsingham already deciphered (*interpretatis*)".[324]

---

[321] Glasgow to ——, Paris, 31 October 1580, *Labanoff*, *VII*, p. 152. Regarding the probable recipient of this letter, and for some biographical details of Ross, cf. *supra* Note 97.

[322] Cf. also Persons, *Notes concerning the English Mission*, C.R.S. *IV*, p. 121.

[323] For Phelippes's stay in France in these years, cf. Wilson to Walsingham, 30 June 1578: " ... Your servant, young Phillips, who is with our ambassador at Paris ... " (*For. Cal. 1578–1579*, p. 37; also Cobham to Walsingham, Paris, 21 April 1580, *Ibid.*, *1579–1580*, p. 247). There are two letters of Phelippes to Walsingham during these years, one from Bourges in Béri, 19 July 1582, and the other from Paris, 13 March 1583 (*Dom. Cal. Add. 1580–1625*, pp. 68 and 86).

[324] The Confessions of Gilbert Gifford, "Parisiis Lutetiorum ex carcere episcopali", 14 August 1588, *Cal. Salisbury MSS. III*, pp. 346–349. The confessions are in Latin and the above passages are on p. 347. Gilbert Gifford had been arrested in a brothel in Paris in December 1587, and was confined in the prison of the Archbishop of Paris. His conversations with Phelippes may have been during his visits to England late in 1585 and throughout 1586, when he was employed by the Government in connection with the Babington plot, or earlier, when Phelippes was in France.

From this friendship with Phelippes, the decipherer, it may be confidently conjectured that it was from him that Morgan derived his knowledge of ciphers which led to his appointment, referred to above, as cipher clerk to the Queen of Scots' ambassador.

Quite in accord with this friendship between the two men, and with his giving information to the English ambassador in Paris, is a draft or summary of a letter in Phelippes's hand endorsed: "Written to Germyn". This latter name was an alias of Morgan known to Phelippes.[325] The text of the paper runs as follows:

"24 May. Fr. [Emb.] advertised that in case her Majesty shall have more dispatches to send than one man can make voyages, I will send another who shall call himself Roland.

Tho. Germin required to send answer of the matters concerning her service sent to Nicholas Cornellis, himself with whome I will deal only hereafter by writing, etc.

I advertise Nicholas Cornellis of the delivery of the packets by a messenger because I am not able to go to R.[326] yet myself my presence being necessary for establishing the intelligence in case of her remove looked for before winter.

I crave to have a calendar of such persons' names as about or in London are servants & friends of E[327] with Tho. Germin his opinion how far every of them hath been is or may be used to the end that I may take my choice according to such further judgment as I may by my experience make of him, to deliver a letter now or then or a message.

I require the address for Scotland with the names of such honest friends as we may be bold to trust in that [the track] over the fells.

Privy tokens of credit and address for both kinds of [friends].

Perfect instructions of the disposition of all the great personages & others about the court towards E.

I promised to send a calendar of SS people to Tho. Germin. Touching Mr. Pagett & Philippes".[328]

---

[325] That this alias of Morgan was known to Phelippes is clear from a letter of Thomas Germyn to Nicholas Cornellys, 3 July 1586, which is endorsed by Phelippes: "From Thomas Morgan to Gilbert Gifford", Cornellys being an alias of the latter (cf. *Scot. Cal. VIII*, p. 498). Cf. also letter of Walsingham to Burghley, 24 August 1580, quoted in the last section.

[326] The R. probably stands for Rouen, though perhaps for Rheims. It must be remembered that Phelippes had been in France soon after Morgan's arrest and imprisonment in the Bastille. A despatch of Stafford to Walsingham, Paris, 15 April 1585, is headed: "Coppy of my letter to Mr. Secretary of the Xth of April 1585 by Mr. Phelippes" (cf. *infra* Note 600).

[327] E probably denotes the Queen of Scots.

[328] Dom. Eliz. 170, n. 89. Uncertain reading are in brackets. The name "Pagett" might be "Bagott", as the writing is very careless. The text is printed, with slight variations, by J. H. Pollen, s.j., *Mary Queen of Scots and the Babington Plot*, p. 102. Pollen

The general drift of the draft or summary, despite the obscurity of some details, seems clear: the secret intelligence was to be established in case of the Queen of Scots' removal to another prison. It was, in point of fact, established after her definitive removal to Chartley before Christmas 1585. Morgan was evidently in the secret with Phelippes who was to establish it, and was asked further to make known to him and through him to the English Government, the names of Mary's friends, whom Morgan had got to know when posing as her loyal servant. There were then, further grounds than at his trial in 1590 the witnesses knew of, for the accusation that Morgan had treated with the servants of the English ambassador and of Walsingham, and was in fact an agent of the English Government.

4. *His faction the cause of division between Mary and her adherents*

To turn now to some further charges that the witnesses in 1590 made against him: they asserted, it will be remembered, that he had sown division and had caused dissensions between the Queen of Scots and her adherents, the Duke of Guise, the Archbishop of Glasgow, Dr. Allen and the Jesuits; that Morgan and Paget had threatened to leave

---

suggested that it was a draft of a letter penned, indeed, by Phelippes, but for Gilbert Gifford to write to Morgan. But this was, as he recognised, pure conjecture. There is not a scrap of evidence for it, and in defect of that, the draft must be taken as that of a letter by Phelippes to the person, indicated by Phelippes himself in the endorsement: namely Germyn, an alias known to him of Thomas Morgan (cf. Note 325). The contents, moreover, agree well with this. The year in which it was written is not stated. The calendarist assigned it to 1584; Pollen to 1586. The former year, however, seems ruled out, as there was no question then of "establishing the intelligence", since the Queen of Scots' channel of secret intelligence had not then been closed by her gaolers; and 1586 appears to be similarly excluded, because by 24 May, the date of the draft, the intelligence was already established. Rather does the intermediate year 1585 suit better the circumstances mentioned. Moreover, in 1586 there was also no question on the part of the Government of the removal of the Scottish Queen, such as appears to be referred to in the draft, except after the Babington plot had been discovered—and this is another reason for not assigning it to 1586. It is true that her removal was considered in 1584, and in the event she was in September of that year removed to Wingfield, only to be taken back to Tutbury in January 1585. But in 1585 also, certainly from the beginning of June there was considerable concern, both on the part of the Queen of Scots and of the Government, to find a new place for the captive, which resulted in her being taken to Chartley just before Christmas. It was, moreover, about Christmas that Phelippes went down to Chartley to arrange for "establishing the intelligence" with the "honest man", the brewer of Burton, just as he paid another visit on 8 July 1586, to bring the fatal letter of Babington. For Phelippes's visit about Christmas 1585, cf. Poulet to Walsingham, 10 January 1586, Morris, *op. cit.*, p. 126; Q. of Scots to Châteauneuf, 24 March 1586, *Labanoff*, *VI*, p. 261. For the identification of the "last messenger" with the first, i.e. Phelippes, cf. Gilbert Gifford to Phelippes, 7 July 1586, Morris, *op. cit.*, p. 216. Morgan, it is to be noted, knew of Phelippes's intended visit to Chartley before it took place! (cf. Morgan to Q. of Scots, 5/15 October 1585, *Murdin*, p. 454; also *infra* Chapter XII, section 1). There are some indications that the Government intended to have had the Babington plot in 1585 (cf. *infra* Appendix V).

her service, if she negotiated with these and that Glasgow, in consequence, had asked to be freed from his post as her ambassador. Of the opposition of the Morgan-Paget faction to Allen there can be no doubt. It was reported by agents and spies of the English Government,[329] as well as by priests, turned informers.[330] Further evidence of it is to be found in the despatches of the Spanish ambassadors in Rome,[331] in the correspondence of Allen himself, and in the letters and memoirs of the Jesuit, Robert Persons.[332]

Amongst other particular manifestations of this continued opposition was their attitude to the seminaries—to dissolve which the English Government made several attempts—and to the mission of priests, especially of Jesuits to England and Scotland.

"About this time also and soon after," wrote Persons, speaking of the years 1583 and 1584, "divers impugnations were attempted at Rome against the seminaries and missions of England, by men of opposite spirit and emulation, some giving up memorials to Pope Gregory the 13 and affirming that it was charges but cast away to maintain them, seeing they were too weak helps to reduce such a great country as England was, and therefore the money were better bestowed upon a maintenance of particular men. Which petition when Pope Gregory would not hearken unto,[333] then they

---

329 Cf. Berden (Rogers) to Walsingham, Rouen, 13 August and 16 December 1585, *Dom. Cal. Add. 1580–1625*, pp. 148 and 158, and *C.R.S. XXI*, pp. 78 and 82; —— to Peter Halins (Phelippes), 2 December 1594, *Cal. Salisbury MSS. V*, p. 26; and Lewkner, *The State of English Fugitives*, 1596, pp. 48–52.

330 Snowden (John Cecil) to Burghley, 23 and 26 May and 7 July 1591, *Dom. Cal. Eliz. 1591–1594*, pp. 42, 46 and 70; J. F[ixer] to Burghley, 23 August 1592, *Ibid.*, p. 254; Dingley (James Younger) to Burghley, 24 and 27 August 1592, to Puckering, 7 September 1592, and his examination, 14 September 1592, *Ibid.*, pp. 255, 257, 267 and 269. Cf. also Confessions of Gilbert Gifford, Paris, 14 August 1588, *ut supra*; and Savage's Confessions, 11 August 1586, *Scot. Cal. VIII*, p. 611.

331 Cf. Olivares to Philip II, 17 January 1587, Simancas, Est. Leg. 948; Same to Same, 30 June 1587, *Ibid.*, Leg. 949, f. 180, and Sessa to Same, 26 October 1597, *Ibid.*, Leg. 967.

332 Cf. Allen to Thomas Throckmorton, 4 January and 20 February 1591 Knox, *Allen*, pp. 320 and 325; Same to Paget, 4 January 1592 (*vere* 1591), Stonyhurst, Coll. M. 129; Persons to Juan de Idiaquez, 1 July 1597, enclosing a brief history of the factions dated 30 June, West. Arch. VI, nn. 41 and 42; Same to Paget, Rome, 20 December 1597, Stonyhurst, Coll. P. 452; to the Same, 14 February 1598, Arch. S.J. Rom. Anglia 31. II. f. 711; to O. Manare, s.j., 20 March 1597, Loyola Archives; to the Same, 14 April 1597, West. Arch. VI, n. 24. There are many references to this opposition in Persons's Memoirs (cf. *Autobiography*, *C.R.S. II*, pp. 31 and 38, *Domesticall Difficulties, Ibid.*, p. 183, and *Notes Concerning the English Mission, C.R.S. IV*, pp. 63, 67, 97 and 121). Cf. also The Memorial for the Archduke Ernest, printed in Knox, *Douay Diaries*, p. 401; the Nuncio to Aldobrandino, Madrid, 30 December 1593, Vat. Arch. Nunz. di Spagna, 46, ff. 788ff; Duke of Feria to Philip II, Brussels, 3 September 1594, Simancas, Est. Leg. K. 1594, f. 76; to the Same, Barcelona, 3 January 1597, Nunz. di Spagna, 51, f. 677; and Feria to Clement VIII, 8 February 1597, West Arch. VI, n. 12; also *supra* Chapter I, section 4.

333 Compare Cardinal Sega's remark *à propos* of the troubles of the English College in 1585, in his report of his visitation of the same College in 1596 (Foley, *Records VI*, p. 10).

went about to persuade his Holiness, that it was cruelty and desperate dealing to send men into England to most certain death. Against which suggestion there be extant letters written as well by Dr. Allen from Rheims anno 1584 as also of Fr. Persons the same year from Paris, to be shown to his Holiness by the Rector of the Roman College, the copies whereof we have seen".[334]

In fact, on account of these representations mentioned by Persons, as well as for other considerations, there was certainly a delay in sending further Jesuits to England or to Scotland.[335]

That both Paget and Morgan supported such views adverse to the mission, in opposition to Allen and Persons, is shown by a letter of Persons to the General of the Society, Claudius Aquaviva. He had earlier suggested that Persons should take charge of the Scottish in addition to the English mission of the Society, and Persons had given reasons to show that this was inexpedient. In this letter he returned to the subject and suggested that Fr. Claude Mathieu, a French Jesuit, should have the responsibility, rather than the Provincial in Paris, Fr. Odo Pigenat.

"If I may be allowed", he wrote, "to state what I think about it I would say that for this charge no man could be so well suited and so pleasing to all concerned as Fr. Claude Mathieu, since Rev. Fr. Provincial has to be so often away from here and is so much occupied with other business that he cannot well attend to these affairs. Further, as I have said before, his Reverence has not the taste for business of this kind, which Fr. Claude has, partly because he has not had very much experience in handling such business and again partly because he is somewhat timid and handicapped by a diffidence which is natural to him. This I do not say to your Paternity by way of complaint of him, but only with the intent that you may be informed how things are here. And there are times when I feel fear that our politiques and rivals, whom we have with us here, such as Morgan, Paget and the rest, who do not greatly approve the Lord's way as beyond their understanding, may discover what is the disposition of the good Father (and certainly they are most active in

---

[334] Persons, *A Briefe Apologie*, 1601, f. 3v. In the margin he referred to a letter of Allen of 2 August and of his own of 15 September 1584. These two particular letters are not now extant, but there is one from Allen on the subject of 5 August 1584 (Knox, *Allen*, p. 236), and two of Persons of 11 June and 13 July also refer to it (*C.R.S. XXXIX*, pp. 201 and 217). Cf. also *C.R.S. IV*, p. 147.

[335] Cf. Persons's letters mentioned above; and for Scotland a Report by a Catholic, probably Fr. J. Tyrie, s.j., written in 1594, which is printed as an Appendix to *Memoirs of Mary Stuart*, by Claude Nau, Ed. J. Stevenson, s.j., Edinburgh, 1883, pp. 135, 138 and 139. Cf. also *C.R.S. XXXIX*, pp. lxiv–lxv.

search of what they want) and may use their knowledge for the purpose of putting discord amongst us of the Society in regard to the
mission of England, for to our part therein all these men, and the
whole of their faction are extremely opposed, though to Mr. Allen
and myself they try to pretend the contrary".[336]

Let that suffice, though a great deal more could be said of this opposition, which continued for years.[337]

As regards the Archbishop of Glasgow, who was working in agreement with the Duke of Guise, the Nuncio and Allen, there is plenty of
evidence to show that the Queen of Scots was, at least for a time,
alienated from him. In 1582 she had showed the fullest confidence in
him. In connection with the enterprise to help her son of that year, she
wrote to him:

"Je trouve bien dangereux d'escrivre aulcune chose au Pape de la
dite entreprise, et le remercier pour semblables occasions par lettres
signées de ma main hors de cyphre, qui se peuvent surprendre,
descouvrir et representer. Le credit qu'il scait que je vous donne en
toutes mes affaires plus importantes, peult assez suppléer en cet
endroit, soit que vous mesmes escripvez a sa Sté en mon nom, me
remettant entièrement à vous de luy mander tout ce qu'il sera
besoing, ou que par son Nunce, aiant en charge de traicter avec vous,
vous trouviez meilleur de luy fere (faire) entendre ce qu'il sera
nécessaire".

A further letter of the 22 April of the same year empowered him to
act without waiting for her advice and orders, as that might cause
delay. The letter runs:

"Je vous ay par cy devant par plusieurs fois mandé que sans attendre
mon advis et commandement, ne pouvant souvent arriver au temps,
vous ne laisiez de pourvoir aux négotiations que vous avez en main
pour mon service selon que de jour á aultre les occurrences se peuvent
presenter. Je vous en prye de rechef affectueusement afin que par
ce moien rien ne demeure en arrière qui puisse servir à l'advancement des dictes nègotiations tendantes à l'honneur de Dieu, re-
stablissement de son Eglise en cest Isle, conservation de ma vie at la
réduction de mon fils à la religion Catholique et Romaine".[338]

Yet early in 1583, in strong contrast to this attitude of trust of only

---

[336] Persons to Aquaviva, Paris, 20 August 1584, Arch. S.J. Rom. Fondo Gesuitico
651.   Italian. The same tactics were pursued by Paget later.
[337] I hope shortly to publish a fuller account of it.
[338] "Extraict des lettres de la royne d'Escosse à Mons. de Glasgo, son ambassadeur
esciptes à Chefield le 2 et 22 Apvril 1582" (Vat. Arch. Nunz. d'Inghilterra II, f. 239).

a few months before, she showed strong resentment against him and undoubtedly this was caused by complaints of him that came from the faction of Morgan and Paget. In a letter to Mendoza of 28 February 1583 she complained bitterly of him that, owing to his ambition, he wanted to have the entire control and direction of her affairs, even independently of herself, and would not tolerate anyone else having a hand in them, showing particular aversion, in this respect, to her servant, the Bishop of Ross.[339] She had determined, in consequence, to communicate with her cousin, the Duke of Guise, only through Morgan, who had done her faithful service, though the Archbishop had made every effort to obstruct him.[340] Again, in a letter of 1 October 1584 to the Master of Gray, who within two or three months was to show his treachery to her whilst on an embassy to Queen Elizabeth, she expressed her anger at Glasgow's alleged conduct. She had understood that, in the name of the Duke of Guise and some individual Jesuits, he managed her affairs in France in a despotic manner. Her Scottish and English adherents there had made incredible complaints against him, as well general as particular, and not only of the backward state and slow progress of her own affairs, but also of the disfavours and wrongs they themselves had suffered at his hands. All were of the opinion that no one could be in his favour who showed dependence on herself; and no order from her, however explicit, was of any avail with him. Several, in fact, had demanded to be freed from her service and to take no further part in her affairs, forcing her in this way, to accede to the request that the Archbishop had so often made in these past years, to be released from his post as her ambassador.[341]

All this receives confirmation from the few extant letters of one of the Morgan-Paget faction, Fontenay, brother-in-law to Nau, the Queen of Scots' French secretary. In these he inveighed strongly against the conduct, as well of the Duke of Guise as of the Archbishop

[339] One cause of the differences between Ross and Glasgow was the former's conduct in connection with the Ridolfi plot and the disclosures he made when imprisoned at that time. He was not trusted by the Archbishop and was thought to be in the pay of the English Government. He does not seem to have been called to participate in the conferences that were held in Paris during the years 1582 to 1584 (cf. Glasgow's letter of 31 October 1580, *Labanoff, VII*, p. 152, and *supra* Note 97; also Shrewsbury and Beale to Q. Elizabeth, 16 April 1583, *Scot. Cal. VI*, p. 393, and W. Robinson to J. Robinson [*Phelippes*], 20 May 1584, *For. Cal. July 1583–July 1584*, p. 504).

[340] Q. of Scots to Mendoza, 28 February 1583, *Spanish Cal. 1580–1586*, p. 446.

[341] Q. of Scots to Gray, Wingfield, 1 October 1584, *Labanoff, VI*, p. 14. It seems odd that the Queen did not see the contradiction between the complaints made against him on the score of his ambition, and his own repeated requests to be released from his post! The true state of things was far other than his adversaries represented (cf. *infra* Chapter VII, section 1).

I

of Glasgow.[342] Thus, in 1585, on his return from a mission to Scotland, he wrote of the Archbishop:

"Had I been fortunate enough to have met with an ambassador as much devoted to your Majesty as to his ambition and his private passions, I should not find myself reduced to this extremity, nor your Majesty for so long to the miseries of your captivity.

It is not too much to say that instead of aiding and encouraging your servants in that which is jointly commanded by your Majesty, he neglects no artifice nor means to traverse them and to endeavour to ruin them utterly.

The ruin of your servants is a small thing if it would not turn to your destruction and undoing. For the last three years that I have had the honour of being in your service, he did not write one single word to me, either in Spain or in Scotland; but what is more, he dissuaded —— from doing so. Madam, were I alone in this complaint, I should be, perchance, less credible; but Mr. Paget, Morgan and other English gentlemen, indeed all those who wish to depend solely upon your Majesty, are in the same, even in worse predicament than myself.

For this cause they have all resolved to quit your service henceforth, and not to put themselves out at all so long as the said Glasgow shall be in his office, infinitely desiring for the good of your affairs, and not for themselves, to have another for ambassador, if it please your Majesty to employ me longer in your service, for if I dare be so bold, I would ask this same grace for myself.

Upon that which your Majesty wrote to me in the month of —— touching the dismissal of the said Glasgow, I was not of opinion that he should then be changed, for the hope that I had of his conversion and the fear of what might befall. But seeing that today everything is going from bad to worse, and that by retaining him your Majesty must of necessity lose many good and faithful English servants, and others not less important to your service than he, forces me to change my opinion, and with them most humbly to beg your Majesty to put another in his place, by whose correspondence we might all respond with one accord to the intentions and designs of your Majesty".

Then, after suggesting that the Bishop of Ross, or Seton might replace Glasgow as her ambassador, he continued:

"The said Glasgow is after sowing a quarrel and keeping Mr. Foljambe apart from the said Paget and Morgan, as he did between

---

[342] Cf. Fontenay to Q. of Scots and Nau, Edinburgh, 15 August 1584, *Cal. Salisbury MSS. III*, p. 47 and *Scot. Cal. VII*, p. 260.

the said Morgan and the Jesuits of his country even whilst I was in Spain, accusing him of many things which he reported of him. I most humbly beg your Majesty to give order concerning this mischief which may arise, and to command the said Foljambe to adhere wholely to the said Morgan and Paget, rather than to the said Glasgow".[343]

In the same letter he wrote of the Duke of Guise:

"His enterprise is altogether contrary to what he told me to say to the King of Scotland on his behalf, that he would be in Scotland without fail with a good army on the —— of —— last past, waiting only for news from the Pope and the King of Spain, which makes me think that he has made use of your Majesty's name as a foundation for his affairs and his undertaking".[344]

Persons himself was well aware of this attempt to destroy the Queen of Scots' confidence in her ambassador and his associates, for he wrote in his Memoirs:

"And first of all the said two [*Morgan and Paget*] in Paris, opposing themselves secretly against the Archbishop of Glasgow, ambassador for the said Queen in Paris, they brake his credit much with the said Queen".[345]

If further confirmation be required of this attempt to besmirch Glasgow in the eyes of the Queen of Scots and so alienate her from her ambassador, it may be found in the letters of Morgan and of his friend, Charles Paget, with whom during these years he was working in close conjunction.[346]

[343] The real reason for Foljambe turning against Morgan was that Morgan was already condemned as a spy, and that no Christian prince would have anything to do with any negotiation in which he had part (cf. Foljambe to Q. of Scots, [March] 1585, and to Curle, [March] 1585, *Scot. Cal. VII*, pp. 589 and 590, quoted *infra* Chapter VII, section 2).

[344] Fontenay to Q. of Scots, 1 [July? August?] 1585, *Scot. Cal. VIII*, pp. 210ff. The calendarist is in error placed the letter in 1586, but the year is clearly indicated "le premier de ... 1585" (cf. *Murdin*, pp. 535–539). Mary herself was at the time opposed to the use of foreign forces to effect her liberation and the like (cf. Q. of Scots to Glasgow, Wingfield, 5 January 1585, *Labanoff, VI*, p. 77). Moreover, the situation in France had changed, owing to the death of Anjou in June 1584—which made it imperative for the Duke of Guise not to leave the country. In March 1585 the Guises and the Catholic party issued a manifesto declaring Henry of Navarre incapable of succeeding to the throne and in July entered into a treaty with Henry III at Nemours.

[345] Persons, *Domesticall Difficulties, C.R.S. II*, p. 184. Cf. also *Notes Concerning the English Mission, C.R.S. IV*, p. 65; and A letter from a Catholic at Brussels to his friend a Monk at Liège, Brussels, 4/14 July 1599, Dom. Eliz. 271, n. 74.

[346] Cf. Paget to Q. of Scots, 18 July 1585, *Scot. Cal. VIII*, p. 26; to the Same, 4/14 February and 31 March/10 April 1586, *Murdin*, pp. 463 and 506; Morgan to Q. of Scots, 18 January 1586, *Scot. Cal. VIII*, p. 189; to the Same, 21/31 March 1586, *Murdin*, p. 481. That Charles Paget was the intimate friend of Morgan is evident from their own letters, as well as from the despatches of the English ambassador, Sir Edward Stafford. Their letters also reveal that they were working in close conjunction. When Paget went to the Spa in 1586, he arranged that Morgan should have all his letters, and decipher them and give directions in his absence (cf. Paget to Q. of Scots, 19/29 May 1586, Morgan to Same, 24 June/4 July and 29 June/9 July 1586, *Murdin*, pp. 516, 520 and 528).

CHAPTER VII

Increasing control taken of Mary's affairs by Morgan and Paget—The Scottish Queen warned against them, and her reception of these admonitions—The Catholic exiles' adverse opinions of Morgan and Paget

1. Increasing control taken of Mary's affairs by Morgan and Paget
Despite her somewhat bitter dissatisfaction with Glasgow in 1583 and 1584, however, the Queen of Scots did not dismiss him from his post as her ambassador in France, possibly because the channel of her secret correspondence was cut for a year or more, beginning about the end of 1584: but even before that she had begun to neglect him and to rely more and more upon Morgan. As early as July 1584, in reply to Englefield's complaint that the Queen of Scots was slow in replying to his letters, Persons wrote:

"Of the Queen of Scots' slow answering of Sir Francis Englefield I cannot guess the cause but that the letters *be not delivered*. Father Persons hath received only once or twice at the farthest now in nine or ten months and that most brief in five or six lines at a time, where Morgan and others receive divers times every month, whereof for mine own part I am very well content: for I have the less business in answering again, and if I could be rid of the whole, it would be great ease and contentment to me, so all parties were satisfied".[347]

No reason was suggested by him for the non-delivery of the letters but, clearly, suspicions were aroused that Morgan, who by this time had become the sole agent of her secret correspondence, was to blame; and a few months later Persons made a request to the Queen of Scots, that,

"if there by any occasion of any business hereafter to be done by me for your Majesty, I desire that the passage of your Majesty's letters to me and mine to you may be recommended affectionately to S.S. [*Morgan*] to be sent with diligence and secrecy".[348]

---

[347] Persons to Englefield, Paris, 24 July 1584, *C.R.S. XXXIX*, p. 224; italics mine.
[348] Persons to Q. of Scots, Rouen, 10 [October ?] 1584, (Postscript), *Ibid.*, p. 246.

A few months after this Godfrey Foljambe, a servant of hers who had fled to Scotland and thence to France after the discovery of the "Throckmorton plot" in 1583, wrote to Curle, her Scottish secretary:

"Your continual silence has greatly afflicted me, who never received any word from you since my departure from England. You have no friend living that loves you more than I, nor that shall venture more for your sake than I will do; and so I pray you to account and make experience; and if any lawful cause I refuse, you hold me for ever condemned. I have written to you divers times and I trust Mr. Morgan has caused [the letters] to be conveyed safely".[349]

That the correspondence was being tampered with is clearly indicated by what another loyal servant of the Scottish Queen, Fr. Henry Samerie, s.j.,[350] wrote to her from Paris in 1584. After protesting his loyalty and stating that he must tell the truth for the honour of God and for the affection he bore her, he continued:

"I make this protestation because clearly they have received here many of the things that were written to your Majesty there, and some in the same terms and words, which has deterred some from writing to your Majesty. The opinion that they have of that here is, that you write it back here to someone, or *that they have counter-ciphers, and that the letters are deciphered before sent.* Wherefore some suspect that necessarily there are some who surreptitiously play you these bad tricks, be it here or there, without that in conscience I tax or suspect anyone in particular, and of these tricks sometimes Monsieur —— and I have spoken, and I have told him of some so evident that he has confessed that there must be something in it, which I have still found in great doubt here, as one cannot believe that your Majesty would do such things".[351]

Later, in a report on Paget in 1599, it was explicitly stated that Morgan and he had interfered with the correspondence.

"Another shrewd suspicion", so runs the document, "of his ill meaning to the Queen of Scots (if he had not rather have it imputed to pride and ambition in himself) was, that he could not endure any

---

[349] Godfrey Foljambe to Curle [March] 1585, *Scot. Cal. VII*, p. 589.

[350] For Samerie, cf. *supra* Note 68.

[351] H. Martelli [*Samerie*] to Q. of Scots, Paris, 28 [October?] 1584, *Scot. Cal. VII*, p. 414. Italics mine. The calendarist assigned the letter to November, but there are indications that it was written earlier. He has made a muddle of the dates of others of Samerie's letters, assigning one from Rome of 4 December and another from Paris of 6 December to the same year. It was quite impossible in those days of slow travel to write a letter in Rome and two days later another from Paris. This letter from Paris should probably be dated November 16, as Samerie stated in it that he was to depart for Rome "to-morrow the 17th", i.e. new style, and in the letter from Rome he reported that he had reached Nancy on his way there at the end of November (cf. *Ibid.*, pp. 464 and 472).

man to have any credit with her but himself and Morgan, and so he brought her to dislike of all other her most faithful friends and servants, as namely, the Duke of Guise, the Bishop of Glasgow, Dr. Allen and Fr. Persons: and this they wrought by corrupting her secretaries (a point that savoureth of treachery) from whom they got a counter-cipher of all her ciphers, so as they had the first view of all letters that came to or from her (for nothing could pass but through their hands) and nothing they would suffer to pass but what themselves liked and allowed of".[352]

It may, then, very well have been that the complaints of the Queen of Scots against Glasgow in 1583 and 1584 that she had received no letters from him for months,[353] had another cause than the neglect of her ambassador, considering that in point of fact he was particularly active on her behalf in those years.[354]

Whatever the truth of the matter, however, it is certain that Morgan and Paget had taken an increasing control of her affairs, and that she herself made more use of them than of her own ambassador. Just after the arrest in Paris of Morgan at the beginning of March 1585 the Nuncio, giving his reasons for not having intervened in favour of the captive Welshman, wrote to Como, the Papal Secretary of State:

"This Morgan is considered by many here, and particularly by the Jesuits, to be a knave; yet the Queen of Scots relies upon him more

[352] A Letter from a Catholic at Brussels to his friend, a Monk at Liège, Brussels, 4/14 July 1599, Dom. Eliz. 271, n. 74. There is a copy of the letter in Phelippes's hand, *Ibid.*, n. 75. The phrase "monk at Liège", which appears in an endorsement in Phelippes's hand, was used to disguise the person to whom the letter was originally addressed, who was a Canon of the church of St. John at Liège. I am indebted to Miss P. Renold for the deciphering, by means of an enlarged photograph, of this man's name from the erased address: Jehan Batson. The photograph also revealed the name of the church in question. Very little is yet known of this man, though he appears, from remarks in his letters to Phelippes, to have been of partly English origin. He acted as a purveyor of news concerning English exiles and other matters, from a markedly anti-Scottish angle, during the years between 1598 and 1602, by letters written under the alias of John Petit. His correspondence with T. Phelippes (addressed to the latter as Peter Haylins), may be seen in the Flanders Correspondence, S.P. 77, vols. 5 and 6, and some of it appears in the *Domestic Calendars*. At least two persons (names erased) who supplied the Canon with information, can also be traced among the same papers, of whom one was the writer of the above letter. His name was carefully scribbled through, and has not yet been deciphered. From Phelippes's endorsements on these papers, it is evident that such reports were forwarded from Liège as received. "John Petit" in a letter to Phelippes from Liège, 30 June 1599, wrote of Charles Paget: "Besides he is an inconstant fellow, full of practices and true to no side whereof I will ere long send you some particulars to prove his falsehood in friendship to sundry he professed friendship to" (cf. R.O. S.P. 77/5, f. 25). It is very probable that the above document provides the "particulars" in question.

[353] Cf. Q. of Scots to Mendoza, 28 February 1583, and the Same to Gray, 1 October 1584, *ut supra*.

[354] For his activity, cf. Persons's letters for these years (*C.R.S. XXXIX*).

than on her own ambassador, as the ambassador himself has told me many times".[355]

Glasgow, indeed, became so discouraged by this that he ceased gradually to deal with her affairs except when necessity forced him to do so. In a despatch to Walsingham in January 1586 the English ambassador, Sir Edward Stafford, reported of Morgan and Paget:

"The rest hate and envy them, because they take all things upon them and specially in Queen of Scots' matters. Glasgow himself, but that he dareth make no show of it, is not of the best contented with them, for they have almost 'liked' him of dealing in any matter of the Queen of Scots but that he must needs deal in".[356]

Furthermore, Paget, with unconscious humour, or more possibly cunning guile, wrote to the Queen of Scots in May of that year:

"And as I have divers times remembered your Majesty, so am I still to put you in mind, that you are to take order that every man at his will and pleasure do not intrude themselves with Princes, and their ministers in your affairs (which I call matters of states of England and Scotland, yourself in right and reason being Queen of them both), without your commission and direction, for that in truth it is against the majesty of your person, which by honest and religious persons is much to be respected, as if you were in the greatest prosperity in the world. But everyone here doth not so, and besides the disobedience showed therein by those lewd and ambitious persons, which do the contrary and take advantage of your adversity (for otherwise they durst not do it) it breedeth infinite contention and hindrance in your affairs".

As a remedy he suggested that she should appoint persons in Spain, France, the Low Countries, Scotland and Rome to take charge, and that she should order all others to concur with them in all matters that tended to the advancement of her service.[357] In her reply the Queen of Scots accepted the suggestion and appointed for charge of her affairs in France, her ambassador, the Archbishop of Glasgow, Charles Paget and Morgan, but added:

[355] Ragazzoni to Como, Paris, 10 March 1585, printed in Knox, *Allen*, p. 434; cf. also *infra* Chapter IX, section 4.
[356] Stafford to Walsingham, Paris, 2 January 1586, *For. Cal. September 1585–May 1586*, p. 276.
[357] Paget to Q. of Scots, Paris, 19/29 May 1586, *Murdin*, p. 516. This scheme of placing ambassadors was revived by Morgan, Paget and their faction in 1589–1590 (cf. Allen to T. Throckmorton, Rome, 20 February 1591, Knox, *Allen*, p. 325; Dingley to Puckering, 7 September 1592, *Dom. Cal. Eliz. 1591–1594*, p. 267; Persons, *A Briefe Apologie*, 1601, ff. 31–33; also *supra* Chapter IV, section 1).

"yet will I not my ambassador do meddle him with the affairs of this side, further than I shall commit him to treat with my 'parents' ".[358]

2. *The Scottish Queen warned against them, and her reception of these admonitions*

It was a fatal mistake on the part of the Scottish Queen thus to by-pass her own ambassador and entrust the management of her affairs to private individuals, such as Morgan and Paget, who had no official standing. Efforts, indeed, were made to warn her of the wrong course she was taking; but it is doubtful whether she ever received most of these letters; and if she did, they were of no avail. Thus, towards the end of 1584, in the letter already quoted above, her faithful servant, Fr. Samerie, s.j., wrote to her:

"The affairs of your Majesty are the affairs of God, and therefore it is necessary to proceed before His divine Majesty in all simplicity; for there is no worldly prudence which can in any way whatever prevail on Him, and I fear that that hinders your affairs very much, or, above all, makes them weaker, because you wish to have too many manners and ways of proceeding which clearly they know here. They say that they have discovered here that your Majesty is trying by all means to put the King of Scots in a bad opinion of the Bishop of Glasgow. Consider well this point, Madam, because it is more important than you think, both in Italy and Spain—and even for the King of Scotland". And further in the same letter: "I will tell you now willingly this one word, but I fear very much that it may not be agreable to you. Nevertheless, I know that it is profitable to you: it is that simply and immediately you should treat of your affairs by the ambassadors, and abandon all private ways; and believe, that without comparison this will be more agreeable to all the princes.... And above all, trust the Duke of Guise, as a principal instrument; for he has very good and very certain intelligence with the others, and they trust him very much. I think, Madam, that these are the most sure ways of advancing your affairs, and that the King of Scotland may be closely united with the said Duke of Guise; for that will remain a greater occasion to the others of good hope in the future".[359]

Again in a letter of May 1585, speaking of the negotiations which the Queen of Scots had entered into with Queen Elizabeth at the end

[358] Q. of Scots to Paget, Chartley, 27 July 1586, *Murdin*, p. 531. "Parents" = her relations in France.
[359] Hieronymo Martelli [*Samerie*] to Q. of Scots, Paris, 28 [October ?] 1584, *Scot. Cal. VII*, pp. 414ff. On the date of this letter, cf. *supra* Note 351.

of 1584, and of the desertion by Mary of the course hitherto contemplated by her adherents for her liberation, he wrote:

"The letters that your Majesty has written, that they only hoped for love and good affection with the Queen of England, have much scandalised the Pope and all the Catholic princes, who are becoming very cold towards your Majesty ... However, I have always advised that it was opportune dissimulation and falsehood. This has not passed without producing suspicion of some here that they were not sufficiently circumspect in handling your affairs. They have failed to help you; but those to whom you entrust your affairs have not been sufficiently faithful, as the Catholic princes have recognised, who have great regret that your affairs go so ill for want of good intelligence; and that this has been added to the rest of your afflictions, to lean too much upon those who have deceived you. I was advertising your Majesty faithfully, but my reasons were suppressed and judged null, saying that I was deceiving myself, your Majesty knowing that I proceed straightforwardly".[360]

Finally, in a further letter of 24 October 1585, having warned her of the sinister effect which the propaganda of the English Government[361] and their agents had had in Papal circles in Rome, he continued:

"Father Claude [*Mathieu, S.J.*] has been at Rome for a long time and is in great credit with the Pope, and labours much for France, England and Scotland, and settles affairs there well; for you will not find such more assured means than he there, for he will not displease the detractors. Princes will stay more on their fidelity of long time tried and known than on those who by detracting put back the affairs of your Majesty, as you have perceived: and to treat of your affairs the princes will not rest on others than the Duke of Guise, the Archbishop of Glasgow, Allen, Fr. Claude and Eusebius

---

[360] La Rue [*Samerie*] to Q. of Scots, Châlons, 18 May 1585, *Scot. Cal. VII*, pp. 687ff. Cf. also Persons's paper on the origin of the Morgan-Paget faction, 30 June 1597, enclosed in a letter to Juan de Idiaquez, 1 July 1597, West. Arch. VI, nn. 41 and 42.

[361] The main idea of this propaganda was to spread the report that there was no persecution in England for religion, that the Queen treated Catholics with commendable clemency, and that, were peaceful methods pursued and all irritation of the Government avoided, some composition, and even a certain degree of toleration might be allowed, not to say the conversion of the Queen herself. Many who propagated such reports were Catholic priests or religious, such as the Jesuit, Richard Bateson, later expelled from the Society, Edward Gratley, Dr. William Gifford, John Cecil, the ex-Jesuit, Thomas Wright, and later the Appellant priests, as well as laymen such as Morgan and Paget. It continued for years, always with the same technique, penetrated to Rome itself, where some members of the Papal court were corrupted, and for a time even deceived two Popes, Gregory XIII and Sixtus V. Cf. also *supra* Notes 214 and 314. I hope shortly to publish a study on the use of propaganda in religious matters by the Elizabethan Government and its effects.

[*Persons*] and I, and on the gentlemen of England and Scotland from here, of whom they shall have sufficient proof of their fidelity, and of those especially whom your Majesty shall choose and of whom they shall be assured: for they wish to proceed seriously and sincerely and not always with distrust and suspicion, and so far and so long as here and there you do not walk this broad road, they will ruin all. Therefore, Madam, I pray you for the honour of God rest yourself here, and they will be very faithful to you and nothing will be wanting to you if so be that you correspond freely with them; and nothing will be done that your Majesty is not advertised of it, and in my own name I promise it to your Majesty, if so be that you follow this road".[362]

Another follower, Godfrey Foljambe, gave her an even more explicit warning. Writing in March 1585, he reported to her from Paris:

"Mr. Arundel has performed many good offices towards your Majesty in this place; by whose means there can hardly any evil intention be contrived against your Majesty but there will be notice thereof obtained out of hand; which intelligence Mr. Arundel is appointed by the Duke to communicate to —— ,who signifies the same to the Duke or the Cardinal of Guise; for in this action each party refuses to deal with Mr. Morgan, who is of all men most suspected to hinder many good attempts enterprised on your Majesty's behalf. By reason whereof it is certain that neither they nor the Prince of Parma will deal in anything he shall manage".[363]

At the same time he wrote to Curle, Mary's Scottish secretary, in even stronger terms:

"The assured bond of friendship which I imagine to be between you and me does not permit that I conceal anything from you—anything that may be prejudicial to your credit or estimation, whereof I have no less regard than of my proper reputation. Yet I am not ignorant

---

[362] La Rue [*Samerie*] to Q. of Scots, Châlons, 24 October 1585, R.O. M.Q.S. XVI, n. 64. Abstracts from the letter are given in nn. 66 and 67. Translation in *Scot. Cal. VIII*, pp. 145ff. The reader will remark the absence from the list of the names of Morgan and Paget, and it seems evident that he was counselling her to deal only with her ambassador and those connected with him.

[363] Foljambe to Q. of Scots, Paris [*March*] 1585, *Scot. Cal. VII*, p. 590. Charles Arundel was obtaining information from the English ambassador. This he stated on oath in an enquiry into the affairs of Aldred held by the Nuncio on 30 September 1585. Arundel said; "that the English ambassador was a relation of his, as also was his wife, and that his association with the ambassador was for just reasons which were known only to the ambassador of Scotland and the Duke of Guise" (Vat. Lib. Chigi, M. II. 47, f. 10ff). Arundel's close friend, Thomas Fitzherbert, was also examined by the Nuncio about the same matter, as this report shows (cf. *infra* Note 651).

that the strings I may play are so unpleasant to you that I may thereby hazard your friendship, whereon I rely more than on any other favour, her Majesty's favour only excepted.

The matter is such as you have been longer acquainted with than myself, albeit not so sufficiently instructed, I suppose, as I have been; which is that Mr. Morgan is not only suspected, but condemned as dealing dishonestly with the virtuous Queen in her causes, as also with the Catholic estate of England. The time and occasion do not serve to set down the particulars. This I can assure you, that the definitive sentence is so arrested,[364] and therewith neither the Pope, the King of Spain, the Prince of Parma, the princely house of Guise, nor any other Catholic prince will deal or employ themselves in any action wherein he shall participate, whereof her Majesty may at divers times have been informed were it not that with great vows he gives assurance that howsoever his actions are, there remain no means possible to impair his credit with her Majesty, which is said to proceed for that whatsoever is pretended to her with his discredit may never come to her hands or hearing. How near this assertion touches you in credit, you may best consider, and also conceive what may be the consequence thereof, if ever God grant her highness liberty in such sort that her best friends may freely discourse with her of these causes.

In sum, if any mishap, which God forbid, betide her Majesty or any overthrow to the Catholics of our country, the whole blame doubtless shall be laid upon him and his adherents.

I deal with you herein as I desire you to do with me, that is, to advertise you of any accident, which may be prejudicial to you, and according to my opinion to advertise [you] what to beware [of] or follow".[365]

Whether the Queen ever received these letters from Samerie and Foljambe, even after the secret correspondence had been reopened at the beginning of 1586, seems very doubtful. She did, however, write to Samerie, assuring him that his communications to her would be secret, except from those who had intelligence with her and the management of her most important affairs, for whose fidelity she was able to answer; that he could write freely and fully of anything of importance that he knew, and that she would interpret it all as proceeding from his affection for her. As for those of her household, they should be obliged to him for being advertised and she would esteem

---

[364] The document has "arrested", but the sense certainly requires some such word as determined, concluded or pronounced—corresponding to one meaning of the French word "arrêter". The paper is a copy in Phelippes's hand.
[365] Foljambe to Curle [March] 1585, *Scot. Cal. VII*, p. 594.

it treason were they to conceal or disguise from her anything that had been written to her.[366] Her other secretary, Nau, too, in a postscript to this letter pledged his faith that all that Samerie might write would be presented to the Queen, "out of cipher down to the smallest jot", and he made a curious protestation, that he would always keep to the duty of an entire Catholic and an honest man, such as he hoped his negotiations with Queen Elizabeth and her Council had made him appear; for had he wished to connive at their pretensions against the Pope, he would have obtained thereby more than he had done for his mistress, the Queen of Scots.[367]

As for Foljambe, the Queen of Scots wrote to him:

"For all you may have heard against Morgan during his adversity, believe upon the experience that I have had of his entire fidelity, he hath proceeded in God's cause and this country, which I esteem mine in principle, as a very sound honest man. And if there be anything in him to be found fault with, it is that he hath been therein but over zealous and affectionate; as you may understand more particularly by Charles Paget who is a gentleman of good credit. I find therefore, right agreable that as you profess the same devotion towards me, and that you desire by your last letters that I inform you of the course I would you should take in those parts, you enter into a near friendship with the said Charles and Morgan and [make an end] of the zizanie which some, to all your prejudice, do what they can to sow amongst you of your nation in those parts".[368]

366 Q. of Scots to La Rue [*Samerie*], Chartley, 30 June 1586, *Scot. Cal. VIII*, p. 484.

367 Nau to La Rue [*Samerie*], 30 June 1586, *Ibid.*, p. 488. The calendarist took it to be a separate letter, but it seems rather to have been a postscript to that of the Queen of Scots to La Rue, of the same date (cf. *Labanoff*, *VI*, pp. 349–352). Despite what Nau said above about the negotiations with Queen Elizabeth at the end of 1584, he could yet, after his arrest in 1586, write to the Council of England: "On my return from my journey to the said Queen your mistress [*Elizabeth*], I protest before the eternal God that I did as much as was in me by every good and advantageous report to establish and maintain a stable course of friendship between the two queens, appeasing as best I could such discontents as might be begotten on the part of the Queen my mistress, the effects not following as she hoped from this course. Whereof her wardens can sufficiently testify how many times I have been reproached by her in their own presence, even to saying that I was deceiving her or that I had allowed myself to be abused. *And in fact her kindred and friends in France conceived so sinister an impression of my negotiations during my said journey, being so much to the advantage of the said Queen your mistress, that even yet they have not been imparted to them in detail, because they found them so disagreable*" (Nau to the Council, 3 September 1586, *Scot. Cal. VIII*, p. 664). Italics mine. More research is needed on Nau's relations with the Queen of Scots. Suffice it to say here that there is some evidence, showing that he was disloyal to her and that the Queen of Scots in the end doubted of his loyalty. On his return to France he made more than one protestation of his innocence which, to one at least, do not sound altogether sincere (cf. Nau's Declaration, B.M. Caligula B.V. 233; but in favour of Nau, cf. Duke of Guise to Archbishop of Glasgow, 15 October 1587, Caligula D. 1, 90).

368 Q. of Scots to Foljambe, Chartley, 29 May 1586, *Labanoff*, *VI*, pp. 330ff. Cf. also *Scot. Cal. VIII*, p. 408.

There is a touch of irony in the Queen's citing Paget as a testimony to the fidelity of Morgan; for he, too, was considered by the Catholic exiles at this time to be no less an agent of the English Government than Morgan.[369] But apart from this, it may be doubted whether this was a reply to the definite charge against Morgan in the letters already quoted, for there is evidence that these statements of Foljambe were withheld from the Queen.[370]

Whether Curle replied to Foljambe cannot now be ascertained, but no reply has so far been discovered. There is, however, a letter to Foljambe from Nau, the French secretary of the Queen of Scots, who deciphered the letters she received from the continent, and who appears to have acquired a dominating influence in her household. In this letter he told him that the Queen of Scots never knew anything of "his advertisement touching Morgan"; that the abuse of Morgan of which he had written, proceeded only out of France, and that some not well-affected to him were very earnest to set up a division between them which could be prejudicial to her interests. He thought he had fully answered the matter by his last and could do no more.[371]

All this has a sinister ring about it. Where else than from France would complaints against Morgan be reported? He was in Paris, still a captive in the Bastille and, as is now known, English Catholics there were keeping a sharp watch on him because of the suspicions aroused by his conduct. This statement of Nau, his blatant assertion that the Queen of Scots never knew of the charges Foljambe had made against Morgan; that they were made by those hostile to him in order to set up a division—this latter part of the assertion being quite untrue, as the history of the past years had shown;[372] and the implication that nothing could be done about it with the Queen of Scots, to whose service it was said to be prejudicial, is all strongly reminiscent of Morgan's own attitude, as reported by Foljambe in his letter to Curle: that there remained no means possible to impair his credit with the Queen, for

---

[369] Cf. *supra* Chapter I, section 3.

[370] Cf. section 1 of this chapter, and Nau to Foljambe, Chartley, 27 July 1586, *Scot. Cal. VIII*, p. 560.

[371] Nau to Foljambe, Chartley, 27 July 1586, *ut supra;* cf. also Same to Same, 30 June 1586, *Ibid.*, p. 489. His "last" appears not to be extant.

[372] Time and time again Allen and Persons had tried to heal the breach, but all to no avail. Persons later recalled these attempts and their failure to Paget himself (cf. Persons to Paget, Rome, 20 December 1597, Stonyhurst, Coll. P. 452. Knox (*Allen*, p. 391) printed a portion of this letter, but the whole should be consulted; an extract is also given in Chapter I, section 6 *supra*. Cf. also Same to Same, Rome, 14 February 1598, Arch. S.J. Rom. Anglia 31. II. f. 711, Persons's *Autobiography, C.R.S. II*, pp. 30–36, and his *Notes Concerning the English Mission, Ibid., IV*, pp. 65, 97, 99 and 121–125).

whatever was reported to her to his discredit would never come to her hands or ears.

Paget himself defended his friend and endeavoured to make the Scottish Queen believe that the complaints against Morgan were due to envy at the favour she showed to him. Thus, in April 1585, shortly after Foljambe had written his letters to her and to Curle, he himself wrote:

"It is a world to see the emulation here and elsewhere in banishment from our nation, and what envy some bear to Mr. Morgan for no other cause but that they find your Majesty bears him special favour. They are strange people, and have strange humours, which I would to God were reformed. Some are angry that they are not employed and favoured by your Majesty as well as Mr. Morgan and others, of whom your Majesty has had long trial of their faithful service, and [who] have ventured their lives and all they have in the world for your Majesty,[373] and they never wetted their fingers or suffered the least inconvenience in the world for your Majesty. They would have authority to prescribe your Majesty who should serve you, and not you to prescribe them.

I note this much to your Majesty by the way, that if at any time such men should discover their humours—which I would be sorry they should—in my simple opinion your Majesty should do well to cut them off. Your Majesty has had sufficient trial of Morgan's fidelity and honesty, and myself, as to confirm as much to your Majesty with twelve years experience of him, so that I assure myself that neither the malicious speech nor practices that shall come against him or any other that has long and faithfully served your Majesty can prevail to the diminishing of your favour towards him in the least jot of the world".[374]

3. *The Catholic exiles' adverse opinion of Morgan and Paget*

The letter of Paget, just quoted, and others of similar import were disingenuous. Envy and malice were not at the back of the complaints against Morgan, but the simple fact that he, as well as Charles Paget, were considered by the Catholic exiles, with but few exceptions, to be spies and agents of the English Government. Already in 1582 they had

---

[373] There is very little evidence that Paget ever ventured anything for the Queen's service, except possibly to lend 3000 crowns, and even this appears to have been repaid.

[374] Paget to Q. of Scots, 27 April 1585, *Scot. Cal. VII*, p. 627; cf. also Same to Same, 18 July 1585 and 4/14 February 1586, *Ibid.*, *VIII*, p. 26 and *Murdin*, p. 463; Morgan to Same, 18/28 January and 21/31 March 1586, *Murdin*, pp. 470 and 481 and *Scot. Cal. VIII*, pp. 189 and 262; and the postscript to Curle, in Morgan to Q. of Scots, 24 June/4 July 1586, *Murdin*, p. 520 and *Scot. Cal. VIII*, p. 461.

been distrusted by the Duke of Guise and the Archbishop of Glasgow, who feared that they might hold secret correspondence with some of the Council in England.[375] The Nuncio's despatch stating that Morgan was considered a knave has already been quoted,[376] as also that of Berden to Walsingham reporting that both he and Paget were held to be spies.[377]

Once her secret correspondence had been reopened at the beginning of 1586, and the Queen of Scots had received them, the letters of Paget and Morgan in their own defence could but enforce, as indeed they were meant to do, her conviction of Morgan's fidelity. But, quite apart from such letters, she was so grateful to him for again becoming the channel of communication with the world and with her adherents outside her prison, that it was incredible to her that he could possibly play her false. She continued, in consequence, to defend him and to have faith in him, so that her Scottish secretary, Curle, could write to Morgan in July 1586:

> "I pray you be of good comfort, and assure yourself that her Majesty is careful thereof, resisting constantly, and rejecting continually, whatever sinister report or opinion can be moved of you concerning your behaviour towards her service, and hers; and believe me (who shall never deceive you, God willing) that you are in the favour and good graces of your good mistress".[378]

The fact is, however, that the unsuspecting Queen was betrayed on all sides. Some years later in a letter to Juan de Idiaquez, Secretary of the Spanish King, in which he gave a brief history of the Morgan-Paget faction, Persons, the Jesuit, wrote:

> "This disagreement first started in the year 1582, when a meeting took place in Paris of the Apostolic Nuncio, the Spanish ambassador, Juan Baptista de Taxis, the Duke of Guise, the Archbishop of Glasgow, the ambassador of the Queen of Scots and others, and it

[375] Cf. *supra* Chapter I, section 2 and Note 9.

[376] Cf. Ragazzoni to Como, Paris, 10 March 1585, *supra* section 1 of this Chapter and Note 355.

[377] Cf. *supra* Chapter I, section 6 and Note 79; also Foljambe to Curle [March] 1585, cited in the last section.

[378] Curle, in a postscript to Q. of Scots to Morgan, 2 July 1586, *Murdin*, p. 519 and *Scot. Cal. VIII*, p. 496. Cf. also Same to O. Lewis, 20 May 1586, R.O. Transcripts 31/9, bundle 82a; to Mendoza, 20 May, and to Glasgow, 28 May 1586, *Scot. Cal. VIII*, pp. 389 and 400; also to Paget, 27 July 1586, *Murdin*, p. 531. That Mary received at least some of the letters of Morgan and Paget known to exist, after the re-opening of her secret correspondence, is clear from her acknowledgement of their receipt (cf. Q. of Scots to Paget, Chartley, 20 May, and to Morgan, 20 May 1586, *Scot. Cal. VIII*, pp. 390 and 392).

was decided that the reduction of the kingdom of England and Scotland must be effected by securing the support of the King of Spain and in no other way.[379]

In pursuance of this decision Fr. Persons and Fr. Crichton were sent (respectively) to Lisbon and Rome to ask for definite aid for Scotland. From this meeting had been excluded Paget and Morgan, who called themselves servants of the Queen of Scots, and who kept up a correspondence with her two secretaries, Nau, a Frenchman, and Curle, a Scotchman, who lived with her in England, and kept her ciphers and had great influence with her: and for that reason these two disgruntled men, who were living in France, so worked upon the secretaries, and the four of them together upon the dethroned queen that they took away from her all liking for and confidence in the course adopted by means of Spain. Fr. Henry Samerie, a French father of the Society, survives to this day as a witness of all this. He lives in Flanders, and at that period was attached to the said queen in England, nominally as her physician and saw what was going on. The Duke of Guise also was a witness of it, so long as he was alive, and he told many people with much feeling, and in particular Fr. Claude Mathieu, S.J., a native of Lorraine, who was his confessor, and Fr. Persons and others that Paget and Morgan had roused distrust between the queen and himself on the score of his being on too intimate terms with Spain and the fathers of the Society.

Besides this, it is well known that these two men at various times tried to persuade the Duke of Guise to take upon himself the liberation of the Queen of Scots and place her on the thrones of England and Scotland, using the power of France and her French friends and excluding the Spaniards. And as the Duke declined to agree to this but determined once more in 1583 to ask again for help from his Majesty of Spain, Charles Paget, not being able to prevent this decision, volunteered to go to England and procure the Earl of Northumberland's collaboration with the Duke. But on his arrival there he did the opposite and prevented him from becoming an ally. This was told to many people afterwards by the Duke of Guise himself. Paget, too, when he was on the point of embarking for England, told William Watts, and English priest, in confidence, that this was his intention.[380] Moreover, it is now known on the testimony of the above-mentioned Fr. Samerie and others, that Paget and

---

[379] For this meeting at which Allen and Persons were present, and for the subsequent negotiations, cf. *supra* Chapter I, section 2, and Note 7.

[380] Persons later recalled this matter to Paget himself (cf. Persons to Paget, Rome 20 December 1597, Stonyhurst, Coll. P. 452, and Same to Same, 14 February 1598, Arch. S.J. Rom. Anglia 31. II. f. 711). Both passages relating to the above are quoted *supra* Chapter I, section 6.

Morgan had, by means of letters, alienated the Queen of Scots herself and caused her to write to the Earl of Northumberland, telling him on no account to associate himself with the Duke of Guise or the Spaniards in this project. And this was done by Paget and Morgan in Paris after they had been reconciled to the Duke of Guise, Dr. Allen and Persons, who out of their desire of peace and union, and to prevent these two men from obstructing their policy further, had admitted them to a share in all their secrets. But these two were never loyal to them afterwards, as the events that followed will show".[381]

He went on, in the same letter, to record these events.

Such then, in the last two chapters, is the evidence, gathered from contemporary documents, in support of the charge against Morgan, made by the witnesses in 1590, that he had sown division, and had caused the Queen of Scots to be alienated from her adherents, the Duke of Guise, the Archbishop of Glasgow, Dr. Allen and the Jesuits; and that Morgan, Paget and others, had threatened to leave her service, if she negotiated with Glasgow, who in consequence had asked to be freed from his post as her ambassador.

[381] Persons on the faction of Paget and Morgan, 30 June 1597, enclosed in a letter to Juan de Idiaquez, Rome, 1 July 1597, West Arch. VI, nn. 41 and 42. Cf. also Memorial for the Archduke Ernest, 1594, Knox, *Douay Diaries*, pp. 401ff; and A Catholic at Brussels to his friend a monk at Liège, 14 July 1599, *ut supra* Note 352; also Northumberland's examination, 11 May 1585, printed in *C.S.R. XXI*, p. 120.

CHAPTER VIII

Morgan and Paget opposed to armed intervention on her behalf, especially by Spain—Queen of Scots' attitude in this matter, 1584-5: her conviction that her chief supporters were acting to her prejudice—Contradictions in the attitude of the Morgan-Paget faction to Spanish aid in 1586

1. *Morgan and Paget opposed to armed intervention on her behalf, especially by Spain*

A further charge against Morgan made by the witnesses in 1590 was this: he—and it is to be understood Paget also, who was working in collaboration with him—had followed the faction of those who proclaimed that the reduction or conversion of the English kingdom could be effected without foreign aid. He had, consequently, been opposed to the use of the forces of foreign princes, especially those of Spain, and had counselled the Queen of Scots not to treat with that country for that purpose. He persuaded her that under cover of her name, and on the pretext of securing her liberation, the leaders of those who relied on Spain, were procuring the conquest of England and Scotland only in the interests of the Catholic King, to the prejudice of her rights and those of her son. The substantiation of this charge is to be found in a consideration of certain propaganda aims of the English Government.

It was a persistent and studied aim of the councillors of Queen Elizabeth, basing themselves on the ideas of Lord Burghley, which found official expression in his *Execution of Justice in England, not for Religion, but for Treason*, of 1583, to spread, even to the court of Rome itself, the idea that there was no real persecution for religion in England, but that all who had been condemned and executed had been so treated only because they had plotted against the state and against the life of the Queen. Her Majesty, it was alleged, being by nature inclined to clemency, if only peaceful methods would be employed by Catholics and all forceful means foreborne which might exasperate the English Government, an accommodation might be reached, with the hope of toleration or liberty of conscience, and even of the conversion of the

Queen herself. The purpose of this propaganda was to sow division among Catholics, and to prevent or at least delay any concerted movement from abroad for the relief of their afflicted brethren both in England and in Scotland.[382]

That Morgan, together with Charles Paget, were leading spirits of the faction among the exiles used by the English councillors to spread these notions there is not the slightest doubt. Both were intimate with Solomon Aldred, who was apparently the first person to be employed by the Government to infect with the propaganda the court of Rome, some Cardinals included; and they continued to treat with him even after Aldred was known to be their agent. Morgan favoured, also, the employment by them of the priests, Edward Gratley and Dr. William Gifford, who had both been won over by Aldred and the English ambassador, Sir Edward Stafford, to assist in spreading this same propaganda, and he deliberately misled the Queen of Scots as to their real intentions.[383] With Dr. Owen Lewis, who himself had in Italy certainly been connected with Aldred's activities, Morgan was in close association. He strove with the rest of the faction to have Lewis raised to the purple, and was angered at the failure of their efforts by the elevation in 1587 to that dignity of Dr. Allen, the leader of the rival party. He was concerned later, with the visit of the Carthusian Prior, Arnold, to Spain in 1589, in order to traduce Allen to the authorities there, and by means of the influence of the Catholic King, to have Owen Lewis made Cardinal as a rival to the recognised leader of the English Catholics.[384] In his letters, moreover, and in those of Paget to the Queen of Scots, Lewis was more than once strongly recommended to her and the suggestion was made that he should be put in charge of her affairs in Rome; and the Queen, in fact, accepted the suggestion and appointed him as her representative there.[385] It was Morgan, finally, whom John Cecil, the priest informer, recommended to the English Government as a suitable instrument for the spread of their propaganda to Spain by way of Savoy.[386]

[382] Cf. *supra* Notes 314 and 361.

[383] Cf. *supra* Note 361 and Chapter III, section 3; also Morgan to Q. of Scots, 24 April and 24 June/4 July 1586, *Murdin*, pp. 510 and 520, and *Scot. Cal. VIII*, pp. 331 and 461.

[384] Cf. *supra* Note 221.

[385] Cf. Morgan to Q. of Scots, 18/28 January, 21/31 March and 24 June/4 July 1586, *Murdin*, pp. 470, 481 and 520, and *Scot. Cal. VIII*, pp. 189, 262 and 461; Paget to Same, 18 July 1585 and 19 May 1586, *Scot. Cal. VIII*, pp. 26 and 385; Q. of Scots to Lewis, 30 April 1586, R.O. Transcipts 31/9, bundle 82a; Same to Morgan, 2 July and to Paget, 27 July 1586, *Murdin*, pp. 519 and 531 and *Scot. Cal. VIII*, pp. 496 and 558.

[386] Cf. *supra* Note 361; also John Snowden [*Cecil*] to Robert Cecil, 20 June and 3 July 1591, Dom. Eliz. 239, nn, 46 and 78, the latter being quoted in Note 229 above.

Similarly, and as was to be expected from one who opposed the use of foreign forces, Morgan's attitude to Spain was one of hostility. Of this also there is no doubt. He revealed it to some extent at his trial in 1590, but apart from that, the small book or tract, which he had earlier encouraged and helped Gilbert Gifford and Edward Gratley to write is proof enough. One of the principal aims of this tract had been to deter English Catholics from supporting any "enterprise" against England, which might be undertaken by the Pope and others for the restoration of the Catholic faith in that kingdom.[387] For this purpose, in addition to its malicious attack on the Jesuits, the book inveighed in most bitter and virulent terms against foreigners and especially against the Spaniards, calling them tyrants, irreligious and atheists, and disseminating many insulting lies about them.[388] The composition of such a work was already being planned, when Gilbert Gifford was in England on his first visit, arriving there in December 1585. The book was actually taken by him on a later visit in 1586, to be presented to Walsingham for printing.[389]

Yet, in spite of their real intentions, Morgan and Paget assisted at the meetings in Paris in 1583 and 1584, of the Nuncio, the Duke of Guise, the Archbishop of Glasgow, Allen and Persons to discuss the "enterprise", and had outwardly agreed to the decisions then made, Paget in 1583 volunteering to go to England, ostensibly to secure support within the kingdom, especially of the Earl of Northumberland, though really to overthrow their endeavours.[390] Later, too, despite his hostile attitude to Spain, Morgan requested the Queen of Scots to

[387] Cf. "Notata contra Edoardum Gratleum," 20 March 1588, Simancas, Est. Leg. 950, f. 113; also *supra* Chapter III, section 3.

[388] "Notata, etc." as in last Note. "And the books are in existence today and are full of a thousand lies and calumnies against the Spanish nation and the intentions of his Majesty in particular". Persons on the factions, 30 June 1597, enclosed in his letter to Juan de Idiaquez, 1 July 1597, West. Arch. VI, nn. 41 and 42. The manuscript of the book was in the hands of the authorities in Rome when the "Notata contra Gratleum" was drawn up and sent to the King of Spain by Olivares, the Spanish ambassador (Olivares to Philip II, Rome, 13 June 1588, Simancas, Est. Leg. 950, f. 112). References are given in it to the folios of the book where proof was found of the statements made in the document. This tract of Gifford, Gratley and Morgan may still be extant in the archives of the Inquisition, where also may be Allen's long relation mentioned by Persons concerning Gilbert Gifford and others. It is to be hoped that some day, when the cataloguing of these archives is completed, access may be granted for the inspection of such documents as deal with English public affairs, as there are indications that these archives contained, at least at one time, valuable documents that might throw considerable light on the history of the English Catholics at this period and later. It was the Congregation of the Inquisition or Holy Office that had particular charge of English affairs.

[389] Cf. Confession of Gilbert Gifford, 14 August 1588, *Cal. Salisbury MSS. III*, pp. 346–349; also Phelippes to Walsingham, 8 July 1586, *Scot. Cal. VIII*, p. 514, and Henry Caesar to Walsingham, Paris, 9 December 1588, printed in Morris, *op. cit.*, p. 385.

[390] Cf. *supra* Chapters I and II.

obtain for him a pension from the King of that country which at that time he was vilifying. The Queen of Scots, in fact, acceded to his request and on her earnest petition, a pension was assigned to him by the Catholic King.[391] Apart from the financial motive—the begging faculty was not undeveloped in Morgan, and both he and his friend, Paget, had always an eye to the main chance—he may have been led to this dishonourable and hypocritical conduct by the desire to conceal his real attitude to Spain. However that may be, there is no doubt, as the Spaniard, Mgr. Peña, Auditor and afterwards Dean of the Rota, later reported, that the Morgan-Paget faction

"held from the beginning as a fundamental principle, to oppose themselves *in secret* to the Jesuits and the Spaniards".[392]

2. Queen of Scots' attitude in this matter, 1584–1585: her conviction that her chief supporters were acting to her prejudice
On her side, it is equally certain that the Queen of Scots was for a time alienated from any "enterprise" and the use of force. In a letter in January 1585 to her ambassador, the Archbishop of Glasgow, she informed him of her resolution to pursue only peaceful methods, namely by negotiating for her liberation with Queen Elizabeth.

"I charge you" she wrote, "to make known to my relations and other friends and servants over there, that I beg them all as well in general as each one in particular to desist from all practices and negotiations, if they have any in hand, that tend to the disturbance of this state, the welfare of which, its peace and preservation I place before any satisfaction and advantage for myself; for I am determined for the future to rely chiefly on the friendship of the Queen, my good sister ... This will serve also as an order to yourself that you on your part eschew all intervention in any affair contrary to this my resolution".[393]

[391] Morgan to Q. of Scots, 18/28 January 1586, *Murdin*, p. 470 and *Scot. Cal. VIII*, p. 189; Q. of Scots to Mendoza, 20 May 1586, *Labanoff*, *VI*, p. 309; Mendoza to Philip II, Paris, 26 June 1586, *Spanish Cal. 1580–1586*, p. 586; Q. of Scots to Morgan, 2 July 1586, *Scot. Cal. VIII*, p. 496, and Philip II to Mendoza, 18 July 1586, *Spanish Cal. 1580–1586*, p. 590.
[392] Peña's Relation, Bib. Vat. Lat. 6227, ff. 77–79, italics mine. For further evidence of Morgan's attitude to Spain, cf. the confession of Savage, 11 August 1586, *Scot. Cal. VIII*, p. 611; the confession of Gilbert Gifford, 14 August 1588, *ut supra*; the examination of the priest, Younger, alias George Dingley, 14 September 1592, referring to Persons's visit to Spain in 1582, *Dom. Cal. Eliz. 1591–1594*, p. 270; Nuncio in Spain to Aldo-brandino, on the English factions, 30 December 1595, Vat. Arch Nunz. di Spagna, 46, ff. 780–795; and Persons to Idiaquez, 1 July 1597, with enclosure of 30 June 1597, *ut supra*.
[393] Q. of Scots to Glasgow, Wingfield, 5 January 1585, *Labanoff*, *VI*, p. 77. Cf. also the Confession of Pasquier, her Master of the ward-robe, 8 October 1586: "She bade the said Archbishop to do as much as should be in him to stop all practices, not only such as

That Glasgow carried out his instructions is clear from a despatch of Stafford, the English ambassador, to Walsingham. Thus, in March 1585 he reported:

"The Queen of Scots wrote, ordering the Bishop of Glasgow to repair to the King and Queen here and declare 'how well she was satisfied of her Majesty, upon whose favour she meant to depend, thanking them for the furtherance that they had given unto it', also to say the same to the Duke of Guise and to require him and all her friends here to 'make no attempts for anything touching her, or if any were made, to break them off, . . . desiring him and all that loved her, to be content with that fortune that she should run, which should be none other than that which it pleased her Majesty to have her to do'.

He came to me and showed me these letters, saying he had delivered them to the King, and that 'he never rejoiced so much at nothing in his life, as this good intelligence'. That he had sent them also to the Duke of Guise, who had sent to stay the Bishop of Ross from going into Scotland, because he would breed no suspicion in men's heads, nor give her Majesty cause for jealousy".[394]

The Queen of Scots was for the time being deceived by these vain hopes held out by the peaceful method of negotiating with Queen Elizabeth. But the Jesuit, Samerie, appears to have been aware of the guile used against her, and as early as May 1585 wrote a warning to her. He gave another warning in October of the same year:

"Madam, I pray you believe me", he wrote, "they have done you very bad service in that they have spread the bruit at Rome everywhere, and to the Pope, that your Majesty is not willing that force should be used, and that you will also leave to the Queen of England and her clemency to determine the matters that your Majesty should agree to. Many English with certain intelligence which they have at Rome and in England spread abroad the bruit that the Queen of England is for the present very benign and clement, and that she no longer prosecutes anyone for the Catholic religion, and that they do not care to use arms against others, that they do not wish and will not permit the foreigner to enter England and that—such is your fortune—they have fallen into so great suspicion of those who

---

[394] Stafford to Walsingham, Paris, 1 March 1585, *For. Cal. August 1584–August 1585*, p. 309.

---

might be prejudicial but even disagreable to the Queen of England, of every kind" (*Scot. Cal. IX*, p. 89); cf. also La Rue [*Samerie*] to Q. of Scots, Châlons, 18 May 1585, *Ibid., VII*, p. 687 (quoted above); and Persons to Idiaquez, 30 June 1597, quoted *supra* Chapter VII, section 3.

have treated of your affairs that no one dares to trust them any longer, and they desire to have another way to signify everything to your Majesty; and the English are in dissension and division. The Pope is after discovering the truth and has written about it to his nuncio. One has the suspicion and almost evident proof that the English, your enemies—I mean the Queen of England and Walsingham—have practised on some of the Cardinals at Rome for your ruin; and we know it is said in high places that they will spend more on that than the Pope will do on all the English seminaries".[395]

This letter was concerned throughout with the propaganda spread by the English councillors, chiefly by means of English Catholics, priests among them, and to the infection by it of some of the Cardinals —not without the expenditure of a good deal of money by the English Government.[396] The reference to those who had treated of her affairs and who were now under grave suspicion, so that her supporters desired to have a new channel of intelligence with her, points to Morgan; for his faction, which was engaged in disseminating this propaganda, was also the group that secretly opposed the use of foreign forces, especially those of Spain, as already shown.

In this connection it must be clearly understood that no objection can be made against men who were honestly convinced that, as a matter of policy, the use of foreign forces, and especially those of Spain, to restore the Catholic faith in England was detrimental, and who, in consequence, inculcated the employment only of peaceful methods. But the dishonesty and iniquity of such men as Morgan lies in their external agreement with the Catholic leaders, who looked to foreign forces for the relief of English Catholics, whilst secretly these same men opposed all their efforts; and again, in their appearing outwardly friendly to Spain and deriving their means of livelihood from its King, yet underhand vilifying and endeavouring to thwart the efforts of that country and its ruler; and finally in consorting with and actually sending into England agents-provocateurs, such as Parry, whilst simultaneously inculcating, though secretly, peaceful and non-violent measures. The contradiction between their outward profession and their conduct is quite apparent: and in effect there was layer upon layer of treachery—and Allen himself, in describing it, used the word of Morgan[397]—in their dealings with the Pope and the Papal Curia, with

[395] La Rue [*Samerie*] to Q. of Scots, Châlons, 24 October 1585, *Scot. Cal. VIII*, p. 145.
[396] Cf. *supra* Notes 314 and 361.
[397] Cf. Allen to Paget, Rome, 4 January 1592 (*vere* 1591), Stonyhurst, Coll. M. 129; to T. Throckmorton, Rome, 4 January and 20 February 1591, Knox, *Allen*, pp. 320 and 325; and Persons to Paget, Rome, 14 February 1598, quoted *supra* Chapter I, section 6.

their Catholic benefactors and their Catholic comrades. It is this contradiction, as revealed in the documents, that is indefensible and needs explanation; and the explanation that fits the facts seems to be that these men were agents of the ruling set in England, working in collaboration with them in spreading their propaganda and in endeavouring to involve Catholics in so-called murder plots.

Evidence is not lacking, either, for the further point that the Queen of Scots was persuaded that the Catholic leaders did not have her interests in view in their plans, but rather those of the King of Spain, thus prejudicing her rights and those of her son. There seems no reason to doubt the truth of the statement of Pasquier, her Master of the wardrobe, who at times helped in putting into cipher and in deciphering her correspondence. According to him she rejected the idea of her liberation by force of arms—referring to the plan of invasion of 1583—because she believed that the leaders in France desired her to renounce her claim to the crown of England to the prejudice of her son.[398]

This statement of Pasquier is supported also by an assertion of Nau. In the course of his statement of 10 September 1586 he said:

"To this intention of employing the said Duke of Guise only in Scotland almost every one of the people of the Church, generally and severally, who were labouring for the religion in England, showed themselves so averse, that the Archbishop of Glasgow informed the said Queen of Scotland that some of them had said to him in these terms: 'If the Queen remains thus obstinate, neither she nor her son will reign'; and that provision would be made without them, and peradventure to their hurt. And in fact *the said Queen of Scotland was advertised that many English had wholly addressed themselves to the King of Spain, proposing to him to invest himself with the crown of England*, in accordance with a book and discourse which had formerly been composed about it between Sir Francis Englefield, and one named Ouan,[399] and as I believe, the Jesuit Persons. Whereat the said Queen of Scotland was much offended, persisting always in not wishing to interfere except about Scotland, as a place where no one could find fault that she and hers should do what seemed good to them".[400]

[398] Articles for Pasquier and his answers, 2 September 1586, *Scot. Cal. VIII*, p. 659; cf. *supra* Chapter I, section 6, where the passage is quoted, and Note 74.

[399] Hugh Owen, a leading Catholic exile in Flanders, who was trusted by the Governors of that country.

[400] Statement of Mons. Nau, 10 September 1586, *Scot. Cal. IX*, pp. 1ff. Italics mine. Cf. also Shrewsbury and Beale to Q. Elizabeth, Sheffield, 16 April 1583, *Ibid., VI*, p. 384. At her trial, the Queen of Scots herself made this statement: "When being prisoner I languished in cares without hope of liberty, and was without all hope to effect those things which very many expected at my hands, declining now through age and sickness, it

Not all the details of this statement appear to be correct, it is true, and Nau himself revealed that he was speaking at times only from report, but it is substantially accurate as to the main point considered here, *viz.* the exclusion of the Queen of Scots and her son from their respective rights to the crown of England. Yet the documents of the negotiations of the Catholic leaders—and they are plentiful—give the lie to this report that had been conveyed to the Queen of Scots from abroad. From whom, then, did she receive it? Certainly not from the Catholic leaders, to the aims of whom it was quite contrary. In view of the evidence already given can there be any doubt that it came from the Morgan-Paget party, who were opposed to the use of force and to any plan of invasion? And this, indeed, is confirmed in a despatch some years later concerning the factions of the English exiles, which was sent to Rome by the Nuncio in Spain. Having referred to the efforts on behalf of the Queen of Scots that had been made on the part of the Duke of Guise, the Archbishop of Glasgow and all those who had looked to the King of Spain for support, he continued:

> "Against all these they [*Morgan and Paget*] sowed suspicion in the mind of the said Queen by means of her two secretaries, how his Majesty and the Duke and the fathers of the Society were treating about dropping the claims of the said Queen to the crown of England, when in verity the whole of their negotiations were on her behalf and to secure her liberation, and of all this deceiving of the Queen there are witnesses still available, Frenchmen of credit who were in England with the said Queen in her house when all this took place".[401]

3. *Contradictions in the attitude of the Morgan-Paget faction to Spanish aid in 1586*

There is, however, as regards the hostile attitude referred to, of the Morgan-Paget faction to Spain and to the use of external forces to restore the Catholic faith in England, a significant contradiction in 1586 that calls for explanation. At the very time that Morgan was aiding Gratley and Gilbert Gifford to compose their venomous brochure

---

[401] Nuncio in Spain to Aldobrandino, Madrid, 30 December 1595, Vat. Arch. Nunz. di Spagna, 46, ff. 788–795. Translation.

---

seemed good to some, that the succession of the crown of England should be established in the Spaniard, or some English Catholic. And when a book was sent unto me to avow the Spaniard's title; which when it was not allowed by me, I incurred displeasure among some" (*State Trials*, 1809 Ed. col. 1188). The document which she referred to was probably that drawn up, not by Englefield and others, but by Robert Highington or Heighton in 1582 (cf. L. Hicks, s.j., *Robert Persons and the Book of Succession, Recusant History*, Vol. 4, No. 3, 1957, p. 105).

attacking Spain, one principal purpose of which, as already stated, was to deter English Catholics from supporting any "enterprise" against England, Morgan's close collaborator, Charles Paget, wrote to the Queen of Scots that she must now look for support only from the King of Spain, "who was willing to do her all good".[402] She eventually followed his advice, because she had realised the utter failure of peaceful methods in the negotiations she had conducted with Queen Elizabeth and her councillors at the end of 1584. But how can the apparently contradictory conduct of the faction be explained: on the one hand attacking Spain and the use of force, and on the other urging the Scottish Queen in the last year of her life to an exactly contrary policy?

The explanation seems to be this. There was no hope of enticing the Queen of Scots to enter into any forceful attempt made by English Catholics to effect her liberation and better the condition of their co-religionists, unless that attempt was supported by foreign forces; and that support, on account of the civil wars in France, could be given only, or preponderatingly, by the King of Spain, in collaboration with the Pope.[403] She had, in fact, but lately rejected such proposals for this very reason.

"I will freely confess to you", she wrote to Mendoza, then Spanish ambassador in Paris, "that I myself was so discouraged from entering into any new attempts, seeing the little effect of previous ones, that I have turned a deaf ear to several overtures and proposals of 'enterprises' which have been made to me during the past six months by the said Catholics, as I had no possible way of giving them a reply based on solid grounds. But now that I have heard *anew* of the good intentions of the Catholic King towards us here, I have written very fully to the leaders of the said Catholics about a plan which I have sent them, to decide among themselves about its execution, stating my opinion on every point; and to gain time I have bidden them to despatch to you with all speed some one from among them, sufficiently instructed to treat with you, according to the general offers already made to you, about all things they will have to request of you in this matter from the King your master".[404]

---

[402] Paget to Q. of Scots, 31 March/10 April 1586, *Murdin*, p. 506 and *Scot. Cal. VIII*, p. 292. Concerning the brochure against Spain, etc., cf. *supra* Note 388.

[403] Hearing that there was a possibility of peace being established in France, Mary wrote to her ambassador in Paris to find out if, in that case, the Duke of Guise would be able to take part in the "enterprise". If so, she thought that it would be better to fix the time for executing it immediately after the conclusion of peace, so that the Duke could use the forces he had in hand, before their dispersal (cf. Q. of Scots to Glasgow, Chartley, 27 July 1586, *Labanoff, VI*, p. 412).

[404] Q. of Scots to Mendoza, Chartley, 27 July 1586, *Ibid., VI*, p. 431. My italics. Cf. also Same to Paget, 27 July 1586, *Ibid., VI*, p. 399: "If his Holiness and the King of

It was, thus, essential that the Queen of Scots should be assured of help from Spain, if she was to be lured into entering into any negotiations with Babington, the leader of a very small group of English Catholics. Failing that, she would have continued to turn a deaf ear to all such proposals from him or others, as indeed, she had been doing during the past six months.[405] It was the part of Charles Paget to give her that assurance.

Paget, therefore, prepared the way by advising her in the letter mentioned above, to rely only on Spain. A few weeks later he told

---

[405] There is something mysterious about these divers "overtures and proposals of enterprises" made to her by English Catholics during that six months, which she mentioned in the letter to Mendoza quoted above. By whom were such overtures and suggestions made? Certainly Mary was convinced that the Catholics were ready to rise (Q. of Scots to Glasgow, 27 July 1586, *Labanoff*, *VI*, p. 412). But what led her to such a conviction? No doubt the letter of Charles Paget of 19 May 1586, relating to her Ballard's visit to Mendoza (cf. *text*), had something to do with it, but it seems probable that these divers overtures and suggested enterprises, made supposedly by English Catholics, played an important part in establishing the conviction. There are two letters which may throw some light on it. Writing to Morgan, 27 July 1586 (*Murdin*, p. 532), she stated: "Neither can I tell by whom to send back my answer again to Poley for his offers made courteously to me, because he hath named no particular man unto me, unto whom he hath committed the sending of his, *which came with an infinite number that divers others confusedly sent me*"; and again, in a letter to Glasgow of the same date, she wrote: "My intelligences begin to be much renewed in *this country, many having addressed themselves to me anew*, by means of whom you will be able henceforth to write to me on all occasions ... " (Q. of Scots to Glasgow, 27 July 1586, *Labanoff*, *VI*, p. 419 and *Scot. Cal. VIII*, p. 555). It is surely strange that neither the letter of Poley, who was, in fact, an agent of the English Government, nor even one of the "infinite number" mentioned by Mary, have been preserved. Did she destroy them as too compromising, and yet keep those of Glasgow, Morgan and Paget and above all the letter of Babington? Or were the letters in reality forgeries, sent to her precisely to convince her that the Catholics were ready to rise, and on the seizure of her papers by the Government were recovered and destroyed? They could never have been used against her or against the Catholics; for they would have been detected as forgeries by those who were supposed to have written them and so weakened the Government's case—a vital point—that the letter of Babington was completely genuine. That such trickery was practised at times on the English Catholics the contemporary historian, Camden, testified (cf. *supra* Note 96, where the passage is quoted). The letter of Poley, Walsingham's agent, was undoubtedly meant to deceive her. It was certainly thought in France that false papers had been foisted on the Scottish Queen, and that it was these that condemned her (Stafford to Walsingham, Paris, 4 April 1587, *For. Cal. June 1586–June 1588*, p. 272). Cf. also "The confession of Thomas Harrison", *Scot. Cal. IX*, p. 530.

Spain will in any way yield to this enterprise, which I desire, they should declare resolutely and plainly without drawing things to length by artificial negotiation and vain hope as hath been done hitherto (as is still so my opinion). I have written to the said Catholics that *before they have sufficient promise and assurance* of the Pope and the King of Spain for accomplishing of that which is required of them, nothing be stirred on this side. For otherwise they shall overthrow themselves without profit". Italics mine. See also Babington's Fourth Examination, Pollen, *op. cit.*, p. 78, and the alleged letter of the Queen of Scots to Babington, *Ibid.*, p. 40 (I use the word "alleged" because there are grave reasons for thinking that it is only in part hers, and that interpolations were added by Phelippes). Cf. also Q. of Scots to Englefield, 27 July 1586, *Scot. Cal. VIII*, p. 555.

her of the visit of a priest, called Ballard, whom he described as very
honest and discreet, and acquainted with all the best Catholics of
England and some of Scotland. He had been sent, according to Paget's
report, to declare the readiness of the most part of Catholics, and even
of schismatics, to take up arms, if assured of foreign help. Having been
taken by Paget to Bernardino de Mendoza, the Spanish ambassador in
Paris, Ballard had declared how many noblemen and knights, armed
and unarmed in the North, in Lancashire and the West country and
other shires were willing to rise in revolt. Many had promised under
oath to do so; and the time was never more suitable, for all the best
Protestant captains and soldiers were with Leicester in Zealand, and
the people themselves were very discontented. He had not stated the
names of the gentlemen who were ready to rise, for he had promised
not to reveal them. Added to this he had given the ambassador information as to the ports. As, however, his information was only general, the
ambassador had instructed Ballard to get further particulars. Once he
was satisfied in these matters by some of the leading and wisest
Catholics in England, the King of Spain, so Mendoza is reported to
have told them, would assuredly give them reasonably speedy relief.
Among such points on which Ballard was to bring back to France
further particulars, were the best ports for landing, Newcastle, Hartle-
pool or Scarborough, and the special measures for ensuring the safety
of the Queen of Scotland. Parma would lead the enterprise from
Flanders with such diligence that the Queen of England would be
taken by surprise, thinking that whatever was intended against her
would come not from Flanders but from Spain. Ballard was shortly
to bring back to France information on these particulars and the Queen
of Scots would then be advertised with all speed.[406] The ambassador
had already in general terms made known these proposals to the King
of Spain, and had, indeed, advised Paget not to write to Mary about
them until the matters had been brought to a better resolution and
more certainty. *But though he had promised Mendoza not to do so*, he
had thought it his duty to make her acquainted with an affair of such
importance. He himself had told the ambassador that if the King of
Spain did not take action against the Queen [*Elizabeth*] this year [*1586*],

---

[406] Gilbert Gifford appears to have been sent in place of Ballard—not, it need hardly
be remarked, by the Catholics, though pretending that he was (cf. Mendoza to Philip II,
Paris, 13 August 1586, *Spanish Cal. 1580–1586*, pp. 603–608). This letter also contains
the purely imaginary state of affairs in England that Gifford put before the gullible
Mendoza; cf. also "Statement of the Provinces of England and their present condition",
Ibid., p. 608.

it would be too late, though he did not reveal to the captive Queen the reasons, if any, for such a statement.[407]

By comparing this account of Ballard's visit to Mendoza with that which the Spanish ambassador himself sent to Philip II, it is clear that Paget heightened the picture of preparations and soundings already made, with his reference to the number of men ready to rise in various parts of the country, the ports available, and the direction of the

[407] Paget to Q. of Scots, 19/29 May 1586, *Murdin*, p. 516 and *Scot. Cal. VIII*, p. 385. Cf. also Morgan to Same, 29 June/9 July 1586, *Murdin*, p. 528 and *Scot. Cal. VIII*, p. 477; and Q. Elizabeth's Instructions to Wotton, 29 September 1586 (*For. Cal. June 1586–June 1588*, p. 96) where, after saying that Ballard was brought by Paget to Mendoza, she continued: "Which two, together with Morgan, a prisoner in the Bastille, persuaded him [*Ballard*] to return to England to deal with the discontented subjects there to enter into actual rebellion, 'joining themselves' to such support, *as they should assuredly shortly receive from the King of Spain* for that purpose". My italics.
    Ballard, it may be remarked, has all the appearance of having been, like William Parry, an agent-provocateur. Why should he have lied to Mendoza? For a lie his statement certainly was, that the greater part of Catholics in England, and even of schismatics, were ready to rise in revolt. There is not the slightest evidence of this apart from these letters. Ballard, in fact, confessed to Gilbert Gifford that unless they obtained the Queen of Scots' authorisation, all would be but wind (G. Gifford to Walsingham, 11 July 1586, printed in Pollen, *Mary Queen of Scots and the Babington Plot*, p. 108. Cf. also the heads of the conference between Ballard and Babington and this Advertiser, *Ibid.*, p. 113). The event proved the falsehood of Ballard's statement to Mendoza. Nor is there any evidence that Ballard was sent to France as these Catholics and schismatics as their representative, though he pretended to be such, just as Gilbert Gifford did a few weeks later, to supplement the false information that Ballard had given to Mendoza, by further fantastic falsehoods (cf. *Spanish Cal. 1580–1586*, pp. 603–610). There is not even evidence to show that Ballard was an emissary of the very small group of Catholics with whom, after his visit to France, he seems to have been more particularly associated, and who were afterwards executed, and conveniently so, before the trial of the Queen of Scots. (cf. Babington's First Confession, Pollen, *op. cit.*, p. 52). To Babington, whom he sought out on his return from France, he falsely represented that the invasion by Spanish forces was imminent, that very summer, in fact, of 1586 (*Ibid.*, Pollen called attention to the discrepancy between Ballard's statement and Mendoza's real message). At her trial, indeed, the Scottish Queen declared that Ballard had formerly been a spy of Walsingham: "But I was told that he had great intelligence with Walsingham and that I must be on my guard" (narrative of the trial, by her physician, Bourgoign, who was present at it, printed in M. R. Chantelauze, *Marie Stuart, Son Proces et son Exécution*, Paris, 1876, p. 523). Châteauneuf, the French ambassador, made the same statement (*Mémoirs sur la Conspiration de Babington, Labanoff, VI*, p. 288). "For on the 4th August Ballard was apprehended and before his apprehension Ballard sent a letter to Mr. Secretary, offering to discover all; myself was the bearer of this letter, and delivered it to one of Mr. Secretary's men" (Statement of John Charnock at his trial, *State Trials*, 1809 Ed. col. 1153). Persons, finally, in his account of the factions, definitely asserted that Ballard was sent to England by Morgan and Paget, as undoubtedly he was, "to negotiate with divers Catholic gentlemen to kill the Queen, whilst on the other hand he was to have dealings with Walsingham, which he had" (Persons's paper on the factions, 30 June 1597, West. Arch. VI, n. 41). Cf. also Persons to Paget, Rome, 20 December 1597, Stonyhurst, Coll. P. 452: "The sending also into England of Ballard and Savage without our privity or even writing one syllable thereof unto us [*Allen and himself*], though the one were a priest, thereby subject to Allen". Also Same to Same, Rome, 14 February 1598, Arch. S.J. Rom. Anglia 31. II. f. 711, and Allen to Throckmorton, Rome, 4 January and 20 February 1591, Knox, *Allen*, pp. 320 and 325. In 1598 Paget shamelessly accused Persons of having sent Savage into England! (cf. Dom. Eliz. 267, n. 67 and Vat. Arch. Nunz. Diverse 264, f. 237, and Persons's Answers to Paget's charges, *Ibid.*, ff. 239–240, enclosed

enterprise from Flanders under the leadership of Parma, to the complete surprise of the Queen of England. Not one of these details was reported by Mendoza, who wisely remarked that more than generalities were required for an affair of such importance. All these details would create, however, in the mind of the Queen of Scots, to whom Paget reported them, an impression of the imminence of the attempt by English Catholics and Spain, and the impression would be further enhanced by Paget's relating his alleged remark to the ambassador that it would be too late if the King of Spain did not act that very year, wisely omitting any reasons he might have had for such an opinion.[408]

A few weeks before Paget wrote his account of Ballard's interview with Mendoza, Morgan in a letter to the Scottish Queen had provoked her to write to Babington, penning, as he had done the year before, a letter for her to send to him in her name—and telling her that Babington had discontinued his dealings with her, as a conveyor of letters, because he had been jealous of her employing Foljambe, to whom he, Babington, thought he should have been preferred. Morgan, therefore, urged her, for the common good, to placate Babington by the enclosed letter.[409] For this statement of Morgan about Babington there is not the slightest evidence beyond his own assertion, and it runs counter

[408] Mendoza's account is in his letter to Philip II, Paris, 11 May 1586, *Spanish Cal. 1580–1586*, pp. 574, 577. On the next day he sent a letter to Juan de Idiaquez, the King's Secretary, ciphered by himself personally, relating that he had been advertised that four men in England, who had the run of Queen Elizabeth's house, had agreed and mutually sworn to kill her, and would advise him on the first opportunity when it was to be effected and whether by poison or by steel (Mendoza to Idiaquez, Paris, 12 May 1586, *Ibid.*, p. 579). Presumably he received this information also from Ballard, or if not from him, from Gilbert Gifford, who was in Paris at the time.

[409] Morgan to Q. of Scots, 29 April/9 May 1586, *Murdin*, p. 513 and *Scot. Cal. VIII*, p. 344. Morgan composed two letters for Mary to send under her own name. The first was enclosed in his letter to her 6 July 1585, o.s. (Morgan to Q. of Scots, 26 July, *vere* 6/16 July 1585, *Murdin*, p. 453). This was acknowledged, as just received, in the postscript of her letter to Morgan, 20 May 1586 (*Murdin*, p. 515): "As the bearer was ready to have been despatched with the foresaid, her Majesty received your letters dated the last of March, 8th and 9th of April, together with another touching Babington of the 6th of July". The first letter to Babington is printed in *Labanoff, VI*, p. 345 as Q. of Scots to Babington, 25 June/5 July, 1586, and by Pollen, *op. cit.*, p. 15. Of this letter Nau stated: "And the first that the said Queen of Scotland wrote to him [*Babington*] was in accordance *with a minute sent word for word ready made by Morgan*" (Nau's Statement, 10 September 1586, *Scot. Cal. IX*, p. 1; italics mine). The second letter Morgan wrote for

in a letter of Persons to Cardinal Cajetan, Naples, 22 August 1598, *Ibid.*, f. 229). Cf. also the letter of a Catholic at Brussels to his friend a monk at Liège, 4/14 July 1599: "One great presumption of his [*Paget's*] double dealing with the Queen of Scots is, that Gilbert Gifford, whom he knew to be a spy for Walsingham and set on by him to entertain the matter of Ballard and Babington till such time as it should be ripe, being apprehended and committed in Paris for his treachery [*December 1587*], there were none that made so great suit for his delivery as Mr. Charles Paget and the Lord Paget his brother ... " (Dom. Eliz. 271, n. 74).

to the confession itself of Babington. In his first examination, after relating his previous conveying of packets to the Queen of Scots on several occasions for the space of two years, Babington continued:

"Being weary of which service (as it was of great danger and more hurtful to this state than before I conceived), I was desirous to cease from further proceedings in that course. This I did three months before her remove from the Earl[410] and ever since till July last past, as I remember, when I received by a boy unknown to me, letters in cipher signifying her discontentment for the breach of intelligence, [and] requiring me to send by that bearer, as I did, certain letters which I had received from Thomas Morgan in April (as I remember) last past [*1586*], directed unto her. Which letters I was earnestly entreated to convey unto her, but did not seek the means: only I kept them safely, *having immediately before sent back unto Morgan another packet* directed likewise unto her, utterly refusing to deal any further in those affairs".[411]

Moreover, a few weeks after Paget's report to the Queen of Scots of Ballard's visit to Mendoza, Morgan informed her that this same Ballard had an affair of consequence in hand but warned her, on account of the danger, not to have any intelligence with him, as he had told Ballard not to have any with her:[412] and all this appearance of care for her safety came from one who had provoked her to get in touch with Babington, with whom both he and Paget knew Ballard was dealing!

The sequence itself of these events is indeed revealing. During the six months previous to July 1586 the Queen of Scots had turned a deaf

[410] The letter of Queen Elizabeth to the Earl of Shrewsbury, in which she informed him that he had been relieved of his charge, and that Sir Ralph Sadleir and Sir Henry Neville had been appointed to have the custody of the Scottish Queen, is dated 1 April 1584 (*Scot. Cal. VII*, p. 54). So, according to Babington's statement, he would have ceased conveying packets about January 1584.

[411] Babington's First Examination, printed in Pollen, *op. cit.*, pp. 50-51. Italics mine.

[412] Morgan to Q. of Scots, 4 July 1586, *Scot. Cal. VIII*, p. 499; cf. also *supra* Note 407, and Q. of Scots to Morgan, 27 July 1586, *Murdin*, p. 532 and *Scot. Cal. VIII*, p. 550.

the Queen to send to Babington was enclosed in his letter to her referred to at the beginning of this Note. This second letter to Babington is printed in *Scot. Cal. VIII*, p. 345. Morgan's letter of 29 April/9 May 1586 was acknowledged as received, in the Queen of Scots' to Morgan, 27 July 1586 (*Murdin*, p. 532 and *Scot. Cal. VIII*, p. 550). This second letter, therefore, came too late, and it was the first, of 1585, that was used. For the significance of this, cf. *The Letter-Books of Sir Amias Poulet*, Ed. J. Morris, s.j., pp. 210-211.

The statement that Morgan *provoked* the Queen of Scots to write to Babington was, according to Burghley, made by Nau: "I think Curle will be more open and yet Nau has amply confessed by his handwriting to have written by the Queen's inditing and her own minute the long letter to Babington, but he would qualify his mistress's fault in that Babington *provoked* her thereto and Morgan *provoked* her to renew her intelligence with Babington" (Burghley to Walsingham, 8 September 1586, *Scot. Cal. VIII*, p. 701). Italics mine.

ear to divers overtures to rescue her from her prison, supposedly made to her by Catholics in England, but probably—for there is no evidence apart from her statement of any such overtures—not unconnected with the "infinite number of letters" from Catholics in England which she mentioned [*see Note 405*] and which have all since mysteriously disappeared. In March of that same year, 1586, despite the hostile attitude to the use of arms, and especially those of Spain, on the part of the Morgan-Paget faction, Charles Paget now advised her to rely only on that country. About this time Babington returned to Morgan packets he had sent him to convey to the Scottish Queen. In April Morgan sent more packets, which Babington did not convey, but kept safely. Further, in May Morgan provoked the captive Queen to get in touch with Babington, giving her a reason, for which there is no evidence, and which from Babington's confession appears quite false, why Babington had ceased to convey letters to her. This was followed, a few weeks later, by Paget sending her an account of Ballard's visit to Mendoza, heightened, as is seen by comparison with Mendoza's own account of the same visit, so as to create the impression of the imminence of Spanish aid. Finally, Morgan some weeks later again, told her of an affair Ballard had in hand, warning her, however, not to have intelligence with him on account of the danger, even though Morgan himself had but lately provoked her to write to Babington, with whom both he and Paget knew Ballard was negotiating.

All these things point not to any concern for the safety of the Queen of Scots, but rather to a subtle conspiracy against her, with Morgan and Paget playing their allotted rôles. Such an interpretation alone explains the letters of Paget in which, despite his earlier opposition to the use of foreign forces and especially those of Spain, he yet recommended her now to rely only on those very forces of Spain, and conveyed to her the assurance of speedy aid from that country. That assurance was vital: without it the Scottish Queen would have turned a deaf ear to any proposal of Babington for her liberation, as she had already done to the others during previous months.

CHAPTER IX

The Parry plot and Morgan's arrest in 1585: imprisonment in the Bastille till 1587—Differences in the
Government's attitude to Morgan after the Parry and
Babington plots—Morgan's use of his imprisonment to
increase his hold over the Scottish Queen—A note of
megalomania in his letters

1. *The Parry plot and Morgan's arrest in 1585: imprisonment in the
   Bastille till 1587*

Much that has been considered in the last two chapters took place
whilst Morgan himself was a prisoner in the Bastille, for he had been
arrested on 1 March 1585, o.s., at the instance of Queen Elizabeth, for
alleged complicity in the Parry plot. He remained in gaol for this
reason until August 1587, but his imprisonment led to no lessening of
his involvement in the affairs of the Scottish Queen whilst she lived,
as will be further shown later. There is no evidence, however, it may
be stated at once, to support the suspicion of the witnesses at his trial
in 1590, that this imprisonment, like that in the Tower in 1572, was
also a sham, a clever ruse to increase his credit with the Queen of
Scots and the English Catholics, made to enable him to carry out his
treacherous designs against them with greater impunity. Indeed, as
regards Queen Elizabeth herself, there seems no doubt that she was
quite sincere in her urgent demands for his extradition. With regard
to the actual "plot" she appears to have been convinced of Morgan's
perfidy, just as she was, and was meant to be, of Parry's, and to have
been genuinely concerned for her own safety;[413] and it was, undoubtedly, she who was the driving force in the matter of his arrest and
imprisonment, and in the question of his extradition.[414] Within a
month after Parry's first questioning she had written three letters on
the subject to the King of France and the Queen Mother; and through

[413] On the Queen's reaction to the Parry plot, cf. Burghley to Walsingham, 4 March
1585 (*Dom. Cal. Eliz. 1581–1590*, p. 230): "Her Majesty occupied with consideration of
her own surety". Regarding the Parry plot itself, cf. *supra* Chapter III, section 2.
[414] "I never saw her Majesty affect any matter so greatly" (Walsingham to Stafford,
7 March 1585, *For. Cal. August 1584–August 1585*, p. 332).

her ambassador, Stafford, and the Earl of Derby, who was in Paris and who in her name had recently conferred the Order of the Garter on Henry III, she demanded that the prisoner be handed over to her. Not content with this she sent a special envoy, William Wade, to France to insist on Morgan's extradition, but without success.[415]

Next year, after the discovery of the Babington plot, in her instructions, dated 29 September, for Edward Wotton, whom she despatched to France to give a report of it to Henry III, and so prepare him for the trial of the Queen of Scots, she incidentally expressed the hope that both Charles Paget and Morgan would be handed over to her.[416] Again in the following December, when she gave audience to Châteauneuf and Henry's special envoy, Bellièvre,[417] whom he had sent to plead for the Queen of Scots, she adverted to Morgan and the question of his extradition.

"To which", reported the ambassadors, "we answered ... 'that if Morgan, having been on her sole account, for a long time detained in a strong prison in France, had plotted a little against her Majesty, he could not do her any harm, as he was in ward; that the Queen of Scotland has fallen into such a miserable state, and has found so many enemies in this kingdom, that there is no need to go and search for them in France to accelerate her ruin; and that it would be deemed a thing too monstrous and inhuman, for the King to send the knife to cut the throat of his sister-in-law, to whom both in the sight of God and man he owed his protection'. We could not believe, but that we had satisfied her with this answer, but she abandoned the subject of Morgan, and flew to that of Charles Paget, saying: 'Wherefore is he not sent?' " Then after the ambassadors had made excuses for not delivering him, the Queen replied, "that the said Paget had promised Monsieur de Guise to kill her, but that she had means enough in Paris to have him killed, if she wished.

[415] Cf. Elizabeth to Henry III, 12 February 1585, to Same, 10 March 1585, and to the Queen Mother, 10 March 1585, *Ibid.*, pp. 272, 237 and 238. Wade's Instructions are dated 10 March 1585, *Ibid.*, p. 238. His mission can be followed in this volume of the *Foreign Calendar*. Taking with him the Queen's letters of 10 March, he arrived in Paris on the 14th of that month and was back in England about 17 April (cf. Edward Burnham to Davison, Barn Elms, 21 April 1585, *Ibid.*, p. 423). A story was put forth by Morgan and Walsingham, that the Duke of Aumâle, under the impression that Morgan was being taken to England by Wade, attacked the envoy near Abbeyville. For the reasons for doubting the truth of the story, cf. Appendix III.

[416] Instructions from the Queen for Edward Wotton, 29 September 1586, *For. Cal. June 1586–1588*, p. 96. In these instructions he was ordered, once he had made known their contents to the King, to return forthwith, without waiting for any further directions. In them, it is to be remarked, that though the Queen of Scots had not by that time been tried, Elizabeth categorically asserted that she was guilty!

[417] From Bellièvre's account, the audience appears to have taken place on 14 December.

She said this on purpose, so loud, that the archers of her guard could hear; and as to Morgan, that he had, *within three months, sent to her 'that if she would please to accord him her grace, he would discover all the conspiracy of the Queen of Scotland'*; adding that he was very ill-guarded in the Bastille, for the Bishop of Glasgow had spoken more than twenty times to him, and that he was free to converse with whomsoever he thought proper".[418]

It is hardly necessary to remark that nothing came of the Queen's complaints; for Henry III had been determined from the beginning not to hand over to her his prisoner, Morgan, and particularly not at this time when to do so might further have endangered the life of the Queen of Scots, whom he was trying to save.

A few weeks later, however, on the occasion of the discovery in January 1587 of the feigned powder-plot to assassinate Queen Elizabeth, of which de Trappes, a member of the French embassy, was accused, William Wade was again sent to France as a special ambassador. In his instructions he was ordered to remind the King of the Queen's often urged request for the delivery of Morgan and Paget, a point which she also stressed to Wade by word of mouth.[419] But it is very noticeable that, though there was even more apparent reason for demanding that extradition at this time, than in the case of Morgan after the Parry plot, the pressure applied and the insistence on the delivery of the two exiles was in no way as vigorous as in 1585, though Henry III strongly suspected and, indeed, was moved to anger by it, that the arrest of de Trappes had been made in part in retaliation for his not having handed over Morgan.[420]

---

[418] Bellièvre and Châteauneuf to Henry III, London, 18 December 1586, printed in A. Strickland, *Letters of Mary Queen of Scots*, London, 1843, *II*, p. 192. Italics mine.

[419] Instructions for Wade (between 15 and 19 January) 1587, *For. Cal. June 1586–June 1588*, p. 189. "From thence I took occasion to urge the delivery of Morgan and Charles Paget, both according to the instructions I received in writing and by word from her Majesty" (Wade to Walsingham and Davison, Paris, 30 January 1587, *Ibid.*, p. 203).

[420] Cf. Stafford to Walsingham, Paris, 24 March 1587, *Ibid.*, p. 250. The so-called plot was discovered early in January 1587, and de Trappes was arrested at Rochester on his way to meet and cross to France with Bellièvre. The story can conveniently be followed in the *Foreign Calendar* and *Scot. Cal. IX*. In the end, though after the feigned plot had served its purpose, Queen Elizabeth, owing to Henry III's counter-measures, and the fear of creating a real breach between the two countries, released de Trappes at the instance of Wade and allowed him to return to France, as Henry III had demanded. She also granted an audience, hitherto withheld, to Châteauneuf and acknowledged the bogus nature of the plot. "Je suis bien aisé", wrote Henry III to her, "que la mensonge dont l'on a voulu imbuir vos aureilles aye esté recognu par vous. Je me promets que aussy me fera elle paroistre que celuy qui a accusé sera puni de tel démerite" (Henry III to Elizabeth, 1 June 1587, *For. Cal. June 1586–June 1588*, p. 310). In a letter to de Courcelles, who was acting at the time as Chargé d'affaires in Scotland, Châteauneuf wrote: "Mr. Wade is also returned, having at length had audience of the King the 6th of this month [*n.s.*], in which

Moreover, when Morgan, on the night of 13 August 1587, was eventually released from the Bastille at the instance of the Nuncio,[421] no complaint was made by the Queen to Henry III; still less was any demand made by her ambassador, Stafford, for his re-arrest, such as he had made in the case of Verstegan a few years earlier. Nor did Morgan himself show any fear of such an event, but with Paget went bragging up and down the streets.[422] In fact, there was a rumour that

[421] Cf. Secretary of State to Nuncio, 24 February and 7 September 1587, R.O. Transcripts 31/9, bundle 82b, and Stafford to Walsingham, Paris, 14 August 1587, *For. Cal. ut supra*, p. 352.

[422] "Mope [*Charles Paget*] and he [*Morgan*] brags up and down the streets, he repairing hither so soon as he understood of the other's delivery" (Lyly to Wade, Paris, 16 August 1587, *For. Cal. ut supra*, p. 355).

Stafford and he told his Majesty, on behalf of the Queen, their mistress, according to the command which they had from her, that she was very sorry to have caused de Trappes to be arrested, and that after having learned the truth of that wherewith it was desired to charge him, as also myself, she had recognised it was but pure calumny, holding us both innocent" (Châteauneuf to de Courcelles, London, 14 June 1587, *Scot. Cal. IX*, p. 444).

There was, possibly, just a grain of truth in Henry III's suspicion that the arrest of de Trappes had been, in part, a retaliatory measure for his refusal to extradite Morgan, but the real reasons were far otherwise. The first of these was to prevent Henry III, through his ambassador, Châteauneuf, continuing to plead powerfully with Elizabeth to spare the Queen of Scots; for after the plot had been discovered Châteauneuf was refused audience, and his communication also with Henry III as far as possible prevented (cf. Stafford to Q. Elizabeth, Paris, 22 January 1587, *For. Cal. June 1586–June 1588*, p. 191). The second reason was to frighten Elizabeth and so to bring pressure to bear upon her to sign the death-warrant of her captive. Châteauneuf was under no illusion on the point. In a letter of 28 January he wrote to de Courcelles: "Moreover, I can have no audience of the Queen, who has sent Wade to the King to complain of me and demand justice. And in the meanwhile the passages have been closed for a fortnight, without my having been permitted to write to the King to advertise him of this calumny, *which has been expressly prepared to ruin the Queen of Scotland*, to hinder my speaking to the Queen, who was incensed by the words of Monsieur de Bellièvre, who was not yet at Canterbury when de Trappes was taken at Rochester, going to seek the Sieur de Bellièvre to cross the Channel with him: and nevertheless, they hindered me from being able to advertise the said Sieur de Bellièvre of this matter, before whom they could have verified the whole" (Châteauneuf to de Courcelles, London, 28 January 1587, *Scot. Cal. IX*, p. 249). And even as early as 12 January, Patrick Gray, the special envoy of James VI, had written: "There is a new conspiracy alleged against the Queen to have been intended, for the French ambassador resident, three of his men taken, but I think it shall prove nothing. Mr. Stafford, who is ambassador for this Queen in France, is touched with it; his brother is taken here. Always it has done this harm in our negotiation that *all this council would not move this Queen to meddle with the Queen of Scotland's blood, till this invention was found forth*" (Gray to the Vice-Chamberlain and Secretary of James VI, London, 12 January 1587, *Letters and Papers Relating to Patrick, Master of Gray*, Bannatyne Club, Edinburgh, 1835, p. 131). Conyers Read remarks that the plot smacks of Walsingham's genius—a curious word to use in this connection (*Mr. Secretary Walsingham, III*, p. 63). Rather does the feigned plot bear all the marks of Burghley's trickery, of which it was not the only example (cf. also R. S. Rait and A. J. Cameron, *King James's Secret*, London, 1927, pp. 130ff). Though cut off from correspondence Châteauneuf managed to get through a letter to de Trappes and a prompt reply from him, thanks to the Jesuit Crichton, whose cell in the Tower was close to that of de Trappes (*Crichton's Memoirs*, printed in J. H. Pollen, s.j. *Mary Queen of Scots and the Babington Plot*, p. 166). Evidently he got this account of de Trappes across to Henry III (Stafford and Wade to Walsingham, Paris, 4 April 1587, *For. Cal. ut supra*, p. 267). My italics above.

he had been set free with the secret connivance of Queen Elizabeth.

"Gilbert Gifford", Stafford reported the day after Morgan's release, "this morning used a speech to one that he met, as though they would have it thought that Morgan was let out by her Majesty's consent underhand . . . to pick out some matter of him for her service".[423]

Some vague hint of this had also been received from England by a certain Massino dal Bene, an intelligencer of the English Government, as he told Stafford on 14 August, not knowing that Morgan had already been set free the previous evening.

"As to Morgan", he later wrote to the ambassador, "so far from saying that when I told you of the report that he was to be set free you laughed at it, I said you were greatly astonished and said that the last discourses you had had with the King on the matter were quite different and you could not think whence the alteration came . . . For the rest I confess that (as I told you) I have had some little hint from England that since the opportunity had passed by, it might be that her Majesty would allow you to employ what you know of for your convenience, but I never said in any way whatever that you had procured it, but spoke with all due discretion and respect".[424]

Whatever truth there may have been in these rumours as regards the Queen's attitude to Morgan in August 1587, there is no reason to doubt that she had genuinely desired his arrest and extradition after the Parry plot in 1585. But that does not mean that her ministers, or some of them, at least, were necessarily of the same mind as herself; for they certainly knew that Parry himself had for a considerable time been their own agent and an agent-provocateur.[425] There was,

---

[423] Stafford to Walsingham, Paris, 14 August 1587, *ut supra*. This despatch Stafford sent in haste by a bearer to announce the release of Morgan "yesternight".

[424] Massino dal Bene to Stafford, s.d. *Ibid.*, p. 381. This letter and others were occasioned by Massino's cousin, the Abbé dal Bene, trying to make trouble for Stafford over the release of Morgan and other matters. That Massino's warning to Stafford was on the 14 August transpires from Stafford's own statement: "That was on the Monday and he [*Morgan*] was let out the Sunday evening before" (*Ibid.*, p. 376). The words in Massino's letter above "that since the opportunity had passed by, it might be that her Majesty would allow you to *employ what you know of* for your convenience", suggests at least, that Morgan was not as he appeared to be and that Stafford knew it. This knowledge may have some connection with that cryptic message he had sent to Burghley some months earlier: "Hasten, I charge you as you will answer it for Morgan and Paget for if you knew as much as I do for your own indemnity you would do it, let your honour know what it is to break our league at this time. If I had not had a clear conscience I might have been afraid, I would to God I had my conscience as clear to Godward as I have in those things that touch her Majesty and especially in that matter of Morgan's and Paget's. I think another would hardly have done so much as I in it, but at my next audience I will do more, it shall not want for that I pray God her Majesty avow me" (Stafford to [Burghley], 22 January 1587, R.O. S.P. 78, Vol. 17, n. 10).

[425] Cf. *supra* Chapter III, section 2.

moreover, a curious delay in sending the Queen's letter to the French King of 12 February 1585, which demanded Morgan's extradition, and Walsingham's own letter of that date on the same subject. These letters were brought over by Shute, Stafford's man, and only reached the ambassador on the 24th of that month.[426] In fact, Stafford had been surprised at learning of Parry's imprisonment in the Tower and of his confession, before he had received an official notification of it.

"News came yesterday", he wrote on 23 February, "which the ill-affected subjects to her Majesty start at greatly: that Dr. Parry is committed to the Tower and has confessed an enterprise against her person, 'procured' from hence. I have heard of it two ways, 'the one from among themselves and that Morgan is greatly amazed of it'; the other, out of Pinart's house. 'I marvel much how they can here come by things out of England afore I have them, and especially touching so near the quick as that doth.' "[427]

This foreknowledge possessed by the exiles, indeed, made the ambassador very apprehensive that Morgan might escape. Reporting on 1 March, o.s., his arrest "this night", he wrote:

"I was never since I came to France troubled more by any one thing [than] for fear he should escape, for I knew of Parry's taking from some of themselves the day before I had your letters, and knew that Morgan was greatly startled at it, and therefore I was afraid he would retire himself".[428]

Yet, though Morgan had known as early as 22 February that Parry had been committed to the Tower and had confessed an enterprise against the Queen procured from Paris and was startled at it, he had made no attempt to hide himself or withdraw from the city and so escape arrest. Could it have been that Walsingham, despite the Queen's wishes, did not himself desire the arrest, and so had delayed sending the despatches, and that Morgan, knowing himself to be an agent of the English ministers, and that he had been acting in that capacity with regard to Parry, felt himself secure, at least in a foreign country?

---

[426] Cf. Stafford to Walsingham, Paris, 24 February 1585, *For. Cal. August 1584– August 1585*, p. 301. The contents of this despatch make it clear that he was referring to these letters. Cf. also Same to Same, Paris, 23 February and 1 March 1585, *Ibid.*, pp. 297 and 309.

[427] Stafford to Walsingham, Paris, 23 February 1585, *Ibid.*, p. 297.

[428] Stafford to Walsingham, Paris, 1 March 1585, *ut supra*. Morgan's surprise was no doubt genuine, for he probably knew that Parry, like himself, was an agent of the English Government.

2. *Differences in the Government's attitude to Morgan after the Parry and Babington plots*

Because of Queen Elizabeth's feelings against him, as has been shown, Morgan's alleged complicity in the so-called Parry plot could not be passed over, whatever her ministers might really have desired in the matter. After the discovery of the Babington plot, however, though the Queen's demands for his extradition from France, together with that of Paget, continued to be made for some months, these seem to have lacked the urgency of the earlier demands, whilst in the action of the Queen's councillors there appears a most striking feature—the almost complete silence which was kept about Morgan's connection with that plot, though this had been very considerable. The official documents are, in this respect, remarkable.

In the Bardon Papers there is a paper headed "Sir Christopher Hatton's Brief of the Case against the Queen of Scots", which ends thus:[429]

"After her intelligence with Babington, she did write to Cha: Pagett, Mendoza, Englefeyld, Lord Pagett, Bis[hop] of Glasco";

and the editor acutely remarks that "it is somewhat curious to find no mention of Thomas Morgan in this list". Had the editor pursued his investigations on this same point with regard to other documents, the almost complete absence of Morgan's name from them would have become, in the words of Alice as her feet disappeared, "curiouser and curiouser". Even in other documents printed in the same volume it is quite noticeable. Thus in "Serjeant Puckering's Notes on the Case against Mary Stuart",[430] the names of Babington, Ballard, Englefield, Charles Paget, Lord Paget and Glasgow all find mention and there is reference to as many as thirteen letters of the correspondence between them and the Queen of Scots, but the name of Morgan is conspicuous by its absence, nor is any letter of his to the Scottish Queen or of hers to him recalled. It is the same again in the documents headed: "Charges against Mary Stuart" and "Brief Notes of Evidence against Mary Stuart".[431] This same exclusion of Morgan's name and of all mention of his letters, though the names and letters of those mentioned above

[429] *The Bardon Papers*, edited by Conyers Read and prefaced by Charles Cotton, *Camden Society, 3rd Series, XVII* (1909), pp. 82–93. The document, printed from the Egerton MSS. is in Hatton's own hand, and the Editor thinks it most likely that Hatton drew it up for the purposes of a speech against Mary, which he delivered in the House of Commons on 3 November 1586 (*D'Ewes*, p. 393).

[430] *The Bardon Papers, ut supra*, pp. 53–64.

[431] *Ibid.*, pp. 77–80 and 81–82.

are recorded, is to be found also in the following documents amongst the Scottish Papers in the Record Office: "The Privity of Nau and Curle to the Conspiracy", "The Privity of the King of Spain", "Plots by Mary", "Proceedings against Mary", and "Crimes chargeable to Mary", in the last of which his name occurs once, but in connection with the Parry plot only.[432] In the list, too, of "Papers Relative to Babington's Conspiracy", preserved at Hatfield amongst Burghley's papers, this same suppression of all reference to Morgan or to his correspondence is noticeable.[433] In a word, in no less than ten documents connected with the Babington plot, in which Charles Paget and others are mentioned and in which accordingly one would expect Morgan's name to appear, it is almost entirely absent.

The same phenomenon is also to be remarked in the trials of the conspirators and in that of the Queen of Scots. In the opening of the trial of Anthony Babington and six of his companions on 13 September 1586, it was stated in the indictment that John Savage "did receive letters from Morgan, William Gifford, and Gilbert Gifford, whereby they did persuade and provoke the said Savage to execute and fulfil his said purpose and determination", and the statement was repeated immediately after the indictment had been read, in the opening speech of the Queen's Counsel, but there is no further reference to Morgan throughout the two days' proceedings.[434] In the trial of Edward Abington and six other persons on 15 September, beyond a reference to Morgan in the indictment, in connection with the sending of Ballard into England, he was passed over in complete silence, though it was Morgan himself who had recommended Abington to the Queen of Scots.[435] It is the same in the trial of the Queen of Scots on 11 October. Morgan is mentioned in connection with the Parry plot, with which she had had nothing at all to do, and his name appears in the copy of a letter read to the court of Mary to Mendoza, but only as one for whom she had desired a pension from the Spanish King. Otherwise there is not a single reference to him or to his correspondence in connection with the Babington plot, for which she was being tried.[436]

[432] Cf. *Scot. Cal. VIII*, p. 678, and *IX*, pp. 64–69, 69–70, 75–76 and 121–127.

[433] *Cal. Salisbury MSS. III*, p. 208.

[434] *State Trials*, London, 1809, cols. 1127–1140. The two references to Morgan occur in cols. 1129 and 1131.

[435] Cf. Morgan to Q. of Scots, 24 June/4 July 1586, *Murdin*, p. 520 and *Scot. Cal. VIII*, p. 461, and Q. of Scots to Morgan, 27 July 1586, *Murdin*, p. 532 and *Scot. Cal. VIII*, p. 550. *State Trials, ut supra*, cols. 1141–1162. The reference to Morgan is in col. 1141.

[436] *State Trials, ut supra*, cols. 1161–1212.

The proceedings at Fotheringay were followed on 25 October, by sentence being pronounced against the Queen of Scots in the Star Chamber before most of the same commissioners who had been present at the trial. A very short account of this gathering appears in the report of the trial itself, but an enlarged version, entitled "Evidence against the Queen of Scots", taken from the Hardwicke State Papers, is annexed to the above in Cobbett's edition. The purpose of the meeting, somewhat reminiscent of the Star Chamber proceedings after the Earl of Northumberland's death in the Tower in June 1585, was to enable the Privy Council to make a recapitulation "of all such proofs as had been made against the Scots Queen, before them at Fotheringay, etc." Nau and Curle were brought before the commissioners and personally avowed and maintained all their confessions and examinations, and details were rehearsed again of Mary's recent correspondence abroad and with Babington. The report of this meeting runs to eight and a half pages, closely printed, yet Morgan's name figures in it only four times near the beginning, though Charles Paget's name appears some twenty-two times, and that of Mendoza not many times less.[436a]

This suppression of Morgan's name and of all mention of his letters is surely remarkable, and especially so when his activities are considered. It was Morgan who had endeavoured to re-open the Queen of Scots' secret correspondence in 1585 by means of Robert Poley who, though in fact acting for the ministers of Elizabeth, was represented by them in 1586 as having been connected with the Babington plot and who, to conceal his real character of a government agent, was for a time imprisoned. He had been again recommended by Morgan to the Scottish Queen for the same purpose of the secret correspondence in 1586.[437] It was Morgan who had introduced to her Gilbert Gifford, and through him had actually re-opened her correspondence, which, though supposed to be secret, was known to the Government from the beginning, and the letters read on their transmission.[438] It was

---

[436a] *State Trials, ut supra*, cols. 1212–1228.

[437] Cf. Morgan to Q. of Scots, 21/31 March 1586 and 10/20 July 1585, *Murdin*, pp. 481 and 446 and *Scot. Cal. VIII*, pp. 262 and 11; to the Same, 18 July 1585, *Scot. Cal. VIII*, p. 25; and of 18/28 January 1586, *Murdin*, p. 470 and *Scot. Cal. VIII*, p. 189; and the Q. of Scots to Morgan, 27 July 1586, *Murdin*, p. 532 and *Scot. Cal. VIII*, p. 550. Cf. also Babington to Nau [June] 1586, Nau to Babington, 13 July 1586, Phelippes to Walsingham, 14 July 1586, Poley's Confessions [August] 1586, and Babington to Poley [August] 1586, *Scot. Cal. VIII*, pp. 492, 521, 523, 595 and 658.

[438] Cf. Morgan to Q. of Scots, 5/15 October 1585, *Murdin*, p. 454, and 18/28 January 1586, *Murdin*, p. 470 and *Scot. Cal. VIII*, p. 189; cf. also *infra* Chapter XII, section 1. Morgan's letter of 5 October was not taken to England by Gilbert Gifford until December, the reason for the delay no doubt being the contemplated removal of the Scottish Queen from Tutbury, which was not carried out till just before Christmas 1585, when she was

Morgan, again, who had provoked her to write to Babington, and had penned a letter for her to send to him in her own name, first in 1585 and again in 1586, and who had pestered Babington to get in touch with her.[439] It was he, too, who had recommended Edward Abington to her.[440] It was Morgan who, with Paget, had sent Ballard back to England after his interview with Mendoza, and had written to the Queen of Scots that Ballard had a project in hand, though warning her not to write to him before it was effected, in case of failure and betrayal,[441] having but a few days previously informed her:

> "There are some good members who await the opportunity of doing a turn of service to her of England which will appease many things (as I hope) if only it please God to assist the enterprise, for which I pray him daily".[442]

Again it was Morgan, who in the same letter had informed her:

> "I wrote to him [*Mendosa*] to remember to advertise your Majesty amply of all matters, whereby you might the better address the affairs of England and Scotland to embrace a good offer for the reparation of all that is amiss. I told Mendoza that he should advise his Master not to apprehend anything past of late in England and Scotland to discourage his former designments, which must be put in execution if his Master would have the public good advanced or repose in his own state. I signified further to Mendoza, that yourself would be able with the King of Spain's lively assistance, to make a good party both in England and Scotland, to embrace any good enterprise, if your intelligence with friends and servants may be continued, as I pray God, it may be".[443]

[439] Cf. Morgan to Q. of Scots, 26 July (*vere* 26 June/6 July) 1585, and 29 April/9 May 1586, and *supra* Note 409, where the references are given.

[440] Cf. *supra* Note 435.

[441] Cf. *supra* Note 412.

[442] Morgan to Q. of Scots, 9 July 1586, endorsed: "Extract of divers poyntes in the intercepted letters arguing the malice of Morgan and the rest of the Scottish Q's servantes in France both against this state and yt. Mis en francoys. July 1586" (*Scot. Cal. VIII*, p. 515). The letter from which the extract was taken is given in both *Murdin* (p. 528) and *Scot. Cal. VIII*, under 9 July 1586, but that date is new style which Morgan, writing from France, used. The passage, in fact, is found also in a letter given in *Scot. Cal.* (*VIII*, p. 477) as a separate letter of 29 June 1586. It is really the same letter, i.e. of 9 July, n.s. and 29 June, o.s.

[443] Morgan to Q. of Scots, 29 June/9 July 1586, *Murdin*, p. 528 and *Scot. Cal. VIII*, p. 477.

---

finally settled at Chartley. She received Morgan's letter on 16 January, o.s. and answered it next day. Cf. Q. of Scots to Morgan, Chartley, 17 January 1586, *Murdin*, p. 469 and *Scot. Cal. VIII*, p. 187; also Morgan to Q. of Scots, 21/31 March, 24 April and 24 June/4 July 1586, *Murdin*, pp. 481, 510 and 520 and *Scot. Cal. VIII*, pp. 262, 331 and 461; and Q. of Scots to Morgan, 20 May and 2 July 1586, *Murdin*, pp. 515 and 519 and *Scot. Cal. VIII*, pp. 392 and 496.

Clearly Morgan was one of the central figures of the plot. Why, then, this repeated omission of his name and of his letters, which has already been indicated? A somewhat similar feature in the dealings of the Queen's ministers with Gilbert Gifford may throw light on the matter. J. H. Pollen has shown that Walsingham was at first made anxious by the flight of Gilbert Gifford, his agent, which as a wise precaution on his own part, Gifford had resorted to before the debâcle of the Babington plot; but that once it was realised that he did not by his flight intend to turn upon his employers, they kept his name out of the trial of the conspirators, so far as was possible.[444] One reason for this was to divert attention from him and so conceal the part he had played in the plot and its discovery, under the direction of Phelippes and Walsingham. Almost from the very moment when the plot was discovered, the Queen and her councillors were concerned with this concealment. As early as 5 August 1586 Walsingham wrote to her that he would observe her commandment

"in keeping to himself the depth and manner of the discovery of this great cause".[445]

Two years later the confession of Thomas Barnes reveals that they were still occupied with this secrecy.[446]

The same preoccupation with secrecy is also noticeable in the correspondence between Phelippes and Richard Bagot between 1588 and 1591. In the Armada year, John Gifford, Gilbert's father, had been imprisoned by the Archbishop of Canterbury, "during the restraint of men of his religion". In spite of this Phelippes authorised him to go to his home at Chillington, Staffordshire, and informed Richard Bagot, the Deputy-Lieutenant of the county, and earlier Poulet's right-hand man, not to interfere, as the deserts of John's son,

---

[444] J. H. Pollen, s.j., *Mary Queen of Scots and the Babington Plot*, pp. cxii–cxv and 119. He was probably in error, however, in thinking that Walsingham, in his letter of 3 September, was referring to Gilbert Gifford. Rather does the context make it clear that he was referring to Lord Paget, cf. *Scot. Cal. VIII*, p. 666 and *supra* Chapter I, section 3.

[445] Walsingham to Q. Elizabeth, 5 August 1586, *Scot. Cal. VIII*, p. 589. Italics mine.

[446] "To the last I answer that I never heard but two ways how the conspiracy was revealed: the first should be by Savage's boy, which was the very general voice almost of all men at that time that I heard talk of it: the second was that it should be descried by my cousin Gilbert [*Gifford*], and that I never heard but once, and that was at Candlemas term last was twelve month, by one Yardley, prisoner in the Clink at that time" (Barnes Confession, 17 March 1588, printed in J. H. Pollen, *op. cit.*, p. 3). Barnes was later employed as an agent by the English Government (cf. *supra* Note 240).

"in that secret negotiation we had two years since with the brewer of Chartley is the cause why he is refused nothing he can demand and enjoy without too scandalous examples".[447]

He warned Bagot, however, that John Gifford must not be told the cause of the favour shown to him. After the imprisonment of Gilbert in Paris, he wrote again to Bagot that the Queen's favour to the father, John Gifford, continued and that if any gentlemen took exception to this treatment, Bagot might tell them that a son of John Gifford had been the instrument of her Majesty's deliverance in the great conspiracy of Babington, which she meant to requite and acknowledge; for the enemies did now know of it, and the man himself was in durance in Paris on account of it, though he hoped, the King prevailing, he would shortly be released.[448] But, though Bagot was allowed to impart this much in explanation of the favourable treatment accorded to John Gifford, though a recusant, the particulars of Gilbert's co-operation with Phelippes and Walsingham were still to be kept secret; for after Gilbert's death in prison in 1591, in another letter to Bagot Phelippes again referred to John Gifford's deserts by the service done by his son to her Majesty in the discovery of the great treason of Babington and the Queen of Scots,

"a thing never to be forgotten though the danger be long over past",

and informed Bagot that although he might impart the cause of the favour shown to John Gifford to others in the county, whose satisfaction it might concern, "the secrets and particularities" must, however, for great causes, still be kept secret.[449]

The reason, then, for the suppression of Gilbert Gifford's name in the account of the trials of the conspirators was obviously to conceal his character of an agent of Phelippes and Walsingham, and the part he had played in the plot and its discovery. As therefore the same feature of deliberate and repeated suppression of the name of Morgan and of all mention of his correspondence is noticeable in an even more marked degree than in the case of Gilbert Gifford, the inference must

[447] T. Phelippes to Richard Bagot, London, 15 August 1588, *Hist. MSS. Comm. Fourth Report*, London, 1874, p. 333, col. 1. Cf. further letters in the same tenor, 8 November 1588, 14 March, 27 April and 16 August 1589 (*Ibid*). By "the brewer of Chartley" was meant the brewer of Burton, whose beer barrels provided the means for Walsingham to acquaint himself with the Queen of Scots' correspondence.

[448] T. Phelippes to R. Bagot, London, 1 August 1590, *Ibid.*, p. 333, col. 1. The "enemies" came to know of part of Gilbert Gifford's activities from his own confession, 14 August 1588 (*Cal. Salisbury MSS. III*, pp. 346ff).

[449] T. Phelippes to R. Bagot, London, 3 February 1591, *Hist. MSS. Comm. ut supra*, p. 333, col. 2. In the same letter he reported Gilbert's death in prison in Paris.

surely be that he, too, was an agent of Queen Elizabeth's ministers, and that by this suppression they wished to conceal the fact, and the part he had played in luring the Queen of Scots to her death. These suppressions, in fact, seem to bear a direct relationship to the commanding importance of the parts played by these two men, Morgan and Gilbert Gifford, in the management of the plot, for no such omissions covered the names of other persons, in particular, as has been noted, that of Morgan's collaborator, Charles Paget.

3. *Morgan's use of his imprisonment to increase his hold over the Scottish Queen*

It has already been stated that the witnesses in 1590 were not justified in their suspicion that Morgan's imprisonment in the Bastille in 1585 was a sham, a ruse to increase his credit with the Queen of Scots; for Queen Elizabeth was undoubtedly genuinely concerned and sincere in her demand for his arrest and extradition, though some reasons have been given for thinking that it was not so with her ministers. Still, the witnesses had this justification for their suspicion, that though Morgan's imprisonment itself was not a sham, he readily adapted it to increase his hold over the Queen of Scots, by using it to arouse her sympathy, as well as to extract money from her. For their parts, too, it would seem that the ministers readily adapted themselves to the new situation.[450]

Morgan's use of his captivity to arouse her sympathy[451] is strikingly evident in his letter to her some weeks after he had been arrested. In it he narrated the circumstances of the arrest, how he had been taken to the house of the Provost's Lieutenant, and a few days later confined a close prisoner in the Bastille, though Thomas Throckmorton had been allowed at times to repair to him. To secure his extradition great efforts had been made by the Earl of Derby—then in France for the investiture of Henry III with the Order of the Garter—though happily so far without success. The expenses of his captivity were very heavy, and he had none to whom he might have recourse save to her. He was, however, ready to endure all things for the cause, even death itself, which would be his fate if he were once put into the power of "her of

---

[450] Cf. *infra* Appendix IV.

[451] The Queen of Scots' reaction to his account of his imprisonment can be seen in the following letters, amongst others: Q. of Scots to Morgan, 17 January 1586 (the first letter to get through after the re-opening of her secret correspondence), *Labanoff, VI,* p. 253 and *Scot. Cal. VIII,* p. 187; to the Same, 20 May 1586, *Murdin,* p. 515 and *Scot. Cal. VIII,* p. 392; to Paget, 2 July 1586, *Labanoff, VI,* p. 358 and *Scot. Cal. VIII,* p. 495.

England".[452] To God, indeed, he had resigned his life and death with all confidence, that He would dispose of his life for His glory. He felt no discouragement in his imprisonment but rather practised patience, though when he called to mind that his captivity and death might cause "decay to her service" then, indeed, was he troubled. Many Englishmen were ready to adventure their lives to prevent his being taken to England,[453] and though the King of France had so far refused to hand him over to the Queen of England despite the offer she had made as an inducement to do so, of two millions of gold, to wage war in Flanders and against the Guise faction in France,[454] the danger still persisted that he might eventually yield; for she had recently sent Wade as a special envoy to urge her demand.[455] This, then, might be his last letter to her Majesty of Scotland and so humbly on his knees he begged her, whatever befell him, to have a gracious memory of him, protesting, as he did twice in the same letter, that he had ever been faithful in her service. Still on his knees, he further requested her to have two masses said daily at St. Paul's for the repose of his soul; and with the advice of Lord Paget, Dr. Lewis, Dr. Allen, Charles Paget, Charles Arundel, Thomas Throckmorton, Richard Gilford and Godfrey Foljambe, friends in his exile, he desired her to give to each of the afore-named and all the friends of his banishment, some jewel in memory of his goodwill to them. He then recommended the various members of his family to her, and begged her to make some gift to the poor that they might pray for his soul, and gave a long list of persons to whom he desired her to give some token in memory of him,[456] adding that there were many others whom friendship bound

[452] Readers will recall how, so far from being ready to endure all things for the cause, he had some years before fled to France to escape imprisonment (cf. *supra* Chapter V, section 4).

[453] It may be remembered that at this very time Morgan was considered by the English exiles to be an agent of the English councillors! Cf. especially Foljambe's letter, *supra* Chapter VII, section 2.

[454] Queen Elizabeth did make an offer at this time to help Henry III with money, but it is quite incredible that she offered such an enormous sum as Morgan mentioned, for his extradition (cf. Nuncio to Secretary of State, 18 April 1585, R.O. Transcripts 31/9, bundle 82a).

[455] Wade's mission can be followed in the *For. Cal. August 1584–August 1585.* He arrived in Paris on Monday, 14 March 1585, o.s. and arrived back in England about 17 April. Queen Elizabeth was evidently convinced of Morgan's perfidy, just as she was, and was meant to be, of Parry's, in connection with which Morgan had been arrested in France. For her letters to Henry III and to the Queen Mother on the subject, which Wade took to France, cf. *supra* Note 415.

[456] The persons named were the following: the Duke of Guise, the Archbishop of Glasgow, the Earl of Northumberland, the Earl of Worcester, Thomas Somerset, Lord Ross, Lord Lumley, Lord Paget, Roger Manners, Dr. Lewis, Dr. Allen, Sir Edward Herbert, Sir Francis Englefield, Charles Paget, William Shelley, Charles Arundel, the

him to remember, but that he would no further trouble her Majesty![457]

Such fantastic heroics sound somewhat hollow, when it is known, from his own testimony, that almost immediately after his arrest, he was assured by the King of France himself that no harm would come to him! In a letter just about a year later, evidently forgetful of what he had written above, he related to the Scottish Queen how some days before his removal to the Bastille, he had protested to the King's Officer that it was a strange proceeding to use him in that manner, he a gentleman, a stranger, and one in no way subject to that realm. Whereupon a gentleman had assured him that he would come to no harm, that the King would not deliver him to England, which indeed later was much pressed. He had replied that he trusted to the honour of his Majesty of France not to abase himself and exalt "her of England" by becoming a means by which she could shed innocent blood. This reply had been taken back to the King, who thereupon had sent a message that Morgan had a right opinion of him and that he, the King of France, would be no officer to the Queen of England, and he had charged the Captain of the place where Morgan then was—the Officer's house—to treat him well, and had assured the prisoner that no harm would befall him.[458]

The use he made of his captivity to extract money from the Queen

[457] Morgan to Q. of Scots, 30 March/9 April 1585, *Murdin*, p. 439 and *Scot. Cal. VII*, p. 602.

[458] Morgan to Q. of Scots, 21/31 March 1586, *Murdin*, p. 481 and *Scot. Cal. VIII*, p. 262. According to his own statement this took place some days before his removal to the Bastille. He was, in fact, taken to that prison four days after his arrest (cf. Derby and Stafford to Walsingham, Paris, 6 March 1585, *For. Cal. August 1584–August 1585*, p. 326, and Thomas Throckmorton to Q. of Scots, Paris, 30 April 1585, *Scot. Cal. VII*, p. 636). Hence, according to his own testimony, it was almost immediately after his arrest that the King of France, assured him that no harm would befall him. Yet, as late as July 1585 he wrote that he was still "being marvellously assaulted by the malice of England" (Morgan to Q. of Scots, 10/20 July 1585, *Murdin*, p. 446 and *Scot. Cal. VIII*, p. 11). As early as 18 April 1585 the Nuncio reported that when Wade pressed Henry III to show regard for Queen Elizabeth and send Morgan to England only to be examined there, giving the Queen's pledge to send him back to France immediately after his examination, the King replied: "Avvenga cio che voglia, egli non voleva far questa indignità" (cf. Nuncio to Secretary of State, Paris, 18 April 1585, R.O. Transcripts 31/9, bundle 82a). There never was any real danger of the King handing over his prisoner, for one reason because he and his ministers were afraid lest so doing they might do harm to others. "For their [*the French*] fear is lest his confession may hurt others, not any account they make of him [*Morgan*]" (Derby and Stafford to Walsingham, 6 March 1585, *For. Cal. ut supra*, p. 326).

two secretaries, Nau and Curle, the Laird of Fernihurst, old Mr. Curle, De Ruisseau, Fontenay, Dr. Astlow, Thomas Throckmorton, Richard Gilford, Foljambe, Liggons and De Courcelles! His remark in the text above that he had taken the advice of the eight persons he mentioned, is not easy to reconcile with his own statement in another part of the same letter that he was kept a close prisoner in the Bastille, with Thomas Throckmorton only as a visitor.

of Scots is shown by his insistence in his letters to her on the very heavy expenses of his imprisonment, and by his statement that in his difficulties he had no one to whom to have recourse save her.[459] That his expenses were heavy at the beginning of his captivity may be conceded, but he continued to play upon that note long after he had been relieved.[460] His removal to the Bastille was, no doubt, meant by the King of France, at least in outward show, as a gesture of goodwill to the Queen of England, to compensate in some degree for his refusal to hand Morgan over to her.[461] But there was also another reason for it—no other than to relieve his prisoner's expenses. In a letter to the Queen of Scots Thomas Throckmorton, after having related Morgan's arrest and his having been taken to the Officer's house, continued:

> "And in the chamber where he was prisoner, three were appointed to remain, five others to watch him from escaping; and all upon his charge, which I assure your Majesty for the time was very great. In the meantime his friends made what means they could both to ease his charges and procure him comfort, and especially your Majesty's ambassador travailed very effectually with the King in his behalf. So did the Nuncio and some others by their procurement. But it was too soon to have any comfortable answer, and they were desired to have patience till the Earl of Derby was departed. Notwithstanding his charges being exceeding great, who so many months lived daily on his purse, to relieve him in that point, it was thought most expedient to send him to the Bastille, where he should need no guard. And so, after four days, thither he was committed, where he remains at this instant at the mercy of God and this King".[462]

Furthermore, at his trial in 1590 Morgan confessed that the King of France had made him a grant of two crowns a day to cover his expenses in the Bastille. From a letter of Glasgow it appears that this grant was made about August 1585, though he stated that it amounted to but one crown a day.[463] But whether it was one or two crowns, it

---

[459] Cf. Morgan to Q. of Scots, 30 March/9 April 1585, *ut supra*.
[460] Morgan to Q. of Scots, 10/20 July 1585, 18/28 January and 21/31 March 1586, *Murdin*, pp. 446, 470 and 481 and *Scot. Cal. VIII*, pp. 11, 189 and 262.
[461] Cf. Derby and Stafford to Walsingham, Paris, 6 March 1585, *For. Cal. ut supra*, p. 326.
[462] T. Throckmorton to Q. of Scots, Paris, 30 April 1585, *Scot. Cal. VII*, p. 636. Shute, Stafford's man, was with the party that arrested Morgan, and Stafford reported the day after his arrest that Throckmorton had been with him when he was taken, and "quaked for fear" (cf. Stafford to Walsingham, Paris, 1/11 March 1585, *For. Cal. August 1584–August 1585*, p. 309).
[463] "I have employed myself in all my audiences for a year past for the liberty of Master Morgan, as carefully and earnestly—as I protest before God and your Majesty—as if he had been my own brother, without gathering other fruit from it than delays from

was sufficient to pay his expenses in the Bastille, which according to his own statement in a letter to Dr. Lewis amounted to four francs a day.[464] Yet as late as March 1586 he was still harping on his heavy expenses, months, that is, after the King had made him the grant.[465] During this same period he also begged her, and with success, to use her influence to obtain for him a pension from the King of Spain,[466] received from her a prebend at St. Quentin's for Gilbert Gifford, and demanded from her the power to appoint to at least two other prebends, not of course for his own interest, as he was careful to tell her, but for hers![467] And this use of his captivity to extract money from the Queen of Scots was also quite successful on his own account, for as soon as she had heard from him of his imprisonment, she ordered her treasurer in France to deliver to Morgan two hundred crowns and assured him that she would see to it that he did not want.[468]

As for his statement in his letter of July 1585 that he was kept close prisoner and deprived of all access of his friends to him, and of all "intelligence" but what he got by extraordinary means,[469] it is clear that from the beginning, even when in the house of the Officer, he was allowed to be visited by Thomas Throckmorton, Charles Paget, the Archbishop of Glasgow, Maldonat from the Spanish embassy and others;[470] and in a letter to the King of France, Queen Elizabeth herself stressed the point that her greatest enemies had been permitted to visit him—a diplomatic exaggeration, no doubt, but with some underlying

---

[464] Morgan to Dr. Lewis in Rome, 18/28 April 1585, *For. Cal. August 1584–August 1585*, p. 416. Though written in the third person—as indeed, was his letter to Dumblane (see Note 229)—the letter is undoubtedly Morgan's, and is endorsed: "A copy of a letter of Thomas Morgan, writ out of the Bastille in Paris to Dr. Lewis in Rome". How did this copy come to the hands of the English Government?

[465] Morgan to Q. of Scots, 21/31 March 1586, *Murdin*, p. 481 and *Scot. Cal. VIII*, p. 262.

[466] Cf. *supra* Note 391.

[467] Cf. Morgan to Q. of Scots, 21/31 March 1586, *ut supra*, and of 24 June/4 July 1586, *Murdin*, p. 520 and *Scot. Cal. VIII*, p. 461. "Now your Majesty may perceive that I demand not the donation of two prebends to serve mine own turn, but yours, as you may perceive, to which end I shall bestow hereafter likewise as many as you shall please to bestow upon me".

[468] Q. of Scots to Morgan, Chartley, 17 January 1586, *Murdin*, p. 469 and *Scot. Cal. VIII*, p. 187. This was the first letter that got through since the interruption of her secret correspondence.

[469] Morgan to Q. of Scots, 10/20 July 1585, *Murdin*, p. 446 and *Scot. Cal. VIII*, p. 11.

[470] Derby and Stafford to Walsingham, 6 March 1585, *For. Cal. August 1584–August 1585*, p. 326.

---

time to time; and eight months since or thereabouts the King's bread, which is a crown a day" (Glasgow to Q. of Scots, Paris, 21 March 1586, *Scot. Cal. VIII*, p. 255). The Nuncio, incidentally, stated that the King was paying Morgan's prison expenses (cf. Nuncio to Secretary of State, Paris, 11 November 1585, R.O. Transcripts 31/9, bundle 82a).

truth in it all the same.[471] Later, too, at the end of April 1585, Throckmorton stated that he had sometimes repaired to him.[472] And Morgan's means of intelligence must, indeed, have been extraordinary, when one considers with what detailed information about current events he filled his letters to the Queen of Scots.

4. *A note of megalomania in his letters*

Whenever Morgan, in the letters of this period, touched on his imprisonment, there is added to his untruthfulness a note of megalomania; but it is a purposeful megalomania to deceive the Scottish Queen and to impress her with the high esteem in which he was held, and the very great importance attached to his own person throughout the entire world. Queen Elizabeth, herself, so he stated, had offered £10,000 for his extradition:[473] from all parts of the world the ambassadors of France had reported, as a matter of consequence and high consideration, the derogatory talk against the King for having imprisoned him, and had unanimously urged his release: the King himself had declared that he would rather have given 50,000 crowns, a very large sum in those days, than have ordered his commitment to prison;[474] yet the league between France and England prevented him from setting him free—and, it may be added—continued to do so for over two years, till a few months after the execution of the Queen of Scots. All, in fine, were concerned about his imprisonment: French ambassadors in every part of the world, the Holy See through its Nuncio, the Cardinal of Guise, the Cardinal of Bourbon, the Duke of Guise and the Duke of Aumâle, the Archbishop of Glasgow, the Spanish ambassador in Paris and the English exiles, many of the last-named being ready to risk their lives to prevent his extradition.[475]

It may well be doubted whether all he had named in his letters did in fact intervene on his behalf. The Papal Nuncio, Ragazzoni, for

---

[471] Q. Elizabeth to Henry III, 10 March 1585, *Ibid.*, p. 337.

[472] T. Throckmorton to Q. of Scots, 30 April 1585, *ut supra*.

[473] Cf. *supra* Note 236.

[474] The King was not told the name of the person for whose arrest he gave an order. This was according to the instructions received by Stafford from Walsingham: "You are not to name the person (though her [*the Queen's*] letter imports that he shall know his name from you) or the place where he may be, lest this purpose should be discovered and its good success 'missed'; but only to desire the King to appoint one (qualified as directed) to execute the charge upon such person and in such place 'as by some especial person belonging unto you he shall be carried' " (Walsingham to Stafford, 12 February 1585, *For. Cal. August 1584–August 1585*, p. 277. Cf. also Throckmorton to Q. of Scots, 30 April 1585, *ut supra*).

[475] Cf. especially Morgan to Q. of Scots, 18/28 January and 21/31 March 1586, *Murdin*, pp. 470 and 481 and *Scot. Cal. VIII*, pp. 189 and 262.

instance, was amongst those whom he asked the Queen of Scots to thank for his intervention.[476] That the Nuncio, however, made any representation at court for his relief and liberation is hardly borne out by his own despatches. The Archbishop of Glasgow, he reported, and some Englishmen had, indeed, desired him to speak to the King in Morgan's favour, but by many in Paris and especially by the Jesuits, this Morgan was considered to be a knave and, as the Nuncio himself had discovered, he had been on terms of intimate friendship with Parry. In consequence, Ragazzoni had refused to intervene, and thought it well to proceed with great caution and restraint, to show that he himself was in no way implicated in that business; and this particularly, as he explained in his despatch, because the English Government had accused his predecessor, Mgr. Rimini, of having suborned Parry to assassinate their Queen. So he awaited counsel and orders from Rome.[477] This came in a reply from the Secretary of State, saying that the Pope praised his caution and restraint, though he gave no weight to what they of England wrote against the former Nuncio; for it was easy to mount charges against one who was dead. But even for this reason, Ragazzoni should persist in his refusal to speak to the King in Morgan's favour.[478]

Later in the year the new Pope, Sixtus V, was brought to think—by what means is not now ascertainable—that the person imprisoned was the ambassador of the Queen of Scots, and out of regard for such a Catholic Queen, who had suffered so much for her religion, he ordered the Nuncio through the Secretary of State to take steps with the King for the liberation of his prisoner, but to proceed in the matter with the prudence and caution that such a negotiation demanded. To this the Nuncio replied that the prisoner was not the ambassador of the Scottish Queen, but one named Thomas Morgan, who though employed by her in some matters, held no official position. Seeing, then, that a mistake had been made as regards the identity of the prisoner and that he, the Nuncio, had been advised to proceed cautiously, he proposed to take no steps until he had received further orders. This Morgan, in fact, had been imprisoned because he had been accused of being implicated in a plot to assassinate the Queen of England undertaken by one, called Parry, who for this cause, or on this pretext, had been hanged. The King, however, showed this consideration for his

---

[476] Morgan to Q. of Scots, 18/28 January 1586, *ut supra.*
[477] Ragazzoni to Secretary of State, Paris, 10 March 1585, printed in Knox, *Allen,* p. 434; also Same to Same, Paris, 18 March 1586, R.O. Transcripts 31/9, bundle 82a.
[478] Secretary of State to Nuncio, 8 April 1585, *Ibid.*

prisoner, that he paid his expenses in prison. Morgan he knew to be a good Catholic and a faithful servant of the Queen of Scots. This reply of the Nuncio satisfied the Pope and Ragazzoni was told to take no action till further orders were given him.[479] No further orders, in fact, appear to have been sent till after the trial and condemnation of the Queen of Scots, when the new Nuncio in February 1587 was bidden to intervene with the King to prevent Morgan's extradition.[480] Thus, for nearly two years after his arrest the Nuncios in Paris took no steps with the King in favour of Morgan, though one of them had been solicited to do so; and all this is in striking contrast to the action of a former Nuncio when Richard Verstegan had been imprisoned in 1583. At that time his remonstrance had led to the liberation of the prisoner only a few days after his arrest, whom he had then advised to leave the country in haste, lest he be re-arrested at the instance of the English ambassador.[481]

One more instance may be given of this trait of megalomania in Morgan's character, which at the same time reveals also his mendacity. Writing to the Queen of Scots on 21 March 1586 he declared:

"And as at liberty, I was ready to serve your Majesty and all yours, most bound so to do; so had I in this captivity, a special regard that your Majesty, or at least your parents [*relations*], *should have the honour of the recovery of my liberty*, for the better encouragement of others to serve your Majesty and them hereafter. But finding nothing done by them in all this time, either for my liberty, or ease of my charges, too heavy for me to bear, which I do not impute to want of good will in your Majesty's parents and ministers, but to the time and difference, and great dissidence between the King of France and all yours, and the diversity of affairs and business they had in so busy a time to compound all matters, and to repair the condition of friends that joined with them in the action. The Lord Paget and Dr. Lewis moved his Holiness in favour of me, who of his goodness, with high words, recommended my case to their Majesties here. The advantage whereof, Paget and Throckmorton took: so by their travail and favour, and Monsieur Villeroy, the King consented to bear the charges of my diet from thenceforth in this captivity".[482]

[479] Secretary of State to Nuncio, Rome, 21 October 1585, Nuncio to Same, Paris, 11 November 1585, and Same to Nuncio, Rome, 2 December 1585, *Ibid.*

[480] Secretary of State to Nuncio, 24 February 1587, *Ibid.*, bundle 82b.

[481] Stafford was very concerned about it and made efforts to have him re-arrested, but he was too late. Verstegan had taken the Nuncio's advice and disappeared. The affair can be followed in Stafford's despatches from November 1583 to March 1584 (*For. Cal. 1583–1584.*

[482] Morgan to Q. of Scots, 21/31 March 1586, *ut supra;* italics mine.

Yet what are the facts? Far from having waited before applying to the Pope, and only having done so after the failure of the Guises to effect anything for his relief, it was, in fact, but a few weeks after his arrest that he had written to Dr. Owen Lewis in Rome, giving him detailed instructions as to how to represent his case to the Pope. Should no new Pope have been yet elected—for Gregory XIII had died on 10 April—he begged the doctor to procure the College of Cardinals to write to the King and the Queen Mother, as well as to the Nuncio, to effect his liberation. The French ambassador in Rome, M. St. Gouard, so he counselled Lewis, should make their Majesties understand the hard interpretation made there of his being imprisoned at the instance of the Queen of England. He might also report that the refusal of the King to deliver him to England was "well taken", and he should advise them to put him at liberty and wish them to be good to him, Morgan being a person of some consequence. At the end of the letter he wisely asked Lewis not to show it to a living soul and begged him to let him know what "comfort he might expect".[483] All this is quite contrary to the impression he wished to convey in the above letter to the Scottish Queen, that so that she might have the honour of his liberation he had waited some considerable time, and had had recourse to the Holy See only when the Guises had failed to effect anything. The "high words" used by the Pope to the King, mentioned in that same letter to her, are similarly purely imaginary, as is shown by the despatches of the Nuncio and the Secretary of State already referred to above.[484] These despatches also reveal that it was not the intervention of the Pope that had led the King to pay Morgan's prison expenses.[485]

These examples must suffice, though to be rightly judged Morgan's megalomania and mendacity should be studied in detail. And what other aim, it must be asked, could he have had in such behaviour save that of deceiving the Queen of Scots?

[483] Morgan to Dr. Lewis in Rome, 18/28 April 1585, *ut supra* Note 464.
[484] Cf. *supra* Notes 477–480.
[485] Glasgow gave the impression that it had been due to his, Glasgow's, efforts (cf. Glasgow to Q. of Scots, 21 March 1586, *Scot. Cal. VIII*, p. 255).

CHAPTER X

Concerning the money found in Morgan's chamber at his imprisonment in 1585—The papers taken at Morgan's arrest: Cherelles's part in saving these, and the motives of his action

1. *Concerning the money found in Morgan's chamber at his imprisonment in 1585*

A considerable amount of both money and papers were discovered in Morgan's chamber when he was arrested on 1 March 1585, and concerning both there are considerable points of interest. Of the money found, it may be remarked at once, that the statements about it are not in agreement one with another, and that there are some very odd circumstances connected with it. At his trial in 1590 Morgan confessed that this money had amounted to between seven and eight thousand crowns,[486] a large sum in the then value of money; but in a letter to the Queen of Scots a month after his arrest, he had declared that it was but six thousand, which is the same figure that Cherelles gave in a letter to her a year later.[487] Stafford, however, writing the day after the arrest, and no doubt deriving his information from his man, Shute, who had assisted at it, reported that the money had amounted to about ten thousand crowns;[488] whilst Charles Paget, after having recovered the money, declared that it was but five thousand.[489]

But, to whom did the money belong? According to a statement of Morgan in March 1585, the representatives of the English Government alleged that it had been sent to him from Spain for services to be rendered, but he furnished no proof of this allegation.[490] The French authorities at first quite naturally considered it to be Morgan's personal property, and many of the English exiles were of the opinion that it was either his, or belonged to the Queen of Scots; and they were

[486] "Sumario de los cargos, etc." Simancas, Est. Leg. 839, f. 21 (*supra* Note 223).
[487] Morgan to Q. of Scots, 30 March/9 April 1585, *Murdin*, p. 439 and *Scot. Cal. VII*, p. 602; Cherelles to Same, 30 March 1586, *Scot. Cal. VIII*, p. 290.
[488] Stafford to Walsingham Paris, 1/11 March 1585, *For. Cal. August 1584–August 1585*, p. 309.
[489] Paget to Q. of Scots, 18 July 1585, *Scot. Cal. VIII*, p. 26.
[490] Morgan to Q. of Scots, 30 March/9 April 1585, *ut supra*.

astonished and even angry that such a large sum had been found in his possession. This was especially the case with Charles Arundel, who at that very time was vainly endeavouring, in his great need, to obtain the repayment of money he himself had earlier loaned, seemingly at Morgan's instance, for the cause of the captive Queen.[491] Morgan himself, however, maintained that with the exception of two hundred crowns which were his, the money belonged to Lord Paget and had been sent from England, and that Lord Paget on his departure for Rome had committed it to Morgan's custody to send to him as required wheresoever he happened to be.[492] In this assertion he was supported, though with some difference of statement, by his friend Charles Paget, Lord Paget's brother.[493] Whatever the truth on this point may have been, this explanation did not lack ingenuity; for Lord Paget, being at the time absent in Rome, could not be interrogated about the matter.[494] When, moreover, Charles Paget demanded, with instance, that the money, as belonging to his brother, should be returned to himself, he appealed for proof of its ownership to an account book of Morgan's that had been seized with his other papers at the time of his arrest. But the book, very conveniently, could not be found.[495]

This fact arouses considerable suspicion that everything was not above board; for Morgan's papers, after having been at first locked up in Secretary Pinart's cabinet, had been handed over for inspection to Cherelles, who had been secretary at the French Embassy in London, and who happened to be in Paris at the time of the arrest.[496] This was

[491] Morgan to Q. of Scots, 10/20 July 1585, *Murdin*, p. 446 and *Scot. Cal. VIII*, p. 11. Concerning Arundel's attempt to obtain a refund of his loan, cf. *infra* Chapter XI, section 2.

[492] Morgan to Q. of Scots, 30 March/9 April and 10/20 July 1585, *ut supra*, and 21/31 March 1586, *Murdin*, p. 481 and *Scot. Cal. VIII*, p. 262.

[493] Paget to Q. of Scots, 18 July 1585, *Scot. Cal. VIII*, p. 26.

[494] Lord Paget arrived in Rome with his two servants 22 February 1585, and was given hospitality at the English Hospice from that date to 19 March (cf. Pilgrim Book of the Hospice, Foley, *Records VI*, p. 556; also Diary of the English College, Rome, *Ibid.*, p. 115).

[495] "The same day I had answer from Brulard [*one of the secretaries of Henry III*], protesting that he had sent all [*Morgan's papers*] that were found in Pinard's cabinet . . . that Charles Paget had been with him and very importunate to demand the money found in Morgan's coffers, saying it was his brother's, and for testimony desired to refer to a book of accounts found in Morgan's study; which Brulard sought for (as he said) in Pinard's cabinet, but could not find, nor ever heard of. But I requested it at his hands, being assured by Shute that there was such a one, and also a book of memorials, which also he [*Brulard*] assured me he never saw or heard of" (Stafford to Walsingham, Paris, 4 May 1585, *For. Cal. August 1584–August 1585*, p. 457).

[496] On Morgan's papers and the way Cherelles juggled with them, cf. *infra* Section 2 of this chapter.

the same Cherelles who had betrayed to Walsingham for a considerable time, when at the embassy in London, the letters of the Queen of Scots, and who according to his own statement had, unknown to others, been an intimate friend of Morgan for some years past.[497] As Morgan's friend, he would naturally have wished to do everything possible to help him—Morgan, in fact, mentioned the services rendered to him by Cherelles on this occasion[498]—and it would have been an easy matter to have produced the account book in support of the assertions of Morgan and Paget that the money taken belonged to the latter's brother. But he did not do so, Paget perhaps acting in conjunction with him and knowing that he would not do so, when he referred to the book for confirmation of his brother's claim to the money. The action of Cherelles certainly suggests that the book contained matter damaging to Morgan.[499]

Furthermore, it certainly seems odd that if the money really belonged to Lord Paget, he should have made the long journey to Rome, taking with him two servants, in order to beg for a pension from the Pope;[500] and then have proceeded thence to Spain to procure the punctual payment of the pension which Philip II had granted him a year or so earlier.[501] These journeys must have entailed considerable expenditure, and he added thereto in Rome by taking into his service the English

[497] " . . . I had the means of doing good service to you and to the said Morgan, and to many others . . . and this so much the more easily that no one knew I had any acquaintance or familiarity with him, with whom, nevertheless, I have been intimate for the last eight years" (Cherelles to Q. of Scots, 30 March 1586, *Scot. Cal. VIII*, p. 290). He was referring to his action as regards Morgan's papers, cf. *infra in text*.

[498] "To save my papers, and especially those about which I was most troubled, Cherelles did me a turn of a very good friend, showing himself very careful of my estate at this stroke, etc. For by good fortune my papers, by order of Brulard and Pinard, fell into the hands of the said Cherelles, and by his friendship I had the favour to withdraw such as I would, for the good of those who had had business with me, and among others the letters of Sir Francis Englefield, and all papers which concerned you, of which I made mention in my last" (Morgan to Q. of Scots, 20 March 1586, *Scot. Cal. VIII*, p. 255).

[499] For Cherelles dealings with Morgan's papers, cf. *infra*. It must always be kept in mind that Walsingham, if Morgan was his agent, would certainly not wish Stafford to know it; for he distrusted Stafford, and set spies to watch him (cf. note appended to Rogers [*Berden*] to Phelippes, London, 15 May 1586, cited in *C.R.S. XXI*, p. 88; [Same] to ——, [June ?] 1586, *For. Cal. June 1586–June 1588*, p. 34; and Stafford to Burghley, 6 November 1586, *Ibid.*, p. 125). Stafford on his part, distrusted Walsingham, for the Secretary of State at times withheld from the Queen Stafford's despatches, and the ambassador had recourse to duplicating them and sending a copy to Burghley.

[500] There are several papers in R.O. Transcripts 31/9, bundle 81, showing Lord Paget's attempts to get money from the Holy See at this time. He does not appear to have been successful.

[501] For his Spanish pension, cf. Mendoza to Philip II, Paris, 9 October 1585 and 11 May 1586, and Q. of Scots to Mendoza, 20 May 1586, *Spanish Cal. 1580–1586*, pp. 550, 577 and 581. Charles Paget reported the arrival of his brother in Madrid in a letter to the Queen of Scots, 4/14 February 1585/6 (*Murdin*, p. 463 and *Scot. Cal. VII*, p. 28, where the same letter is placed under the wrong year, as is clearly to be seen, firstly from the

organist Peter Philips, who then travelled with him to Spain.[502] More-over, Thomas Rogers or Berden, Walsingham's spy, who as a pre-tended Catholic consorted freely with the English exiles, and whose factual information, apart from his interpretation of it, is generally fairly accurate, if at times somewhat out of date, actually threw doubt on the alleged purpose of Lord Paget's journey to Rome, just because Lord Paget had no great need of money, *having recently received £6000 from England*.[503] Stafford, too, later remarked that Lord Paget and others had made banks in France before they had come to that country and were well stored.[504]

If, however, Lord Paget had received money from England, as both Morgan and Rogers asserted, the question imposes itself, from what source did it come? Certainly it was not derived from Lord Paget's estates, for they had been confiscated on his flight from England late in 1583,[505] and the revenues derived from them were later applied to pay the expenses of the household at Chartley where, from before Christmas 1585 the Queen of Scots was imprisoned.[506]

These odd circumstances: the withholding of Morgan's account

---

[502] Cf. A. G. Petti, *Peter Philips, Composer and Organist 1561–1628, Recusant History*, *Vol. 4*, no. 2, p. 49, and Note 2 of that article, where Philips's own statement is quoted from Archives du Royaume de Belgique, Papiers d'Etat et de l'Audience, 1398 t.

[503] T. Rogers (or Berden) to Walsingham, 18 October 1585, *Dom. Cal. Add. 1580–1625*, p. 154.

[504] Speaking of the command of Mendoza to the Spanish pensioners in Paris to go to Flanders in preparation for the Armada, Stafford reported to Walsingham that Mendoza had said that Westmorland would soon be restored to his estates; whereupon Westmorland had answered, "he should be beholding to him when he were in it [*England*], for so great a good, but for preparing himself without means he could not do that which he had good will to do, as my Lord Paget there and others had, that had made banks afore they came and were well stored to do it" (Stafford to Walsingham, 24 April 1588, *For. Cal. June 1586–June 1588*, p. 597). Of course, this may only be what Lord Paget gave out to explain his supply of money.

[505] "Lord Paget and [Charles] Arundel tell me that the Queen of England has con-fiscated all their goods" (Nuncio to Secretary of State, Paris, 20 February 1584, Vat. Arch. Nunz. di Francia, XVII, f. 66).

[506] Cf. Darell's Account of Money Received, etc. 20 April 1583 to 3 April 1586, printed in J. Morris, s.j. *The Letter-Books of Sir Amias Poulet*, London, 1874, p. 183; Poulet to Walsingham, Chartley, 27 December 1585; to Lord Treasurer, 27 December 1585, 10 January and 7 March 1586, *Ibid.*, pp. 121, 123, 129 and 158. Cf. also *Accounts and Papers relating to Mary Queen of Scots*, Ed. A. J. Crosby and J. Bruce, Camden Society, 1867, pp. 1–6; Roger Cave to Burghley, Stamford, 28 June 1584, Inventory of goods and chattels belonging to Thomas, Lord Paget, etc. 17 August 1584, Thomas Gresley, Sheriff of Staffordshire, and others to the Council, 23 November 1584, and Note of articles of furniture, etc. needful to be conveyed to Tutbury for the use of the Queen of Scots, etc. 2 February 1585, *Dom. Cal. Eliz. 1581–1590*, pp. 186, 196, 213 and 226.

---

reference in it to Morgan's imprisonment, which did not begin till 1/11 March 1585, and then by the reference to the Earl of Northumberland's death, which was not till 21 June 1585. Boyd also printed a precis of the same letter under 6 February 1585/6, in *Scot. Cal. VIII*, p. 219).

book by Cherelles, and the receiving of money from England by Lord Paget after his estates had been confiscated and their revenues collected to be put to other purposes than his own support, suggest, at least, that the money found in Morgan's coffers, whether really assigned to Lord Paget or not, was from the English Government, to be used for the purposes prescribed by them, which the account book might have disclosed. One of these purposes may well have been to continue the bribing of highly placed persons in the Papal court. Solomon Aldred, the initial instrument used for that purpose, was by then known to be Walsingham's agent, and was no longer able to go to Rome for that end without danger of arrest and imprisonment.[507] The petitioning for a pension, which on several grounds he does not seem to have needed, would have provided Lord Paget, if he was indeed so employed, with an excellent cover for such activity.[508]

Finally, two further disagreements may be noted between the statement of Thomas Morgan and those of his friend, Charles Paget, with regard to the money found in the former's room. Morgan reported that apart from two hundred crowns of his own, the money belonged to Lord Paget; Charles Paget, on the other hand, declared that it belonged to his brother,

> "*and other gentlemen on this side the sea, being 5000 crowns, and that no part of it Mr. Morgan's or your Majesty's, as the bruit perhaps may run*".[509]

He further stated that he himself, without any help from her ambas-

---

[507] Cf. *supra* Chapter III, section 3, Notes 214, 314 and next Note.

[508] To add to the suspicious circumstances, there is a letter of Lord Paget to the Council some weeks before his journey to Rome, saying that apart from his departure from England without licence, for reasons of conscience, for which he begged them to intercede for her pardon, he had done nothing to offend the Queen, that he had been loyal to her and had a mind to continue to be so (Lord Paget to the Council, Paris, 12 October 1584, *Dom. Cal. Add. 1580–1625*, p. 128). This letter, enclosed in one to his sister, Lady Lee, he begged Stafford to forward, which the latter did (Lord Paget to Stafford, Paris, 13 October 1584, *Ibid.*, p. 128). Whereupon Walsingham replied that her Majesty was offended with the ambassador for forwarding the letter to the Council. He also, curiously enough, warned Stafford himself from having anything to do with Lord Paget, which the ambassador evidently thought strange and at which he took umbrage. (Walsingham to Stafford, 26 October 1584, and Stafford to Walsingham, 3 November 1584, *For. Cal. August 1584–August 1585*, pp. 119 and 138.) To this Walsingham replied that he was not to send letters of men of mark among the fugitives, but that he could allow those of the inferior sort to have access to him—which is certainly somewhat odd. Can it have been that Walsingham, who distrusted Stafford—the distrust was mutual—wished the ambassador not to enquire into Lord Paget's activities? For a later letter of Walsingham in which he referred to Lord Paget as "our friend beyond the sea", cf. *supra* Chapter I, section 3.

[509] Cf. Morgan to Q. of Scots, 10/20 July 1585, *Murdin*, p. 446 and *Scot. Cal. VIII*, p. 11, and Paget to Same, 18 July 1585, *Ibid.*, p. 26. Italics mine.

sador, the Archbishop of Glasgow, had recovered the money, whereas Morgan informed the Queen that the money had actually been restored to the said ambassador for Lord Paget's use.[510] Both these latter statements can hardly be true; for it is extremely improbable that Charles Paget, having recovered the sum without any aid from Glasgow—a fact which he stressed—would then have handed over his brother's money to the Archbishop for the use of that brother. Be this as it may, the general aim of Morgan and Paget is sufficiently evident: to disabuse the Queen of Scots of any idea that the money as a whole was either Morgan's or hers. Hence Morgan, twice calling God to witness that it was not so,[511] begged the Queen to let him know if she had received any sinister information about him. It must be admitted, however, that the disagreements revealed in all these statements, the withholding of the account book by Cherelles, when its production might have supported Lord Paget's claim to ownership of the money in question, and the difficulty, if it really was his, in assigning the source of it, all suggest that the whole affair was not straightforward.

2. *The papers taken at Morgan's arrest: Cherelles's part in saving these, and the motives of his action*

Besides the money found in Morgan's coffers, there were also seized at his arrest all his papers. According to his own statement, having anticipated that some action might be taken against him, he had taken occasion to go through all his letters and writings; and after his arrest he wrote to the Queen of Scots, assuring her that amongst those that had been seized there was no paper from her or any concerning her, save a short ciphered letter from Sir Francis Englefield, which had reached him the very night he was arrested. There was also a packet of "letters in blank", which he had prepared some time before to be addressed to Germyn Ireton, and even in these there was no matter to cause her anxiety. Charles Paget also wrote to assure her that there was not a paper that touched her.[512]

The representatives of Queen Elizabeth, on the other hand, had clearly hoped to find useful information in the papers, and from the very moment of his arrest showed a lively interest in and concern for them. Shute, Stafford's man, who had assisted at the arrest, sealed with

[510] *Ibid.*

[511] Morgan to Q. of Scots, 30 March/9 April and 10/20 July 1585, *ut supra.*

[512] Morgan to Q. of Scots, 30 March/9 April, *ut supra*, and Paget to Same, 27 April 1585, *Scot. Cal. VII*, p. 627.

his seal the packet into which the papers were made; and Stafford himself requested that he should be present when the packet was opened.[513] He made a strong protest when he found that the French authorities had not complied with his request, but had entrusted the papers to one of their own officials to be examined in private.[514] Queen Elizabeth herself sent a vigorous and angry protest to the King of France and the Queen Mother, at her ambassador not having been allowed to inspect Morgan's ciphers and writings—a worse insult, so she declared, than the refusal to extradite the prisoner, as if the King made more account of a villain than a prince.[515] Time and again demand was made that the papers be handed over to her ambassador: indeed, one gathers the impression from the documents that greater insistence was made about this than on the extradition of Morgan himself; but always the demand was met by one excuse after another for not doing so.[516] Clearly, the French authorities were determined not to part with the papers without a previous private examination of them by one of their own officials; and this, as well as the refusal to deliver up the prisoner himself was, as Derby reported, not out of regard for Morgan, but for fear that hurt might thereby ensue to others, among them, no doubt, was included the Scottish Queen.[517]

The Frenchman who was deputed to go through the papers was Cherelles, a former secretary of the French embassy in London, who happened at the time to be in Paris. He has left an account of how he carried out his task, which to some extent can be verified from other sources. In a letter to the Queen of Scots a year or so after Morgan's arrest, when he was again in England, after recalling what he had done on that occasion, and how he had carried out the King's command about the papers in a short time, he continued that,

"in this matter I had the means of doing good service to you and to the said Morgan, and to many others of your good and faithful servants, and this so much the more easily that no one knew I had any acquaintance or familiarity with him, with whom, neverthe-

[513] Stafford to Walsingham, Paris, 1 March and 4 May 1585, *For. Cal. August 1584– August 1585*, pp. 309 and 457.

[514] Stafford to Walsingham, Paris, 6 March 1585, *Ibid.*, p. 326.

[515] Elizabeth to Henry III, 10 March and to the Queen Mother, 10 March 1585, *Ibid.*, pp. 337 and 338. Wade, too, was instructed to protest that Morgan's papers, sealed up with the seal of her ambassador's servant, had been carried away without her consent and privity (cf. Wade's Instructions, 10 March 1585, *Ibid.*, p. 338).

[516] Cf. Derby and Stafford to Walsingham, 6 March 1585, Stafford to Same, 19 March, Wade and Stafford to Same, 23 March, and Stafford to Same, 4 May 1585, *Ibid.*, pp. 326, 359, 373 and 457.

[517] Derby and Stafford to Walsingham, 6 March 1585, *ut supra*.

less, I have been intimate for the last eight years, having known him to be a faithful servant of your Majesty.

There were among the papers thirty two alphabets of divers ciphers, among which was the one which he had with your Majesty, and also many packets in cipher for you and many others:[518] and seeing how much the ambassador, Stafford, daily urged the King to have the papers and ciphers which had been seized at the said Morgan's lodging put into his hands to be sent to his mistress, and knowing that many of the Council were of opinion that his Majesty should deliver them up to him, and even the person of the said Mr. Morgan, for which he made great request, I surreptitiously did so much by means of Monsieur de Châteauneuf, that Monsieur de Villeroy adopted the opinion that that would be greatly prejudicial in these parts for the service of the King and all the Catholics of this realm in general; in such wise that he sought the King expressly the next day, and persuaded him that he ought in no wise to do it, at least as regarded delivering the person; and as to the papers and ciphers, since the secretary of the said Stafford had already seen that they had been taken, one could hardly deny them to him: having heard which, and the gentlemen of the Council having sent to fetch me the next day, and commanded me to carry to the said Mr. Stafford the papers and ciphers of the said Mr. Morgan, and of many others mentioned, your servants, persons of this realm, being sensible of their extreme anguish on this account, I resolved to set all the said ciphers aside, and for every one in such characters to make another, which instead of availing them afterwards, would only amuse, being nevertheless quite useless; and thus I withdrew from the papers all those which were of importance, and only left those which were of no moment. And having had the whole carried with the said ciphers to the said Mr. Stafford, I told him that the gentlemen of the Council had commanded me to bring them to him and leave them with him, provided that he would give me a receipt for them, signed by his hand; with which being vastly pleased, he immediately laid his hand upon the said ciphers, and sent to fetch some letters in cipher that he had intercepted; and seeing that the same characters were in the said ciphers as in his letters, he was persuaded that these were what he wanted; and thereupon he expressed to me the great obligation that the Queen, his mistress, was under to the King for dealing so frankly and openly with her, and that he would go and thank his Majesty. But after having broken his head for some days upon the said ciphers he could never get a word of intelligence. Meanwhile, having returned to the

[518] This hardly agrees with what Morgan wrote to the Queen a year earlier (cf. Morgan to Q. of Scots, 30 March/9 April 1585, referred to above).

gentlemen of the Council, I laid all these proceedings before them, whereat they laughed much, and were very glad that I had thus rid myself of that matter.

Since then, Madam, by order of the said gentlemen of the Council, I have put all the said papers into the hands of Mr. Charles Paget[519] to restore to the said Mr. Morgan, without his having lost a single one of importance to him; and he has caused him to receive all the good treatment he could desire in the place where he is; a hundred other particulars having happened on this subject, with which I will not importune your Majesty, although I am sure you would have been pleased to hear them in detail if I had had the honour to have been able to speak freely to you. I so far persuaded Monsieur de Villeroy, who does me the honour to believe me, that he has now as good an opinion of the said Mr. Morgan as others had desired to give him a bad impression, saying that he was a maker of plots and practices for and against many states of Christendom; who has since told me many times, and Monsieur de Châteauneuf the same, that if they had been at court they would have hindered that mistake from being made of having taken him, much less made him prisoner. I am sure that the said Monsieur de Villeroy will not allow any harm to be done to him, and I for my credit, and the command that your Majesty sent me by Monsieur Nau, will give him all the assistance that shall be in my power, loving him greatly for the fidelity he shows to the service of your Majesty".[520]

Cherelles's trickery, recorded in this letter, deceived the astute Stafford only for the moment. In a letter to Walsingham in May 1585, he dealt with the handing over of the papers.

"I send you herewith" he wrote, "what Brulard sent me of Morgan's writings, viz. nine divers ciphers; a little book of the life of one Edward Throgmorton;[521] the request of the gentlemen of Suffolk to her Majesty, and the confession of one, William Lewis, in English.[522]

[519] Compare: "By my own travail only, without the help of your ambassador, I have recovered into my hands the money and papers which were found in Mr. Morgan's chamber" (Paget to Q. of Scots, 18 July 1585, *Scot. Cal. VIII*, p. 26). His own travail, from Cherelles's account, certainly does not appear to have been much, as regards the papers, but he may have agreed with him beforehand on the above procedure.

[520] Cherelles to Q. of Scots, 30 March 1586, *Scot. Cal. VIII*, p. 290.

[521] This young man had been a student of the English College, Rome, had died there 18 November 1582, and had been received into the Society of Jesus on his death-bed. The Life has often been ascribed to Bd. Robert Southwell, but the ascription is not absolutely certain. A translation of it from a Latin manuscript at Stonyhurst is printed in Foley, *Records IV*, pp. 288ff. The copy of the Life in the Record Office is, no doubt, that mentioned by Stafford and sent by him to Walsingham.

[522] According to his confession, William Lewis was supposed to have been sent over with the consent of Queen Elizabeth to murder Morgan. Stafford took hold of the man and "stayed" him in his house for a time, but protested to the King of France that the

There is nothing else worth looking into, the rest being a book of the Bishop of Ross on the Queen of Scots' title; a letter to Charles Paget from the counsellors of Rouen about a trifling process, and other things of no moment, as Shute can tell you, who was present both at the taking and at my receiving of them, and could best guess what quantity was missing.

They were brought to me by Arnault [*Cherelles*] who was Mauvissière's secretary in England, and is now one of the secretaries of the King's Chambers.[523] I laid afore him all the ciphers and the letter of Morgan's in cipher that you sent me in the summer, to see if any of them would decipher it, but they would not;[524] whereupon I desired him to tell M. Brulard that if no others were sent to me I should be fain to complain to the King. Shute, also affirmed afore him that there wanted a great many things of those that were wrapped in a cloth and sealed up by him".[525]

Despite, however, the complaints of Stafford, no more papers of Morgan were given to him. Those that Cherelles had extracted and retained from the packet were handed over by him to Morgan's friend

[523] Cherelles returned to England with the new ambassador, his cousin Châteauneuf, about August 1585 (cf. Arnault [*Cherelles*] to Walsingham, Paris, 16 February 1585, in which letter he told Walsingham of his promise to accompany Châteauneuf when he came to London to take up his post as ambassador. *Ibid.*, p. 285).

[524] Stafford was referring to a letter of Morgan to Sir Francis Englefield, 22 July 1584, found in an intercepted packet for Spain, which seemed to contain something touching the succession, but the names being in cipher, and single symbols not being decipherable, Walsingham had sent it to Stafford in the hope that someone in Paris might be able to decipher it—evidently without success (cf. Walsingham to Stafford, 10 December 1584, and Stafford to Walsingham, 29 December 1584, *Ibid.*, pp. 185 and 207).

[525] Stafford to Walsingham, Paris, 4 May 1585, *Ibid.*, p. 457. The account book of Morgan, already referred to, was one of the things which Shute averred to have been amongst the papers seized and sealed.

Queen would rather lose the best morsel in her realm than seek the murder of anybody by extraordinary means; and that as he himself was also touched in it, he further protested to the King that he had never heard of any such thing; and that, although if Morgan were condemned by justice, for lack of a hangman, he would willingly hang him himself, yet not for the best duchy in England would he favour his murder or anyone else's by extraordinary means. If anyone in her realm had practised any such thing, or used her name in it, he was sure her Majesty would punish him as he deserved. Though Lewis stood to it that Topcliffe had used all manner of speeches, as were recorded in the confession, Stafford discounted the whole business and let Lewis go quietly back to his master, believing that the confession had been sent among the papers purposely to see whether he would be moved by it or no. He asserted that Topcliffe had never written to him in his life about it, or about anything else, but had sent a letter to his wife recommending Lewis without naming the matter, which Stafford took "not well sending him for such a purpose (if it be true)". Were he a private person he would write to Topcliffe but being as he was, he begged Walsingham to do so. He would seek as much as he or any man living to have justice upon such a villain as Morgan, but he could not "take it well to be put before the world as a shrouder of a murderer or any villainy" (cf. Stafford to Walsingham, Paris, 4 May 1585, *For. Cal. August 1584–August 1585*, p. 457).

and collaborator, Charles Paget.[526] The statement, therefore, at his trial in 1590, about these papers seized in 1585 in Morgan's lodgings, was substantially correct.[527]

A further question about his papers arises, however: was it really the Queen of Scots whom Cherelles was protecting by his action?[528] Despite his letter to her, quoted above, claiming that it was so, certain evidence decidely points to a negative answer to the question. For it was this same Cherelles who, when secretary of the French ambassador, Mauvissière, whilst pretending to be a friend of the Scottish Queen, had delivered to Walsingham copies of her letters.[529] After his return to London in August 1585 with his cousin, Châteauneuf, the new ambassador, suspicion was soon aroused in the French authorities that he had been corrupted by Walsingham, and in consequence Châteauneuf, without apparently being told the reason, was ordered to send him back to France.[530] Knowing that he was recalled, Cherelles obtained permission, at a time when the Queen of Scots was being kept under the strictest surveillance, to pay her a visit at Chartley, though only a few months before, on his return from France, he had not been allowed to visit her in connection with her dowry, despite her earnest request to Queen Elizabeth for him to do so.[531]

This visit to Chartley he used to good effect, and obtained from the captive Queen a gift of five hundred crowns for the services he had rendered her! His letter to Nau on his return from

[526] Cherelles to Q. of Scots, 30 March 1585, *ut supra.*

[527] Cf. *supra* Chapter IV, section 2.

[528] At the time he wrote his letter to her, he had received notice to return to France, though probably not informed of the reason—the suspicion aroused that he had been corrupted by Walsingham (cf. next Note).

[529] The copies of the letters are in his handwriting (cf. *Labanoff, V*, pp. 429 and 430). Note also Cherelles's letter there printed, begging that his knavery might be kept secret; for he would not have it discovered for all the gold in the world, on account of the shame that would come upon him, and possibly the loss of life, which he considered secondary to his shame! Cf. also *Ibid.*, p. 361. His knavery probably began soon after April 1583, for H. Fagot, a spy in the French embassy in London, informed Walsingham in that month that Cherelles could be bought! (Cf. H. Fagot to Walsingham, 29 April 1583, *Scot. Cal. VI*, p. 430, and *supra* Note 89, where the letter is quoted).

[530] Cf. Glasgow to Q. of Scots, 21 March 1586, *Scot. Cal. VIII*, p. 255; Rogers (or Berden) to ——, [June?] 1586, *For. Cal. June 1586–June 1588*, p. 34. Speaking of Stafford, Rogers wrote: "that he imparteth also his said secrets to Charles Arundel and that he told him that M. Arnault [*Cherelles*], that lately attended upon the French ambassador here was a spy for the right honourable, your good master [*Walsingham*] and that he gave him at his first entertainment a chain of gold, upon his promise to perform that office; which matter was delivered to the Queen Mother, who presently was much perplexed with the matter, and gave orders to remove him from hence" Cf. also *supra* Note 363.

[531] Cf. Requests of the Queen of Scots to Queen Elizabeth, 17 August 1585; Q. of Scots to Mauvissière and Another, 6 September 1585, and Poulet to Walsingham, Tutbury, 7 September 1585, *Scot. Cal. VIII*, pp. 67, 93 and 99.

Chartley reveals both his hypocrisy and his greed, the root cause of his treachery.

"I say, praying you humbly, Sir," he wrote in the course of this letter, "as you are a good and faithful witness that I have lost no occasion these ten years past of doing humble and faithful service to the Queen, your good mistress, which has been in my power, as her Majesty has done me the honour to testify to me the thanks that she gave me for the same, and having resolved to continue all my life to do as much as shall be possible to me, seeing that so fine an occasion presented itself at the coming of Monsieur de Châteauneuf into this kingdom, where I judged well the need there was to establish her service. I thought that, cost what it might, I ought not to fail to come hither for that purpose.[532] But having already rendered all my kinsfolk ill content at the long time they deem I have lost in the past, and knowing that they would never approve of my voyage without some apparent reason, I was constrained to tell them I was coming to gather some fruit of my labours and recompense for my past services, and that having never cost the Queen [*of Scots*] anything, as you know, she would not deny me some good present".

He then discussed with Nau the possibility of obtaining another five hundred crowns from the Scottish Queen, payable on her seignorial rights in France,[533]—and all this from one who, indubitably, had copied her letters and delivered the copies to Walsingham! Furthermore, in a letter of 2 April 1586 he reported to her the plan of sending him as ambassador to the King of Scots, and that he had waited from day to day to find some means of being able to write to her about it in order to know in what way he could serve her in that capacity; but that the delay had caused the appointment of the Baron d'Esneval in his place.[534]

[532] Of course this was not the reason. He had already betrayed her letters, and his return to England had probably been concerned with Walsingham. The appointment of Châteauneuf, who was, so Walsingham reported, devoted to the Guises, was unwelcome to the English Secretary of State. He even suggested to Stafford that he might work diplomatically for the continuance of Mauvissière as ambassador, as the latter had ceased his secret dealing with the Queen of Scots. To have such a man as Cherelles at the embassy, when the new ambassador came, would be a safeguard for Walsingham's purposes (cf. Walsingham to Stafford, 3 December 1584, on hearing that Mauvissière was to be recalled and Châteauneuf appointed in his place. *For. Cal. August 1584–August 1585*, p. 174). Cherelles informed Walsingham as early as February 1585, that he had promised to accompany his cousin, Châteauneuf, when he took up his post in London (cf. *supra* Note 523).

[533] Cherelles to Nau, 22 March 1586, *Scot. Cal. VIII*, p. 278. He was still in England when he wrote this letter.

[534] Cherelles to Q. of Scots, London, 2 April 1586, *Ibid.*, p. 297. The French authorities, it may be remarked, would hardly have appointed as ambassador to the King of Scots, one

In the light of these facts, then, is it even remotely probable that it was any interests of the Queen of Scots that Cherelles desired to protect, as he pretended, by his action with regard to Morgan's papers—Cherelles who had treacherously delivered copies of her letters to Walsingham, and who at the time of Morgan's arrest was still corresponding and on friendly terms with him,[535] and who, during his second stay at the embassy in London was recalled, because of suspicion about his integrity? It was, indeed, not the Queen of Scots he was protecting, but Morgan, who had been his secret friend for eight years.[536] Had the papers, the account book amongst them, fallen into other hands, they might have been damaging to Morgan and revealed matter to confirm the conviction of most of the English exiles that he was an agent of the English Government. So much, then, for the seizure of his papers and their subsequent history.

[535] Cf. his letters to Walsingham, Paris, 17 October 1584, 16 February and 4 March 1585, *For. Cal. August 1584–August 1585*, pp. 109, 285 and 323.
[536] Cf. Cherelles to Q. of Scots, 30 March 1586, quoted above in the text.

---

who was recalled from England because they suspected he had been corrupted by Walsingham. The suspicion, in fact, arises that the suggested plan of placing him as ambassador to the King of Scots came from Cherelles himself, after he knew he had been recalled from England, not uninfluenced by Phelippes or Walsingham; for at that very time these two were seeking to have someone in Scotland who was trusted by the Queen of Scots but who was, in fact, in the service and pay of the English Government (cf. Phelippes to Walsingham, 19 March 1586, *Ibid.*, p. 253). Cherelles, from their point of view, would have been an excellent choice for ambassador.

CHAPTER XI

Morgan's familiarity with Gilbert Gifford, Walsingham's agent—Morgan and Paget accused of controlling
the Queen of Scots' dowry in France—Morgan's claim
to have acted with the consent or command of the
King of Spain

1. *Morgan's familiarity with Gilbert Gifford, Walsingham's agent*
A few more points from the charges of 1590 against Morgan still
remain to be considered. One of these, it will be recalled, was his
familiarity and dealings with Gilbert Gifford, Walsingham's agent.[537]
Of his friendship with Gifford there is, indeed, not the slightest doubt.
It was Morgan who persuaded him and set him on to deal with Walsingham;[538] and it was Morgan who introduced him to the Queen of
Scots,[539] and endeavoured to persuade him to stay in England despite
his own wish to return to France.[540] On Gifford's return to Paris at

[537] That Gilbert Gifford was Walsingham's agent is made clear by his correspondence
with Walsingham and Phelippes. Pollen printed some of the letters and referred to others
in his *Mary Queen of Scots and the Babington Plot*, pp. 110–130. The following, in
addition may be noted: Thomas Wilsdon [*Gilbert Gifford*] to Walsingham, 1 June 1586,
Harleian MSS. 288, f. 161, which is in Gifford's hand; Nicholas Cornellys [*Gifford*] to
Phelippes, 7 July 1586, also in his hand, calendared in *Scot. Cal. VIII*, p. 512; G[*ilbert*]
G[*ifford*] to Walsingham, 11 July 1586, also in his hand, *Ibid.*, p. 517; to Walsingham,
12 July 1586, Harleian MSS. 286, f. 136; to Phelippes, [*c.* June] 1587, Dom. Eliz. 200,
n. 65. A letter of Phelippes to Gifford was intercepted by the Catholics (cf. Gifford to
Phelippes, 6 February 1588, Dom. Eliz. 208, n. 28, and Notata contra Giffordium,
20 March 1588, Simancas, Est. Leg. 950, f. 114). Cf. also Gifford's Confession, 14 August
1588, *Cal. Salisbury MSS. III*, p. 346, and Gerard Gifford [*Gilbert's brother*] to Phelippes,
27 December 1588, Dom. Eliz. 219, n. 41.
[538] Cf. Gifford's Confession to the Archbishop of Paris, Dom. Eliz. 219, n. 14; his
Confession, 14 August 1588, *ut supra*, and Gifford to his brother Gerrard, 12 October
and 16 December 1588, Dom. Eliz. 217, n. 3 and 219, n. 13.
[539] Cf. Morgan to Q. of Scots, 5/15 October 1585, *Murdin*, p. 454 and *Scot. Cal. VIII*,
p. 120, cited *infra* Chapter XII, section 1. This was the first letter to get through to the
Queen after the stopping of her secret correspondence about the end of 1584, just as her
reply to it of 17 January 1586 (*Murdin*, p. 469 and *Scot. Cal. VIII*, p. 187) was the first
from her to reach Morgan after that closure. Cf. also Morgan to Q. of Scots, 18/28
January 1586; Paget to Same, 31 March/10 April 1586; Q. of Scots to Morgan, 20 May
and 2 July 1586, *Murdin*, pp. 470, 506, 515 and 519 and *Scot. Cal. VIII*, pp. 189, 292,
392 and 496.
[540] Cf. Morgan to Q. of Scots, 18/28 January 1586, *ut supra;* of 21/31 March, 29 March,
8 April and 24 April 1586, *Murdin*, pp. 481, 505 and 510 and *Scot. Cal. VIII*, pp. 262/
288 and 331; Q. of Scots to Morgan, 2 July 1586, *ut supra;* Gifford's two confessions, *ut
supra*.

the end of May 1586, he was taken by Charles Paget the next day to the Bastille where Morgan welcomed him with delight, though he was sorry, on the other hand, that he had not stayed in England as he had tried to induce him to do.[541] Eventually, at Morgan's continued instance, he agreed to return there on the pretext of presenting to Walsingham the book against the Jesuits and the Spaniards which Morgan had helped him and Gratley to compose.[542] It was Morgan, again, who directed his activities in England, often writing to him for that purpose, whilst Gifford on his part, kept Morgan informed of his negotiations and talks with Walsingham.[543] Then, it was through Morgan's persuasion that Gifford endeavoured to lure his cousin, Dr. William Gifford, to cross to England as a cover for his own activities.[544] Morgan also induced Gilbert's father, John Gifford, to write

[541] "Arrived at Paris the last of May the first man I met withal was Monsieur Charles Paget who rejoiced greatly to see me. The next morning we went to the prison. The gratulation of Morgan I cannot express, only he was sorry of my departure, . . . He bade me in any wise continue my credit with your honour, seeming very willing that I return which albeit I plainly denied declaring the manifest danger which I said could not possibly in time but fall to me. Nevertheless he urged that my credit with your honour would colour the matter well enough, and I ought to spare no travail in so great a service which as he said, cannot be done without . . . Your honour may consider whether it be convenient I promise him to return which willingly I would not truly, except it be thought necessary, for that he will not be so free with me unless I were there present" (Thomas Wilsdon [*G. Gifford*] to Walsingham, 1 June 1586, Harleian MSS. 288, f. 161).

[542] Cf. Gifford's Confession to the Archbishop of Paris, and that of 14 August 1588, *ut supra*. For the book, cf. *supra* Chapter III, section 3, and Note 388.

[543] "Haec autem gesta sunt in primo meo in Angliam reditu ubi quamdiu manseram, et quos sermones cum Walsingham habueram, particulatim de die in diem Morgano significavi, scripsit autem Morganus ad me saepius de eadem re" (Gifford's Confessions, 14 August 1588, *Cal. Salisbury MSS. III*, p. 347). "Morgan was the first and principal author of all my actions in England . . . but in the end all this course will return on its source and author which is Morgan" (Gilbert Gifford to Gerard Gifford (his brother), 16 December 1588, Dom. Eliz. 219, n. 13, calendared under 6 December). Cf. also the only two letters of Morgan to Gifford that seem to have survived: Thomas Germyn [*Morgan*] to Nicholas Cornellys [*Gifford*], 4 July 1586, and Thomas Sansellen [*Morgan*] to Nicholas Cornellys, 9 July 1586 (*Scot. Cal. VIII*, pp. 500 and 515). Both letters are in Morgan's hand.

[544] Cf. Gifford's Confession, 14 August 1588, *ut supra*, and Morgan to Q. of Scots, 24 April 1586, *Murdin*, p. 510 and *Scot. Cal. VIII*, p. 331. In his letter of 1 June 1586, Gilbert recommended Dr. Gifford to Walsingham's care: "The book [*against the Jesuits and Spaniards*] is in hand and I doubt not will be of great importance; only my fear is lest D. Gifford for want or fear of it should faint not, for truly he hath no maintenance. He would willingly leave Reims, if otherwise he could live, and then they lose their only countenance and credit as all the world knoweth. I tell him he shall want nothing and I beseech your honour at this beginning help him forward, for once being gone from thence he can never return" (Thomas Wilsdon [*Gilbert Gifford*] to Walsingham, 1 June 1586, *ut supra* Note 541. The letter is in Gilbert's own hand. Walsingham's agent, Solomon Aldred, had already reported in April Dr. Gifford's willingness to promote division amongst the Catholic leaders (cf. Aldred to Walsingham, 24 April 1586, *Dom. Cal. Add. 1580–1625*, p. 174; also *supra* Note 361 and *infra* Chapter XII, section 3. Concerning a design for his coming to England with a Government passport, cf. *infra* Note 746.

to the Queen of Scots, and induced her, in turn, to write to him, thanking him for his son's services.[545] Finally, it was Morgan who gave him money and supported him, and obtained for him from the Scottish Queen a prebend at St. Quentin's.[546] Many of the facts about Gifford's activities, here indicated briefly, were undoubtedly known to those who accused Morgan of familiarity with him; for during his imprisonment in the Archbishop's prison in Paris Gifford had made more than one confession, and the details of that of 14 August 1588, in particular, to which reference has been made in the notes, had become fairly widely known.

2. *Morgan and Paget accused of controlling the Queen of Scots' dowry in France*

A further charge of the witnesses was that Morgan and Charles Paget had obtained the control and disposal of the Queen of Scots' dowry in France, and by that means, if public report was to be believed, had enriched themselves, whilst the Scottish Queen became embarrassed in her financial affairs. It is to be noted, in this accusation, that there is a distinction made between the categorical assertion that the disposal of the dowry had passed into the hands of Paget and Morgan, and the further charge that they had enriched themselves thereby, which was based only on public report. Persons, who is generally reliable in his relation of facts, and who, being in the midst of affairs from 1581 to 1585, was well acquainted with the Archbishop of Glasgow, the Queen's ambassador, certainly supported both accusations.

"And first of all" he wrote in his *Domesticall Difficulties*, "the said two in Paris [*Paget and Morgan*], opposing themselves secretly against, the Archbishop of Glasgow, ambassador for the said Queen in Paris, they brake his credit much with the said Queen and wrung from him in time the administration of the Queen's dowry in France, which was some 30,000 crowns a year, by which they were able to pleasure much their friends and hinder their adversaries".[547]

---

[545] Cf. Morgan to Q. of Scots, 24 June/4 July 1586, *Murdin*, p. 520 and *Scot. Cal. VIII* p. 461. The letter which he penned for her to send in her name is presumably that of Q. of Scots to John Gifford [July] 1586, *Scot. Cal. VIII*, p. 560. Cf. also Same to Morgan, 27 July 1586, *Murdin*, p. 532 and *Scot. Cal. VIII*, p. 550.

[546] Cf. Morgan to Q. of Scots, 24 June/4 July 1586, *ut supra;* also Gifford's Confession, 14 August 1588, *ut supra;* "Pecunias nullas a Walsinghamo recepi, nisi paulo ante apprehensionem meam Parisiis, quin illud in genere Morgano innotuit, novit utique me pecunias ab illo recepisse".

[547] *A Storie of Domesticall Difficulties*, *C.R.S. II*, p. 184. The date of composition of this treatise of Persons is given in his own hand "anno jubilaei 1600". H. Samerie, s.j., also referred to the control of her dowry falling into other hands: " . . . and that it was

Lewkner, again, implied that Morgan had at one time been the receiver of her dowry, but Lewkner mixed the statement with many details which are demonstrably untrue.[548] A century later Anthony à Wood, basing himself in part on Lewkner, positively asserted that the Queen of Scots made Morgan her receiver of the profits of her dowry.[549]

It would certainly seem that the rents from some of her estates were overvalued at the time when her dowry was assigned to her. The troubles, moreover, in France during the civil wars affected, for the worse, her property in particular; and the King of France forced her, in favour of the Duke of Alençon, to exchange her estates in the Duchy of Touraine for some others, the rents of which, however, could not be collected. Whether for this cause or not, the King owed her at the time of her death a very considerable sum; nor, apparently, was her uncle, the Cardinal of Lorraine, above exercising liberality at her expense.[550] The real villain, however, appears to have been her treasurer, Dolu. Before ever Morgan went to France Dolu, whether through carelessness or dishonesty, had mishandled her finances. In several letters the Scottish Queen expressed great dissatisfaction with the state of affairs under his management, and on occasions asked

---

[548] "Notwithstanding all which, so effectual and forcible were the means with which they [*the Jesuits*] practised against him [*Morgan*] that they got him to be imprisoned in Paris, laying to his charge that he was an intelligencer for Sir Francis Walsingham, a traitor to the service of the Queen, his mistress, and from time to time a discoverer of her practices, and withal procured the said Queen to conceive exceedingly ill of him, and taking the receiver-ship of her dowrie in France from him, to bestow the same upon the Bishop of Ross" (Lewkner, *The State of the English Fugitives*, London, 1596, p. 51). It was certainly not the Jesuits who had Morgan imprisoned in Paris, but Queen Elizabeth herself, as has been shown; nor did the Queen of Scots conceive an ill opinion of him, but quite the reverse, as is evident from her own letters. There is not a particle of evidence that she took the receiver-ship from Morgan, if he ever had it, and gave it to the Bishop of Ross and it is in itself extremely improbable. Lewkner, indeed, mixed so much fiction into his grain of fact, that unless supported by other evidence, all his statements must be received with extreme caution.

[549] *Athenae Oxoniensis*, Ed. London, 1813, *I*, p. 605. From Anthony à Wood the statement passed to *Murdin*, p. 439 note. Lingard, too, probably on Murdin's authority or that of Wood, asserted the same (cf. Lingard, *History of England*, London, 1888, *VI*, p. 404). Neither Wood nor Murdin knew of the document "Sobre el negotio de Morgan" at Simancas (see Chapter IV *supra*), nor of Persons's *Domesticall Difficulties* (*C.R.S. II*).

[550] Cf. Q. of Scots to Glasgow, June 1574, *Labanoff, IV*, p. 175; Note of Glasgow on the Dowry of the Queen of Scots, *Scot. Cal. V*, p. 224; Q. of Scots to Glasgow, 10 July 1581, *Labanoff, V*, p. 238 and *Scot. Cal. VI*, p. 40; to Same, 8 November 1582, *Labanoff, V*, p. 339 and to Mauvissière, 12 August 1585, *Ibid., VI*, p. 195. For the debt due to the Queen by the French King at the time of her death, cf. *Parties dues par le Roy à la déffunte Royne d'Escosse*, printed by Teulet, *Relations Politiques de la France et de l'Espagne avec l'Ecosse au XVIe siècle*, 1862, *IV*, p. 205.

---

not without cause that some snatched away from your Majesty's hands all your revenue ... " He had just referred to a report that she had wasted it on superfluities (La Rue [*Samerie*] to Q. of Scots, Châlons, 24 October 1585, *Scot. Cal. VIII*, p. 145).

advice from her uncle and from the Archbishop of Glasgow and from the Bishop of Ross, as to finding one suitable to take his place as treasurer.[551] Nothing, however, seems to have come of it, and Dolu continued in office for some years, and her affairs in the same state of mismanagement, despite her frequent complaints,[552] though in 1580 he appears to have been replaced by Cherelles's brother.[553] It had been agreed, indeed, that the treasurer should send her yearly two thousand crowns for her expenses,[554] but it is very doubtful whether she received such a sum regularly. As late as 1583 the mishandling of her dowry was the subject of strong complaints by Glasgow, and appears to have been common knowledge.[555] Certainly she was often in stress for want of money, and never more so than in 1585, as is shown by her letters to Mauvissière asking for financial help,[556] though she did receive, apparently from her dowry, £190 about the end of that year.[557]

One source of trouble appears to have been the number of French officials who battened on her estates. In 1580 Mauvissière, the French ambassador in England, reported to Burghley that 33,000 crowns were

[551] Cf. Q. of Scots to Burghley, 9 February 1574, *Labanoff, IV*, p. 103; Declaration of the Q. of Scots, as regards her dowry, 29 April 1574, *Ibid.*, p. 137; Q. of Scots to Glasgow, 8 May, June and 4 September 1574, *Ibid.*, pp. 161, 175, and 216; Memorial sent by her to France, 22 September 1574, and her letter to Glasgow and the Cardinal of Lorraine, 9 January 1575, *Ibid.*, pp. 229 and 248.

[552] Cf. Q. of Scots to Dolu, 10 March 1576, *Ibid.*, p. 304; Same to Mauvissière, 12 March 1576, *Scot. Cal. V*, p. 214; to Glasgow, 21 May and 1 June 1576, *Labanoff, IV*, p. 311; to Same, 31 August 1577, and Nau to his brother, 31 August 1577, *Scot. Cal. V*, pp. 239 and 241; Q. of Scots to Glasgow, 6 November 1577 to Cardinal of Guise, 2 January 1578, and to Glasgow, 24 June 1579, *Labanoff, V*, pp. 2, 13 and 83.

[553] "Arnold [*i.e. Cherelles*], Mauvissière's secretary, has stayed here ever since my coming. His brother is now made the Scottish Queen's treasurer, and she has appointed Arnold a pension of 2000 francs" (Cobham to Walsingham, 13 January 1580, *For. Cal. 1579–1580*, p. 128). Later he reported: "Arnold, secretary of Mauvissière, is still here. His brother has now received his patent from the Scottish Queen to be her treasurer, and enters into the accounts of his office at midsummer" (Same to the Secretaries, Paris, 29 February 1580, *Ibid.*, p. 171). In 1581 Nau's brother was qualified by Mary as "Conseiller et Secretaire de nos finances", at which time Ruisseau, Nau's brother-in-law, had the management of part of the revenues (cf. *History of Mary Stewart by Claude Nau*, Ed. J. Stevenson, s.j. Edinburgh, 1883, pp. xxi–xxii, note, and the authorities there cited). Some details of Cherelles's career will be found in Chapter X, section 2.

[554] Cf. Requests by Q. of Scots for passports, 22 July 1578, *Scot. Cal. V*, p. 303, and Mauvissière to Burghley, 2 June 1580, *For. Cal. 1579–1580*, p. 287.

[555] "He [*Glasgow*] greatly complains of the evil usage of the Queen of Scots here, in matter of her dower, and I hear of everybody that it is so" (Stafford to Walsingham, 27 October 1583, *For. Cal. July 1583–July 1584*, p. 172).

[556] Cf. Q. of Scots to Mauvissière, 7 September 1584, 6 February, 9 March, 24 March, 15 May, 12 July and 16 November 1585, *Labanoff, VI*, pp. 6, 92, 117, 140, 169, 188 and 233.

[557] "She received from you not long since £190. Cherelles has written to Nau that one, Bonruam, your servant, told him that he had received £198 for the Queen's use; by which account there should be £8 remaining in your hand"! (Poulet to Walsingham, Chartley, 25 January 1586, *Scot. Cal. VIII*, p. 201).

mortgaged to such persons since the time she had been Queen of France, and that this was a first charge on her dowry.[558] The same point was made by Morgan some years later.

"A gentleman of this country," he wrote to her on 21 March 1586, "with whom I had honest friendship in this place, being a personage of account, and knowing my devotion towards your Majesty, by way of discourse with me talking of your Majesty, told me that your Majesty in this time being spoiled of your right, was evil served in the affairs of your dowry, and for your Majesty's service wished me to advise that you should put your dowry to farm for three, four, five or six years, and so should you have yearly answered 30,000 crowns, and have substantial farmers to pay the same in Paris, or where you shall appoint, and so be the better able to help your affairs and such as depend upon you, and are employed in your service ... yet the daily decay I hear to be in your Majesty's dowry, and the necessity of reparation which your state and affairs require, do move me in duty and conscience to tell your Majesty what I have heard offered in this point, whereof it may please your Majesty to think. And as you shall think good to propound to your Council, that for your urgent affairs you must retrench the multitude of chargeable officers that you have to small profit to you, and let your dowry to farm, to your best advantage, and therein require their sincere advice and assistance, though perhaps to some of them this motion will not be acceptable; and indeed if your Majesty were in your pristine state, I would not in haste make this motion unto you to make any alteration in your said dowry".[559]

What lay behind this suggestion, it is now impossible to say, but with the knowledge of his other activities it is difficult to believe that the suggestion was made solely in the interests of the Queen of Scots. At least it shows some attention on Morgan's part to her dowry; and there the matter must be left for lack of direct evidence.

Of course, if Morgan and Paget did obtain in some way control of her dowry—and it may be remarked that the treasurer, Dolu, was a friend of the former—it is not to be expected that their letters to the Scottish Queen would have given any direct reference to it; for naturally they would not have desired her to know of it. But there are certainly some odd features in the statements about money which occur occasionally in their correspondence. Take, for instance, the

[558] Mauvissière to Burghley, 2 June 1580, *For. Cal. 1579–1580*, p. 287. Cf. also *Estat des Gaiges des dames, damoiselles, gentilshommes et autres officiers domestiques de la Reine d'Escosse, etc. 1566–1567*, in Teulet, *op. cit., II*, pp. 268–281.

[559] Morgan to Q. of Scots, 21/31 March 1586, *Murdin*, p. 481 and *Scot. Cal. VIII*, p. 262.

case of the money lent by Charles Arundel. Late in 1583 or early in 1584 Morgan, without the Queen of Scots' previous knowledge,[560] raised a loan of some six thousand crowns for her service, Arundel and Charles Paget each contributing three thousand crowns, though what the service was the documents do not reveal.[561] Also, in some way, he guaranteed and made himself responsible for its repayment. No matter how he tried, however, Arundel, even when in great need, could never obtain from Morgan the refunding of his money. In a letter of 4 January 1585, Paget wrote to the Queen of Scots that Charles Arundel three days earlier had burst out in a "marvellous passionate humour", and by deep oaths had sworn before Morgan and himself that he would within six days return to England if he could not get repaid the money he had loaned earlier in her service. To avoid the danger that might ensue to her by his return Paget had offered to lend him five hundred crowns in his necessity, but Arundel had refused it. Paget, therefore, with difficulty had collected one thousand crowns from his own resources,[562] and had asked Glasgow to give it to Arundel as if it came from the Queen's officers, but could not persuade him to do so.[563] In the end, Morgan himself had presented the crowns as though the money had come from the Queen's resources.[564] Such was Paget's story, and Morgan's was similar. But some months later, Rogers alias Berden, the spy, gave a rather different account of Arundel's loan and of the attitude of Paget and Morgan to it. He reported to Walsingham that the reason for Arundel's coming to Paris had been to receive there from the officers of the Queen of Scots three thousand crowns that he had laid

---

[560] She stated this very definitely: "Albeit it was done before I was aware thereof" (Q. of Scots to Morgan, 2 July 1586, *Labanoff*, *VI*, p. 354).

[561] Cf. The account given to Mendoza by Gorion, the Queen of Scots' apothecary, when he reached Paris from England in 1587 (Mendoza to Philip II, Paris, 24 October 1587, printed in A. Teulet, *op. cit.*, *V*, pp. 497ff; also The Attestation of Elizabeth Curle, who had accompanied Gorion on his visit to Mendoza, given some years later, 1 October 1592 (B.M. Cotton MSS. Caligula IX, ff. 29–30)).

[562] Morgan, on the other hand, stated that the thousand crowns were furnished from Lord Paget's store, as well as from Charles Paget's (cf. Morgan to Q. of Scots, 21/31 March 1586, *Murdin*, p. 481 and *Scot. Cal. VIII*, p. 262).

[563] Had Glasgow yielded to do so, it would have amounted to a tacit acknowledgment by him that the debt was the Queen's, not Morgan's. Beyond Rogers's report below, and the statements of Morgan and Paget, there is no evidence that the loan was really for the Queen's service. It was certainly raised, as she herself declared, without her previous knowledge and consent, and evidently she did not know for what purpose it had been made, though she accepted responsibility for it on the statements of Morgan and Paget (cf. Q. of Scots to Morgan, 2 July 1586, *Labanoff*, *VI*, p. 354).

[564] Cf. Paget to Q. of Scots, 4/14 January 1585, *Murdin*, p. 435 and *Scot. Cal. VII*, p. 524; to Same, 18 July 1585, *Scot. Cal. VIII*, p. 26; Morgan to Same, 5/15 January 1585 and 21/31 March 1586, *Murdin*, pp. 456 and 481 and *Scot. Cal. VII*, p. 529 and *VIII*, p. 262.

out in England about her affairs. The money had been promised him several times, but only three or four hundred crowns had been paid to him a year since, and one hundred lately. The rest he could not get; for Paget and Morgan hindered it on account of some old quarrel, which Arundel grieved over. The tension, indeed, between Arundel and Paget had grown so great that the former would have slain him with his dagger, had not Hamilton and the Earl of Westmorland prevented him.[565]

This statement of Rogers, certainly, can hardly be reconciled with those of Paget and Morgan. Nor is the further assertion, made by them, at all probable, that Arundel had threatened to return to England within six days, if the loan was not repaid; for according to Morgan's own statement in the same letter in which he related Arundel's alleged conduct about the loan, the Earl of Leicester had lately sent over a man to France to murder Arundel who, therefore, from Morgan's own words, would hardly have been likely to make himself more accessible to his enemy and expose himself to greater danger by returning to England.[566] As will be shown later, both Morgan and Paget were bent on denigrating Arundel, not only to the Queen of Scots, but also to the Pope and to the King of Spain, and the above assertion made by them may well have been part of the process.

The Queen of Scots, on her part, though the loan had been raised without her knowledge and consent, was very concerned, when she heard of it, that the creditors should be reimbursed for such a long-outstanding debt. She had, evidently, been given to understand that the respective representatives in Paris of the Pope and the King of Spain had guaranteed its repayment.[567] When, however, Philip II in 1586 sent money to France to be used for her liberation, Morgan and Paget cooly suggested that part of the money should be diverted to repay the debt![568] To this suggestion the Queen turned a deaf ear, insisting that the money had been given by the King of Spain for a

[565] Rogers [*alias Berden*] to Walsingham, Paris, 16 December 1585, *Dom. Cal. Add. 1580–1625*, p. 158.

[566] Cf. Morgan to Q. of Scots, 5/15 January 1585, *ut supra*. The incident, if it ever really occurred, may be connected with the appearance in 1584 of *Leicester's Commonwealth*, which exposed the Earl's evil life and which naturally enraged him. Arundel was almost certainly concerned with the composition and publication of this "chronique scandaleuse" (cf. L. Hicks, s.j., *The Growth of a Myth: Father Robert Persons, S.J. and Leicester's Commonwealth, Studies*, Spring 1957).

[567] Cf. Q. of Scots to Mendoza, 2 July, to Morgan, 2 July, and to Glasgow, 12 July 1586, *Labanoff, VI*, pp. 352, 354 and 362. Cf. also Paget to Q. of Scots, 18 July 1586, *Scot. Cal. VIII*, p. 26.

[568] Cf. Morgan to Q. of Scots, 21/31 March 1586, and Paget to Same, 31 March/9 April 1586, *Murdin*, pp. 481, 506 and *Scot. Cal. VIII*, pp. 262, 292.

definite purpose and must be applied to that and to no other.[569] She also informed Morgan that the debt amounted to five, not six thousand crowns; for, as he might recall, she had already caused her treasurer to pay him one thousand.[570] It is to be noted, also, that the Scottish Queen, when she knew of Paget's giving sixty crowns to Ballard and getting thirty crowns from Glasgow to present to Poley, referred in her letters to the repayment of these sums from her dowry,[571] but though she mentioned in her correspondence the money owed to Paget and Arundel, she never suggested that Paget should be reimbursed the thousand crowns that he had reported that he had given to Arundel from his own resources, though pretending that the money had come from the Queen's. Of course, the thousand crowns she had caused her treasurer to pay, and which she recalled to Morgan's memory, may have been refunded to Paget, but there is not a hint of this in her letters. It may be that she suspected or was informed that the money Paget had caused to be paid to Arundel really came from her own dowry. At all events, in her final instructions before her execution, she begged Mendoza, through Gorion, to ask the King of Spain to pay three thousand crowns to Paget, two thousand to Arundel,[572] and another thousand to the person whom Glasgow and Morgan would name, and in this manner discharge both her own conscience, and that of Morgan.[573] The King appears to have complied with her dying wish, and so ended the story of the loan.[574]

Another odd feature in the references to money that occur in the letters of Morgan and Paget is this. On 18 July 1585, the latter reported to the Queen of Scots that Glasgow had stormed against her treasurer because he, Glasgow, could obtain no money from him, and he added that in this the treasurer had acted wisely, retaining it for her service according to her orders, suggesting by this latter remark that Glasgow

---

[569] Q. of Scots to Paget, 27 July, to Glasgow, 27 July, and to Mendoza, 27 July 1586, *Labanoff, VI*, pp. 399, 412 and 431. Labanoff, for no apparent reason, gives the date of these letters as 17 July. They are dated at the ends of the letters 27 July, and the Queen of Scots generally used old style.

[570] Q. of Scots to Morgan, 2 July 1586, *ut supra*.

[571] Cf. *infra* Notes 577 and 580.

[572] He had already received 1000, as stated above.

[573] Mendoza to Philip II, Paris, 24 October 1587, enclosing Gorion's relation, printed by Teulet, *op. cit., V*, pp. 497ff; also The Attestation of Elizabeth Curle, 1 October 1592, *ut supra* Note 561: "Et pour cause son intention estoit et ainsy l'avoit déclaré a ladite damoiselle Curll que le dit Sr. Thomas [*Morgan*], en aultre en son nom requerreroit sa Majesté Catholique d'Espagne, son frère, de vouloir donner ordre que la dite some de six mils escus, ainsy levez et employez pour son service, fusse réimboursée tant à sa descharge et de sa conscience que du dit Morgan".

[574] Philip II to Mendoza, Le Prado, 27 November 1587, in Teulet, *op. cit., V*, p. 504.

did not require the money for that purpose.[575] Yet, only on the previous
day he had written to her, complaining that he could by no means obtain
a warrant from Glasgow to have thirty pistolets or crowns from the
treasurer to give to Poley, and that the Archbishop had supplied the
money from his own resources, but added that Morgan stood charged
to repay it to Glasgow.[576] There is a strange inconsistency here, and
the latter statement, moreover, is hardly in agreement with what
Morgan himself had written to the Queen about the same matter but
a few days earlier, viz. that he had merely promised the Archbishop
to write to her that the thirty crowns should be repaid to him.[577]

From time to time, too, Paget and Morgan paid money to her
supposed servants. They persuaded Dolman, a Marian priest, to
return to England, and Paget gave him sixty crowns for his charges
there, stating in his report of it, that it was for her service, though what
service Dolman rendered her does not appear.[578] When Ballard, also,
was sent back to England after his interview with the Spanish ambassador in Paris in 1586, Paget presented him with sixty crowns, as his
journey, so he reported, was for the Queen's service and the common
cause.[579] Gilbert Gifford, likewise, was furnished with money for the
same reason. But for these two, if reliance can be placed on the letters
of Paget and Morgan, the money was provided, not from the Queen's
dowry, but from their own resources. The Queen, indeed, thanked Paget
for giving the money to Ballard and said that she had written to her
ambassador, Glasgow, to see to it that it be refunded without delay.[580]

To these instances a contrast is afforded by the case of Jonas
Meredith. Some time in 1585 Charles Arundel was accused, seemingly
by Paget, of being a spy and the Nuncio in Paris, having been ordered
to look into the matter, after careful investigation declared Arundel
innocent.[581] The latter, whether as a counter-move to this attack on

---

[575] Paget to Q. of Scots, 18 July 1585, *Scot. Cal. VIII*, p. 26. Cf. also Glasgow to
Same, 21 March 1586, *Ibid.*, p. 255.
[576] Paget to Q. of Scots, 17/27 July 1585, *Murdin*, p. 453 and *Scot. Cal. VIII*, p. 25.
[577] "I have promised by my writing to the said Lord of Glasgow to save him harmless,
which I trust your Majesty will do by repayment of the said sum according to his expecta-
tion and my promise made in his behalf" (Morgan to Q. of Scots, 10/20 July 1585,
Murdin, p. 446 and *Scot. Cal. VIII*, p. 11). Cf. also Glasgow to Same, 21 March 1586,
Ibid., p. 255, and Q. of Scots to Glasgow, 28 May 1586, *Ibid.*, p. 400: "I hear that the
thirty crowns which you caused to be delivered to a man, named Poley, has been returned
to you".
[578] Paget to Q. of Scots, 4/14 January 1585, *Murdin*, p. 435 and *Scot. Cal. VII*, p. 524.
[579] Paget to Q. of Scots, 19/29 May 1586, *Murdin*, p. 516 and *Scot. Cal. VIII*, p. 385.
[580] Q. of Scots to Paget, 27 July 1586, *Labanoff, VI*, p. 399.
[581] Rogers [*or Berden*] to Walsingham, Paris, 30 September 1585, printed in *C.R.S.
XXI*, pp. 80–81. The enquiry held by the Nuncio, 30 September 1585, seems to have had
a definite connection with this charge (cf. Notes 615 and 638).

himself or before it, laid an information in Rome against both Paget and Morgan, and these two sent the exiled priest, Jonas Meredith,[582] there to uphold their credit. In reporting this, Rogers, the spy, expressly added that Paget and Morgan furnished the funds for Meredith's journey at the Queen of Scots' expense,[583]—and this, it must be remembered, at a time when even the Queen's own ambassador,

[582] The career of this priest, Jonas Meredith, a Welshman, like his friend Morgan, contains many curious features. He entered the seminary at Douay in 1574, was ordained in 1576 and left for England on 16 September of that year (Knox, *Douay Diaries*, pp. 6, 7, 105, 110 and 260). By July of the next year he was in prison (*Ibid.*, pp. 124 and 125), on the charge of "uttering lewd words", and on this occasion his confession seems to have been used to arrest his associates and charge them (*Dasent, IX*, p. 389 and *X*, p. 5). He was released or escaped soon after, for he returned to Douay on 16 September 1577, and left again on 1 October to enter the newly established English College in Rome (Knox, *op. cit.*, pp. 129 and 130). In the trouble that ensued in the College in 1578 and 1579 he supported Maurice Clenog and the Welsh party (Persons to Good, 1579, *C.R.S. II*, p. 150). Having taken the oath of the College (*Ibid.*, p. 132), he left for the English mission on 4 November 1579 (Annual Letters of the College, 1579, Foley, *Records VI*, p. 68). Sledd, the spy, who is not always accurate, gives his name as Meridaye, and the day of his departure as October 26 (Sledd's Diary, Yelverton MSS. XXXIII, now B.M. Addit. 48029, printed *C.R.S. LIII*, pp. 193ff). Arriving at Douay Seminary, by then transferred to Rheims, on 19 December, he left for England on 7 January 1580 (Knox, *op. cit.*, p. 159). Soon after his arrival he was captured but set free upon a recognisance (Names of such persons convented before the Commissioners for causes ecclesiastical in London and released upon bonds, Harleian MSS. 360, f. 49). As the documents connected with the affair show, he had some obscure connection with the Throckmorton-Paget plot, and he appears to have been again imprisoned, for he was among the priests exiled in 1585 (Knox, *op. cit.*, pp. 13 and 289). In a list of prisoners in 1586, it is noted that he had been already exiled (*C.R.S. II*, p. 277). Early in 1586 he was sent to Rome by Morgan and Paget to defend them against Arundel's charges, as stated above in the text (see also next Note). Arriving in Rome on 1 April (Pilgrim Book, Foley, *Records VI*, p. 558), he was soon on his way back. At Modena he was met by Garnet and Southwell, and accompanied them to Parma and Piacenza (Southwell to Agazzari, Brera, 26 May 1586, *C.R.S. V*, p. 307). He was sent back to England by Morgan in 1586 on the passport of Walsingham, which Gilbert Gifford had brought over to France for his cousin, William Gifford (cf. *infra* Note 746). By August 13 of the same year Meredith was once more in prison (Prison List, *C.R.S. II*, p. 268), and in the list of prisoners to be disposed of [December] 1586, he was noted by both Berden and Phelippes as having been exiled before and as worthy to be hanged, the latter adding that he might do harm "on the other side", i.e. overseas (*C.R.S. II*, p. 272). He was nevertheless not executed, even though in a later list of prisoners, 30 September 1588, he was numbered among those who from their own confessions were guilty of treason or felony (*C.R.S. II*, p. 282). In April of the same year Anthony Bacon, in return for the kindness shown to him in France, pleaded for his release (A. Bacon to Walsingham, April 1588, *Dom. Cal. Add. 1580–1625*, p. 251). His name appears on the list of priests for Wisbech (*C.R.S. II*, p. 278), and in the Armada year he is mentioned as one of those "who will take the Queen's part" (*C.R.S. V*, p. 155). To Wisbech Castle he was eventually sent and his name occurs in the list of priests imprisoned there in 1595 (Harleian MSS. 6998, f. 20 and Dom. Eliz. 199, n. 91). In the quarrels that occurred among the prisoners there he took the side of Bagshaw and his party (cf. *The Wisbech Stirs, C.R.S. LI*).

[583] "Thomas Morgan and Paget have appointed Jonas Meredith the late banished priest to go up to Rome to salve their credit, which is impaired by Arundel and his party. His charges is borne by them, but out of the Scots Queen's purse. Arundel hath sent Articles to Rome before against Meredith to have him into the Inquisition, if it may be" (Rogers, alias Berden, to Walsingham, Paris, 12 January 1586, printed in *C.R.S. XXI*, p. 84). The charges against him are presumably still in the Inquisition Archives.

Glasgow, was unable to draw at need even a penny from her resources.[584] And, it may be added, that nowhere in the correspondence between Morgan and Paget and the Queen is this journey of Meredith mentioned, still less that she had been made to provide the money for it. The whole incident, undoubtedly, points to collusion between the two men and the Queen's treasurer, and lends some support to the statement of the witnesses at Morgan's trial in 1590, and to Persons's explicit assertion, quoted above, that these supposed servants of the Queen wrung from Glasgow the administration of her dowry.

It may be that the proposition made by Morgan to the Queen in 1586 was an attempt to regularise this situation. In the letter of 21 March of that year, already cited, after suggesting that the Queen should lay up a store of money on her side for any purpose that was needed, and a similar store in France to be placed in the hands of Glasgow or Fontenay, he continued:

"And for that Paget and I live here (which is an exceedingly chargeable place) for no other cause but to assist your service, and to entertain intelligence with that country and people, by whose labour many good offices are to be done, both there and towards Scotland, it shall be most expedient for the good of your service that it may please your Majesty to give order likewise to such here as shall have charge of the said crowns, that whensoever Paget or I jointly or severally shall demand some crowns, the same be delivered unto us, or to either of us, wherein we shall not exceed, but consider as becometh your present estate, and withal I promise your Majesty for mine own part, as I dare also for Paget, by the duties we owe to your Majesty, never to bestow any of the said crowns, but to continue and advance your service in such cases, as yourself, upon notice thereof, shall full well allow; and although it is a jealous matter and a jealous charge, to intermeddle with money matters, and distribution of the same, yet under correction, I know by long experience, and by the occasions daily occurring, that it is very necessary that your Majesty give this credit, as is said, for the good of your own service, which may not be suffered to go to decay. This motion I would never make to your Majesty, but attend your pleasure in all things as becometh me to do, but alas! your Majesty is sequestered from us, and by that means not able to lay down your pleasure in things so speedily, as your service requireth, whereby many opportunities and occasions for the advancement of your service are lost, or at least hindered; and it is a pitiful case considering your dignity, and what

[584] "It is not in my power to draw one penny from your monies at need" (Glasgow to Q. of Scots, 21 March 1586, *Scot. Cal. VIII*, p. 255).

dependeth of your life and service, that there is nothing to be had here for the good thereof in cases so much importing your Majesty; but your Majesty's poor banished servants do deduct from their own ordinary provision, to them assigned by God's goodness and yours".[585]

What were the many opportunities and occasions for this advancement of her service, which he mentioned, he wisely did not specify. And what, it may be asked, had become of her dowry, that a store of money was needed in France? Could Morgan and Paget draw upon that dowry to send Meredith to Rome in their own cause, and yet nothing from it be available for the Queen's service? It was in this same letter, too, that Morgan, having got to know that some twelve thousand crowns were being sent from Spain to be employed for her liberation, coolly suggested that six thousand of them be used to pay the debt to Paget and Arundel. At all events, it seems clear enough, that he was demanding *carte blanche* for Paget and himself to use her money at demand. The Queen, in fact, replied through Glasgow, that she would furnish as well as she could what was needed in England for the maintenance of her intelligence, but that it was not in her power to do more and provide a store of money in France; and she begged her ambassador to communicate her reply to Morgan and Paget, recommending to him, at the same time, the payment of their pensions.[586]

3. *Morgan's claim to have acted with the consent or command of the King of Spain*

One final point with regard to Morgan's trial in 1590 must here be considered. It will be recalled that he then stated in his defence that that all that he had done, had been done with the consent and by the command of the King of Spain. This plea had, indeed, caused the Duke of Parma to delay subjecting Morgan to "rigorous examination", whilst he awaited the King's instructions. From Morgan's continued imprisonment for over two years, it may be inferred that the King's reply was not favourable to him, and later events certainly do not support his statement. After being released from prison and exiled from Flanders by Parma about June 1592, Morgan went eventually to Italy, and appears to have entered into the household of one of the

---

[585] Morgan to Q. of Scots, 21/31 March 1586, *Murdin*, p. 481 and *Scot. Cal. VIII*, p. 262.

[586] Q. of Scots to Glasgow, 12 July 1586, *Labanoff*, *VI*, p. 362.

Pope's nephews, probably through the influence of his friend, Dr. Owen Lewis, Bishop of Cassano.[587] In 1594 he journeyed to Spain, and Aldobrandino, the Papal Secretary of State, wrote to the Nuncio there to recommend him to the Spanish King, as the Pope had been asked to do so by a person of great authority; but the Nuncio was first to discover the nature of his business, and to see if it was worthy of receiving the support of the Holy See.[588] Whether on account of this caution or because of his efforts, after the death of Cardinal Allen in October 1594, to have Owen Lewis promoted to the place of the dead Cardinal, enquiries were soon made about Morgan; and the Governor of Flanders, the Archduke Ernest, was ordered by the King of Spain to find out why Parma in 1590 had imprisoned him—and this despite the fact that Morgan had come to Spain loaded with letters of recommendation from prelates and Cardinals. In obedience to Philip II's order the Archduke sent the King the summary of Morgan's trial held in 1590;[589] and as a result of this Morgan was exiled from Spain by the King about May 1595, just as he had been from Flanders by Parma three years earlier.[590] This fact certainly gives no support to his statement that he had done all with the consent and by command of the King of Spain.

[587] Cf. W. Gifford to T. Throckmorton, 7 May 1595, *Dom. Cal. Eliz. 1595–1597*, p. 37. Gifford, however, may have meant that he was with the Pope's nephew, General Aldobrandino, who was sent on a special embassy to Spain at the end of 1594.

[588] Aldobrandino to Nuncio, Cajetan, 2 April 1594, R.O. Transcripts 31/9, bundle 84a. The person of authority mentioned in this letter was almost certainly Owen Lewis, Bishop of Cassano (cf. Cresswell, s.j., to Aldobrandino, Madrid, 25 September 1595, Vat. Arch. Borghese III, 124, g. 2, f. 77). Ross, in a letter to T. Throckmorton, Brussels, 8 May 1595, and T. Wright in his Examination [June ?] 1595, mention Morgan as being in Spain (*Dom. Cal. Eliz. 1595–1597*, pp. 38 and 156).

[589] Cf. Archduke Ernest to Philip II, Brussels, 10 December 1594, Simancas, Est. Leg. 607, f. 105. Cf. also *Cal. Salisbury MSS. V*, p. 35, where the name "Rergel" should read "Paget", as the Spanish document makes clear.

[590] "Morgan came to Spain, loaded with letters from prelates and Cardinals and, I think, from the Pope, as well as from the Duke of Savoy and the Infanta—all procured by means of the bishop [*Owen Lewis*] whose agent he was in Madrid until he was exiled from the States of the King as he was from Flanders by the Duke of Parma" (J. Cresswell, s.j., to Aldobrandino, Madrid, 25 September 1595, *ut supra*, translation from original. "On hearing of Allen's demise, he [*Morgan*] made every effort to obtain the promotion of the Bishop of Cassano to the dignity thus vacated. But after the fact of his banishment from Flanders, and the reasons thereof came to light, he was once more expelled the dominions of the Catholic King, which he left in the month of May; where he may be at present is more than anyone seems able to tell" (Cardinal Sega's Report on his Visitation of the English College, Rome, dated 4/14 March 1596, Foley, *Records VI*, p. 15. Cf. also Persons's *Certayne Aparent Judgments*, C.R.S. *II*, p. 206).

CHAPTER XII

Some matters arising from Morgan's correspondence which call for explanation—Some other points about the closure of the Queen of Scots' secret correspondence—Morgan's recommendations of doubtful characters to the Scottish Queen: hostile attitude of his faction to her known followers—The fate of a book attacking Morgan and Paget after her death: conclusion

1. *Some matters arising from Morgan's correspondence which call for explanation*

There remain to be considered some points from Morgan's letters that did not come within the compass of the witnesses' knowledge at his trial in 1590. One of these—and a very remarkable one—is that he appears to have had advanced information on the plans of the English councillors with regard to the Queen of Scots before they were put into execution, as for instance, in the case of the closure of her secret correspondence. By 5 December 1584 Sir Francis Englefield in Spain had been informed by Morgan that the channel for her secret letters had been closed.[591] Yet, the fact is that by that date the closure had not yet been effected. The Scottish Queen herself stated that it was since 20 December that she had received no letters from abroad.[592]

---

[591] "At my writing of my last [letter], dated 15 December, upon an advice from Morgan that his means of convoy to you had failed, I meant to have stayed my pen for a time till I should have some necessary or some comfortable, matter to give you, and find some way that it might come to your hands" (Englefield to Q. of Scots, 2/12 January 1585, *Scot. Cal. VII*, p. 521). But the fact that on that very date, 2/12 January, he had received one from her dated 30 October, made him write again in the hope that his letters would get through. This hope was vain; for the Queen of Scots in her letter to him of 20 May 1586, stated that she had received his of 15 December 1584 and 12 January 1585 only in April 1586, (cf. Q. of Scots to Englefield, 20 May 1586, *Ibid., VIII*, p. 388). Englefield, being in Spain, would have used the Gregorian calendar, 15 December and 12 January, new style, being 5 December and 2 January, old style. The English Government had always been anxious about the Queen of Scots' correspondence by her secret agents, for example, cf. *supra* Chapter V, section 2. Francis Throckmorton, too, was, according to the Government's account, first arrested because they suspected him of having been a conveyor of her letters, cf. *supra* Notes 89 and 102.

[592] "Since the 20th of December eighty-four, I received none of yours nor of others abroad, neither any other intelligence of the world stirring in any part at all" (Q. of Scots to Englefield, Chartley, 20 May 1586, *Labanoff, VI*, p. 323).

Thus, the incoming post was not cut off till after 20 December, fifteen days, that is, after Englefield had received news from Morgan that the convoy of letters had failed. Allowing time, then, for a letter from Morgan in Paris to reach Englefield in Madrid, it seems clear that Morgan knew of the closure of the secret channel at least three weeks before it was actually effected. As regards the outgoing post, a letter from the Queen of Scots dated 21 January 1585 certainly got through; for it reached Gabriel Denis in Flanders, to whom it was directed, not in 1586, when the channel of communication had been re-opened, but in 1585, when the closure was in force.[593] So the outgoing post was not cut off till after 21 January. How, then, could Morgan have had the idea of the closure, and have warned Englefield that it had been effected some weeks before it actually happened, unless he had had information from England that such a stoppage was intended by the ministers of Queen Elizabeth?[594]

There appears to be another instance of this anticipatory knowledge on the part of Morgan in connection with the proposed removal of the Queen of Scots from Tutbury. Towards the end of September 1585, as the Earl of Essex had objected to his residence at Chartley being chosen for her next prison, two other houses were suggested for the purpose, one at Tixall, belonging to Sir Walter Ashton, the other at Chillington, the house of John Gifford, the father of Gilbert Gifford, the agent of Walsingham and Phelippes.[595] On 10 October, on receipt of Poulet's first report, which was favourable, Walsingham wrote to say he was glad that he found Gifford's house so suitable.[596] On further information, however, Poulet raised serious objections to it: the brew-house was very small and there was no common brew-house in the town, so another would have to be built, which would entail considerable delay; the strength, too, of the house itself left much to be desired, and those "well-affected in religion" were all some ten miles distant, with the solitary exception of Mr. Lyttleton, who lived

[593] "The last letters he received from her Majesty were dated the 21st of January 1585; since which he had written to her on the 1st of July and the 18th of August" (Gabriel Denis to Q. of Scots, Brussels, 4 October 1585, *Scot. Cal. VIII*, p. 118).

[594] In the instructions given by Queen Elizabeth, 4 March 1585, to Sir Amias Poulet when he was about to take over the task of gaoler to the Queen of Scots, some stress was laid on the prevention of any secret correspondence, by means of her servants (cf. *Scots. Cal. VII*, p. 385).

[595] Cf. Walsingham to Poulet, 21 September 1585, quoted in J. Morris, s.j., *The Letter-Books of Sir Amias Poulet*, p. 94; Same to Same, 26 September 1585, concerning Gifford's house, *Ibid.*, p. 98. In a letter of 27 September Poulet supported Ashton's entreaty that his house should not be chosen, *Ibid.*, p. 98.

[596] Cf. Poulet to Walsingham, 3 October and Walsingham to Poulet, 10 October 1585, *Ibid.*, pp. 99–100 and 100–102.

within three or four miles of the house. As for Mr. John Gifford, he had two brothers, near neighbours to the house, one of them rich and of good credit in the shire, and both of them backward in religion, so the said house seemed to be barren of good neighbours.[597] These objections prevailed, and by 26 October the choice of Chillington had been abandoned and Chartley once more chosen, despite Essex's unwillingness to have his house used for the purpose.[598] It is to be noted that the first mention of Chillington was in a letter of 26 September, and that it was not till 3 October that Poulet gave his first report on it.

Yet, as early as 5 October o.s. Morgan showed considerable interest in this house of Gifford, in his letter to the Queen of Scots, which was to be one of the first letters from him to re-open the secret correspondence.

"It may please your Majesty," he wrote, "many of sundry nations and honourable members have found the means to visit me in this undeserved captivity of mine, and among others there was with me of late one named Gilbert Gifford, a Catholic gentleman to me well known for that he was brought up in learning of this side the seas this many years past, where I have been always his friend to my power, as I would be profitable to all that deserve well.

The said gentleman returneth to his country, and offered to do me all the friendly offices that he may do. His father is named John Gifford, a Staffordshire man, a gentleman of a good house and well friended in that country, but he is at present a prisoner for our religon at London, and so he hath been of a long time.

The said John Gifford hath a brother named Robert Gifford, who is also a Catholic gentleman, and dwelleth within ten miles or thereabouts of the place of your continuance. These Giffords be kinsmen and friends to Baynard [*Francis Throckmorton*], and to Barasino [*Thomas Throckmorton*], and otherwise well disposed towards your Majesty.

Knowing the honesty and faith of these gentlemen and considering their habitation and credit in their country, and as far as I can perceive your intelligence discontinued (though in that point both before and sith my captivity I remembered to discharge my duty as shall appear unto your Majesty, if they on that side perform their part according to my careful and ample instructions given in that behalf), I thought it my part for the more surety and increase of the number of your servants and advancement of your service, to deal

---

[597] Poulet to Walsingham, Tutbury, 16 October 1585, *Ibid.*, pp. 102–108.
[598] Poulet to Walsingham, 26 October 1585, *Scot. Cal. VIII*, p. 136.

with the said Gilbert to pratique with his parents and friends for the furtherance of the same.

This he promised to put in execution with care, and I hope he will show his good will and diligence in the cause. He required my letters to your Majesty, thereby to give him credit and a mean to enter into intelligence with your Majesty. For this purpose I gave him these few lines, assuring myself of his faith and honesty, and for such I recommend unto your Majesty the persons above-named.

I have been in hand with the bearer [*Gilbert Gifford*] to place some honest gentleman and woman to serve your host and hostess for your sake, whereby your service may be the better advanced. He is also instructed how to pratick with your host, his people and such as depend of him or his wife. He is also instructed how to haunt the market-towns adjoining the place of your continuance, to see whether he may thereby find any of your Majesty's people. In all these points he hath promised to travail effectually.

I have dealt with him to see if he can place himself to serve your host. This he will attempt. Yet his coming from these parts will be suspicious in the sight of the curious and watchful sort that have a special regard to all such as be placed about your host, whereof I gave the bearer warning, leaving him nevertheless to use his own discretion when he came to the country and saw the condition and state of things.

His uncle Robert above-named was acquainted with your host in this country. I have instructed the bearer to cause his uncle to visit your host and to renew with him their former acquaintance,[599] whereby some familiarity may be drawn between them, under colour whereof somewhat may fall out of to your Majesty's advantage. This I desire, as God knoweth, who knoweth my heart, and that I have no other desire in this life but to serve God, your Majesty and my country. Thus with my prayers in this captivity for your preservation and consolation. I most humbly take my leave and commit your Majesty to God who even preserve your Majesty.
Written this 15th of October [*n.s.*]

Your Majesty's most humble and obedient
faithful servant during life to command.

P.S. It is very like that one Phelippes hath great access to your host in this time and peradventure hath some charge under him. It is the same Phelippes of whom I made mention heretofore. If you do use him according to my former instructions, it may be that he may be recovered to your service, but try him long and in small matters

---

599 Compare this with Poulet's opinion of John Gifford's brothers, *supra*.

before you use him, being a severe Huguenot, and all for that state, yet glorious and greedy of honour and profit. By this means he may perhaps be won to your service, but I dare not assure you of him as I would I could; but present commodity and preferment hereafter will weigh much with him, and I told him heretofore upon such conference as passed between him and me, and upon hope that he gave me to serve and honour your Majesty, whereof he seemed well pleased, and told me that he would do good offices.[600] If he be there you may cause some of your principal people to take him in hand, and to let him know that you have been well informed of him, and of his good dispositions towards your Majesty, and assure him and his friends that you will acknowledge their good wills, and so see how far he can be wrought to your service.

The said Gilbert is instructed how to send your letters to my hand to these parts".[601]

As will be shown later, Gilbert Gifford on crossing to England stayed some time in the house of Phelippes and then, under his supervision, caused the above letter to be delivered to the Queen of Scots, by then at Chartley, thus supplying one channel for the re-opening of her secret correspondence. In view of this and of Morgan's intimacy with Phelippes, already instanced, can the interest in the Giffords, shown in this letter, be simply regarded as pure coincidence, or does it not point rather to Morgan's having been informed of the suggested move of the captive Queen to John Gifford's house at the very time it was being considered within the closed circle of Queen Elizabeth's ministers? Another point, moreover, endorses this impression. From his reference to Gilbert's uncle Robert Gifford's dwelling "within ten miles or thereabouts" of her place of "continuance", it would appear

---

[600] Was Morgan here referring to a conference with Phelippes as far back as 1578–1583, when the latter had been in France, or to a more recent one? There is a despatch of Stafford to Walsingham, 10 April 1585, headed "Coppy of my letter to Mr. Secretary of the Xth April 1585 by Mr. Philippes" (R.O. French Correspondence). The copy was presumably sent to Burghley, as it is endorsed by him. The heading certainly indicates that Phelippes was with Stafford in Paris at that date, and the conference of Morgan with him may have taken place on the occasion of this visit. It seems probable that Phelippes had been sent to explore the situation and get assurance of the safety of communication with Morgan by letter now that he was in prison. His being in France at this time also fits very well with his letter to Morgan of 24 May [1585], cf. *supra*, Chapter VI, section 3, and Note 328.

[601] Printed by J. Morris, s.j., *op. cit.*, pp. 112–115. As it now survives the letter is a copy in Phelippes's hand. Morgan would have used new style, being in France, so the date of the letter in the old style used in England would be 5 October. The bearer of the letter, Gilbert Gifford, did not, in fact, cross to England till December. Berden (or Rogers) referred to Gifford's "capture" on landing in England, in his letter to Walsingham, 28 December 1585: "There is news of his [*Gifford's*] apprehension at the coast whereof here is great sorrow, and they [*the Catholic exiles*] are the willinger that I should venture home by reason of his apprehension" (printed in *C.R.S. XXI*, pp. 83–84).

that when he wrote this letter Morgan may have believed that the Queen had, in fact, already been moved to Chillington. Poulet's objection to that house as lacking in "good neighbours", including among those who were "backward" John Gifford's two brothers, establishes their proximity to Chillington, and thus makes it unlikely that Morgan was referring to her old prison at Tutbury, since that place was too far away for his remark about Robert Gifford to be applicable.

The postscript to the letter, suggesting that Phelippes was likely to visit the Queen, certainly suggests the hypothesis that Morgan had some advance knowledge of the proposed plans concerning the prisoner. Though his letter, which was to be taken to the Queen by Gilbert Gifford, was written on 5/15 October, Gilbert did not, in fact, bring it till December when he crossed to England. There he stayed for a time in London, lodging in Phelippes's house, and paid, from time to time, visits to the French ambassador, Châteauneuf.[602] The postponement of his journey to England and his stay in London were probably due to the delay in the removal of the Queen of Scots from Tutbury to Chartley, which was actually made just before Christmas 1585. But once she was settled at Chartley Phelippes did pay her a visit, as Morgan had suggested, and spoke with her; and Gilbert Gifford also visited the neighbourhood, and had Morgan's letter of 5 October delivered to her. She received it on 16 January.[603] Is, then, the mention of a likely visit of Phelippes, in Morgan's letter, also to be explained as a pure coincidence, or does it not rather indicate that Morgan himself knew beforehand that Phelippes was to make that visit? And whence would he have learned of it but from Phelippes himself, or from one of the councillors?[604]

<hr/>

[602] Cf. *Mémoire de M. de Châteauneuf sur la Conspiration de Babington, Labanoff, VI,* pp. 274ff.

[603] Q. of Scots to Morgan, Chartley, 17 January 1586, *Murdin,* p. 469 and *Labanoff, VI,* p. 253. She stated in this that she had received his letter of 5 October "yesterday".

[604] That Phelippes was at Chartley for more than three weeks at about Christmas is known from the Queen of Scots' letter to Châteauneuf, 24 March 1586, *Labanoff, VI,* p. 261; and Poulet to Walsingham, Chartley, 9 and 25 January 1586, *Scot. Cal. VIII,* pp. 181 and 201. From the Queen's letter it is clear that she thought it was Phelippes whom Châteauneuf had employed to convey his letter to her. In this she was mistaken. The messenger employed was Robert Poley, who was the first to be used to re-open the secret correspondence, and not Gilbert Gifford as is usually thought (cf. *infra* Appendix IV). In contrast, however, to what Morgan had written of Phelippes, she warned Châteauneuf that if he had, as she thought, employed him, he was to have nothing more to do with him, for though Phelippes had offered to do her service, she knew he was "playing a double game". Even as late as 27 July 1586, she could not believe that he was the man who had been recommended to her by Morgan and wrote to enquire about it: "I remember of one, named Philippes", she wrote, "a gentleman whom you had dealt withal

Again, Morgan appears to have known of the Queen of Scots'
earlier removal to Tutbury in 1585, before the change of prisons had
been effected. She actually left Wingfield on 13 January 1585, stayed
at Derby that night, and arrived at Tutbury the next day. Yet, already
on 5 January, Morgan wrote to her:

"I hear of your removing to the castle of Tutbury, to the guard of
Lord St. John; but of his deportments towards your Majesty I do not
hear". In view of this Dolman was about to return to England. This
Marian priest, he continued, "is a grave man, and one that hath great
acquaintance and credit among the Catholics of that realm, besides
the particular familiarity that he hath with some nigh in blood to the
said Lord St. John, as I wrote to your Majesty already.[605] Whereof
I hope that before this day he hath some contentment, if my letters
be come to your hands, as I hope they be, or shall come shortly,
by the grace of God . . . the said Dolman is persuaded to return into
England, as I am sure Paget hath written to your Majesty at large
at the present".[606]

Paget had, indeed, written "at large" just the day before—which
affords an interesting sidelight on the way in which Morgan and Paget

---

[605] This letter appears not now to be extant.

[606] Morgan to Q. of Scots, 5/15 January 1585, *Murdin*, p. 456 and *Scot. Cal. VII*,
p. 529. Lord St. John made strong objection to being appointed gaoler to the Queen of
Scots, and on 4 January Burghley wrote confidentially to Walsingham: "Her Majesty
very earnestly, by my Lord Steward and me, has charged my Lord St. John to make
himself ready to take the charge of the Scottish Queen, and he very peremptorily delays
it, I cannot say refuses. But I may write, he would not accept it, but rather offers, in a
sort, imprisonment. Since this, I alone have dealt with him, and found him, upon my
violent persuasions, with fear of her Majesty's indignation, that he would obey. But,
upon this report, her Majesty resolved that though he would, he should not, and commanded my Lord of Leicester, my Lord Chamberlain, and me to show to him her
displeasure; wherewith the good gentleman is sore troubled. And now, hearing from you
of Sir Ralph Sadleir's sickliness, she has commanded me to write to Rycott to Sir Amias
Poulet, whom I think she will send to ease Mr. Sadleir until she be otherwise advised.
Of this none knoweth but myself" (*Scot. Cal. VII*, p. 524).

---

long ago to have served me, about Secretary Walsingham. There is one of that name who
had been here five or six days with my keeper about Christmas, and whom at that time I
made be sought about, to try if he had been your man or not. But neither on his side or
mine could know the same, no more than I have yet done in the space of a fortnight that
he hath of late been here and departed but this day: albeit myself and some of mine have
given him occasion to have declared himself at hunting and otherwise if he had been the
man you wrote of. This Philippes is of low stature, slender every way, dark yellow haired
on the head and clear yellow bearded, eated in the face with small-pox, of short sight,
thirty years of age by appearance and as is said Secretary Walsingham's man: which I
have thought good hereby to utter, to the end against his next return, in case it happen,
I may before by you, if it be possible be informed by these signs whether it be your man
or not, and accordingly to use him" (Q. of Scots to Morgan, Chartley, 27 July 1586,
Labanoff, VI, p. 420 and *Scot. Cal. VIII*, p. 550). From this letter, it would almost seem
that Morgan had again recommended Phelippes to the Scottish Queen for his visit to
Chartley in July, just as he had done before his visit there before Christmas.

were working in conjunction. Dolman, he reported to the Queen of Scots, was "of comely personage", and when attired like a gentleman of good calling, as he usually was, might be taken for a Justice of the Peace.[607] He was well acquainted in Staffordshire and Derbyshire and *about Tutbury*. At his persuasion he was to return to England within ten days, take the name of Alyson and, under that alias, to write in cipher to him from time to time. He would also write to the Queen and enclose Paget's letter to her.[608] From these two letters, it would certainly seem that both Morgan and Paget knew of the Queen of Scots' removal to Tutbury in 1585 before the change of prisons had been effected. Was this also just coincidence, or does it not rather suggest that Morgan was in fact in touch with the Government and its plans?

The answer that he was in touch with the Government can hardly be doubted, in view of the already quoted letter of Phelippes to Morgan, of 24 May 1585.[609] There is, moreover, a document of 1586, in Poley's hand and endorsed by him: "The Principall particulars of 2 letters from Mor: and Pag: of Januar. 6".[610] The person to whom the letters were directed is not mentioned, but from the contents it appears to have been some one who was able to obtain directives from the Government on matters of policy. This person may well have been Phelippes, for the name "Poley" was added by him underneath the above endorsement. The former document of 24 May put down some points of advice and enquiry from Phelippes to Morgan, the later does the same in reverse, implicating Charles Paget as well as the Welsh exile: and it is significant that many of the particulars on which information was required appear later in the letters of the two exiles. The document runs:

"They advise and require
1. That the Packet may be speedily delivered, and a sure intelligence made with the Queen of Scots.[611]

[607] Berden (alias Rogers), the spy, cited this description of him, when commenting on the list of "Prisoners to be disposed of", July 1586, *C.R.S. II*, p. 256, which shows that the intercepted correspondence had already by that date been shown to a man of his subordinate position. For J. H. Pollen's comments on this, cf. *Ibid.*, p. 253.

[608] Paget to Q. of Scots, 4/14 January 1585, *Murdin*, p. 435 and *Scot. Cal. VII*, p. 524. The calendarist omitted the words "about Tutbury".

[609] Cf. *supra* Chapter VI, section 3.

[610] R.O. M.Q.S. Vol. 17, n. 2. The version in *Scot. Cal. VIII*, p. 178 contains inaccuracies.

[611] It will be shown in Appendix IV that Poley, the Government agent, though naturally unknown as such to the French ambassador, was the first messenger sent by him to the Queen of Scots to re-open the channel of her secret correspondence. He was sent by Châteauneuf on 1 December 1585, and returned to him on 20 February 1586, the

2. That, for sure advertisement to the King of Scots, safe recourse may be made to the L. Prior Seton, into Scotland, by a special token.[612]

3. That Pan (after the Packet delivered here) go first and confer with them in France, before he pass into Holland to Blo: [*Blunt*][613]

4. That Pan (as in a matter of pinciple purpose) labour, inform, and practise with the French ambassador, that an absolute union may be settled and observed between the French King and the Duke of Guise.[614]

5. That they be informed what course Char: Arundel and Fitz-herbert hold with Mr. Secretr: Walsingham.[615]

[612] Alexander Seton, Prior of Pluscardine, though by conviction and sympathy a Catholic, was a complete time-server as regards the outward profession of that religion until some time before his death in 1622, when he publicly declared his adherence to the old faith. He was much trusted by James VI. Morgan urged the Queen of Scots to take him into her service, in a letter of 21/31 March 1586, *Murdin*, p. 481. A few days later Charles Paget echoed Morgan's recommendation: "For your conveyance into Scotland", he wrote, "if your Majesty think so good, it is meet you understand of certainty, either by Lord Claude [*Hamilton*], or the Prior of Seton, how your son standeth affected towards the Queen of England. For if any about him [*James VI*] affected to the Queen of England should discover the intelligence, and especially the Master of Gray, it were that which would breed much inconvenience, etc." (C. Paget to Q. of Scots, 31 March/10 April 1586, *Murdin*, p. 506 and *Scot. Cal. VIII*, p. 292). In January Morgan had urged her to use Poley for the conveyance of letters, especially to Scotland. (Morgan to Q. of Scots, 18/28 January 1586, *Murdin*, p. 470 and *Scot. Cal. VIII*, p. 189. Cf. Phelippes to Walsingham, London, 19 March 1586, *Scot. Cal. VIII*, p. 253; cf. also *infra* Appendix IV.

[613] "Pan" appears to have been an alias of Poley. In January Morgan wrote to the Scottish Queen to use Poley, stating that he was a Catholic, and that Blunt had "placed him to be Sir Philip Sydney's man, that he may more quietly live a Christian life". In March of the same year he again strongly recommended him to her, adding that it was by his advice that he had been placed with Lady Sydney, the daughter of Walsingham, and by that means "ordinarily in his house and thereby able to pick out many things to the information of your Majesty". Later in the same letter he told her that Christopher Blunt or Blount who was in Holland with Leicester, had sent for Poley to come to him (Morgan to Q. of Scots, 18/28 January and 21/31 March 1586, *ut supra*). A few days later Paget endorsed Morgan's words. "There be two others", he wrote, "which be in practice to gain others to serve your Majesty for intelligence, whereof the one is called Poley, a great friend to Christopher Blunt, of whom I suppose your Majesty hath heard heretofore. Morgan and I have had conference with the said Poley, and hope he is in such place, being servant to Sir Philip Sydney, and thereby remaining with his lady, and in house with Secretary Walsingham, so as he shall be able to give your Majesty advertisement from time to time" (Paget to Q. of Scots, 31 March/10 April 1586, *ut supra*). Neither Blunt nor Poley was then a Catholic, as Morgan represented them to be. Cf. *infra* Appendix IV.

[614] The idea of the underling, Poley, influencing the ambassador borders on the absurd, though what lay behind the suggestion is not clear. After Poley's return to Châteauneuf on 20 February, he was distrusted by him because he had brought back no message from the captive Queen (cf. Appendix IV).

[615] This query could hardly have been answered otherwise than by Walsingham himself or by someone in his confidence. A curious situation, indeed, had developed at the beginning of 1586, as regards the two exiles mentioned. In 1586 Charles Arundel

delay, no doubt caused in part by her removal to Chartley just before Christmas, when Phelippes stayed there for three weeks or so (cf. Châteauneuf to Q. of Scots, 6 and 30 March 1586, *Scot. Cal. VIII*, pp. 247 and 288; Q. of Scots to Châteauneuf, Chartley, 31 January 1586, *Ibid.*, p. 205; the Same to Same, 24 March 1586, *Labanoff, VI*, p. 261; and Morgan to Q. of Scots, 21/31 March 1586, *Murdin*, p. 481 and *Scot. Cal. VIII*, p. 262.

6. That they may understand what is intended here for the employing of Don Antonio: how many ships: of what burden: how furnished: who be the captains: and what the enterprise.[616]

7. That the Catholic part be encouraged, and put in hope, that the

---

[616] "Don Antonio is still in England, and is writing a book to the Queen, and would have of her support of 10,000 men to assist him to enter into Portugal, which maketh Princes believe that he hath special credit with the Portuguese" (Morgan to Q. of Scots, 29 June/9 July 1586, *Murdin*, p. 528 and *Scot. Cal. VIII*, p. 477). Don Antonio was illegitimate son of the brother of King John III of Portugal and pretender to the Portuguese crown.

---

had been denounced to the Queen of Scots and later accused to Rome of being a spy of the English Government, from which charge he had been cleared by the investigations of the Nuncio in Paris (cf. *infra* this chapter, section 3). Both Arundel and his close confidant, Thomas Fitzherbert, were in fact endeavouring to hoodwink the English Government. The former was related to Sir Edward Stafford, the English ambassador in France, as well as to his wife, whom he visited and from whom, as also from Lily, the ambassador's secretary, he obtained information (cf. The Process before the Nuncio, Paris, 30 September 1585, Vat. Lib. Chigi II, 47, ff. 10ff; also Notes 363 and 651). Arundel certainly later had the full approval of the Spanish ambassador for his recourse to Stafford, and was rewarded for his services by an extra grant of money from Philip II (cf. *infra* Note 648, where the references are given). Gilbert Gifford, the Government agent in fact endeavoured, though falsely, to excuse his own intelligence with the English councillors by pleading that he was but imitating Arundel and Fitzherbert: "I swear" he wrote to Thomas Throckmorton, "that I never wrote them anything that I was not certain had come to their ears before; touched no private affairs save in my own defence, and have done nothing for which I had not the consent of the best Catholics. In temporising with them I act as does Charles Arundel in haunting the house of their ambassador; as Suigo has done by consent of Don Bernardino [*de Mendoza*], and Fitzherbert to Walsingham" (Gifford to T. Throckmorton, prison in Paris, 22 January 1588, *For. Cal. June 1586–June 1588*, p. 670). Whether Stafford was playing false to the English Government, or was genuinely deceived, is a debatable point, but in January 1586 he certainly gave a strong recommendation of Fitzherbert to Walsingham. "I pray, Sir," he wrote, "be a means to procure some favour for Fitzherbert that is here, for besides that I think I durst assure you that on this side of the sea there is not an honester man to his country of his religion than he, the well-dealing with him may put courage into many others that have but a prick of conscience and not evil will to the state" (Stafford to Walsingham, Paris, 2 January 1586, *For. Cal. Sept. 1585–May 1586*, p. 276; also Same to Same, Paris, 15 April and Aldred to Walsingham, 14/24 April 1586, *Ibid.*, pp. 550 and 714). But not all agreed with Stafford's estimate, and but a few weeks before Stafford's letter, quoted above, Rogers (or Berden), Walsingham's spy, who was pretending to be a Catholic, and who frequented the company of Fitzherbert, denounced both Arundel and his confidant ([Rogers, or Berden] to Walsingham, Paris, 6 December 1585 (wrongly ascribed by the Calendarist to Barnes), *Dom. Cal. Add. 1580–1625*, p. 157; also Same to Same, Paris, 16 December 1585 and 12 January 1586, printed in *C.R.S. XXI*, pp. 82 and 84; cf. also *infra* Note 651).

It was, doubtless, this division of opinion as regards the two exiles that had led Morgan and Paget to request information as to what courses they held with Walsingham. The Secretary, in fact, took the view of his spy and not that of the ambassador (cf. Fitzherbert to Walsingham, Paris, 31 March 1586, *For. Cal. September 1585–May 1586*, p. 503; Stafford to Walsingham, Paris, 15 April 1586 and Aldred to Same, 14/24 April 1586, *ut supra*).

In March 1586 Charles Paget, having presumably received the information required, nevertheless gave the Queen of Scots a false account of both Arundel and Fitzherbert, making them out to be "advertisers" of the Queen of England (cf. Paget to Q. of Scots, Paris, 31 March/10 April 1586, *Murdin*, p. 506 and *Scot. Cal. VIII*, p. 292; also *infra* section 3 of this chapter).

Pope's levying of money and men, with the Kings of Spain and France his preparation to sea, extendeth and will conclude in some notable enterprise behoveful for the common cause, and every particular.[617]

8. That they be advertised what is done, or said of the Earls of Arundel and Northumberland: what becometh of Shelley, and how the indictments proceed against the L. Paget, his brother Charles.[618] and others.

9. That Blo: [*Blunt*] be dealt with to practise deliverance of some important Town in Holland unto the King of Spain; or to undertake the convey of some other notable enterprise touching the defeat of the Earl of Leicester: whereunto they offer the joining of many fit helps, and instruments, the best on the other side: and that they may have a cipher procured from Blo: for the entertain, and recourse of those circumstances".[619]

Such, then, are the points of these two letters of Morgan and Paget on which they sought advice. Some of the information acquired was passed on to the Queen of Scots, though given a false twist, in their subsequent letters to her. The points confirm the evidence already given that these two supposed friends of that Queen, were receiving directives from the English Government, probably through Phelippes.

There is a further short and undated letter in the hand of Poley which points to the same conclusion. The last paragraph runs:

[617] Cf. *supra* Chapter VIII, section 3.

[618] The Calendarist has misread "Charls" and given "Earls".

[619] In March 1586 Morgan wrote to the Scottish Queen that Blunt "hath also sent the said Poley an alphabet to be sent to me, which I have this day received. I know Blunt's mind, and confidence he hath in me, more than in most men living, having been his friend in prosperity, and his greatest distress. He hath some charge and credit where he is, and his meaning is for the service of God and advantage of the King of Spain; to further the delivery of some notable towns in Holland and Zealand to the King of Spain and his ministers, wherein nevertheless he desireth to proceed with my poor advice and labours, himself being in a notable place to do great service to all Christendom, by aiding the expulsion of heretics, etc." (Morgan to Q. of Scots, 21/31 March 1586, *Murdin*, p. 481 and *Scot. Cal. VIII*, p. 262). There is no evidence that Blunt was ever helped by Morgan either in his prosperity or his great distress. He was still quite young when Morgan left England in 1575, and matriculated at Douay about 1577 (Knox, *Douay Diaries*, p. 277). Nor is there the slightest evidence that Blunt had any intention of delivering towns in Holland and Zealand to the Spanish forces. Quite the contrary, for on sending him home after having been dangerously wounded, Lord Willoughby wrote in January 1589: "During the last four years, he first led his Excellency's troop and then 'a band of ordnance of her Majesty's.' This was equal to a Colonel's rank, which is 'even in a manner with Knighthood.' Has accordingly knighted him, 'though he be not peradventure as rich a Knight as another' " ... (Lord Willoughby to Walsingham, The Hague, 22 January 1589, *For. Cal. January–July 1589*, p. 53). Blunt was a follower of Leicester and had given up his Catholic religion at this time (cf. *infra* section 3 of this chapter); though he was reported to "have been reconciled to the Church of Rome", when engaged with Essex in the Irish expedition (Bishop of Meath to Sir R. Cecil, Dublin, 23 October 1599, *Cal. Salisbury MSS. IX*, p. 375).

"He doth much fear that the Rutters [*i.e. Reiters*] levied (as I told him) by the princes of Germany in aid of the King of Navarre, will either much hinder or prolong the Guises' attempt in France. He received no packet from the King these 30 days: Neither he nor we have any letter from Paget or Morgan since his first coming: of whose slackness being somewhat suspicious, not knowing what they fear or intend, I dare not too boldly enter with him, for discovery of such as repair to, or give him intelligence, for as they with us, so must we with him proceed. And further as your honour shall advise".[620]

It must be remembered, too, that Morgan and Paget sent their letters to the Queen of Scots through the channel of the French embassy in London.[621] But Poley's statement that neither he, Châteauneuf, nor "we" had received letters from them since the first coming of the

[620] Poley to [Walsingham?], R.O. M.Q.S. 16, n. 9. The Calendarist assigned the letter to "about July 1585", but it should rather be referred to the end of October of that year. The "he" appears to be Châteauneuf, the new French ambassador, who arrived in England at the end of August 1585, and with whom Poley was to have dealings, pretending to be a friend of the Scottish Queen, though in reality he was an agent of the English Government (cf. *infra* Appendix IV). In the first part of the letter Poley reported: "He says that this practice and tumult shall hardly prevail against or endanger the King of Scots: and that before the next attempt he shall be sufficiently assured". This seems to refer to the sending of the exiled Protestant lords back to Scotland in October 1585: Stafford declared on the 20th of that month that Châteauneuf had reported the despatch of the Scottish lords to the border (cf. Extracts from Stafford's letters, 20 October 1585, *For. Cal. September 1585–May 1586*, p. 118). Stafford's letter of 24 October shows Châteauneuf's concern at this event (*Ibid.*). Yet the fact that the ambassador, as reported by Poley, stated that the scheme would not prevail, indicates that the news of the seizure of Stirling and the capitulation of James had not yet been received by him. Stirling was captured at the beginning of November, and immediately after its capture the Master of Gray reported the success "of the plot", to the English court in a letter of 6 November (cf. Tytler, *History of Scotland, VIII*, p. 242). This, then, would place Poley's letter in the latter part of October.

With regard to the reiters mentioned in his letter, there were negotiations more or less continuously throughout 1585 and 1586 for Queen Elizabeth to loan money for the recruitment of these German mercenaries. Ségur-Pardailhan came to England for this purpose in June 1585, but returned in July with little more than a promise of meagre help if certain conditions were fulfilled (cf. Walsingham to Stafford, 20 July 1585, *For. Cal. August 1584–August 1585*, p. 618). After Henry III's agreement with the Guises at Nemours 7 July 1585, the King of Navarre's need for such troops became more pressing (cf. Walsingham to Burghley, 29 September 1585, *Scot. Cal. VIII*, p. 114), and in October the Sieur de Guitry was to be sent to England to obtain the desired pecuniary help (Duke Casimir to Walsingham, Heidelberg, 21 October 1585, *For. Cal. September 1585–May 1586*, p. 107; Ségur-Pardailhan to Burghley, Frankenhal, 22 October and Walsingham to Duke Casimir, 3 November 1585, *Ibid.*, pp. 109 and 113). It was not, however, till September 1586 that actual steps were taken to supply the money, and the reiters eventually invaded Lorraine in 1587 and were decisively defeated at Auneau in November of that year. Poley may have been referring to these negotiations begun in 1585, and conveying to the French ambassador the false impression that the reiters had already been levied, as his phrase "as I told him" suggests. But he may also have been referring to the small body of these mercenaries, which in 1585 Henry of Navarre recruited at his own expense (cf. Lawrence Stone, *Sir Horatio Palavicino*, Oxford, 1956, p. 118).

[621] There are no letters in 1585 from Morgan and Paget to her after July till that of Morgan of 5/15 October 1585, introducing Gilbert Gifford (cf. *supra*; also next section).

ambassador, suggests, to put it no stronger, that besides sending letters for the Scottish Queen, as arranged, to the ambassador, they were also communicating with the English Government: and Poley's concern that no letter from them had been received since the arrival of Châteauneuf at the end of August 1585, would seem to point to their regular correspondence with the English ministers. This letter, then, still further confirms the above conclusion that Morgan and Paget were their agents and acting in collusion with them.

2. *Some other points about the closure of the Queen of Scots' secret correspondence*

There are further points arising from the letters of Morgan and Paget which call for explanation. They knew, for instance, that the English Government had in late December 1584 blocked the channel for the Queen of Scots' incoming secret correspondence: Englefield, in Spain, was informed of it by Morgan as early at 5 December 1584, in advance of the actual closure, as already shown in the last section. Yet, despite this, they continued to write regularly to the captive Queen. There are nearly as many letters of theirs in 1585, during the suspension, as there are for 1586, when the correspondence had been re-opened: and every month up to the end of July, with the exception of June, has its letter or letters. After July 1585 there are no more letters until that of Morgan of 5/15 October of that year. This letter Gilbert Gifford was to carry to England to re-open the secret correspondence but, as already stated, Gifford did not cross to England until December 1585,[622] and it was not till 16 January 1586, after the Queen of Scots was settled at Chartley, that she received the letter.

This re-opening of the secret correspondence at the beginning of 1586 repeated the pattern of 1585 in Morgan's and Paget's letters to the Queen. The correspondence again ended in July. The last letter of Morgan was of the 4 July 1586, two weeks or so before the supposed fatal letter of the Queen of Scots to Babington, about the 17th of that month, and a few weeks before the Government took action against the conspirators. Paget, it may be noted, had withdrawn to the Spa near Liège, outside the jurisdiction, that is, of the King of France, his last letter to the Queen being dated 19 May 1586. The letters of 1586, particularly those of Paget—for there were reasons, as already explained on an earlier page, for keeping Morgan's name out of the process as far as possible—were used as evidence of the plot, both against the

[622] Cf. section 1 of this chapter.

conspirators and, especially, against the Queen of Scots at their trials. There are definite indications that Queen Elizabeth's ministers had at first intended the "plot" to have taken place in 1585, but for certain reasons, explained later, their plan was postponed about July 1585 to the following year.[623] Moreover, from these letters of Morgan and Paget in 1585, it is clear that Robert Poley, the Government agent, was to have been used in 1585 to re-open the channel of communication, just as Gilbert Gifford, another Government agent, was actually so employed in 1586.[624] The repeated pattern is unmistakeable. Can, then, the conclusion be avoided, that the reason why Morgan and Paget continued to write to the Queen of Scots in 1585, despite their knowledge that the letters would not reach her then, was that they were advised to do so by the councillors of Queen Elizabeth: their letters being required, according to their plan, as evidence against her in 1585, just as letters of 1586 were actually so used in that year; and that the reason why the correspondence of 1585 ceased after July was because the plan had then had to be postponed till the following year?

The plea of Morgan and Paget, moreover, for breaking off relations with Blunt and Poley in 1585 enforces these conclusions, for that plea was entirely bogus. In a letter to the Queen of Scots of 18 July 1585, Morgan wrote:

"This morning I was informed by Barasino [*Thomas Throckmorton*], a careful servant to your Majesty, that Poley, mentioned in my former letters, wrote hence to England to Blunt, named in my former letters,[625] of my captivity and the difficulty that he found here to speak with me. But this much was written before he spoke with me, and now I hear that the said Poley's letters were intercepted at the port in England and sent to the Council; whereby both Blunt and the other are like to fall into trouble, to my grief, or at least they will be dealt withal to abuse your Majesty on that side and myself on this side; which has moved me—though I have a good conceit of Blunt —to stay an ample despatch and instructions that I had made ready for Blunt, for the furtherance of your Majesty's service, being right sorry for the evil accident happened to both of them, if it be true, as I pray God it be not. But if the one or the other be discovered to have intelligence with me, they will be so watched by that side that they shall not be able to serve your Majesty. Whereof I thought it my bounden duty to advertise your Majesty, and to wish you to stay

[623] Cf. *infra* Appendix V. [624] Cf. *infra* Appendix IV.
[625] Cf. Morgan to Q. of Scots, 10/20 July 1585, *Murdin*, p. 446 and *Scot. Cal. VIII*, p. 11. This was Christopher Blunt or Blount, cf. *supra* Note 619.

till this matter be better cleared, from accepting of any service at Blunt's hands, if he happen to offer you any. Yet I am of opinion that he will not be made an instrument to deceive your Majesty. But fearful and careful I am in such cases as import your Majesty's service, as I ought to be, and shall be whilst I live".

He went on to state that he knew not the truth of the matter, that it would be a great loss to lose the services of Blunt, and left it to her own wisdom, whether or not to see how things were by trying him by letters in blank between her and the French ambassador.[626]

It is hardly necessary to add that there is no trace or even the slightest echo of such a letter having been intercepted, or of Blunt or Poley having been called in question by the Council, as Dr. Astlowe, Dr. Good and others were in 1574. Nor is this at all surprising; for Blunt and Poley were acting with Queen Elizabeth's ministers. Blunt himself confessed as much in his plea for mercy to the Queen after the Essex riot in 1601, begging that her Majesty be

> "particularly informed and remembered of those great services which he did in laying the way open to the Earl of Leicester and Mr. Secretary Walsingham for the discovery of all the Queen of Scot's practices".[627]

Morgan, indeed, in his letters represented Blunt as a Catholic, fawning upon and serving under Leicester only to escape the persecution at home, and so be able to live a Christian life![628] But this, too, was false. Blunt, it is true, had been brought up as a Catholic at the seminary of Douay, but he changed his religion, as a letter of his to Walsingham shows.[629] The whole purpose, in fact, of the lying story put out by

---

[626] Morgan to Q. of Scots, 18 July 1585, *Scot. Cal. VIII*, p. 25. Compare Paget to Same, 15 July 1585, *Ibid.*, p. 23. "Her Majesty has been advertised by Morgan and him of Blunt's good affection towards her, and that he sent one hither on purpose, called Poley, to get credit. Poley on his first arrival here has committed an error in writing hence to Mr. Christopher Blunt something concerning Mr. Blunt, and presuming that by the credit he had by Blunt it might safely have passed the ports, he sent it by an ordinary messenger, so that it was taken. Thinks he is taken also. Does not know what will become of the matter, but hurt he can do none, because they trusted him with nothing". He then advised her to handle the matter discreetly.

[627] Examination of Sir Christopher Blunt, printed in the *Correspondence of James VI with Sir Robert Cecil and others*, Camden Society, 1861, pp. 107–110. Cf. also *infra* Appendix IV, where the parts played by Blunt and Poley are discussed more at length.

[628] Cf. Morgan to Q. of Scots, 10/20 July 1585, *ut supra;* Same to Same, 18/28 January and 21/31 March 1586, also Paget to Same, 31 March/10 April 1586, *Murdin*, pp. 470, 481 and 506 and *Scot. Cal. VIII*, pp. 189, 262 and 292.

[629] "To you my soul was ever known; God hath altered me for my opinion in religion, and I not altered it to please any man but to save my soul; yet have I enemies that inform my Lord of the contrary, and that at my departure I said I would live and die a papist. You know better; wherefore as occasion is offered, certify for me both his Lordship and

Morgan and Paget was to explain why they had ceased recommending Blunt and Poley, now that the Government had postponed their plan till the following year. In 1586, indeed, they resumed their recommendation of both of these English agents, as instruments for re-opening the secret correspondence, and this without any explanation of the alleged episode of the intercepted letter of 1585!

3. *Morgan's recommendations of doubtful characters to the Scottish Queen: the hostile attitude of his faction to her known followers*

In connection with events discussed in the preceding pages it may pertinently be asked, was it not strange, if he was really the careful servant he claimed to be, that Morgan should have recommended to the Queen of Scots as many as three persons who were working against her in co-operation with the English Government: Christopher Blunt, Robert Poley and Gilbert Gifford, not to mention Thomas Phelippes himself. Nor do these exhaust the doubtful characters suggested to her as willing and suitable agents to help her. There is, for instance, William Greene, alias Gabriel Blunt, whom he recommended to her no less than three times,[630] and to whom he wrote to her that he had sent a cipher for him to use in correspondence with her. He further, penned a letter for her to send to him in her own name; and though there is not the slightest evidence that she had ever had anything to do with him, or had even heard of him before this recommendation of him, that letter begins:

"Good Gabriel Blunt, it is *long* since I have been very well informed of your virtuous family and friends by my old, good servant Thomas Morgan".[631]

The whole letter, in fact, smacks of trickery on Morgan's part; for William Greene, or Gabriel Blunt, was as Phelippes knew, a close follower of the Earl of Leicester, her deadliest enemy.[632] Morgan

[630] Morgan to Q. of Scots, 7 December 1584, *Scot. Cal. VII*, p. 478; Same to Same, 10/20 July 1585 and 21/31 March 1586, *Murdin*, pp. 446 and 481 and *Scot. Cal. VIII*, pp. 11 and 262.

[631] Enclosed in Morgan to Q. of Scots, 7 December 1584, *ut supra*, in which for the first time he had recommended Greene to her. Italics mine.

[632] "Blunt, one W. Green, my Lord of Leicester's man" (Phelippes's comment in "The Plot against England", 4 September 1586, in Phelippes's hand, *Scot. Cal. VIII*, pp. 675–678). In the list of Gentlemen following in the train of the Earl of Leicester, there is mentioned a William Greene as having two servants and two horses, and assigned to the ship "The Flying Hart of Hull" (*Spanish Cal. 1580–1586*, p. 555).

her Majesty, who otherwise will believe of me as she heareth, because she knows me not, nor the faithful service I vow to do her" (Blunt to Walsingham, Flushing, 3 June 1588, *For. Cal. XXI*, part *IV*, p. 451).

himself knew it, but as in the case of Christopher Blunt, gave the explanation to the Queen of Scots, that "he followeth Leicester to seek thereby quietness to live a Christian life"![633]

Others recommended by Morgan would also repay investigation, such as Robert Bruce, the Scottish spy, William Langharne, secretary to Sir Walter Raleigh, Thomas Markham and the priest Edward Gratley, "a sweet soul of God" and devoted to the Queen of Scots, according to Morgan, yet the same who betrayed the Earl of Arundel and later, at the instance of Dr. Allen, was imprisoned in the Inquisition in Rome for his treachery to the Catholic cause and his heretical leanings.

In sharp contrast with the recommendation of such men as the above, was the attitude of the Morgan-Paget faction to the Catholic leaders and genuine servants of the Queen of Scots. Some account has already been given of the conduct of these men to Allen and Persons,[634] as also of their attempt to destroy the confidence of the Scottish Queen in her own ambassador, the Archbishop of Glasgow, as well as in the Duke of Guise.[635] Their conduct towards Charles Arundel was in no way dissimilar. Of his fidelity to the Queen of Scots and to the Catholic cause there can be no doubt. He had had considerable part in the composition in 1584 of *Leicester's Commonwealth* which, though considered a "chronique scandaleuse" was in reality a political tract in defence of the Queen of Scots, as Walsingham at once recognised.[636] In March of the following year, 1585, Godfrey Foljambe wrote to her:

> "Mr. Arundel has performed many good offices towards your Majesty in this place; by whose means there can hardly any evil intention be contrived against your Majesty but there will be notice thereof obtained out of hand"...[637]

It was Arundel, moreover, who in April of that same year warned the Pope that the councillors of Queen Elizabeth were bribing one of the Cardinals in Rome;[638] and it was probably through him also that the true character of Cherelles, as a spy of Walsingham, was revealed, and the opportunity of further treachery on his part curtailed by his being

[633] Morgan to Q. of Scots, 10/20 July 1585, *ut supra*.
[634] Cf. *supra* Chapter VI, section 4.
[635] *Ibid.* and VIII, section 2.
[636] Cf. L. Hicks, s.j., *The Growth of a Myth: Fr. Robert Persons, S.J., and Leicester's Commonwealth, Studies*, Spring 1957.
[637] Foljambe to Q. of Scots, Paris [March] 1585, *Scot. Cal. VII*, p. 590.
[638] Cf. Charles Arundel to Gregory XIII, Paris, 10 April 1585, Vat. Arch. Nunz. di Francia XVII, f. 399 and R.O. Transcripts 31/9, bundle 82a. For further references about this matter cf. *supra* Notes 214, 314, 363 and 615.

P

recalled to France.[639] Yet, as early as 1585, Arundel was represented to the Queen of Scots by Paget as about to return to England to the peril of herself and her cause, from which peril she was saved only by Paget's devotion in sacrificing one thousand crowns;[640] and later in that same year he was accused in Rome of being a spy of the English Government. However, when the charges were investigated by the Nuncio in Paris, on orders from Rome, Arundel was found to have been entirely innocent. The accusation was supposed, not without a high degree of probability, to have come from Charles Paget, possibly by means of his brother, Lord Paget, who was in Rome in that year.[641] Not long after these investigations, however, despite the fact that he had been declared innocent, Paget wrote to the Queen of Scots:

"I am credibly informed, that Mr. Charles Arundel is already gained, and promised he shall have his pardon, and be restored to his living, and that now is gone into Spain for some time to discover what preparation the King of Spain maketh to the sea. And so having advertised the Queen of England what he can learn he is presently after to return to England, and for the accomplishment of this journey, he hath already taken money of the Queen of England. In truth, Mr. Arundel hath been in wonderful passions, and unruly courses, which maketh me think this aforesaid to be the more true".[642]

Actually, on Arundel's going to Spain, he was denounced as a spy to the Spanish ambassador in Paris, who accordingly wrote to the King to be on his guard. In a second letter of the same date Mendoza reported that an English priest, then at Rouen, whom he knew well for a good soul, had informed him that Arundel had gone to Spain by orders of the Queen of England to discover what was being done there, she having supplied him with money for the purpose. Despite his

---

[639] "A report of him [*Cherelles*] has been made to their most Christian Majesties that Walsingham should have won him to the devotion of the Queen of England, and caused a chain of two hundred crowns to be given him, and on this account the said Sieur de Chasteauneuf has been told to send him back hither with all diligence" (Archbishop of Glasgow to Q. of Scots, 21 March 1586, *Scot. Cal. VIII*, p. 255). The spy Rogers, alias Berden, reported that the report had been made by Charles Arundel, who had had it from Stafford (cf. Rogers to ——, [June ?] 1586, and *supra* Note 530, where the passage is quoted).

[640] Cf. *supra* Note 564 for references to Paget's and Morgan's letters on this matter. They were never silent about their own "services" to the captive Queen: it is a feature that strikes the student of their correspondence.

[641] Cf. Rogers (alias Berden) to Walsingham, Paris, 30 September 1585, printed in *C.R.S. XXI*, p. 80; also Notes 363 and 615.

[642] Paget to Q. of Scots, 31 March/10 April 1586, also Morgan to Same, 21/31 March 1586, *Murdin*, pp. 506 and 481 and *Scot. Cal. VIII*, pp. 292 and 262.

indebtedness to the family of the Earl of Arundel, his conscience, so the priest had stated, had forced him to make this charge. All this had confirmed Mendoza's suspicion, he said, so the King should order Sir Charles Arundel to return.[643]

From Mendoza's account there is no doubt that the priest-informer was no other than Edward Gratley,[644] who has been more than once referred to already. But it may still pertinently be asked, what was this priest, Gratley, himself doing at the very time when his tender conscience forced him to accuse Charles Arundel to the Spanish ambassador in Paris of being a spy of the English Government? With Gilbert Gifford and Morgan he was engaged in composing the book against the Spaniards and the Jesuits which Gifford was shortly to take to Walsingham when he went back to England! With Dr. William Gifford, Gilbert's cousin, he was meeting Aldred,[645] Walsingham's agent, with a view to spreading the false propaganda put out by the English Government and to sowing dissension among the Catholic leaders. In this connection he was taken by Aldred secretly to see Stafford, the English ambassador in Paris, and was for some months in correspondence with Walsingham himself; and this with the approval of Morgan who, lest rumour of these dealings with her enemies might reach her, gave a lying report of them to the Queen of Scots.[646] Finally, Stafford himself planned to plant this same Gratley on the household of Mendoza, the Spanish ambassador, to play the spy—the very thing of which he had accused Charles Arundel.[647]

[643] Two letters of Mendoza to Philip II, both dated 11 May 1586, *Spanish Cal. 1580–1586*, pp. 574 and 577. To the second letter the King appended a note: "It will be well to send him away, and give him fresh attendants".

[644] The mention of the priest being at Rouen and of his connection with the Earl and Countess of Arundel makes it certain that Gratley was Mendoza's informant. Writing in December 1588 Henry Caesar, an intelligencer, informed Walsingham that Gilbert Gifford had accused Arundel to the Spanish ambassador of being a spy of her Majesty of England, but he did not state the date when the accusation had been made (Caesar to Walsingham, Paris, 9 December 1588, printed in J. Morris, s.j., *The Letter-Books of Sir Amias Poulet*, p. 385). It is possible that Gilbert Gifford did so on this occasion, for he had returned to France at the time; but he was certainly not the person to whom Mendoza referred, for he was not then a priest, nor had he had any acquaintance with the Earl and Countess of Arundel, as had Gratley. Charles Arundel was but a rather distant relation of the Earl. For Gratley's connection with the Earl and Countess, cf. *C.R.S. XXI, passim*.

[645] Solomon Aldred to Walsingham, 24 April 1586, *Dom. Cal. Add. 1580–1625*, p. 174; also *supra* Chapter III, section 3, and Note 214.

[646] Cf. the letters of Aldred, March and April 1586, and those of Gratley, under the name of John Foxley, April to June 1586, in *Dom. Cal. Add. 1580–1625;* also *supra* Note 361. Cf. also Morgan to Q. of Scots, 24 April 1586, *Murdin*, p. 510 and *Scot. Cal. VIII*, p. 331.

[647] Cf. Aldred to Walsingham, 14/24 April 1586, *ut supra*, and Stafford to Same, Paris, 15 April 1586, *For. Cal. September 1585–May 1586*, p. 550.

This attempt, however, to destroy the repute of Arundel with the Spanish authorities failed, as had their previous attempt to do so with the Roman authorities; for certainly, later in that same year, 1586, Charles Arundel had regained, if indeed he had ever really lost it, the confidence both of Mendoza and of the King of Spain.[648] But what can these repeated efforts to denigrate him in Rome, in Paris, in Spain and to the Queen of Scots have been but a deliberate intrigue to destroy his authority and influence with the Catholic powers? For Arundel, as appears from Foljambe's letter already quoted, knew too much, having obtained information from Sir Edward Stafford, the English ambassador, and also from his wife, Lady Sheffield, herself a cousin of Arundel.[649]

Morgan and Paget, moreover, always displayed themselves as very anxious to re-start the secret correspondence of the Queen of Scots, and as making great efforts to find persons to undertake the task, but their instruments for the purpose were all agents of the English Government: Christopher Blunt, Robert Poley and Gilbert Gifford. Yet when, very soon after the channel of her secret letters had been closed, Thomas Fitzherbert had volunteered to go to England and find means to re-open it, they brushed aside his offer as unnecessary.

"I have sent divers letters to your Majesty from Scotland and England", wrote Foljambe from Paris to the Scottish Queen, "but never received any answer to any of them, which I ascribe to want of 'intelligence' [*i.e. communications*]. For the reparation whereof I travail by an honest and well qualified gentleman, Mr. Thomas Fitzherbert, who would have undertaken the journey if it had been so thought good by Mr. Paget and Mr. Morgan, who 'seemed' to me that your Majesty stood in need of no such service".[650]

And this at a time when the channel of communication was closed!

[648] Cf. Mendoza to Philip II, Paris, 8 November 1586, and Juan de Idiaquez to Mendoza, 18 December 1586, *Spanish Cal. 1580–1586*, pp. 648 and 679; also *supra* Note 615.

[649] Cf. Mendoza to Philip II, 8 November 1586 and Juan de Idiaquez to Mendoza, 18 December 1586, *ut supra;* G. Gifford to T. Throckmorton, 22 January 1588, and Stafford to Walsingham [January] 1588, *For. Cal. June 1586–June 1588*, pp. 670 and 661; also the Examination of Charles Arundel and Thomas Fitzherbert, before the Nuncio in Paris, 30 September 1585 (reference as in Note 615). As Berden, pretending to be a Catholic, was closely associated with Fitzherbert, it is very probable that he was referring to this examination in his letter to Walsingham, Paris, 30 September 1585 (printed in *C.R.S. XXI*, p. 80). Cf. also Discorso del Sig^r. Tomaso Fitzherberto, etc., 1602, Arch. S.J. Rom. Angl. 36. 1, f. 100. Though there are other copies of this document, a margin note in this particular one states that Arundel's information about the bribing of the Cardinals was derived from Lady Sheffield.

[650] G. Foljambe to Q. of Scots, March 1585, *Scot. Cal. VII*, p. 590.

It was this Fitzherbert that Paget later traduced to the Queen of Scots, for in March 1586 he wrote to her:

"That Fitzherbert, which I recommended to your Majesty, without my privity is become the Queen Mother's man here: and as I am informed, is an advertiser for the Queen of England, and therefore is permitted to receive what benefits he can out of England, and, as I suppose, shall have leave to return when he will".[651]

In the light of the facts above-narrated, considered in conjunction with all the evidence already given, does not the conclusion impose itself that Morgan and Paget were but the puppets of Queen Elizabeth's councillors, carrying out their orders in sowing dissension among Catholics, blackening the characters of their leaders and attempting to destroy the confidence of the Catholic powers in them, in which, indeed, they succeeded for a time, even in Rome itself?

4. The fate of a book attacking Morgan and Paget after her death: conclusion

To what extent Morgan and Paget were made fully cognisant of the aim of Queen Elizabeth's ministers to bring the Queen of Scots to her death may possibly be arguable, but that they were disloyal to her on many counts and were responsible, whether knowingly or not, for her fate appears, from the documents, to be beyond dispute. That, at least, was the conviction of the majority of the Catholic exiles who had not, at that time, all the evidence now available. That conviction they expressed after her execution in a book attacking both men, which was so damaging that Lord Paget, whether on his own initiative or on the orders of the English ministers, bought up the whole edition, with few exceptions, and had them destroyed. Some years after Mary's death, a Catholic in Brussels wrote of Paget:

"In these tragical actions some upon good and probable grounds do suppose that he [*Charles Paget*] was not altogether sound to the Queen of Scots, but that he played two parts in one, and thereupon

---

[651] Paget to Q. of Scots, 31 March/10 April 1586, *Murdin*, p. 506 and *Scot. Cal. VIII*, p. 292. There is a letter of Fitzherbert's to Walsingham, it is true, of this time; and Stafford wrote in his favour to the Secretary of State. But he was playing a part with Walsingham as well as with Stafford, in furtherance of the Catholic cause, just as Charles Arundel was doing, whose confidant he was. Fitzherbert had acted similarly with the Government agent, Aldred, as the Nuncio's report of 30 September 1585 shows, learning from him, indeed, of the bribing of the Cardinals in Rome, and Aldred began to suspect him (cf. *supra* Notes 214, 363, 581 and 615). His whole career, in fact, shows his loyalty to the cause of the English Catholics. Cf. also Introduction to *Letters of Thomas Fitzherbert, C.R.S. XLI.*

some of her servants made a book and printed it in Paris wherein they charged Morgan and him to have been the causers of her destruction. The whole impression of which book the Lord Paget bought up and caused it to be burnt, some few only escaping the fire which are extant to this day to be seen.[652]

One great presumption of his double dealing with the Queen of Scots is, that Gilbert Gifford (whom he knew to be a spy for Walsingham, and set on by him to entertain the matter of Ballard and Babington till such time as it should be ripe) being apprehended and committed in Paris for his treachery, there was none that made such great suit for his delivery as Mr. Charles Paget and the Lord Paget, his brother, who laboured so earnestly in the matter that they had obtained his liberty, but that Dr. Pierce and some others opposed themselves and procured justice to take due course. Divers English gentlemen fugitives in these countries, upon this and other presumptions of his disloyalty to the Queen of Scots, accused him and Morgan thereof to the Duke of Parma, who caused Morgan to be committed and both him and Mr. Paget to be examined in justice, and how far forth things were proved against them the process can show. But being a matter that belonged not to the Duke of Parma to punish, as not concerning the King, his master, nor his own government, the issue thereof was that Morgan for another cause was banished out of these countries, and both he and Mr. Paget held by the said Duke, and by the commissioners that examined the cause, for knaves and traitors even after".[653]

It seems highly probable that the book mentioned in the above letter was written after some knowledge of Gilbert Gifford's activities had come to light on his being imprisoned in Paris in December 1587, though it does not appear to have been the same book as that to which Stafford referred in a letter to Burghley in April 1588:

"I have sent Mr. Secretary", he wrote, "and desired him to show it to your Lordship the villainest book that ever was set out, for there [is] not possibly another yet to be got; they be sold so secretly. I am, as I write to him, [in] a perplexity what to do; whether to complain earnestly or so seek to have it suppressed, or by fear kept to have it come no further abroad than it is. I have resolved to deal with Pinard, to show him the beginning and the ending, which is most

---

[652] It will be recalled that it was Lord Paget who had protected them in Flanders, and that it was only when he was ill to death, that proceedings could be taken against Morgan in 1590 (cf. *supra* Chapter IV, section 1, and Charles Browne to Philip II, 22 February 1590, Simancas, Est. Leg. 599, f. 87).

[653] A Catholic at Brussels to his friend a Monk at Liège, 4/14 July 1599, Dom. Eliz. 271, n. 74. Concerning the recipient of this letter, cf. *supra* Note 352.

villainous, and by the example of that which was done in England when Simiers was there, which they have set down, though falsely in the Epistle, wish that he would move the King, either by punishing it as that was, or by suppressing it at this time, show the like good part to her Majesty. And that I take the best course, considering the time, and will follow it till I have further direction".[654]

Though it is not now possible to say whether or not Lord Paget had instructions to take the action already described above with regard to the book attacking Morgan and his brother, Charles, it can hardly be doubted that it was this same book to which reference was made in a letter of the spy, Thomas Barnes, who had himself taken an important part, as Walsingham's agent, in the Babington plot, to Thomas Phelippes:

"There is another book going to press", he wrote from Flanders, "which answers that was written in France concerning the death of the Queen of Scotland wherein it toucheth Ch. Paget and Morgan somewhat sharply. It is printed by one Clitheroe a priest remaining now at Anvers by the advice and direction of Ch. Paget especially. It doth pestilently discover many things. As soon as it is extant I will send you one".[655]

Phelippes appears not to have shared Barnes's apprehension about the uncovering of hidden dealings in the new book then in the press, for he remarked in this reply:

"It maketh no great matter what they write. We know what we have done and let them mend themselves as they can".[655a]

[654] Stafford to Burghley, Paris, 7 April 1588, *For. Cal. June 1586–June 1588*, p. 585. The book in question in this letter was probably a work in French, entitled *Martyre de la Royne d'Escosse, Douanière de France*, published anonymously in 1587, and re-published several times in the next two years. In the account of the Queen of Scots' life given there, many important persons in England and Scotland, but in particular Walsingham, were severely dealt with, though Morgan and Paget were little mentioned. In the Epistle introducing this book occurs the reference to Simiers mentioned by Stafford. With regard to the book burnt by Lord Paget, it may be remarked that Gilbert Gifford had been arrested on the previous 9 December, o.s.

[655] α [T. Barnes] to John Wytsande [T. Phelippes], 26 November 1589, n.s. Dom. Eliz. Add. Vol. 31, n. 82. The handwriting is that of Barnes, thus the interpretation of the cipher sign with which this and other similar letters are signed. Neither the book, of which most copies were burnt, nor Paget's answer to it, have so far been identified amongst the contemporary literature concerning the death of the Queen of Scots. The priest, William Clitheroe, had helped Paget earlier with another book, though it seems doubtful that it was ever published (cf. Rogers (or Berden) to Walsingham, 13 August 1585, *Dom. Cal. Add. 1580–1625*, p. 148 and *supra* Note 77). Something of Barnes's part in the Babington plot can be seen J. H. Pollen, s.j., *Mary Queen of Scots and the Babington Plot*, Edinburgh, 1922.

[655a] Draft in Phelippes's hand, dated London, 14 December 1589, answering Barnes's letter of 26 November, Dom. Eliz. Add. Vol. 31, n. 90.

He was no mean manager of tortuous affairs, and his schemes had evidently been cleverly enough arranged to render ineffectual the revelations of any disgruntled or frightened participators. What is clear, however, even from these meagre accounts about the book attacking them, is that Morgan and Paget were considered by certain of their contemporaries to have been responsible, in some way, for the death of the Scottish Queen.

It would be a difficult matter to draw together briefly all the threads of the many incidents dealt with in these pages. Some of them are, in themselves, trivial, and taken separately could be discounted. Their true effect is cumulative. As might be expected, many of the affairs of men such as Morgan and Paget were intended to be kept secret, or at most to leave only isolated traces, not readily interpreted. Years of work piecing together scraps of such information has necessarily yielded a somewhat untidy narrative, unamenable to summarising. In general, however, it may be said that, whilst Charles Paget has been largely ignored, where Morgan's career has been considered at all, historians seem rather to have ascribed his conduct during the years of his supposed service to the Queen of Scots to extreme folly, and not to disloyalty on his part. Such a view seems only possible because no co-ordination of evidence about him has hitherto been attempted, for such folly as is suggested would surely have to be that of a complete simpleton. That is certainly not the picture of him which emerges, either from his own letters, or from the testimony of his contemporaries: and from the abundant and converging evidence considered in this study, their verdict seems unavoidable that he was not, despite his frequent protestations and outward show, Mary's loyal servant during the period of her imprisonment in England, but was, on the contrary, an agent of the English councillors. On the same grounds, it emerges that Charles Paget, though in a less prominent way, played the same rôle, in conjunction with Morgan, his great friend.

Their careers as intriguers, in one sphere or another, were by no means circumscribed by their connection with the Scottish Queen's affairs, as has been shown, in part, in the foregoing pages, nor did either change his ways after her execution. Much evidence exists in English, foreign and ecclesiastical sources, to show how amply, and for how long, these two adventurers earned the distrust of so many of their English Catholic contemporaries in exile. The full story of their doings lies, however, far outside the scope of this particular study, for both men survived into the early years of the next century.

APPENDIX I

The Bogus Papal League of 1580 (*cf. Chapter II, section 5, Note 129*)

At the meeting in the Star Chamber on 23 June 1585 concerning the treasons of the Earl of Northumberland and his alleged suicide in the Tower two days before, Popham, the Attorney-General, in his speech referred to a Papal league of 1580, stating

"that in a letter sent to the same Allen from Rome, touching audience given by the Pope to the ambassadors of certain foreign princes, between the Pope and whom a league was agreed on against the Queen's Majesty, there were enclosed certain articles, containing in effect, that the realm should be invaded with 20,000 men, at the charge of the said Pope and princes; that her Majesty should be deposed, and some English Catholic elected king. That it was confessed that the coming over of so many priests into the realm, was to win great numbers to the Catholic party, to join (if opportunity served), either with foreign invasion, or with tumult at home".[656]

There is a further elaboration of the story in an earlier document, Thomas Norton's "Chain of Treasons".[657] This will be discussed

---

[656] *Somers Tracts I*, p. 215. The vagueness of the printed pamphlet should be compared with the definite details given in the Salisbury draft (cf. Note 76). "John Hart, seminary priest," it runs, "deposed on oath 31 December 1580, that about February then last, Dr. Allen (with whom the said Hart was very inward) received a letter from Rome, with articles enclosed, touching an audience given by the Pope to the ambassadors of Spain and Florence who had agreed on a league against the Queen of England, which articles by Dr. Allen's command he copied and was forbidden to speak of. The effect of which was that the realm should be invaded by 20,000 men, and the most part at the King of Spain's charge; that her Majesty should be deposed, some English Catholic elected king, etc. The said Hart in another examination 3 November 1581, said that the coming over of so many priests was to win great numbers to the Catholic party to join (if opportunity served) either with foreign invasion or tumult at home" (*Cal. Salisbury MSS. XIII*, p. 272).
  In the alleged articles themselves (cf. *Cal. Carew MSS. II*, p. 288 and *Venetian Cal. 1558–1580*, p. 649), it may be noted in passing, that the army was considerably bigger, amounting to 33,000 infantry and 2600 horse, besides the German troops which had gone to Spain. It is rather suspicious that the 20,000 mentioned in the draft above, is the exact number put down by Lennox in his plan of 1582 (cf. *Kretzschmar*, p. 122).

[657] Yelverton MSS. XXXIII, now B.M. Addit. 48029, ff. 58–62v. This document was certainly written before the martyrdom of George Haydock or Haddock, 5 February 1584, as he is referred to in it as again to be examined: it was probably composed with reference to Francis Throckmorton's prosecution. Thomas Norton died 10 March 1584.

223

later, but it may be said here, that once allow that the alleged Papal
League was purely fictitious, it contains blatant falsehoods, especially
as regards Allen and the Bishop of Ross. Finally, at the trial of the
Earl of Arundel in 1589 there was a further addition. Hart, a seminary
priest, so Popham then asserted, had affirmed on oath 31 December—
the year now being stated as 1581, and not, as in the earlier Salisbury
manuscript, 1580—that

> "Allen was in Norfolk to have talked with the Duke, but spoke
> not with him, and said it had been good for the Duke that Allen
> had spoken with him".[658]

That such a league in 1580 was bogus, was shown some years ago
by J. H. Pollen, s.j., though the hoary legend still appears from time
to time in historical works.[659] He sums up his argument: "A negative
conclusion [*the fact that there are no documents about the negotiations for
such a league in the respective archives*], would have been of little value,
if it had only been the question of finding one particular document.
But that is not the contention. The point is that a compact, such as this
professes to be, could never come into existence by the sudden simul-
taneous freak of the representatives of three great Powers. It presumes
previous and subsequent correspondence, instructions, powers,
drafts, cautions, ratifications on a very large scale. The archive
argument turns on the inexplicable absence, from these large and well
preserved national archives [*e.g. the Vatican, Spain and Tuscany
(Florence)*], of an intercorrespondence which ought to have been
copious in each".[660] This argument, indeed, could be reinforced by
comparing this absence of documents in these archives, with the
number of documents still preserved concerning the attempted league
for the invasion of England in the years 1582 to 1584.[661] The very
idea, in fact, of Philip II entering such a league in 1580 is quite out of
accord with his position and activities of that year. Apart from the
struggle in the Netherlands, he was far too concerned with the conquest
of Portugal in 1580, to think of joining a league for the invasion of
England, of which the greater part of the expense, according to the

---

[658] "Popham's Brief", printed in *C.R.S. XXI*, p. 290, from B.M. Egerton MSS. 2074,
f. 81. This Brief of 1589 is substantially a repetition of Popham's speech in the Star
Chamber on 23 June 1585.

[659] E.g. R. B. Merriman, *The Rise of the Spanish Empire, IV*, New York, 1934, p. 516.

[660] J. H. Pollen, s.j., *The English Catholics in the Reign of Queen Elizabeth*, London,
1920, p. 239, n. 1. The so-called Papal league of 1580 is discussed, *Ibid.*, pp. 234–243.

[661] Cf. *Kretzschmar*, pp. 123–215. Further documents are to be found in Knox, *Allen*,
pp. 175–264 and 419–434, and in Thomas Phillipps, *De Conquestu Angliae*, 1869.

Salisbury manuscript, was to be borne by him.[662] Nor is it in accord with his bickering with the Pope over their proposed respective payments in the plans of invasion of the years 1582 to 1584, and his persistent refusal to grant military aid to effect them. That the Government knew all this is clear.[663]

But to return to Hart who, so it was alleged, had received the articles of the league under great secrecy. There is extant, indeed, an extract from Hart's examination of 31 December 1580,[664] but there is nothing in it to support the above statements, rather the reverse: for Hart there explained the relaxation, as regards the English Catholics, of the Bull of Excommunication of Pius V, granted by Gregory XIII on 14 April 1580, at the petition of the Jesuits, Persons and Campion, so that without scruple of conscience her Catholic subjects could obey and serve Queen Elizabeth, as their legitimate sovereign. As for Allen going to Norfolk, even had it been true, as Nicholas Fitzherbert[665] and other authors after him have since repeated, and for which there appears to be no strictly contemporary evidence—for Fitzherbert wrote over forty years after the supposed talk with the Duke of Norfolk, and may, indeed, have taken the notion from the Government pamphlet—the statement itself is altogether beside the mark: for Allen, not yet a priest, left England for the last time in 1565, some years even before the Queen of Scots fled to England: at a time, that is, when there was no question of the Duke of Norfolk, a Protestant, conspiring against the Government.

As to Allen's having received a letter from Rome "in February last" [*i.e. 1580*], enclosing the articles of the alleged confederation, it must be remembered, as Allen himself pointed out, that he was still in Rome, when the confederation was supposed to have been concluded, viz. at an audience of 18 February; nor did he leave Rome to return to Rheims till 25 February,[666] that is, two days after the news of the supposed league was sent from Rome.[667] It is, moreover, quite incredible that Allen should have ordered Hart to copy the articles of

[662] Cf. *supra* Note 656.
[663] Cf. *supra* Chapter II, section 5.
[664] Dom. Eliz. 144, nn. 64 and 65.
[665] Cf. *Nicolai Fitzherberti de Alani Cardinalis Vitae libellus*, Rome 1608, reprinted in Knox, *Allen*, p. 6.
[666] Cf. The Diary of Sledd, the spy, who accompanied the party, under date 25 February 1580, Yelverton MSS. XXXIII (printed *C.R.S. LIII*). Allen had been in Rome on business connected with the new English College there, since 26 September 1579.
[667] Cf. *Cal. Carew MSS. II*, p. 288, where it is stated that the articles were sent from Rome on 23 February.

the alleged treaty, for he considered it to be bogus, as it certainly was;
and he pointed out the absurdity of the Government's charge in the
Proclamation of 15 July 1580, that the exiles had published them.

"Further", he wrote, "invocating upon his soul, that he never knew,
saw, nor heard, during his abode in the Court there [*Rome*], of any
such writings, as are mentioned in the said Proclamation of July,
containing certain articles of confederation of the Pope, King of
Spain and other Princes, for the invasion of the Realm: nor ever
afterwards gave counsel to publish any such thing, though he were
in Rome at the day of the date that some of those copies, which afterwards he saw, when they were common to all the world, do bear.
Being also most assured that no other English Catholic would or
could be the author thereof, nor (as it may be thought) any other of
those Princes, or their ministers, that are pretended to be of the foresaid league: being neither wisdom nor policy, if any such thing were
intended (as we verily think there was not) much less if it were never
meant, to publish any such libels, to give the Realm warning purposely to provide for it, especially all the world knowing, that the
pinching of the poor Catholics at home (a lamentable case) is
their sense and repay for all adverse accidents abroad".[668]

Nor is the statement that Hart, being very inward with Allen, was
ordered to copy the articles, borne out by Hart's alleged letter to
Walsingham of 1 December 1581. In that letter he suggests that he
might be sent back to Rheims, where in view of the sufferings he had
been reported to have undergone at the hands of the Government,
Allen would reveal secrets which hitherto he had imparted only to a
few seniors and not to him.

"If I were now with him in this case", he wrote, "I should be so
much made of as I can not express it in any words, and I think verily
he would now make me privy to very many things which hitherto,
mistrusting my constancy in this behalf, and by this that now I have
said, having most certain tokens of the same, he hath kept secret
from me and others of my calling, imparting them only to a very
few (all which I know very well) of the chief seniors in the house.
So that if he should perhaps herein be more circumspect than they
(as it is very like he will) yet I have very vehement conjectures of
coming to some knowledge of matters by others about him, with
whom he often dealeth very secretly, and for the causes which now

---

[668] Allen, *An Apologie and True Declaration of the institution and endevours of the two
English Colleges, etc.* Mounts in Henault, 1581, ff. 15–15v. Cf. also Allen, *A True Report
of the Death and Martyrdom of Twelve Reverend Priests*, 1583, ed. J. H. Pollen, s.j.,
London, 1908, p. 9.

I said are no less fond of any that shall suffer in the cause, than he, but much more talkative".[669]

The whole letter should be read, but whether written by Hart, or fabricated by the Government—for they never dared to use it, nor does it fit in with Hart's career—it does suggest the precise opposite of the Government's statement that Hart was so inward with Allen as to have been let into such a high secret as the alleged confederation for the invasion of England, and that he was ordered to copy the articles thereof but not to speak of them. The latter remark is particularly inept, seeing that the Government had declared in its own Proclamation of 15 July 1580, that the exiles themselves had actually published them. In a word, it is quite impossible from the documents to make a consistent story on the part of the Government. That, however, did not hinder them from adhering to their statements about Hart's confession supposedly made a year before the letter just quoted, nor from using the same in evidence against two Earls, the Earl of Northumberland in 1585, and the Earl of Arundel in 1589.

Though Pollen, as already stated, showed that the alleged confederation in 1580 was a complete fiction, he did not pursue the subject further and investigate who was responsible for the story of the league and its articles. Such evidence as is extant suggests, to put it no stronger, that the story of the treaty emanated from some members of the Elizabethan Government. It is to be noted that, according to the documents handed to the Venetian Ambassador, Priuli, by Cobham, the English ambassador in Paris, the alleged confederation was concluded in an audience given by the Pope to the ambassadors of the King of Spain and Tuscany on Thursday, 18 February 1580—a slight slip in the date, for 18 February in 1580 fell on a Friday, not on a Thursday, and a slip that would hardly have been made at Rome so soon as the 23 February, when the articles were supposed, according to the Carew manuscript, to have been despatched from there.[670] It is further to be noted that Norton the rack-master, in his "Chain of Treasons", gave further details.

"There is also", he wrote, "special provision agreed among them that the abbeys, bishoprics, and ecclesiastical livings in England be bestowed only upon Englishmen and this portion of the treaty seemeth to be added by Allen who was a third capitulator in the same articles. And so concurred the three commissioners for that cause,

[669] J. Hart to Walsingham, 1 December 1581, Dom. Eliz. 150, n. 80. Italics mine.
[670] Cf. *supra* Note 667 and *Venetian Cal. 1558–1580*, p. 649.

Englefield in Spain for the laity of England, Ross for the Queen of Scots and Allen for the clergy of England, joining with the Pope himself and the devil for them all. . . .

This confederacy and all these articles thereof have been confessed in the Tower by Hart, who was the person of all the seminarians most near in secret with Allen and he confesseth that Allen himself did show him these articles and did cause him to write them out and that Allen received them from Rome written with hand wherein Allen received his ordinary intelligence from the Pope, which he supposeth to be the hand of Doctor Owen Lewis".

Requisite qualities were also, according to Norton, laid down for the person to be elected King, such as that he should be English, a Catholic, a bachelor, approved of by the Pope, and enjoying "the general favour of the seminarians and busiest Papists in action".

"Those" accordingly, "that had the service committed unto them to examine Hart, did most earnestly press and urge him to tell who was the noble person to be elected, which thing Hart refused to declare, pretending that he knew it not. Being still pressed, though he knew not certainly who should be elected, yet to utter to what noble person the favours and wishes of the seminarians did most incline or they would be most glad to have so advanced or they liked best . . . he made no direct answer but gave commendation to the Lord Henry Howard".[671]

Such were some of the details supplied by Norton, and it may be remarked in passing, that Allen, according to this Puritan rack-master, was one of the "capitulators" of the treaty, yet from Allen's own statement, he knew nothing of it while in Rome when it was concluded; and further that the "seminarians" appear to have been cognisant of a great deal of what was, according to the story, a "top secret", revealed only to Hart, because he was so "inward with Allen", who had ordered that it should not be divulged! These additional and fictitious details are to be found only in this document; which certainly points to their having been fabricated in Government circles in England. This, in turn, suggests, at least, that the alleged articles themselves had a similar origin.

The first person to report on the supposed league was the English ambassador in Paris, Sir Henry Cobham, a strong Puritan and follower of Walsingham, as was Norton. As early as January 1579, when Queen Elizabeth, in an audience granted to Mendoza, the Spanish ambassador,

---

[671] Reference as in Note 657. The use of the word "seminarian" occurring in this manuscript is exceptional, I think, in the Government circles of the time.

mentioned the league of Catholic princes being formed against her, Mendoza replied that he himself knew of no such league, but added:

> "*I was, however, certain some of her ministers would like to arouse her suspicions by saying that something of the sort was being done, as they wished to break her alliance with your Majesty and the house of Burgundy, and attach her to the French. Besides which, her ambassador in France persists in his news about such a league, as he is a great heretic, and is inspired by certain people of the same sort here*".[672]

What Mendoza reported of Cobham was certainly true, and it is surely strange that more than a month before the audience of 18 February 1580, when the contracting parties were supposed to have agreed upon the said league, Cobham should have reported that it had been already concluded.[673] At the same time he endeavoured, though not with great success, to convince the Venetian ambassador in France, Priuli, that the league was already in existence.[674] It was Cobham, too, who reported the false news that the excommunication of Elizabeth had been renewed by the Pope at the beginning of January 1580 and secretly printed, and that the Queen's Catholic subjects had been absolved from their oath of allegiance.[675] In another despatch, he stated:

> "I send a copy of Pope Pius' bull, renewed against the Queen and an indulgence procured by Bernardino [*Mendoza*] to infect her subjects".[676]

Now all this was certainly faked; for Gregory XIII, so far from renewing the excommunication and absolving the Queen's subjects from their allegiance, conceded, as already stated, on 14 April 1580, a relaxation of it as regards English Catholics, so that they could without scruple, recognise the Queen as their legitimate sovereign: as, indeed, did Campion and his companion martyrs in 1581. The supposed league, again, was frequently mentioned in Cobham's despatches, bearing out Mendoza's earlier remark that he persisted in reporting it.[677]

---

[672] Mendoza to Philip II, London, 27 January 1579, *Spanish Cal. 1568–1579*, p. 632; italics mine.

[673] Cobham to Burghley, Paris, 13 January 1580, *For. Cal. 1579–1580*, p. 127.

[674] Priuli to the Signory, Paris, 16 January 1580, *Venetian Cal. 1558–1580*, p. 627; cf. also Same to Same, 23 February 1580, *Ibid.*, p. 630.

[675] Cobham to Walsingham, 20 February 1580, *For. Cal. 1579–1580*, p. 157.

[676] Cobham to [the Secretaries], Paris, 29 February 1580, *Ibid.*, p. 171.

[677] Cf. Cobham to Walsingham, 20 and 21 February 1580; to Leicester, 21 [?] February; to Sir H. Sidney, 21[?] February; to Q. Elizabeth, 23 February; to the Secretaries, 29 February and 20 March; to Walsingham, 25 March; to Q. Elizabeth, 15 April; to [Walsingham], 12 July 1580, *Ibid.*, pp. 160, 164, 171, 192, 202, 231, 235 and 355.

It was from France, too, where Cobham was in touch with the Huguenots, that the articles of the alleged league were first brought to England. About the middle of June 1580, after Henry III had resolved to use force against his Huguenot subjects, their leader, the Prince of Condé, came secretly to England, to beg help from Queen Elizabeth and—no doubt to enforce his appeal—brought the articles of the fictitious league to her and her Council.[678] A fortnight or so later Cobham enclosed a copy of the articles in one of his despatches, and in a further despatch reported that they had been delivered to him by the Bishop of Ross, who had affirmed that Bishop Goldwell and the priests coming to England were to be instruments of the confederation.[679] A few days later, the articles appeared in Waterford, published by a gentleman from Devon, called William Eve, who stated that

> "*the same was commonly abroad in England, and that himself had given out twenty copies of it. Being demanded where he had it,* [he] *said it was delivered to him by Mr. Harry Bourchier, brother to the Earl of Bath*".[680]

Meanwhile the league had been referred to in the Proclamation of 15 July 1580. William Eve, it is true, was imprisoned by Pelham's orders, but there is no evidence that the Council of England ever took measures against him, rather the reverse. He appears to have been soon released; for the Council on 8 October of that year wrote to the Lord Treasurer to allow one, William Eve, to transport two hundred quarters of wheat from Devon and Cornwall to Ireland, provided he brought a certificate from the Lord Deputy or some other officer of credit, that the wheat had been bought there; and the identity of the two names, and the man's connection with Devon and Ireland, certainly suggest that this William Eve is the same person who brought the articles to Ireland.[681] Nor is there any evidence that Henry Bourchier

---

[678] Cf. The Prince of Condé to Walsingham, Sandwich, 18 June 1580, *Ibid.*, p. 311. Cobham reported his intended visit on 15 June (Cobham to the Queen, 15 June 1580, *Ibid.*, p. 305). At the end of the articles in the Carew MSS. is recorded: "These articles were brought by the Prince of Condé to the Queen's Majesty and her Council" (*Cal. Carew MSS. II*, p. 288).

[679] Cobham to [Walsingham], Vanves, 12 July 1580, *For. Cal. 1579–1580*, p. 355, where he also stated that he had enclosed the articles in his last despatch, presumably that of 7 July.

[680] Cf. Nicholas White, Master of the Rolls, to the Earl of Leicester, 21 July 1580, enclosing the articles of the alleged confederation, a document entitled "Eves Seditious Libel" (*Cal. Carew MSS. II*, p. 288). Italics mine. Cf. also Lord Justice Pelham to the Mayor of Waterford, Limerick, 26 July 1580 (*Ibid.*, p. 281); and Pelham to the Council in England, Asheton, 30 July 1580 (*Ibid.*, p. 287).

[681] The Council to the Lord Treasurer, 8 October 1580, *Dasent XII*, p. 227.

was ever interrogated about the articles and their dispersion by him, all which is very strange, seeing that according to Burghley's statement in the Proclamation of 15 July 1580, it was the Catholic exiles who

> "had caused to be devised in writings and the same published, that the Pope, the King of Spain and some other princes are accorded to make a great army to invade this realm of England and other her Majesty's dominions".[682]

It was certainly not usual for the Government to show such "insouciance" about those who spread such writings of the exiles: it is possibly a unique example.

Burghley's statement was, of course, somewhat stupid, as Allen was quick to point out,

> "being neither wisdom nor policy, if any such thing [*invasion*] were intended, (as we verily think there was not) much less if it were never meant, to publish any such libels, to give the Realm warning purposely to provide for it".[683]

Indeed, grave suspicion cannot but arise that Burghley made the statement to cover the secret fabrication and dispersion of the articles by the Government itself. That would explain why no action appears to have been taken against William Eve and the brother of the Earl of Bath by the Council, or against anyone else for that matter. Nor could the Government really believe that the King of Spain would invade England in 1580, his attentions being concentrated on the occupation of Portugal, besides the recovery of Flanders. As early as 1 June a spy in Spain, who as he himself stated, had taken great pains to discover the truth, informed the Government that there was no foundation for the reports given out by divers persons, that great preparations were being made in Spain for England ("that part"), and that the King with his army would be wholly occupied with Portugal that year.[684] That Philip would be unable to send his forces abroad was confirmed later by Fernihurst, who had come recently from Spain and reported that the King would not be able for twelve months to "address an army for any place".[685]

[682] Cf. "A Proclamation against Traitors and seditious rumours", dated 15 July 1580. A printed copy is preserved in the collection made by Humfrey Dyson, 1618, *Queene Elizabeth's Proclamations 1559 to 1602*, B.M. G. 6463. The draft, amended by Burghley, is in Dom. Eliz. 140, n. 18.

[683] *An Apologie, etc.* f. 15v, as in Note 668.

[684] Roger Bodenham to Dr. Wilson, San Lucar, 1 June 1580; to Burghley, San Lucar, 1 June 1580, *For. Cal. 1579–1580*, pp. 284 and 285.

[685] Cobham to the Secretaries, Blois, 10 December 1580, reporting the statement (*Ibid.*, p. 504).

Q

Finally, although Cobham and the Government knew of the articles by late June or early July, it was only about 2 December that the English ambassador made another attempt to convince the Venetian ambassador, Priuli, of the supposed confederation, by handing him a copy of them, of which, apparently, Priuli *had previously not been cognisant*. Cobham, indeed, had little success, for Priuli proved critically sceptical and drily reported:

"I will contrive to ascertain whether I have been told the truth, because these English are so artful in their negotiations that I cannot be sure that this story may not have been their invention, or if not entirely so, at least to some extent".[686]

Nor is there any further reference to the alleged league in his published despatches.

Such then is the evidence, and it certainly suggests that the fictitious league with its articles was fabricated by some members of the English Government. Several reasons, indeed, arising from the documents, can be adduced for their having done so. The first was to induce Queen Elizabeth to agree to more repressive measures against her Catholic subjects by the falsely alleged renewal of her excommunication, the threat of invasion by the Catholic powers, and the allegation that the priests were coming to England to form a party there to aid it. Moreover the people, too, needed to be persuaded to acquiesce in these intended repressive measures by rousing national sentiment, which was done by the Proclamation 15 July, in which priests, and those who supported them, were linked with the fictitious league for the invasion of the realm; for certainly this fabrication was so used in the trial of Campion and his companions in November 1581. Allen was, probably, not far from the truth when he wrote:

"And it verily may be thought (and so it is certain that *some of the principal ministers of the forenamed Princes have answered, being demanded thereof*) that the Protestants having exercised skill and audacity in such practices and counter practices (of which France, Flanders, Scotland, and other countries have so lamentable experience) did contrive them [*the libels or articles*] to alter her Majesty's accustomed benignity and mercy towards the Catholics, into such rigour of justice as in the said Edict [*of 15 July*] is threatened".[687]

The second reason for their invention may have been to influence the Queen to grant to the Huguenots the aid that Cobham and

[686] Priuli to the Signory, Moret, 2 December 1580, *Venetian Cal. 1558–1580*, p. 649.
[687] *An Apologie, etc. ut supra*, f. 16. Italics mine.

Walsingham so much desired. It is surely significant that on his visit to England the Prince of Condé should have brought to the Queen and her Council the articles of the alleged league; that Cobham, but a few days after that visit, should also have sent a copy of them; and that a few days after this a further copy should have been received in Ireland—and this at a time when the Venetian ambassador in Paris apparently knew nothing of them. Granted the bogus character of the league and its articles, can one say that the timing of all these notices of it was purely fortuitous?

A third reason may be adduced, such as Mendoza himself mentioned, namely to persuade the Queen to break with Spain and to lead her to attempt again the formation of a counter league of Protestant princes— a favourite plank in the policy of Walsingham and Cobham—after the failure to form such in the immediately preceding years.[688]

It must not be forgotten, either, that this was not the first time that the Government had dealt in a fictitious Papal league. To mention but one other example, when the Emperor in 1567 sent Count Stolberg to England to invite Queen Elizabeth to join a general league against the Turk, the story of a fictitious Papal league against her was used as the reason for refusing the Emperor's request, Stolberg being assured, as soon as he arrived at Dover, by the person sent to meet him, that such a Papal league against the Queen was a reality. This person, indeed, promised that he would give him the heads of the agreement between the Pope, the King of Spain and the King of France, to prove the truth of what he had asserted. It was the Spanish ambassador, Guzman de Silva, who exposed the fictitious nature of this alleged league, and who was convinced that it had been forged by the Elizabethan ministers to give them an excuse for refusing the invitation of the Emperor, as, indeed, it was so used by the Queen herself for that effect.[689]

Whatever the origin, however, of the bogus league of 1580, the Government were certainly lying in their statements about Hart's confessions concerning it, and that may well be the reason why they omitted mention of his name in the printed pamphlet about Throckmorton, for fear that he would give them the lie; nor was he called as a witness in the trial of Campion in 1581, or his confessions used in his

[688] Cf. Cobham to Walsingham, 21 February and 25 March 1580; to Burghley, 30 October; to the Secretaries, 12 October; to Walsingham, 19 November; to [Walsingham], 28 November 1580, *For. Cal. 1579–1580*, pp. 160, 202, 436, 448, 487 and 498.

[689] Cf. Guzman de Silva's despatches, 21 and 26 June 1567, *Spanish Cal. 1558–1567*, pp. 646 and 649; and of 16 February and 20 March 1568, *Ibid., 1568–1579*, pp. 8 and 15.

own trial on the day after that of Campion, though if true, they would have been most effective for the Government's purpose. Hart, though condemned to death, was not executed, but was kept in prison until January 1585, when he was exiled with other prisoners.

The documents themselves, indeed, give a glimpse of how evidence was fabricated by the Government, and thus may serve as a warning, not naïvely to accept statements emanating from this source, about alleged confessions that are no longer extant, but to receive them with extreme caution.

APPENDIX II

Crichton's Paper (*cf. Note 72*)

The story put out by Walsingham, that a plan of invasion, written in Italian was found when Crichton, the Jesuit, was captured at sea in 1584[690] and, though torn up by him and divers pieces lost, yet by joining the recovered fragments together, the sense of the document was revealed, is, when critically examined, an extremely "tall" one.[691] The torn-up pieces, if they ever existed, are no longer extant, but there has survived an English translation of the document, as reconstructed from the fragments.[692] This official English translation runs in Knox's book to some seven quarto pages and is, in fact, a very complete synopsis of Lennox's plan of invasion, as modified by the Duke of Guise and his collaborators about May 1582—a plan, it must be recalled, that had been abandoned by the September of that year because Philip II refused to aid its execution with his armed forces, and because Lennox's power was overthrown by the capture of James VI in the Raid of Ruthven on 22 August 1582.[693] Knox, who appears not to have known of the original modified plan of Lennox, asserted of the reconstructed paper of Crichton that "there is no pretence of giving more than the substance of the discourse". This is a gross understatement. A comparison of the paper said to have been put together from the torn fragments, with the original plan in Kretzschmar, reveals a truly surprising agreement, even to the order of the paragraphs! One section only is in a different place, and even in that section the order of the many paragraphs is followed, and in two places, where the original has some animadversions on Queen

---

[690] Crichton was captured at the end of August or the beginning of September 1584 (cf. *supra* Note 72).

[691] Cf. Walsingham to Sadler, 16 September 1584, Sadler's *State Papers*, 1808, Ed. *III*, p. 168.

[692] Dom. Eliz. 173, n. 4. Strype (*Annals*, 1824 Ed. *III, I*, p. 602) printed his extracts from another manuscript (B.M. Cotton MSS. Julius F. VI, 58). Knox (*Allen*, p. 485) printed the document from a third contemporary copy, in the Westminster Cathedral Archives, which is somewhat more complete than that preserved among the Domestic Papers, Elizabeth. I have used Knox's printed version for convenience.

[693] Cf. *supra* Chapter I, section 5. The original plan, with an English translation is printed in *C.R.S. XXXIX*, pp. 148ff; cf. also *Kretzschmar*, pp. 135ff.

Elizabeth's private life, there are blank spaces left in the English translation of the torn-up document. Walsingham was certainly understating the case, when he wrote to Sadler that despite the document having been torn up and some pieces lost, the sense of it was recovered. It is a truly marvellous work of reconstruction! His story was probably put out as a cover, to conceal how such a document came into the possession of the Government; for it is known that they had tried to obtain the original documents concerning the invasion from the effects of the late Nuncio in France, Castelli, who had died 27 August 1583. Writing a year or so before Crichton's capture to Robert Beale, who was acting as Secretary of State in the absence of Walsingham in Scotland, Cobham, the English ambassador, reported from Paris:

> "After the death of the Pope's Nuncio I used my best means to recover those memorials and writings specified in your letter, but could never do so".[694]

In the confessions of Crichton, moreover, taken in French at the time of his capture, there is no mention of such a document, but there is mention of a letter which he had in his hand when arrested and tore up. When he was asked why he had torn it up, he replied that it was a cipher alphabet, which the Archbishop of Glasgow had given him, addressed to the Archbishop's nephew, Fentry, for their correspondence, and which he had been charged to destroy, if pursued or taken prisoner, which is extremely probable. Nor is there a hint of this cipher or any paper being reconstructed from the torn pieces and sent to Walsingham. Further, Addy, the secular priest captured with Crichton, confessed that any letters he had had from the Bishop of Ross, whose chaplain he had been, to his friends, had been carried away in the ship with the Jesuit, Gordon, who had been allowed to go free.[695] Davison, indeed, had seen an original letter to Fentry and an abstract of an instruction given by the Bishop of Ross to his servant, copies of which he sent to Walsingham, but he did not refer to any document that had been torn up.[696] It is also to be noted that these documents were only copies and further that they were enclosed in a letter to Walsing-

---

[694] Cobham to Beale, Paris, 12 October 1583, *For. Cal. July 1583–July 1584*, p. 135. Could it have been that the Government obtained copies later, after Morgan and Paget had been admitted in 1583 to the secrets of the leading supporters in France of the Queen of Scots (cf. *supra* Chapter I, section 5)? There is, however, no evidence to prove this.

[695] Cf. Confessions of Crichton and Addy in French, undated, Dom. Eliz. 173, nn. 2 and 3.

[696] "The Jesuits who are drawn home are by proclamation commanded to avoid the country within a month under pain of death. But how it will be executed his honour will hear hereafter. That they hope better he may perceive somewhat by the copy of a letter

ham, on the day *after* Walsingham had reported the news to Sadler of the torn-up document found when Crichton was captured.[697] Nor is there any mention of such a document in Crichton's own account of his capture.[698] There seems, in fact, no reason at all why Crichton should have been carrying about him, when there was always danger of being captured, the plan of invasion of 1582, which he knew had been abandoned two years before, especially seeing that a new plan had been drawn up since then.[699] It is true that in the summary of a speech of the Lord Chancellor, there is a reference made to Crichton's confession, in which he asserted that the Jesuit had confessed to have received the discourses, Latin, Italian and French, from his superior, and to have said that the author of the Italian discourse "should hardly be discovered". A note, however, in the margin of the Chancellor's speech gives the name of "George Golbert".[700] The person so signified was probably intended to be George Gilbert, who was well known to the English Government, but he had been in Rome when the conferences about Lennox's plan were held in Paris in April–May 1582, and so could not have taken part in drawing up the modified plan of Lennox, supposed to have been reconstructed from the pieces thrown away by Crichton.[701] The copy, indeed, of this plan, as modified by the Duke of Guise and his collaborators, was conveyed to Rome by Crichton himself to give to the Papal Secretary of State, and the copy in Spanish was either sent to Spain by De Tassis, the Spanish agent in Paris, or else was taken there by Persons.[702] It would seem, then, that if George Gilbert is the person named in the margin, the Italian "discorso" mentioned in the alleged confessions of Crichton, was not the Lennox plan as modified but some other document; for Crichton

[697] Cf. *supra* Note 691.

[698] Printed by J. H. Pollen, s.j. in *Mary Queen of Scots and the Babington Plot*, Edinburgh, 1922, pp. 151ff.

[699] Cf. Disegno per l'impresa d'Inghilterra, enclosed in the Nuncio, Castelli's despatch of 20 June 1583, *Kretzschmar*, p. 168.

[700] Cf. what T. F. Knox calls "Confessions of Fr. William Creighton, s.j. in the Tower 1584", (Knox, *Allen*, pp. 432–434, printed from Cotton MSS. Galba C. X, 322).

[701] George Gilbert had been sent to Rome as the bearer of Allen's letter to Como, 20 December 1581 (Knox, *Allen*, p. 106), and remained there till his death, 6 October 1583. He had been the inseparable companion of Persons in England, but the pursuit of him by the Government had been so keen, that the Jesuit persuaded him, not without difficulty, to leave England (cf. Persons to Gregory XIII, London, 14 June 1581, *C.R.S. XXXIX*, p. 64).

[702] Cf. *C.R.S. XXXIX*, p. lii.

to Fentry, the original whereof he saw, and by the abstract of an instruction given by the Bishop of Ross, amongst other things, to his servant taken by the Flushingers, both of which he encloses" (Davison to Walsingham, 17 September 1584, *Scot. Cal. VII*, p. 333).

knew that that plan had been drawn up at the conferences of April and May 1582, at which Gilbert had not been present, and so could not have been the author of it.

The story of Walsingham was, in fact, a fabrication, just as were the articles of the alleged Papal league of 1580. Lingard, however, followed by Froude, made the story more incredible still by saying that the torn pieces of the document had been cast into the sea, whence they were recovered.

But to return to what Knox published as the "Confessions of William Creighton, s.j., in the Tower 1584": this document is all in one hand and is undated, though "1586" has been written on it in another hand.[703] It begins, not on folio 322, as one would gather from Knox, but on folio 321, and is a summary of or points for a speech made by the Lord Chancellor, possibly at the beginning of Parliament in 1584. Knox omitted folio 321, and also the last folio, and printed the middle folios of the speech as the Confessions of Crichton. The Chancellor's statements about Crichton's confessions cannot by any critical historian be labelled "Crichton's confessions", especially as Goverment statements about confessions not now extant are, as already shown, unreliable. It was quite unpardonable of Knox to print these statements and call them "The Confessions of Creighton": for it was to mislead the reader completely as to the true nature of the document. The only confessions of the Jesuit about this affair that are extant are those in French, to which reference has already been made,[704] though there are also interrogatories, dated 3 January 1585, but without replies.[705] These documents, however, do not support the story put out by Walsingham.

[703] B.M. Cotton MSS. Galba C. X, 322.

[704] Cf. *supra* Note 695.

[705] Dom. Eliz. 173, n. 3. There is one other short confession signed by Crichton, dated 15 February 1585 (Dom. Eliz. 176, n. 54), but this refers to the so-called Parry plot, from which he exculpated himself, which exculpation was confirmed by Parry himself.

APPENDIX III

The Attack on William Wade (*cf. Note 415*)

There is a curious incident related by Morgan in connection with William Wade's mission to demand his extradition from France in March 1585. In a letter to Dr. Owen Lewis, he wrote:

"The bruit went far and near that Mr. Morgan should be delivered [*to England*], whereupon they of the house of Guise, having in singular recommendation the old service of Mr. Morgan to her Majesty of Scotland and to some of them also, laid wait for Wade his return, thinking Mr. Morgan should have been in his company, about Abbeville in Picardy, where M. d'Aumâle, cousin-germain to M. de Guise, commanded much. Wade was assaulted in the highway, accompanied with four, and was well beaten, and Wade detained in ward by the command of M. d'Aumâle until he found the truth that Mr. Morgan was not of the company. The French king being hereof informed, wrote to M. d'Aumâle to put Wade to liberty, and so he did, and made humble suit to his Majesty to do the like with Mr. Morgan who should have been rescued, as you may perceive, if the King had sent him to England".[706]

Thomas Throckmorton also referred to the incident. In a letter to the Queen of Scots a few days later than the above letter of Morgan, he wrote:

"But *infine* he [*Wade*] received a plain conclusion negative, and so departed three days before Easter very much discontented and was in his return taken by a few soldiers about Abbeville, whom he takes to be of the Duke of Aumâle's company and all his packets rifled and himself stayed for a time till upon the King's letters to the Duke he was delivered".[707]

Apart from this account, which sounds like an echo of Morgan's written a few days earlier, there are two other references to the

[706] Morgan to Dr. Lewis in Rome, 18 April 1585, *For. Cal. August 1584–August 1585*, p. 416. The only other allusion to the incident by Morgan was in his letter to the Queen of Scots, 10/20 July 1585 (*Murdin*, p. 446 and *Scot. Cal. VIII*, p. 11). There all he wrote was that if he had been sent to England, d'Aumâle was prepared to rescue him.
[707] Throckmorton to Q. of Scots, 30 April 1585 (*Scot. Cal. VII*, p. 636). Throckmorton used the new style. Easter in that style fell on 21 April in 1585, whilst in the old style it fell upon 3 April, and three days before that would be 31 March, and Wade had not left by that date.

occurrence, one in a letter of Edward Burnham, the other in one of Poulet. Burnham, a servant of Walsingham, had been sent by him to Davison at the Hague, and on his return, writing from Barn Elms, Walsingham's house, he reported the return of Wade from France three days before he himself had arrived back in England, adding that Wade had been stayed by the Duke of Aumâle at Pont de Rémi by Abbeville, who took his letters but had used him courteously, opened none but the King's letter to her Majesty, and after dinner let him go.[708] Walsingham, on his part, had lost no time in reporting the incident to Poulet;[709] and the way the latter used it, according to Walsingham's direction, to brow-beat the defenceless captive Queen gives some insight into the characters of these savage Puritans at the beginning of their final attack upon her. In a letter to the Secretary of State, Poulet wrote:

> "I had just occasion in my last speech with this Queen to tell her, *according to your direction*, that it was not enough that some of her Ministers had not long sithence practised most execrably the utter ruin of her Majesty [*Elizabeth*], but that now also, very lately, the Duc d'Aumâle had rifled one of her Highness' servants in his return out of France, of all his letters and papers,[710] which must be said to have been done either by her assent or for her sake, and that it could not be but that these bad offices falling out daily in this sort, must breed jealousy and mistrust in the Queen my mistress.
>
> She protested that she knew nothing of it, adding that this Duke was a mere stranger unto her, and that she had never seen him. I answered that he knew her to be his kinswoman, and was content to give testimony of his good effection towards her by doing wrong to the Queen's Majesty".[711]

This unreasonable harshness may be more explicable, though not more excusable, if, as certain indications show, it was the intention of Walsingham and his fellows to have had the "Babington Plot" in that year, 1585.[712]

[708] Edward Burnham to Davison, Barn Elms, 21 April 1585, (*For. Cal. ut supra*, p. 423). He stated that he had arrived back on 20 April, so Wade would have returned on the 17th.

[709] Poulet to Walsingham, Tutbury, 2 May 1585, referring to a letter of Walsingham's of the 18 April, the day after Wade's return, informing him of it (cf. *Scot. Cal. VII*, p. 642).

[710] J. Morris, s.j., notes that in his next letter "we learn that this was William Waad or Wade" (*The Letter-Books of Sir Amias Poulet*, p. 16, n. 1).

[711] Postscript to Poulet to Walsingham, Tutbury, 27 April 1585 (*Ibid.*, pp. 10–16). Italics mine. The Queen of Scots had had nothing to do with Parry's plot, to which Poulet also referred, as Walsingham very well knew.

[712] Cf. *infra* Appendix V.

However it be, despite the above references to the attack on Wade, there are reasons for thinking that the incident was purely imaginary or faked. In the first place, as Wade had but four men with him, it would not have been difficult for d'Aumâle to have ascertained whether Morgan was one of them before he stayed the ambassador, or according to Morgan, assaulted him in the highway. Furthermore, Burnham's account by no means agrees with Morgan's in detail. According to the former Wade was but stayed, used courteously and dismissed at once after dinner, only the King's letter having been read; whereas according to Morgan there was a fight, Wade was well beaten, and kept in ward until the king had been informed and had sent a letter to d'Aumâle to release him, which certainly would have taken some considerable time. A further reason for thinking the incident imaginary and a conclusive one is this. Had it really taken place there would surely have been some echo of it in the diplomatic correspondence of the time—a complaint, at least, from the Queen of England to Henry III for such a serious violation of the rights and status of her ambassador. Yet, neither in the letters of Walsingham to Stafford, nor in those of Stafford himself, is there the least mention of the incident; still less is there any letter on the subject from Queen Elizabeth to Henry III.[713] Moreover, if it really did occur, Walsingham must be credited with prophetic foresight, the only error being as regards the identity of the ambassador; for in a letter to Stafford *a month before the incident is said to have taken place*, he wrote:

"I pray God Morgan may be delivered to the Earl of Derby before these come to your hands. I never saw her Majesty affect any matter so greatly. The French Ambassador here is doubtless moved by the ill-affected to stay his delivery. The Earl *must take good heed between Abbeville and Montereau lest an ambush be laid to intercept him*; I have written to advise him to leave that way and to pass along the sea-side".[714]

This letter of Walsingham, a month before the supposed incident,

---

[713] Compare the immediate reaction of Henry III à propos of the de Trappes incident (cf. *supra* Chapter IX, section 1 and especially Note 420). "He [*Henry III*] told me again", Stafford reported, "that he took it very unkindly to be injured; that it was a wrong to all ambassadors and especially to him that had not deserved to be wronged at any man's hands" (Stafford to Burghley, Paris, 23 January 1587, *For. Cal. June 1586–June 1588*, p. 198). In a letter to Elizabeth Henry III again raised the same point: "that she had suffered him [*Châteauneuf*] to be treated in a manner so unworthy of the respect in which all ambassadors should be held" (Henry III to Elizabeth, Paris, 26 January 1587, *Ibid.*, p. 199).

[714] Walsingham to Stafford, 7 March 1585, *For. Cal. August 1584–August 1585*, p. 332. Italics mine.

suggests at least, that the story emanated from his household at Barn Elms, whence Burnham wrote his account of Wade, not Derby, having been stayed near the same Abbeville. The letter itself is, surely, too extraordinary to have been the result of mere coincidence. It is just possible that the incident did take place, but that the persons who made the assault were not Aumâle's men but Walsingham's, the attack being part of the "build-up" against Mary, Queen of Scots. It is noticeable, certainly, how quickly Walsingham seized the opportunity of making her responsible for it. If the attack did not take place, or was made not by Aumâle, it would account, indeed, for the complete silence regarding the alleged incident in the diplomatic correspondence. It is also strange that Morgan, who from his own account was a close prisoner and deprived of all ordinary intelligence, should have related the story but a day or two after the event was supposed to have taken place! But, whatever the explanation, Morgan's account, when contrasted with that of Burnham, reveals his characteristic megalomania.

APPENDIX IV

Who was the first Messenger employed to re-open the Queen of Scots' secret correspondence? (*cf. Chapter XII, sections 1 and 2*)

Gilbert Gifford is usually regarded as having been the first who essayed to re-open the channel of secret correspondence for the Queen of Scots, after it had been closed throughout the year 1585. But, in point of fact, he was not the first, for there were two messengers sent to restart communications. The first, originally an unnamed person, —his identity will be discussed later—was despatched by the French ambassador, Châteauneuf, on 1 December 1585, and returned to him on the 20 February 1586: the second was Gilbert Gifford, who was sent by the ambassador a little later than the first man. In a letter to the Queen of Scots, 6 March 1586, Châteauneuf wrote:

"Seeing Madam, that to my great regret I had no letters in cipher from your Majesty, I did my utmost to find a man who would carry some to you at any price. Having done so, I promised him fifty crowns and advanced the half of it, with a letter of mine which he assured me he would deliver to some one of your people and bring me an answer: upon which I was to give him the rest. He went hence the first of December, and I did not see him again till the twentieth of February, when he told us that he had delivered my said letters in cipher to Pasquier but without bringing me the said answer, which keeps me from as yet delivering the rest to him, and moreover that your Majesty has sent me no word".[715]

The messenger to which he referred in this letter was not Gilbert Gifford, whom according to Châteauneuf's own statement he did not despatch till later, and who returned to him on 1 March.[716] The fact, moreover, that Châteauneuf had discovered two messengers to restart the secret correspondence is confirmed by a letter of Glasgow to the Queen of Scots, 21 March 1586. In this her ambassador reported what

[715] Châteauneuf to Q. of Scots, 6 March 1586, *Scot. Cal. VIII*, p. 247.
[716] Cf. *Mémoire de Monsieur de Châteauneuf sur la Conspiration de Babington, Labanoff VI*, pp. 274ff.

he had learnt in conversation with the Duke of Guise, that Monsieur de la Chastre had heard from his brother-in-law in London [*Château-neuf*] that he had already found two persons for the re-opening of communications with the Queen.[717]

It may be remarked, *en passant*, that as this unnamed messenger was on trial, neither Châteauneuf nor the Scottish Queen put anything of importance in their respective letters.[718] She did, however, somewhat unwisely, send by him a completely new cipher for the ambassador to use in his secret letters to her.[719] For some reason she began to fear that her letter had not been delivered to Châteauneuf by this first messenger; so on 31 January she sent a duplicate by another messenger who, no doubt, was Gilbert Gifford.[720] Her fears were justified since, as shown above, the ambassador on 6 March reported that the unnamed messenger had brought no answer from the Queen, when he had returned on 20 February. In consequence, the ambassador would not pay him the other twenty-five crowns that had been promised him.[721]

It seems highly probable, moreover, that the letter committed by Châteauneuf to the unnamed messenger, was not delivered by him personally to the Queen of Scots' servant, Pasquier, but by Phelippes himself; for writing to the ambassador and referring to this incident, she said:

"I desire to know the name of him to whom you have addressed your-self, so that I shall be able to recognize him: and thereupon I shall be able to enlighten you. If it is, as I think, one named Philippes, servant of Walsingham, who about Christmas stayed in this house for more than three weeks, beware of further committing yourself

---

[717] Glasgow to Q. of Scots, 21 March 1586, *Scot. Cal. VIII*, p. 255.

[718] See their own statements to this effect, in Châteauneuf of Q. of Scots, 30 March 1586, and Q. of Scots to Châteauneuf, 31 January 1586 (*Ibid.*, pp. 289 and 204).

[719] The real reason for not writing anything of importance appears to have been that she thought Phelippes was the messenger employed by Châteauneuf and knew that he was playing a double game (Q. of Scots to Châteauneuf, 24 March 1586, *Labanoff VI*, p. 261 and *Scot. Cal. VIII*, p. 284). The Queen of Scots, as Dowager Queen of France and sister-in-law to Henry III, was entitled to have secret correspondence with the ambassador of France, a fact which is rarely if ever mentioned, just as the total illegality of her imprisonment is glossed over far too often.

[720] Q. of Scots to Châteauneuf, 31 January 1586, *ut supra*. The letter of 5 October 1585, that Gifford had been commissioned by Morgan to have delivered to her, reached her on 16 January, and was answered by her the next day (Q. of Scots to Morgan, 17 January 1586, *Murdin*, p. 469 and *Scot. Cal. VIII*, p. 187).

[721] Châteauneuf to Q. of Scots, 6 March 1586, *ut supra*. Cherelles, too, reported that they had been deceived: "I have induced Monsieur de Châteauneuf to seek some means to write secretly, thinking finally to have found one, wherein we have found ourselves deceived, as the said Sieur de Châteauneuf told me he had given your Majesty to understand" (Cherelles to Q. of Scots, 2 April 1586, *Scot. Cal. VIII*, p. 297).

to him. For although he has promised to do me service, I know that he is playing a double game".[722]

Had Phelippes succeeded in gaining her confidence, as this letter shows that he tried to do, it seems very likely that he would have continued this direct approach; but from her own letters it is clear that he failed to do so, and thus had recourse, by means of Gilbert Gifford, to the more complicated and cumbersome process of the beer-barrel of the Burton brewer, which has since caused many a head-ache to historians.

But who was this unnamed messenger to whom was committed the first attempt to re-open the secret correspondence? Châteauneuf himself later reported, in answer to the Queen's enquiry, that he was a small fair man, who had been a servant of Stafford, the English ambassador in France, and that his name was Motin. Not all these details are necessarily correct, nor the name his real one, for Châteauneuf was reporting what the messenger had told him, who, being in reality an agent of the English Government, would not have given very much correct information. There are, indeed, solid reasons for considering the messenger to have been no other than Robert Poley. Writing to the Queen of Scots on 18 January 1586, Morgan reported:

"Charles Paget and I recommended some English in London to the French ambassador, to do him pleasure and service there; and amongst others, one Robert Poley, who hath given me assurance to serve and honour your Majesty to his power, being but a poor gentleman".

Then after having said that the French ambassador and his secretary, Cordaillot, had since reported favourably of him, he concluded:

"I think the said Poley be at this time in the parts of Tutbury, where that Queen's horses be, for that Blunt hath given credit to the said Poley, to the end he might thereby do some service to your Majesty;[723] and I gave Blunt a few lines to make an intelligence for

---

[722] Q. of Scots to Châteauneuf, Chartley, 24 March 1586, *Labanoff VI*, p. 261. Châteauneuf replied on the 30 March giving a description of the messenger and also the name he gave himself (cf. Châteauneuf to Q. of Scots, 30 March 1586, *Scot. Cal. VIII*, p. 288).

[723] "As to Blunt", wrote Châteauneuf, "he is in Flanders with the Earl of Leicester. I knew him: he visited me once or twice on behalf of his master; I had no other secret understanding with him. But I hear he is an honest man and one upon whom your Majesty might rely" (Châteauneuf to Q. of Scots, 30 March 1586, *ut supra*). Doubtless the information of his "honesty" came from Morgan, who in several letters both in 1585 and in 1586 strongly recommended him to the Queen of Scots and always in association with Poley (cf. Morgan to Q. of Scots, 10 July 1585, 18 July 1585, 18 January 1586 and 21 March 1586, all which letters are in the *Scot. Cal. VIII*, and most of them are given in full in *Murdin*). The "credit" that Blunt gave of Poley was to the French ambassador, judging by subsequent events.

your Majesty. But as far as I perceive, Blunt hath recommended the same to the said Poley to labour the delivery [of] the same".[724]

In a later letter Morgan reported that Poley had carried out his task.

"Having written thus far", he wrote on 21 March 1586, "I received letters out of England from London from Poley, in my former letters mentioned, who writeth unto me, that he hath been in the parts where your Majesty remaineth and there addressed the means to convey such letters, as I commended to his care, to serve to make an intelligence with your Majesty. We have applied him this twelve months, or thereabouts, and have found him to deal well, and very willing to serve your Majesty, as Paget can tell you. He was first recommended unto to me by Christopher Blunt, who never abused me, but continued well affected to serve and honour your Majesty; and I am of opinion, that you entertain the said Poley, who, by Blunt's labours and my advice, is placed with the Lady Sidney, the daughter of Secretary Walsingham, and by that means ordinarily in his house, and thereby able to pick out many things to the information of your Majesty. Blunt and he, in favour of your Majesty and by my instruction, have done notable service to the French ambassador at his first arrival in England.[725] when as he was so narrowly looked unto, as few or none of the English durst approach his house, much less confer with him or any of his house. According to your wisdom your Majesty may in ordinary sort entertain Poley in writing, and use his labour for the convoy between your Majesty and the French ambassador, and give order there or here to us for some consideration of his service, which with time may be very profitable for us".[726]

From these two letters it seems clear that Poley was to be used as a convoy of secret letters to the Queen of Scots, and that by the second letter of Morgan, of 21 March, he had been so employed. These dates fit in very well with that of the ambassador's own letter of 6 March reporting the messenger's return.

Robert Poley, of course, was an agent of the English Government and more particularly, at first, of Leicester. In a letter early in 1585

---

[724] Morgan to Q. of Scots, 18/28 January 1586, *Murdin*, p. 470 and *Scot. Cal. VIII*, p. 189. Of Poley's earlier connection with Walsingham, cf. *supra* Note 315.
[725] About August 1585.
[726] Morgan to Q. of Scots, 21/31 March 1586, *Murdin*, p. 481 and *Scot. Cal. VIII*, p. 262. Cf. also Paget to Same, 31 March 1586, *Murdin*, p. 506 and *Scot. Cal. VIII*, p. 292; and "Particulars of two letters from Morgan and Paget, 6 January 1586", M.Q.S. XVII, n. 2, and *Scot. Cal. VIII*, p. 178. The last-named document is quoted in full and discussed in Chapter XII, section 1.

he clearly revealed his attempts to be employed by the Government.[727]

"My three years past determination", it runs, "Right honourable, to do her Majesty and the state some special service, to be proved by witness of others, mine own proceedings, and all circumstances; which my most earnest suit ten months past, and many times since, to the next in court, and nearest at home, to Mr. Secretary for mine entertainment, and direction in the same service, will I hope persuade your honour that my reserving of Morgan's letter, (as a testimony to be shewed Mr. Secretary of my credit with him)[728] my recourses to Norris in the Marshalsea, (to entertain his and others' opinion and report of me to Morgan, if it were required)[729] and my receiving, and keeping of a few purposeless Books from the said Norris, with what else I have coldly done, as seeming to favour their religion, or cause, will I hope, as I said, confirm your honour's judgements of my loyalty, and behoveful service intended: and to acquit me of, and from all sinister reports or conceits for that part: wherein if your honour (for more confirmation) vouchsafe a probable, and irreproveable witness, I humbly beseech, that Thomas Audely, a Spanish merchant (and of their language, manners and customs much skilful) dwelling at the Plough in Thames Street near the custom house, may be called: with him, being a very good Protestant, and most affectionate subject, I have much conversed for three years past; him, (he always instantly persuading me thereunto) I made privy with mine intent, (but not intended course of service) to deal with Mr. Secretary: he accompanied me to Greenwich, to Otelands, to St. James, to Seething Lane where I attended Mr. Thomas Walsingham for my secret recourse to Mr. Secretary: But all to lost labour then, and my distress now: lastly (about iij or iiij months since) Mr.

[727] Poley to the Earl of Leicester, undated, R.O. S.P. 78 (France), 17, n. 26 bis. This letter is wrongly calendared under 1587 (*For. Cal. June 1586–1587*, p. 288). The Calendarist, misled by the mention of Parliament in this undated letter, assigned it to that year, but the reference to the priest Richard Norris, and other prisoners banished with him, shows that it belongs to 1585, for they were exiled on 21 January of that year. The Parliament mentioned in the letter is not, as the Calendarist supposed, that of 1587, but that which began on 23 November 1584, and which was prorogued on 29 March 1585. The names of the exiled prisoners, that of Richard Norris among them, are given in the Royal Commission, 15 January 1585, authorising their banishment (Dom. Eliz. 176, n. 9). Allen referred to their having been exiled on 21 January, in his letter to Como, Rheims, 28 February 1585 (Knox, *Allen*, p. 248); cf. also the Nuncio to Como, Paris, 4 February and 3 March 1585, R.O. Transcripts 31/9, bundle 82a, and *C.R.S. V*, pp. 102–103.

[728] Apparently he did not know at this time that Morgan himself was an agent of the English Government, which is not surprising.

[729] Norris was imprisoned in the Marshalsea on 17 December 1581 (Prison Lists in *C.R.S. II*, pp. 233 and 236). He was still there late in July 1584 (Nicholas Parker to Walsingham, Ratton, 24 July 1584, *Dom. Cal. Eliz. 1581–1590*, p. 192). Banished with other prisoners on 21 January 1585, he returned to England on 28 May of the same year, and later went to Spain, where he died in 1590 (Knox, *Douay Diaries*, pp. 206 and 230).

R

Audely requested me to acquaint him with Mr. Christopher Blount for that he, having married a niece kinswoman of your honour's first wife,[730] was determined by her to move some suit to your lordship; where I took advantage earnestly to persuade him to offer unto your honour his service for Spain, for which doubtless he is much sufficient; which, after many debatings between us, he condescended to do, and then brought I Mr. Christopher Blount to his house: And then went your honour immediately to Killingworth; and he since hath been delayed by means of your honour's great business of Parliament, and other occurrents: This man hath known mine intent, and proceedings to do her Majesty and your honour some acceptable service, and, I presume would be bound life for life for my true accomplishment in the same: Further whereas Mr. Secretary in my late examination did charge me as justly to be suspected by your honour, and him, as procurring, or knowing the procurers of certain libels, against her Majesty, the State, and other persons of honour, published:[731] I humbly and dutifully protest that I am utterly innocent, and in no circumstance to be touched, either in any such traitorous libelling, or other undutiful practice against her Majesty, or the State whatsoever; neither is there any dependence or comformity, Right honourable, that I having carried iij or iiij years intent to serve the State in like discoveries, and most instantly labouring mine admittance, and direction in the same for x or xij continual months last past, should either in the mean time myself commit any offence of like quality; or knowing of others procuring should conceal the same: And yet further, under your honour's patience, if it be demanded why I have not in these iij or iiij years' intent, endeavoured to discover some practice either foreign, or at home against the state; I humbly answer, that, if at mine own election, without your honour's, Mr. Secretary's, or some others of her honourable Council's consent, and direction, (for which consent and direction from Mr. Secretary I have laboured a whole year) I should have insinuated the conversation of any at home, or abroad suspected for religion, or practice against the state; and not in convenient time (as often it must needs fall out) detected anything; then should I have been directly charged as a practiser with them,[732] neither should

---

[730] Presumably Amy Robsart.

[731] Referring probably to *Leicester's Commonwealth*, cf. L. Hicks, s.j., *The Growth of a Myth, Studies*, Spring 1957.

[732] William Parry was tried for treason at Westminster on 24 February 1585 and condemned (cf. *supra* Chapter III, section 2). It has been suggested that the downfall of this agent-provocateur, which he certainly was, was due to his not having such a licence or direction in the particular case of Neville; and Poley may possibly have had this case in mind (cf. Conyers Read, *Mr. Secretary Walsingham*, London, 1925, *II*, p. 402. Conyers Read's treatment of the Parry Plot, however, is far from satisfactory, cf. L. Hicks, s.j., *The Strange Case of Dr. William Parry, Studies*, September 1949).

my close intent have availed for excuse: But here I most humbly beseech your honour, so far as may conforme with your pleasure and wisdom either to direct, or licence me in some course of discovery and service either abroad or at home; but rather I wish with Morgan, because my plat being laid that way, my credit is both enough with him, and also much with some of them which were last sent over, as Norris the Priest, and the rest. And I no whit mistrust, the grounds being secretly laid, and so kept, but that in short time, I shall accomplish some thing both worthy her Majesty's and your honour's acceptance, and also sufficient to countervail and recompense any the offences and misbehaviours of my youth past and lost.

Your honour's most humble and ever at command.

Rob: Poly.

His petition to be employed was evidently accepted, for he was sent over by Blunt to Morgan, who recommended both of them to the Queen of Scots.[733] A few days later, however, Morgan warned her that one of Poley's letters to Blunt had been intercepted and sent to the Council, and that in consequence both were likely to fall into trouble.[734] But, as already shown, Poley was employed in December of that year to re-open the channel of her secret correspondence, and Phelippes, having himself failed in his own direct approach to the captive Queen, suggested that Poley should be used to carry letters containing secret matter for Scotland, which Gilbert Gifford would obtain from the French ambassador. Thus, on 19 March 1586—the date should be noted—Phelippes wrote to Walsingham:

"The ambassador himself [*Châteauneuf*] has been anxious to find some apt means to send a packet into Scotland with some secret matters. I thought good to send your honour a word hereof to the end that if Poley be not attainable, you may think of some other who will deliver it, and the secret party[735] shall demand the same. If Poley received it, do not think but that he will send it to you, for as appears from Morgan's last he is recommended as a fit man for that convoy of Scotland.[736] Poley I think may be sent to the ambassador to see what he will offer touching the convoy of these letters;

---

[733] Morgan to Q. of Scots, 10/20 July 1585, *Murdin*, p. 446 and *Scot. Cal. VIII*, p. 11. Cf. also Paget to Same, 17/27 July 1585, *Murdin*, p. 453 and *Scot. Cal. VIII*, p. 25.

[734] For the bogus character of Morgan's report, and the reasons for it, cf. *supra* Chapter XII, section 2.

[735] Gilbert Gifford.

[736] He appears to have been referring to Morgan's letter to the Queen of Scots, 18/28 January 1586, in which he had written of Poley: "[He] hath been heretofore in Scotland, and knows the best ways into Scotland. If you know not how to be better served for conveyance to Scotland, you may cause the ambassador [*Châteauneuf*] to address the said Poley with your letters to Scotland. But order must be taken to make his

which if he commit to Poley, you shall either have it outcarried at their costs or else know Poley thoroughly.[737] My secret friend shall know what becomes of it. If they do not commit it to Poley, it may please you to consider how it may be conveyed otherwise, and give me direction, and my secret friend shall accept it, and call for the packet at your pleasure".[738]

In this letter Phelippes appears to have been by no means sure that the ambassador would hand Poley the letters: no doubt because, as Phelippes knew, Poley had not brought an answer from the Queen of Scots to Châteauneuf's letter, as had been expected, and might, on that account, not be trusted by the ambassador. His suggestion that the employment of Poley, if possible, for the convoy of Scotland would save costs, as the Queen of Scots or the French ambassador would have had to pay them for that journey, seems to be almost an echo of Morgan's remark in his letter of 18 January 1586, that order would have to be taken to make the charges in such a voyage!

Finally, the close association of Poley with Blunt is evident from all these letters of Morgan. Blunt was represented as directing the young man, who was at his devotion: and it was, doubtless, to the employment of Poley as the first messenger that Blunt referred in his plea for mercy to Queen Elizabeth, after the Essex riot in 1601.

[737] He seems to have meant that there was no danger; for, either Poley would give Walsingham the letter before taking it to Scotland, or if he did not, then Walsingham would know him to be playing false, and would be able to stop him before he reached Scotland.

[738] Phelippes to Walsingham, London, 19 March 1586 (*Scot. Cal. VIII*, p. 253). In the same letter he warned Walsingham that Justice Young was "putting his foot into it" by having a spy of his own about the ambassador, and asked the Secretary of State to give Young a peremptory order to cease from that activity! It may be remarked that there are reasons for thinking that the Government intended originally to have had the "Babington plot" in 1585, in conjunction with the great onslaught on Catholics in that year. Poley was to have been used for the convoy of the secret correspondence of the Queen of Scots; but for certain reasons the plan was postponed (cf. Appendix V). In 1586, also, Poley, as shown above, was used for the same purpose. His part has, in fact, been rather played down by historians. It was by Burghley that Poley was assigned Anthony Hall's house for a time, for the purpose of entrapping Babington and the other conspirators. Hall himself referred to this in a letter to Burghley some years later, detailing the services he had rendered. "Also my house", he wrote, "was possessed at your Honour's commandment certain days and nights, whereby Ballard, the priest, and Babington, with others of that traitorous crew were apprehended in a garden near my house. Testes Mr. Philips and Mr. Francis Mills [*Walsingham's secretary*]" (A. Hall to Burghley, 13 January 1593, Strype, *Annals IV*, p. 232). Cf. also Phelippes to Walsingham, 3 August 1586, *Scot. Cal. VIII*, p. 584, and *Autobiography of William Weston, S.J.*, in J. Morris, *Troubles of our Catholic Forefathers, II*, pp. 167–169.

charges in such voyage" (*Murdin*, p. 470). The knowledge of Phelippes that the ambassador was anxious to send some secret letters to Scotland, may have been derived from Cherelles, who was in the pay of Walsingham, and who on account of such suspicion was recalled about this time by the Queen Mother (cf. *supra* Chapter X, section 2).

"He doth also desire", he wrote, "that her Majesty be informed of such things as he hath verbally delivered and lastly that her Majesty may be particularly informed and remembered of those great services which he did in laying the way open to the Earl of Leicester and Walsingham for the discovery of all the Queen of Scots' practices".[739]

At all events it would be difficult to find any other episode to which his plea could have referred. It was Blunt who sent Poley to Morgan in 1585, though clearly not without Morgan's suggestion, and in that year he was sent back by Morgan to the Queen of Scots for the conveyance of her secret correspondence;[740] just as he was again recommended to her by Morgan for the same purpose in 1586. How and why Poley was "called off" in 1585, will be explained below in Appendix V.

[739] Examination of Sir Christopher Blunt, printed in *The Correspondence of James VI with Sir Robert Cecil and others, Camden Society,* 1861, pp. 107–110. Cf. also *supra* Chapter XII, section 2.

[740] Morgan to Q. of Scots, 10/20 July 1585, *ut supra* and 18 July 1585, *Scot. Cal. VIII,* p. 25; Paget to Same, 15, 17 and 18 July 1585, *Scot. Cal. VIII,* pp. 23, 25 and 26.

APPENDIX V

Was the "Babington Plot" originally planned for
1585? (cf. Chapter XII, section 2)

There are definite indications that Queen Elizabeth's councillors at
first intended the plot, known later as the Babington plot, to take place
in 1585, after their failure early in that year, at the time when Dr.
Parry was condemned, to bring the Queen of Scots to trial, owing to
the opposition made to that step by Queen Elizabeth herself.[741]
Leicester's men, Blunt, Poley, and the like were to have been employed,
though Phelippes was probably the directing mind behind the plan.
In March or April of that year, 1585, he made a journey to France,
possibly to explore the situation created by Morgan's recent imprisonment in the Bastille;[742] and in the May following wrote that letter to
Morgan which clearly shows that he was working in conjunction with
him, and despite the obscurity of some parts of it, sufficiently adum-
brates the future, by its demand to know the names of the Queen of
Scots' friends, and its reference to opening her "intelligence".[743]
Morgan and Paget continued to write letters to her to the end of July
1585, though they knew that the channel of the secret correspondence
was closed; for those letters would be needed for sending to her when
it was re-opened, just as in fact happened in 1586. Poley, under the
direction of Blunt, was the one chosen to re-open the correspondence,
and both were highly recommended to the captive Queen by Morgan
in a letter of 10 July 1585. Only a few days before this he had penned
a letter for her to send to Babington in her own name.[744] But all this
activity was broken off, the excuse being the absurd story that a letter
of Poley had been intercepted which might bring Blunt and Poley
into suspicion—absurd because Blunt and Poley were really agents of

741 Cf. Q. Elizabeth to Q. of Scots, 22 March 1585, and Same to Poulet, 13 September
1585, *Scot. Cal. VII*, p. 597 and *VIII*, p. 102.
742 Cf. *supra* Note 600.
743 Cf. *supra* Phelippes to Germyn [*Thomas Morgan*], 24 May [1585], Chapter VI,
section 3 and Note 328.
744 Morgan to Q. of Scots, 10/20 July 1585, *Murdin*, p. 446 and *Scot. Cal. VIII*,
p. 11. On the letter for Babington of 6 July 1585, cf. *supra* Note 409.

the English Government, though naturally not known as such to the Queen of Scots.[745] Furthermore, in 1585 Dr. William Gifford, then teaching at Rheims, was to have been induced to come to England, a passport being sent to him for that purpose; just as in 1586 another attempt was made to get him to England, a passport being again provided, so that he might be used as a cover for the work of his cousin, Gilbert.[746] At the end of 1585 and the beginning of 1586 Morgan and Paget began again to write to the Queen of Scots, which they had ceased to do after July 1585: Gilbert Gifford was sent over as one who would help to re-open the secret correspondence, and was highly recommended by Morgan to the Queen of Scots: Blunt and Poley were again recommended to her by him, and the latter was the first messenger employed in the attempt to re-start that correspondence.[747] The captive Queen was provoked by Morgan to write to Babington, as in 1585, and again a letter was penned by him for her to send to Babington in her own name[748] but, since it arrived too late, the letter Morgan had written for the purpose the previous year was used. It was this letter, which the Queen of Scots sent to Babington on 25 June 1586, which was, according to the testimony of her Secretary, Nau, "word for word ready made by Morgan".

It would, indeed, be difficult to explain this parallelism between the actions of the Government's agents in 1585, and of the same in 1586, except on the hypothesis that the councillors of Queen Elizabeth had intended at first to have had the plot in 1585, when they had created a favourable situation, except for one factor and that a decisive one, which despite all their efforts they failed to control, and which imperatively forced them to postpone their plan till the following year.

The factor in question was the situation in Scotland. The English councillors could not venture to proceed against the Queen of Scots till assured that no trouble, in consequence, would arise from that

[745] Cf. Morgan to Q. of Scots, 18 July 1585, *Scot. Cal. VIII*, p. 25.

[746] The passport for 1585 is referred to in R. Persons, *A Manifestation of the Great Folly*, etc. 1602, f. 99, where a marginal note mentions a passport sent by Walsingham for Dr. W. Gifford, dated 14 May 1585. The other passport, issued early in 1586, was acknowledged in W. Gifford's letter to Walsingham, 18 April 1586 (Knox, *Allen*, p. 262), and at its close he said that he awaited Walsingham's "particular directions" by his kinsman Gilbert [*Gifford*], as to what services he might do, so long as he had "assurance of his conscience". This passport, in which the name was to be inserted, was used to send back the priest Jonas Meredith (cf. Note 582) to England (Confession of Gilbert Gifford, 14 August 1588, *Cal. Salisbury MSS. III*, p. 347). Cf. also [G. Gifford] to [Phelippes], [December] 1586, *Scot. Cal. IX*, p. 219 and cf. *supra* Note 544.

[747] Cf. Appendix IV.

[748] On the two letters, one in 1585 and the other in 1586, sent by Morgan for the Queen to send to Babington in her own name, cf. *supra* Note 409.

country, and of that they could have no assurance in 1585.[749] With the execution of Gowrie on 2 May 1584, and the flight and banishment of the Protestant Lords, Angus, Mar and Glamis, with their chief followers, the English party in Scotland was for the time being overthrown and Arran in complete control of the government. Throughout 1584 and 1585 the ministers of Queen Elizabeth tried to remedy matters by various schemes and plots,[750] but it was only in October of the latter year that the situation there began to be restored. In that month, with the connivance and active participation of Queen Elizabeth, her ministers and Wotton, her special ambassador in Scotland, the banished Protestant Lords, Mar and Glamis, re-entered Scotland with an army, seized Stirling, overwhelmed Arran, and made James subservient to them. There followed long negotiations for a league and close alliance between James and Elizabeth, which was eventually signed in July 1586.

It was on 18 July of the previous year, 1585, it may be remembered, that Morgan broke off the Blunt-Poley affair by the story of Poley's intercepted letter. It was earlier in that same month that Leicester had written:

"I now begin to fear Scotland, and that there is great dissimulation by Arc. there and his mistress".[751]

And in a letter of the day following, Walsingham reported to Wotton:

"Our ambassador doth also assure us, that there is no sound dealing. I have acquainted the known friend,[752] to the end he may communicate the same unto 39. His sincerity towards us deserveth plain dealing at our hands. I am presently greatly perplexed with our uncertainty in the causes of weight now in hand. I fear lack of resolution will work our confusion".[753]

It was this fear of the state of affairs in Scotland that led, about July 1585, to the plot being abandoned by the English councillors and postponed till the situation had been remedied and they could feel

---

[749] "It was to them [*Burghley and Walsingham*] therefore of the utmost consequence, that the league between England and Scotland should be concluded before they made their great effort against Mary" (Tytler, *History of Scotland*, *VIII*, p. 229).

[750] For these attempts to restore the situation, cf. Tytler, *op. cit.*, *VIII*, Chapter V, and Conyers Read, *Mr. Secretary Walsingham*, *II*, pp. 206ff.

[751] Copy of a minute from my Lord of Leicester, 10 July 1585, printed in J. Morris, *The Letter-Books of Sir Amias Poulet*, p. 67. The "Arc." probably stands for Archibald Douglas.

[752] Probably Archibald Douglas.

[753] Walsingham to Wotton, 11 July 1585, the *Hamilton Papers*, *II*, p. 660.

secure of James. Even as late as 24 May 1586 Walsingham showed his anxiety lest the treaty of close alliance between James and Elizabeth might not be concluded;[754] and a few days later he wrote to Burghley:

> "There can fall out for the present nothing as dangerous as a breach with Scotland, and therefore passion must be laid aside, or else all will be marred. I pray your Lordship that the King of Scotland and his colleagues may receive some good advice how to govern himself in this cause".[755]

Once assured of this treaty, the Babington plot followed with truly extraordinary rapidity. It would certainly seem that much careful and very detailed research remains to be done, if the full truth concerning that plot and, indeed, of the whole decade, is ever to be ascertained.

[754] Cf. Walsingham to Gray, 24 May 1586, *Scot. Cal. VIII*, p. 397.
[755] Walsingham to Burghley, Barn Elms, 3 June 1586, *Scot. Cal. VIII*, p. 417. James was making difficulties about one or two points in the proposed treaty—one being the amount of pension.

INDEX